Oscar Wilde in Quotation

Oscar Wilde in Quotation

3,100 Insults, Anecdotes and Aphorisms, Topically Arranged with Attributions

Tweed Conrad

McFarland & Company, Inc., Publishers
Jefferson, North Carolina, and London

LIBRARY OF CONGRESS CATALOGUING-IN-PUBLICATION DATA

Conrad, Tweed.
Oscar Wilde in quotation : 3,100 insults, anecdotes and aphorisms,
topically arranged with attributions / Tweed Conrad.
p.   cm.
Includes bibliographical references and index.

ISBN-13: 978-0-7864-2484-9
(softcover : 50# alkaline paper) ∞

1. Wilde, Oscar, 1854–1900 — Quotations.
I.   Conrad, Tweed, 1967–
PR5812.C66   2006   828'.809 — dc22   2006003781

British Library cataloguing data are available

On the cover: Oscar Wilde, 1882 *(Library of Congress)*

Manufactured in the United States of America

McFarland & Company, Inc., Publishers
Box 611, Jefferson, North Carolina 28640
www.mcfarlandpub.com

To my family and friends.

Contents

Contents

Preface

Jotting down Oscar Wilde's quotations began as a hobby one long, snowy winter in Minnesota several years ago. I had developed an avid interest in Oscar Wilde during my time in the theatre and thus began collecting rare Wilde books and recording his amusing quotations merely for personal pleasure. As the quotations began to fill page after page, it soon became apparent that they should be organized in some manner. This seemed a relatively simple task since categories naturally appeared to present themselves in accordance with Wilde's favorite topics. Certain quotations, however, fit quite well in more than one category based upon their broader content. In such cases, I attempted to slot them where they would appear most at home.

The real pleasure (and work) came with the intensive organizing *within* each individual category, where I attempted to create a cohesive flow of Oscar's ideas whenever possible. Sometimes the quotations seem to be telling us a story chronologically and other times they appear in delightful contradiction to each other. As the work progressed, the categories would change somewhat as their contents increased and decreased, with the end result being the 67 categories found in this volume.

What had started as a hobby turned into an obsession; the manuscript grew into a collection of Oscar Wilde quotations that is the largest published to date, which differentiates this book from its predecessors. Previous collections of Oscar Wilde quotations have listed only the title of the work without the precise source and page numbers. Finding such limited citations unsatisfactory, I chose to provide the title, source, edition and page number from which each quotation was pulled. This allows the reader a chance to research and explore a favorite quotation within its original context.

The content and context of Oscar Wilde's work covers a vast amount of ground. Wilde's character Prince Paul (in *Vera, or the Nihilists*, p696) expressed that his only desire for immortality was to "invent a new sauce." Oscar Wilde, thankfully, far exceeded this humble culinary goal with an extraordinary body of work that quite literally speaks for itself. One has merely to peruse the index of this collection to get a clear picture of the subjects that predominated his thoughts, life and work. The titles of the 67 categories present a summarized version of this, as they range from "Happiness" and "Flowers" to "Pain, Sorrow and Suffering." The heights of success and the depths of despair were areas in which Wilde himself was all too familiar. His complex life is beyond the scope of this book and we can safely leave that to many past, present and future biographers, but what we can easily extrapolate from the work at hand is that Oscar Wilde had attained a full spectrum of life experience that he successfully transferred onto paper for the benefit of humanity. Perhaps it was this very breadth of interest and experience that gave Oscar Wilde the ability to empathetically and humourously display such a wide variety of characters and situations in his work.

One of the keynotes of Wilde's writing is the talent he had for presenting our foibles in black and white and transforming them into the timeless truths of human nature. The same treatment by another hand could easily have turned them into vinegar, but with his deft touch they become only more flavourful with age. Through his filter, our most glaring faults became mere eccentricities, our bad habits conversation fodder and our flaws food for thought.

It could be a flaw that "Most people are other people. Their thoughts are someone else's opinions, their life a mimicry, their passions a quotation" (*De Profundis*, p114). Yet, it is this very sentiment that inspired the collection of these quotations and that perhaps places this book in your hands today. Oscar Wilde is one of the most quoted and quotable authors of all time. In fact, he was so quotable that he regularly quoted himself! This "self-plagiarism" occurs throughout his writings, lectures and personal letters, as you will soon observe. Perhaps he felt that a good phrase is a terrible thing to waste — or to use just once. Along these lines, you will find that in this very volume we have resorted to the use of secondary sources for a number of quotations whose original attribution to Wilde was unverifiable. One major such contributor to this collection is Hesketh Pearson's *The Wit and Wisdom of Oscar Wilde* (1946). Pearson's thorough investigation of his subject as well as his full utilization of the works available at the time have made his book a classic. I have also chosen to draw from personal memoirs such as Frank Harris's

Oscar Wilde (1916) and Robert Sherard's *Oscar Wilde: The Story of an Unhappy Friendship* (1908) in order to round out our picture of Wilde as seen through the eyes of friends.

The completion of this collection was due largely in part to the recent publication of *The Complete Letters of Oscar Wilde* (2000), edited by Oscar Wilde's own grandson, Merlin Holland. Holland's monumental editorial work records hundreds of pieces of previously unpublished personal correspondences, providing an excellent and much awaited supplement to the public writings of Oscar Wilde. With this new information we can peek backstage to see a more private side of Wilde and to observe that he displayed just as much brilliance in his personal letters as in his public works. This is just another confirmation of his uniquely individual brand of genius.

The whole of Oscar Wilde's writings reveal only a portion of Oscar the man. Who was this greater than life character who still captures the world's imagination and remains such a solid presence in the literary and theatrical world? What might it have been like to sit next to him a London dinner party, or to have been part of his inner circle of friends? Besides his genius at the writing table, Oscar Wilde was reportedly a genius at the dinner table; by all accounts, his conversational skills were unmatched. In *Oscar Wilde: His Life and Wit*, Hesketh Pearson tells us that Desmond MacCarthy said, "He was probably the greatest self-consciously deliberate master of the Art of Conversation who has talked in the English language."

It is most regrettable that we lack audio recordings of Oscar Wilde's voice because apparently it was exquisite. Actress Lily Langtry described his voice as "one of the most alluring voices that I have ever listened to." Vincent O'Sullivan described the happiness of visiting Wilde as being "rather like the emotion of going to hear some Schubert music, well sung, well played." Actor Franklin Dyall recalled, "Wilde's voice was of the brown velvet order — mellifluous — rounded — in a sense giving it a plummy quality — rather on the adenotic side — but practically pure 'cello — and very pleasing."

Perhaps the most poignant memory (taken from *The Complete Poems of Lord Alfred Douglas, 1928)* is in the form of a poem written one year after Wilde's death by his former love, Lord Alfred Douglas:

I dreamed of him last night, I saw his face
All radiant and unshadowed of distress,
And as of old, in music measureless,
I heard his golden voice and marked him trace
Under the common thing the hidden grace,
And conjure wonder out of emptiness,
Till mean things put on beauty like a dress
And all the world was an enchanted place.
And then methought outside a fast locked gate
I mourned the loss of unrecorded words,
Forgotten tales and mysteries half said,
Wonders that might have been articulate,
And voiceless thoughts like murdered singing
    birds.
And I woke and knew that he was dead.

Fortunately, Oscar Wilde still reaches out to us through his literary legacy across time and space, continuing to live on in our hearts, thoughts and, of course, our words.

Source Abbreviations

CC	Constable and Company, *Aspects of Wilde*
CG	Carroll and Graf, *Oscar Wilde*
GC	Greening and Company, *Oscar Wilde: The Story of an Unhappy Friendship*
HBC	Harcourt, Brace and Company, *Oscar Wilde Discovers America*
HBP	Harper and Brothers Publishers, *Oscar Wilde: His Life and Wit*
OWC	Oxford World's Classics, *The Soul of Man and Prison Writings*
SC	Signet Classics, *The Picture of Dorian Gray and Selected Stories*
UB	University Books, *The Three Trials of Oscar Wilde*
Works	*Complete Works of Oscar Wilde*

1

About Oscar, by Oscar

1. I want to eat of the fruit of all the trees in the garden of the world. *Quoted in Oscar Wilde: His Life and Wit* (*HBP*, pp35–6)

2. I want to stand apart, and look on, being neither for God nor for his enemies. This, I hope, will be allowed. *Letter to Mrs. R.B. Cunninghame Graham* (*Letters*, p403)

3. Be warned in time, James; and remain, as I do, incomprehensible: to be great is to be misunderstood. *Letter to James Whistler* (*Letters*, p250)

4. I have never given adoration for anybody except myself. *The Three Trials of Oscar Wilde* (*UB*, p129)

5. In case I become bankrupt I suppose the autographs will fetch something.... *Letter to Reginald Harding* (*Letters*, pp23–4)

6. I worked at it as a boy; I wanted a distinctive handwriting; it had to be clear and beautiful and peculiar to me. At length I got it but it took time and patience. I always wanted everything about me to be distinctive. *Oscar Wilde, by Frank Harris* (*CG*, pp260–1)

7. Would that I could live up to my blue china! *Oscar Wilde Discovers America* (*HBC*, p10)

8. You have heard of me, I fear, through the medium of your somewhat imaginative newspapers as ... a young man to whom the rush and clamour of reality of the modern world were distasteful, and whose greatest difficulty in life was the difficulty of living up to the level of his blue china — a paradox from which England has not yet fully recovered. *Art and the Handicraftsman lecture* (*Uncollected*, p116)

9. I have nothing to declare [in customs] but my genius. *Oscar Wilde, by Frank Harris* (*CG*, p44)

10. When I had to fill in a census paper I gave my age as 19, my profession as genius, my infirmity as talent. *Quoted in Oscar Wilde: His Life and Wit* (*HBP*, p44)

11. There is nothing [I] would like better in life than to be the hero of such a *cause celebre* and to go down to posterity as the defendant in such a case as "Regina vs. Wilde!" *Oscar Wilde, by Frank Harris* (*CG*, p15)

12. God Knows! I won't be a dried up Oxford don, anyhow. I'll be a poet, a writer, a dramatist. Somehow or other I'll be famous, and if not famous, I'll be notorious. Or perhaps ... I'll rest and do nothing ... These things are on the knees of the gods. What will be, will be. *Quoted in Oscar Wilde: His Life and Wit* (*HBP*, p31)

13. ... I shall now live as the Infamous St Oscar of Oxford, Poet and Martyr. *Letter to Robert Ross* (*Letters*, p1041)

14. If I spent my future life reading Baudelaire in a cafe, I should be leading a more natural life than if I took to hedger's work or planted cacao in mud-swamps. *Letter to Robert Ross* (*Letters*, p790)

15. ... how I loathed your regarding me as a *"useful"* person, how no artist wishes to be so regarded or so treated; artists, like art itself, being of their very essence quite useless. *De Profundis* (*OWC*, p142)

16. Between me and life there is a mist of words always. I throw probability out of the window for the sake of a phrase, and the chance of an epigram makes me desert the truth. Still I do aim at making a work of art.... *Letter to Arthur Conan Doyle* (*Letters*, p478)

17. REPORTER: And what will your next lectures be about?

OSCAR WILDE: Oh, they will begin at the

doorknob and end with the attic. Beyond that there remains only heaven, which subject I leave to the church. *Oscar Wilde Discovers America (HBC, p180)*

18. ... at present I am deep in literary work, and cannot stir from my little rooms over the Seine till I have finished two plays. This sound ambitious, but we live in an age of inordinate personal ambition and I am determined that the world shall understand me, so I will now, along with my art work, devote to the drama a great deal of my time. The drama seems to me to be the meeting place of art and life. *Letter to Clarisse Moore (Letters, pp204–5)*

19. While the first editions of most classical authors are those coveted by bibliophiles, it is the second editions of my books that are true rarities, and even the British museum has not been able to secure copies of most of them. *Quoted in Oscar Wilde: His Life and Wit (HBP, p215)*

20. Robbie's refusal to interest himself in my poem I feel is inartistic of him — my work as a poet is separate from my life as a man — and as for my life, it is one ruined, unhappy, lonely and disgraced. *Letter to Leonard Smithers (Letters, p1004)*

21. I am glad you like that strange coloured book of mine [The Picture of Dorian Gray]: it contains much of me in it. Basil Hallward is what I think I am: Lord Henry what the world thinks me: Dorian what I would like to be — in other ages perhaps. *Letter to Ralph Payne (Letters, p585)*

22. If I have good health, and good friends, and can wake the creative instinct in me again, I may do some more in art yet. *Letter to Selwyn Image (Letters, p879)*

23. Nothing really at any period of my life was ever of the smallest importance to me compared with Art. But in the case of an artist, weakness is nothing less than a crime, when it is a weakness that paralyses the imagination. *De Profundis (OWC, p42)*

24. ... my reckless pursuit of mundane pleasures, my extravagance, my senseless ease, my love of fashion, my whole attitude towards life, all these things were wrong for an artist. *Letter to Arthur L. Humphreys (Letters, p880)*

25. My existence is a scandal. But I do not think I should be charged with creating a scandal by continuing to live: though I am conscious that I do so. *Letter to Robert Ross (Letters, p979)*

26. I was a problem for which there was no solution. *Letter to More Adey (Letters, p995)*

27. I could not bear life if I were to flee. I cannot see myself slinking about the continent, a fugitive from justice. *Oscar Wilde: The Story of an Unhappy Friendship (GC, p161)*

28. Somehow I don't think I shall live to see the new century — if another century began and I was still alive, it would really be more than the English could stand. *Oscar Wilde, by Frank Harris (CG, p348)*

29. ... the world is angry because their punishment has had no effect. They wished to be able to say "We have done a capital thing for Oscar Wilde: by putting him in prison we have put a stop to his friendship with Alfred Douglas and all that that implies. But now they find that they have not had that effect, that they merely treated me barbarously, but they did not influence me, they simply ruined me, so they are furious." *Letter to Robert Ross (Letters, p993)*

30. I think that I could live through one year's imprisonment.... Not two years — not two years. *Oscar Wilde: The Story of an Unhappy Friendship (GC, pp172–3)*

31. Something is killed in me. I feel no desire to write. I am unconscious of power. Of course my first year in prison destroyed me body and soul. It could not have been otherwise. *Letter to Robert Ross (Letters, p1095)*

32. I knew quite well that this action of mine would with many people damage my already damaged reputation, and that it would sadly try some of my best friends, whom I had already tried a great deal. *Quoted in Oscar Wilde: His Life and Wit (HBP, p269)*

33. I want to get to the point when I shall be able to say, quite simply and without affectation, that the two great turning points of my life were when my father sent me to Oxford, and when society sent me to prison. *De Profundis (OWC, p99)*

34. I remember, that as I was sitting in the dock on the occasion of my last trial listening to Lockwood's appalling denunciation of me

... and being sickened with horror at what I heard. Suddenly it occurred to me, *"How splendid it would be, if I was saying all this about myself!"* I saw then at once that what is said of a man is nothing. The point is, who says it. A man's very highest moment is, I have no doubt at all, when he kneels in the dust, as he beats his breast, and tells all the sins of his life. *De Profundis* (*OWC*, p145)

35. When I was a boy my two favourite characters were Lucien de Rubempre and Julien Sorel. Lucien hanged himself, Julien died on the scaffold, and I died in prison. *Aspects of Wilde* (*CC*, p36)

36. I hope soon to begin a new play but poverty if degrading with its preoccupation with money, the loss of many friends, the deprivation of my children, by a most unjust law, by a most unjust Judge, the terrible effects of two years of silence, solitude and ill-treatment — all these have, of course, to a large extent, killed if not entirely that great joy in living that I once had. However, I must try.... *Letter to Georgina Weldon* (*Letters*, p1080)

37. I told you that I was going to write something: I tell everybody that. It is a thing I can repeat each day, meaning to do it the next. But in my heart — that chamber of dead echoes— I know that I never shall. It is enough that the stories have been invented, that they actually exist; that I have been able, in my own mind, to give them the form which they demand. *Quoted in Oscar Wilde: His Life and Wit* (*HBP*, p320)

38. I don't think I shall ever write again: *la joie de vivre* is gone, and that, with will-power, is the basis of art. *Letter to Carlos Blacker* (*Letters*, p1035)

39. I was a man who stood in symbolic relations to the art and culture of my age. I had realised this for myself at the very dawn of my manhood, and had forced my age to realise it afterwards. Few men hold such a position in their own lifetime and have it so acknowledged. It is usually discerned, if discerned at all, by the historian, or the critic, long after both the man and his age have passed away. With me it was different. I felt it myself and made others feel it. *De Profundis* (*OWC*, p95)

40. I became the spendthrift of my own genius, and to waste an eternal youth gave me curious joy, Tired of being on the heights I deliberately went to the depths in the search of new sensations. What the paradox was to me in the sphere of thought, perversity became to me in the sphere of passion. Desire, at the end, was a malady, or a madness, or both. I grew careless of the lives of others. I took pleasure where it pleased me and passed on. I forgot that every little action of the common day makes or unmakes character, and that therefore what one has done in the secret chamber one has some day to cry aloud on the housetops. *De Profundis* (*OWC*, pp95–6)

41. The trivial in thought and action is charming. I had made it the keystone of a very brilliant philosophy expressed in plays and paradoxes. *De Profundis* (*OWC*, p49)

42. The gods had given me almost everything. I had genius, a distinguished name, high social position, brilliancy, intellectual daring: I made art a philosophy, and philosophy an art: I altered the minds of men and the colours of things: there was nothing I said or did that did not make people wonder: I took the drama, the most objective form known to art, and made it as personal a mode of expression as the lyric or the sonnet, at the same time that widened its range and enriched its characterisation: drama, novel, poem in rhyme, poem in prose, subtle or fantastic dialogue, whatever I touched I made beautiful in a new mode of beauty: to truth itself I gave what is false no less than what is true as its rightful province, and showed that the false and the true are merely forms of intellectual existence. I treated Art as the supreme reality, and life as a mere mode of fiction: I awoke the imagination of my century so that it created myth and legend around me: I summed up all systems in a phrase, all existence in an epigram. *De Profundis* (*OWC*, p95)

43. There is before me so much to do, that I would regard it as a terrible tragedy if I died before I was allowed to complete at any rate a little of it. *De Profundis* (*OWC*, p104)

44. Oh Frank, you would turn all the tragedies into triumphs, you are a fighter. My life is done. *Oscar Wilde, by Frank Harris* (*CG*, p262)

45. I turned the good things of my life to evil, and the evil things of my life to good. *De Profundis* (*OWC*, p99)

46. I know you all think I am wilful, but it is the result of the nemesis of character, and the bitterness of life. I was a problem for which there was no solution. *Letter to More Adey* (*Letters,* p995)

47. Nemesis has caught me in her net: to struggle is foolish. *Letter to Carlos Blacker* (*Letters,* p921)

48. For myself, I really am quite heartbroken. Nemesis seems endless. *Letter to Carlos Blacker* (*Letters,* p920)

49. Robbie wrote to me "Remember always that you committed the unpardonable and vulgar error of being found out." *Letter to Leonard Smithers* (*Letters,* p1004)

50. You may talk as you please, Frank, but you will never get me to believe that what I know is good to me is evil. Suppose I like a food that is poison to other people, and yet quickens me; how dare they punish me for eating of it? *Oscar Wilde, by Frank Harris* (*CG,* p292)

51. ... that talk about reformation, Frank, is all nonsense; no one ever really reforms or changes. I am what I always was. *Oscar Wilde by Frank Harris* (*CG,* p240)

52. I will not talk to you about it, Frank; I am like a Persian, who lives by warmth and worships the sun, talking to some Eskimo, who answers me with praises of blubber and night spent in ice houses and baths of foul vapour. Let's talk of something else. *Oscar Wilde, by Frank Harris* (*CG,* p285)

53. FRANK HARRIS: You often talk now as if you had never loved a woman; yet you must have loved — more than one.

OSCAR WILDE: My salad days, Frank, when I was green in judgment, cold of blood. *Oscar Wilde, by Frank Harris* (*CG,* p282)

54. The first these ten years [regarding sex with a female prostitute], and it will be the last. It was like cold mutton ... tell it in England, for it will restore my character. *Quoted in Oscar Wilde: His Life and Wit* (*HBP,* p301)

55. Oscar was NOT a man of bad character; you could have trusted him with a woman anywhere. *Oscar Wilde, by Frank Harris* (*CG,*

p333) and The Three Trials of Oscar Wilde (*UB,* p78)

56. The three women I have most admired are Queen Victoria, Sarah Bernhardt, and Lily Langtry. I would have married any one of them with pleasure. *Aspects of Wilde* (*CC,* p25)

57. If the life of St. Francis awaits me I shall not be angry. Worse things might happen. *Letter to Robert Ross* (*Letters,* p885)

58. I have got to make everything that has happened to me good for me. The plank-bed, the loathsome food, the hard ropes shredded into oakum till one's fingertips grow dull with pain, the menial offices with which each day begins and finishes, the harsh orders that routine seems to necessitate, the dreadful dress that makes sorrow grotesque to look at, the silence, the solitude, the shame — each and all of these things I have to transform into a spiritual experience. There is not a single degradation of the body which I must not try and make into a spiritualizing of the soul. *De Profundis* (*OWC,* p99)

59. I still recognise that I have only at last come to the complete life which every artist must experience in order to join beauty to truth. *Quoted in Oscar Wilde: His Life and Wit* (*HBP,* p322)

60. I must say to myself that I ruined myself, and that nobody great or small can be ruined except by his own hand. *De Profundis* (*OWC,* p94)

61. Terrible as what you did to me was, what I did to myself was far more terrible still. *De Profundis* (*OWC,* p95)

62. For my own sake I must forgive you. One cannot always keep an adder in one's breast to feed on one, nor rise up every night to sow thorns in the garden of one's soul. *De Profundis* (*OWC,* p94)

63. To each of us different fates have been meted out. Freedom, pleasure, amusements, a life of ease have been your lot, and you are not worthy of it. My lot has been one of public infamy, of long imprisonment, of misery, of ruin, of disgrace, and I am not worthy of it either.... *De Profundis* (*OWC,* p129)

64. As I sit here and look back, I realise that I have lived the complete life necessary to the artist: I have had great success, I have had great failure. I have learned the value of each....

Quoted in Oscar Wilde: His Life and Wit (HBP, p321)

65. I have had my hand on the moon. What is the use of trying to rise a little way from the ground? *Aspects of Wilde* (CC, p35)

66. No man of my position can fall into the mire of life without getting a great deal of pity from his inferiors; and I know that when plays last to long, spectators tire. *My* tragedy has lasted far too long: its climax is over.... *Letter to Robert Ross* (Letters, p669)

67. My cradle was rocked by the Fates. Only in the mire can I know peace. *Letter to Carlos Blacker* (Letters, p921)

68. What kills one is uncertainty, with its accompanying anxiety and distress. *Letter to More Adey* (Letters, p804)

69. Peace is as requisite to the artist as to the saint: my soul is made mean by sordid anxieties. It is a poor ending, but I had been accustomed to purple and gold. *Letter to H.C. Pollitt* (Letters, p1103)

70. ... all I want is peace: all I ever wanted was peace.... *Letter to More Adey* (Letters, p808)

71. I am dying, as I've lived, beyond my means. *Oscar Wilde, by Frank Harris* (CG, p315)

72. Every one is born a king, and most people die in exile, like most kings. *A Woman of No Importance* (Plays, p177)

73. Why have you brought me no poison from Paris? *Oscar Wilde: The Story of an Unhappy Friendship* (GC, p157)

74. He seems to have expressed a desire to be buried in Paris. *The Importance of Being Earnest* (Plays, p386)

75. He died abroad; in Paris, in fact. *The Importance of Being Earnest* (Plays, p386)

76. Yet all is well; he has but passed
To life's appointed bourne:
And alien tears will fill for him
Pity's long-broken urn,
For his mourners will be outcast men,
   And outcasts always mourn.
The Ballad of Reading Goal (OWC, p185)

77. I have lost the mainspring of life and art, *la joie de vivre*: it is dreadful. I have passions and pleasures, and passions, but the joy of life is gone. I am going under: the morgue yawns for me. I go and look at my zinc-bed there. *Letter to Frank Harris* (Letters, p1025)

78. OSCAR WILDE: I have had a dreadful dream. I dreamt that I was dining with the dead.
REGINALD TURNER: My dear Oscar, I am sure you were the life and soul of the party. *Oscar Wilde, by Frank Harris* (CG, p341)

79. When the last trumpet sounds, and we are couched in our porphyry tombs, I shall turn and whisper to you "Robbie, Robbie, let us pretend we do not hear it." *Quoted in Oscar Wilde: His Life and Wit* (HBP, p333)

80. Would you like to know the great drama of my life? It is that I have put my genius into my life — I have put only my talent into my works. *The Three Trials of Oscar Wilde* (UB, p27)

81. I wrote when I did not know life; now that I do know the meaning of life, I have no more to write. Life cannot be written; life can only be lived. *Quoted in Oscar Wilde: His Life and Wit* (HBP, p330)

82. Close the eyes of all of us now and fifty years hence, or a hundred years hence, no one will know anything about Curzon or Wyndam or Blunt. Whether they lived or died will be a matter of indifference to everyone; but my comedies and my stories and "The Ballad of Reading Gaol" will be known and read by millions, and even my unhappy fate will call forth world-wide sympathy. *Oscar Wilde, by Frank Harris* (CG, p260)

83. ... the world is slowly growing more tolerant and one day men will be ashamed of their barbarous treatment of me, as they are now ashamed of the torturings of the Middle Ages. The current opinion is making in our favour and not against us. *Oscar Wilde, by Frank Harris* (CG, p292)

84. Yes; I am a dreamer. For a dreamer is one who can only find his way by moonlight, and his punishment is that he sees the dawn before the rest of the world. *The Critic as Artist* (Works, p1155)

85. I could have become anything. But have I not chosen the better part? *Oscar Wilde: The Story of an Unhappy Friendship* (GC, p39)

86. I was quite amazing. *Oscar Wilde: The Story of an Unhappy Friendship* (GC, p19)

87. After all, I had a wonderful life, which is, I fear, over. But I must dine once with you first. *Letter to Frank Harris* (Letters, p1025)

2

Actors and Acting

88. The world is a stage, but the play is badly cast. *Lord Arthur Savile's Crime* (*SC,* p273)

89. Actors are so fortunate. They can choose whether they will appear in tragedy or in comedy, whether they will suffer or make merry, laugh or shed tears. But in real life it is different. Men and women are forced to perform parts for which they have no qualifications. Our Guildensterns play Hamlet for us and our Hamlets have to jest like Prince Hal. *Lord Arthur Savile's Crime* (*SC,* p273)

90. I love acting. It is so much more real than life. *The Picture of Dorian Gray* (*SC,* p95)

91. Their [actor's] disguises off the stage are bewildering. *Letter to Edward Strangman* (*Letters,* p916)

92. [Being natural] is such a very difficult pose to keep up. *An Ideal Husband* (*Plays,* p229)

93. OLIVER SHREINER: I live in the East End because there the people don't wear masks.

OSCAR WILDE: And I live in the West End because there they do. *Quoted in Oscar Wilde: His Life and Wit* (*HBP,* p150)

94. As a rule, people who act lead the most commonplace lives. They are good husbands, or faithful wives, or something tedious. *The Picture of Dorian Gray* (*SC,* 124)

95. Just as work is the curse of the drinking classes of this country, so education is the curse of the acting classes. *Oscar Wilde, by Frank Harris* (*CG,* p98)

96. ... acting is no longer considered absolutely essential for success on the English stage. *The American Invasion, Court and Society Review* (*Uncollected,* p36)

97. For anybody can act. Most people in

England do nothing else. *Letter to the Editor of The Daily Telegraph* (*Letters,* p519)

98. It is not good for one's morals to see bad acting. *The Picture of Dorian Gray* (*SC,* p100)

99. ... she acted badly because she had known the reality of love. *The Picture of Dorian Gray* (*SC,* p124)

100. ... no amount of advertising will make a bad play succeed, if it is not a good play well acted. *Letter to Marie Prescott* (*Letters,* p203)

101. For without quick and imaginative observation of life the most beautiful play becomes dull in presentation, and what is not conceived in delight by the actor can give no delight at all to others. *Henry the Fourth at Oxford, Dramatic Review* (*Uncollected,* p80)

102. For delightful as good elocution is, few things are so depressing as to hear a passionate passage recited instead of being acted. The quality of a fine performance is its life more than its learning, and every word in a play has a musical as well as an intellectual value, and must be made expressive of a certain emotion. *Hamlet at the Lyceum, Dramatic Review* (*Uncollected,* p76)

103. [George] Alexander doesn't act on stage; he behaves. *Oscar Wilde, by Frank Harris* (*CG,* p289)

104. When a man acts he is a puppet. When he describes, he is a poet. *The Critic as Artist* (*Works,* p1123)

105. ... the stage is only "a frame furnished with a set of puppets." *Letter to the Editor of The Daily Telegraph* (*Letters,* p518)

106. There are many advantages in puppets [as opposed to live actors]. They never argue. They have no crude views about art. They have no private lives. We are never bothered by accounts of their virtues, or bored by recitals of their vices; and when they are out of an engagement they never do good in public or save people from drowning; nor do they speak more than is set down for them. They recognize the presiding intellect of the dramatist, and have never been known to ask for their parts to be written up. They are admirably docile, and have no personalities at all. *Letter to the Editor of The Daily Telegraph* (*Letters*, p519)

107. ... select only *young* actors— there are possibilities of poetry and passion in the young— and picturesqueness also, a quality so valuable on the stage. Shun the experienced actor: in poetic drama he is impossible. Choose graceful personalities— young actors and actresses who have charming voices— that is enough. The rest is in the hands of God and the poet. *Letter to Michael Field* (*Letters*, p570)

108. DORIAN GRAY: But an actress! How different an actress is! Harry! Why didn't you tell me that the only thing worth loving is an actress?

LORD HENRY: Because I have loved so many of them, Dorian. *The Picture of Dorian Gray* (*SC*, p68)

109. When she acts, you will forget everything. These common rough people, with their coarse faces and brutal gestures, become quite different when she is on the stage. They sit silently and watch her. They weep and laugh as she wills them to do. She makes them as responsive as a violin. She spiritualises them, and one feels that they are of the same flesh and blood as one's self. *The Picture of Dorian Gray* (*SC*, pp96–7)

110. To whatever character Miss Terry plays she brings the infinite charm of her beauty, and the marvelous grace of her movements and gestures. It is impossible to escape from the sweet tyranny of her personality. *Olivia at the Lyceum, Dramatic Review* (*Uncollected*, p955)

111. ... in Miss Terry our stage possesses a really great artist, who can thrill an audience without harrowing it, and by means that seem simple and easy can produce the finest dramatic effect. *Olivia at the Lyceum, Dramatic Review* (*Uncollected*, p955)

112. [Lily Langtry's] figure is molded like a Greek statue. She is not petite, but I would not say that she is tall. She is of perfect artistic height. When she has studied her art she will be able to act Shakespeare's Rosalind in a way in which most of us have never seen the part done. *Oscar Wilde Discovers America* (*HBC*, p217)

113. I call him [Mr. Irving] a great actor because he brings to the interpretation of a work of art the two qualities which we in this century so much desire, the qualities of personality and of perfection. *Hamlet at the Lyceum* (*Uncollected*, p76)

114. The actor is unconscious of our presence; the musician is thinking of the subtlety of the fugue, and the tone of his instrument; the marble gods that smile so curiously at us are made of insensate stone. But they have given form and substance to what was within us; they have enabled us to realise our personality; and a sense of perilous joy, or some touch or thrill of pain, or that strange self-pity that man so often feels for himself, comes over us and leaves us different. *The Portrait of Mr. W.H.* (*Works,* p343)

115. What then shall we say of the material that the Drama requires for its perfect presentation? What of the Actor, who is the medium through which alone the Drama can truly reveal itself? Surely, in that strange mimicry of life by the living which is the mode and method of theatric art, there are sensuous elements of beauty that none of the other arts possess. Looked at from one point of view, the common players of the saffron-strewn stage are Art's most complete, most satisfying instruments. *The Portrait of Mr. W.H.* (*Works,* pp323–4)

116. Perfect heroes are the monsters of melodrama, and have no place in dramatic art. *Olivia at the Lyceum* (*Works,* p956)

117. The play [Vera] is meant, not to be read, but to be acted, and the actor has always a right to object and to suggest. No one could recognise the artist's right more than I do in the matter. The only reason, to speak honestly, that the play is as good an acting play as it is, is that I took every actor's suggestion I could get. *Letter to Richard D'Oyly Carte* (*Letters*, p151)

118. From the point of view of form, the type of all the arts is the art of the musician. From the point of view of feeling, the actor's craft is the type. *The Picture of Dorian Gray* (*SC*, p18)

119. Well, there *is* a good deal to be said for blushing, if one can do it at the proper moment. *A Woman of No Importance* (*Plays*, p199)

120. ... the essence of good dialogue is interruption. All good dialogue should give the effect of its being made by the reaction of the personages on one another. It should never seem to be ready made by the author, and interruptions have not only their artistic effect but their physical value. They give the actors time to breathe and get new breath power. *Letter to Marie Prescott* (*Letters*, p204)

121. ... dialect should be only indicated: an attempt to reproduce it exactly [is] bad art. *Aspects of Wilde* (*CC*, p22)

122. The actor is the critic of the drama. He shows the poet's work under new conditions, and by a method special to himself. He takes the written word, and action, gesture and voice become the media of revelation. *The Critic as Artist* (*Works*, p1131)

123. ... you know how difficult a *comedienne* is to catch. Their disguises off the stage are bewildering. *Letter to Edward Strangman* (*Letters*, p916)

124. In the comedy scenes people should speak out more, be more assertive. Every *word* of a comedy dialogue should reach the ears of the audience. *Letter to George Alexander* (*Letters*, p514)

125. To be conventional is to be a comedian. To act a particular part, however, is a very different thing, and a very difficult thing as well. *Letter to the Editor of The Daily Telegraph* (*Letters*, p519)

126. An audience looks at a tragedian, but a comedian looks at his audience. *Henry the Fourth at Oxford, Dramatic Review* (*Uncollected*, p81)

127. This full recognition of the actor's art, and of the actor's power, was one of the things, consequently, that we owed to Shakespeare. *The Portrait of Mr. W.H.* (*Works*, p322)

128. When a great actor plays Shakespeare.... His own individuality becomes a vital part of the interpretation. *The Critic as Artist* (*Works*, p1131)

129. People sometimes say that actors give us their own Hamlets, and not Shakespeare's.... In point of fact, there is no such thing as Shakespeare's Hamlet. If Hamlet has something of the definiteness of a work of art, he has also all the obscurity that belongs to life. There are as many Hamlets as there are melancholies. *The Critic as Artist* (*Works*, p1131)

130. But to Shakespeare, the actor was a deliberate and self-conscious fellow worker who gave form and substance to a poet's fancy, and brought into Drama the element of a noble realism. *The Portrait of Mr. W.H.* (*Works*, p322)

131. Yet Shakespeare himself was a player, and wrote for players. He saw the possibilities that lay hidden in an art that up to his time had expressed itself in bombast or in clowning. He has left us the most perfect rules for acting that have ever been written. He created parts that can be only truly revealed to us on the stage, wrote plays that need the theatre for their full realization, and we cannot marvel that he so worshipped one who was the interpreter of his vision, as he was the incarnation of his dreams. *The Portrait of Mr. W.H.* (*Works*, p324)

132. To say that only a woman can play the passions of a woman, and that therefore no boy can play Rosalind, is to rob the art of acting of all claim to objectivity, and to assign to the mere accident of sex what properly belongs to imaginative insight and creative energy. *The Portrait of Mr. W.H.* (*Works*, p330)

133. [Shakespeare] protests against other difficulties with which managers of theatres have still to contend, such as actors who do not understand their words; actors who miss their cues; actors who overact their parts; actors who mouth; actors who gag; actors who play to the gallery; and amateur actors. *Shakespeare on Scenery, Dramatic Review* (*Uncollected*, pp71–2)

134. MARION TERRY: Oh, well, you know, Mr. Wilde, you can lead a horse to water, but you can't make him drink.

OSCAR WILDE: No, Terry. But you have a circus. In that circus is a ring. A horse enters the ring and approaches a trough of water. The ringmaster cracks his whip and says, "Drink!" and the horse drinks. That horse, Terry, is the actor.

MARION TERRY: So, Mr. Wilde, you compare the stage to a circus?

OSCAR WILDE: Ah, yours was the metaphor. *Aspects of Wilde* (*CC*, pp20–1)

135. We are sorry, too, to find an English dramatic critic misquoting Shakespeare, as we had always been of the opinion that this was a privilege reserved especially for our English actors. *A Cheap Edition of Great Men, Pall Mall Gazette* (*Uncollected*, pp71–2)

136. ... all the arts are free in England, except the actor's art. *Letter to William Rothenstein* (*Letters*, p532)

137. Why should not degrees be granted for good acting? Are they not given to those who misunderstand Plato and who mistranslate Aristotle? And should the artist be passed over? No. To Prince Hal, Hotspur and Falstaff, D.C.L.'s should be gracefully offered. *Henry the Fourth at Oxford* (*Uncollected*, p82)

138. Well, if I am not to be allowed to go on the stage, I must be allowed to be part of the audience at any rate. *Lord Arthur Savile's Crime* (*SC*, p271)

139. It is a humiliating confession, but we are all of us made out of the same stuff. In Falstaff there is something of Hamlet, in Hamlet there is not a little of Falstaff. The fat knight has his moods of melancholy, and the young prince his moments of course humour. Where we differ from each other is purely in accidentals: in dress, manner, tone of voice, religious opinion, personal appearance, tricks of habit and the like. The more one analyses, the more all reasons for analysis disappear. Sooner or later one comes to that dreadful universal thing called human nature. Indeed, as any one who has ever worked among the poor knows only too well, the brotherhood of man is no mere poet's dream. *The Decay of Lying* (*Works*, pp1075–6)

140. ... in each play there was some one whose life was bound up in mine, who realized for me every dream, and gave shape to every fancy. *The Portrait of Mr. W.H.* (*Works*, p344)

141. As the inevitable result of this substitution of an imitative for a creative medium, this surrender of an imaginative form, we have the modern English melodrama. The characters in these plays talk on the stage exactly as they would talk off it; they have neither aspirations nor aspirates; they are taken directly from life and reproduce its vulgarity down to the smallest detail; they present the gait, manner, costume and accent of real people, they would pass unnoticed in a third-class railway carriage. And yet how wearisome the plays are! They do not succeed in producing even that impression of reality at which they aim, and which is their only reason for existing. As a method, realism is a complete failure. *The Decay of Lying* (*Works*, pp1079–80)

142. ... Art being to a certain degree a mode of acting, an attempt to realise one's own personality on some imaginative plane out of reach of the trammeling accidents and limitations of real life.... *The Portrait of Mr. W.H.* (*Works*, p302)

143. The actor's aim is, or should be, to convert his own accidental personality into the real and essential personality of the character he is called upon to impersonate, whatever the character may be; or perhaps I should say that there are two schools of actors— the school of those who attain their effect by the exaggeration of personality, and the school of those who attain it by suppression. *Letter to the Editor of The Daily Telegraph* (*Letters*, p519)

144. ... the personality of the actor is often a source of danger in the perfect presentation of a work of art. It may distort. It may lead astray. It may be a discord in the tone or symphony. *Letter to the Editor of The Daily Telegraph* (*Letters*, p519)

145. For while we look at the dramatist to give romance to realism, we ask of the actor to give realism to romance. *Henry the Fourth at Oxford, Dramatic Review* (*Uncollected*, p82)

146. Perhaps one never seems so much at ease as when one has to play a part. *The Picture of Dorian Gray* (*SC*, p187)

3

America and Americans

147. Americans dance better than the British. *Oscar Wilde Discovers America* (*HBC*, p176)

148. America is one long expectoration. *Oscar Wilde Discovers America* (*HBC*, p181)

149. The Americans are not uncivilized, as they are so often said to be, they are *de-civilised*. *Oscar Wilde Discovers America* (*HBC*, p32)

150. I believe a most serious problem for the American people to consider is the cultivation of better manners among its people. It is the most noticeable, the most painful, defect in American *civilization*. *Oscar Wilde Discovers America* (*HBC*, p389)

151. The Americans are certainly great hero-worshippers, and always take their heroes from the criminal classes. *Letter to Norman Forbes-Robertson* (*Letters*, p164)

152. English people are far more interested in American barbarism than they are in American *civilization*. *The American Invasion, Court and Society Review* (*Uncollected*, p36)

153. I have met minors: they are big-booted, red-shirted, yellow bearded and delightful ruffians. *Letter to Mrs. George Lewis* (*Letters*, p154)

154. For our aristocracy they have an ardent admiration; they adore titles and are a permanent blow to Republican principles. *The American Invasion, Court and Society Review* (*Uncollected*, p37)

155. My lord, I will take the furniture and the ghost at a valuation. I come from a modern country, where we have everything that money can buy; and with all our spry young fellows painting the Old World red, and carrying off your best actresses and prima-donnas, I reckon that if there were such a thing as a ghost in Europe, we'd have it at home in a very short time in one of our pubic museums, or on the road as a show. *The Canterville Ghost* (*Works*, p184)

156. SIR THOMAS: The Americans are an extremely interesting people. They are absolutely reasonable. I think that is their distinguishing characteristic.... I assure you there is no nonsense about the Americans.

LORD HENRY: How dreadful! I can stand brute force, but brute reason is quite unbearable. There is something unfair about its use. It is hitting below the intellect. *The Picture of Dorian Gray* (*SC*, p56)

157. [American] men are entirely given to business; they have, as they say, their brains in the front of their heads. *Personal Impressions of America lecture* (*Works*, p941)

158. There is no such thing as a stupid American. Many Americans are horrid, vulgar, intrusive, and impertinent, just as many English people are also; but stupidity is not one of the national vices. *Oscar Wilde Discovers America* (*HBC*, p281)

159. The crude commercialism of America, its materialising spirit, its indifference to the poetical side of things, and its lack of imagination and of high unattainable ideas, are entirely due to that country having adopted for its national hero a man who, according to his own confession, was incapable of telling a lie, and it is not too much to say that the story of George Washington and the cherry-tree has done more harm, and in a shorter space of time, than any other moral tale in the whole of literature ... and the amusing part of the whole thing is that the story of the cherry-tree is an absolute myth. However, you must not think that I am too despondent about the artistic future either of

America or of our own country. *The Decay of Lying* (*Works*, p1081)

160. There is no country in the world where machinery is so lovely as in America. *Personal Impressions of America lecture* (*Works*, p938)

161. [In America] everybody seems in a hurry to catch a train. This is a state of things which is not favourable to poetry or romance. Had Romeo or Juliet been in a constant state of anxiety about trains, or had their minds been agitated by the question of return-tickets, Shakespeare could not have given us those lovely balcony scenes which are so full of poetry and pathos. *Personal Impressions of America Lecture* (*Works*, p938)

162. America is the noisiest country that ever existed. One is waked up in the morning, not by the singing of the nightingale, but by the steam whistle. It is surprising that the sound practical sense of the Americans does not reduce this intolerable noise. All art depends upon exquisite and delicate sensibility, and such continual turmoil must ultimately be destructive of the musical faculty. *Personal Impressions of America lecture* (*Works*, p938)

163. I saw some designs on your vases done by someone who, I should say, had only five minutes to catch a train ... the institution of pottery should not be a refuge for people who cannot draw nor asylum for the artistically afflicted. *Oscar Wilde Discovers America* (*HBC*, p200)

164. One is impressed in America, but not favourably impressed, by the inordinate size of everything. The country seems to try to bully one into a belief in its power by its impressive bigness. *Personal Impressions of America lecture* (*Works*, pp938–9)

165. We in England have no idea of the distances in your country. The impression there seems to be that all of the large cities are located in the suburbs of New York; then come the Rocky Mountains, next the Indians, then San Francisco and the ocean. We do not understand that large cities like Chicago and Cincinnati are located in the heart of the country. *Oscar Wilde Discovers America* (*HBC*, p205)

166. LADY CAROLINE: I believe this is the first English country house you have stayed at, Miss Worsley?

HESTER: Yes, Lady Caroline.

LADY CAROLINE: You have no country houses, I am told, in America?

HESTER: We have not many.

LADY CAROLINE: Have you any country? What we should call country?

HESTER: We have the largest country in the world, Lady Caroline. They used to tell us at school that some of our states are as big as France and England put together.

LADY CAROLINE: Ah! you must find it very draughty, I should fancy. *A Woman of No Importance* (*Plays*, p127)

167. You call America a country, but I call it a w-o-r-l-d. *Oscar Wilde Discovers America* (*HBC*, p155)

168. American humour has no real existence. Indeed, so far from being humorous, the male American is the most abnormally serious creature who ever existed. He talks of Europe as being old; but it is he himself who has never been young. He knows nothing of the irresponsible light-heartedness of boyhood, of the graceful insouciance of animal spirits. He has always been prudent, always practical, and pays a heavy penalty for having committed no mistakes. It is only fair to admit that he [the American] can exaggerate; but even his exaggeration has a rational basis. It is not founded on wit or fancy; it does not spring from any poetical imagination; it is simply an earnest attempt on the part of the language to keep pace with the enormous size of the country. It is evident that where it takes one twenty-four hours to go across a single parish, and seven days' steady railway traveling to keep a dinner engagement in another state, the ordinary resources of human speech are quite inadequate to the strain put on them, and new linguistic forms have to be invented, new methods of description, resorted to. But this is nothing more than the fatal influence of geography upon adjectives; for naturally humorous the American man certainly is not. *Oscar Wilde Discovers America* (*HBC*, p281)

169. Your newspapers are comic without being amusing. *Oscar Wilde Discovers America* (*HBC*, p179)

170. ... the advice to read the daily papers as a method of acquiring judgment and good sense is an excellent bit of American *humour*. *Letter to A.P.T. Elder* (*Letters*, p249)

171. In America the president reigns for four years, and Journalism governs for ever and ever. *The Soul of Man* (*OWC*, p23)

172. LADY HUNSTANTON: What are American dry goods?

LORD ILLINGWORTH: American novels. *A Woman of No Importance* (*Plays*, p136) and similar quotation in The Picture of Dorian Gray (*SC*, p55)

173. I don't think I like American inventions. Arthur. I am quite sure I don't. I read some American novels lately, and they were quite nonsensical. *Lord Arthur Savile's Crime* (*SC*, p284)

174. What can Americans know about English literature? *Oscar Wilde, by Frank Harris* (*CG*, p296)

175. But, as in your cities so in your literature, it is a permanent canon and standard of taste, an increased sensibility to beauty (if I may say so) that is lacking. *The English Renaissance of Art lecture* (*Uncollected*, p21)

176. ... I don't know where I am, but I am among canyons and coyotes — one is a sort of fox, the other a deep ravine: I don't know which is which, but it does not really matter in the West: they have such a strong objection to literature that they always use different words for the same object every day. *Letter to Mrs. Bernard Beere* (*Letters*, p152)

177. If you expect an English gentleman to come to your country, you must improve the character of your journalism. I do not intend to come to this city [Washington D.C.] again until this sort of thing is changed. *Oscar Wilde Discovers America* (*HBC*, 82)

178. The newspapers are far from representing the true public opinion of the American people on art questions. I have met as intelligent, appreciative, sympathetic people on my travels as in the highest art and social centers of England. *Oscar Wilde Discovers America* (*HBC*, p336)

179. All Americans lecture, I believe. I suppose it is something in their climate. *A Woman of No Importance* (*Plays*, p167)

180. There is, I think, no country in the world where there are such appreciative audi-

ences as I saw in the United States. *Letter to Marie Prescott* (*Letters*, p215)

181. She behaves as if she was beautiful. Most American women do. It is the secret of their charm. *The Picture of Dorian Gray* (*SC*, p51)

182. American youths are pale and precocious, or sallow and supercilious, but American girls are pretty and charming — little oases of pretty unreasonableness in a vast desert of common sense. *Personal Impressions of America lecture* (*Works*, p941)

183. I am charmed with American beauty. They possess a certain delicacy of outline surpassing English women. *Oscar Wilde Discovers America* (*HBC*, p64)

184. Every American girl is entitled to have twelve young men devoted to her. They remain her slaves and she rules them with charming nonchalance. *Personal Impressions of America lecture* (*Works*, p941)

185. She dresses exceedingly well. All Americans do dress well. They get their clothes in Paris. *A Woman of No Importance* (*Plays*, p136)

186. On the whole, American girls have a wonderful charm, and, perhaps, the chief secret of their charm is that they never talk seriously, except to their dressmaker, and never think seriously, except about amusements. *The American Invasion, Court and Society Review* (*Uncollected*, p37)

187. The first thing that struck me on landing in America was that if Americans were not the most well-dressed people in the world, they are the most comfortably dressed. *Personal Impressions of America lecture* (*Works*, p938)

188. Many American ladies on leaving their native land adopt an appearance of chronic ill-health, under the impression that it is a form of European refinement.... *The Canterville Ghost* (*Works*, p185)

189. ... as there is neither romance nor humility in her love [the American woman], she makes an excellent wife. *The American Invasion, Court and Society Review* (*Uncollected*, p39)

190. America is the only country where Don Juan is not appreciated. *Oscar Wilde Discovers America* (*HBC*, p154)

191. American women are bright, clever, and wonderfully cosmopolitan ... they take their dresses from Paris and their manners from Piccadilly, and wear both charmingly. They have a quaint pertness, a delightful conceit, a native self-assertion. They insist on being paid compliments, and have almost succeeded in making Englishmen eloquent. For our aristocracy they have an ardent admiration; they adore titles and are a permanent blow to Republican principles. In the art of amusing men they are adepts, both by nature and education, and can actually tell a story without forgetting the point — an accomplishment that is extremely rare among the women of other countries. It is true that they lack repose and that their voices are somewhat harsh and strident when they land first at Liverpool; but after a time one gets to love these pretty whirlwinds in petticoats that sweep so recklessly through society and are so agitating to all duchesses who have daughters. There is something fascinating in their funny, exaggerated gestures and their petulant way of tossing the head. Their eyes have no magic or mystery in them, but they challenge us for combat; and when we engage we are always worsted. *The American Invasion, Court and Society Review* (*Uncollected,* p37)

192. Still, they [American women] never really lose their accent: it keeps peeping out here and there, and when they chatter together they are like a bevy of peacocks. Nothing is more amusing than to watch two American girls greeting each other in a drawing-room or in the Row. They are like children with their shrill staccato cries of wonder, their odd little exclamations. Their conversation sounds like a series of exploding crackers; they are exquisitely incoherent and use a sort of primitive, emotional language. After five minutes they are left beautifully breathless and look at each other half in amusement and half in affection. If a stolid young Englishman is fortunate enough to be introduced to them he is amazed at their extraordinary vivacity, their electric quickness of repartee, their inexhaustible store of curious catchwords. He never really under-

stands them, for their thoughts flutter about with the sweet irresponsibility of butterflies; but he is pleased and amused and feels as if he were in an aviary. *The American Invasion, Court and Society Review* (*Uncollected,* p37)

193. In the art of amusing men [American women] are adepts, both by nature and education, and can actually tell a story without forgetting the point — an accomplishment that is extremely rare among the women of other countries. *The American Invasion, Court and Society Review* (*Uncollected,* p37)

194. American women are charming, but American men — alas! *Quoted in Oscar Wilde: His Life and Wit* (*HBP,* p67)

195. For the strange thing about American civilization is that the women are most charming when they are away from their own country, the men most charming when they are at home. *Oscar Wilde Discover America* (*HBC,* p152)

196. At home, the American man is the best of companions, as he is the most hospitable of hosts. The young men are especially pleasant, with their bright, handsome eyes, their unwearying energy, their amusing shrewdness. They seem to get a hold on life much earlier than we [English] do. At an age when we are still boys at Eton, or lads at Oxford, they are practicing some important profession, making money in some intricate business. Real experience comes to them much sooner than it does to us that they are never awkward, never shy, and never say foolish things except when they ask one how the Hudson River compares to the Rhine, or whether Brooklyn Bridge is not really more impressive than the dome at St. Paul's.... Bulk is their canon of beauty and size is their standard of excellence.... *Oscar Wilde Discover America* (*HBC,* pp152–3)

197. Their education is quite different from ours. They know men much better than they know books, and life interests them more than literature. They have no time to study anything but the stock markets, and no leisure to read anything but the newspapers. Indeed, it is only the women in America who have any leisure at all; and, as a necessary result of this curious state of things, there is no doubt but that, within a century from now, the whole culture of the New World will be in petticoats. *Oscar Wilde Discover America* (*HBC*, p153)

198. LADY CAROLINE: ... These American girls carry off all the good matches. Why can't they stay in their own country? They are always telling us it is the Paradise of women.

LORD ILLINGWORTH: It is, Lady Caroline. That is why, like Eve, they are so extremely anxious to get out of it. *A Woman of No Importance* (*Plays*, p135) and similar quotation in The Picture of Dorian Gray (*SC*, p51)

199. LORD HENRY: It is rather fashionable to marry Americans just now, Uncle George.

LORD FERMOR: I'll back English women against the world.

LORD HENRY: The betting is on the Americans.

LORD FERMOR: They don't last, I am told.

LORD HENRY: A long engagement exhausts them, but they are capital at a steeplechase. They take things flying. *The Picture of Dorian Gray* (*SC*, p51)

200. LORD HENRY: Dorian is far too wise not to do foolish things now and then, my dear Basil.

BASIL HALLWARD: Marriage is hardly a thing that one can do now and then, Harry.

LORD HENRY: Except in America. *The Picture of Dorian Gray* (*SC*, p88)

201. On the whole, the great success of marriage in the States is due partly to the fact that no American man is ever idle and partly to the fact that no American wife is considered responsible for the quality of her husband's dinners. In America, the horrors of domesticity are almost entirely unknown. *Oscar Wilde Discovers* (*HBC*, p153)

202. Even the American freedom of divorce, questionable though it undoubtedly is on many grounds, has at least the merit of bringing into marriage a new element of romantic uncertainty. When people are tied together for life they too often regard manners as a mere superfluidity and courtesy as a thing of no moment; but where the bond can easily be broken, its very fragility makes its strength and reminds the husband that he should always try to be pleasing, and the wife that she

should never cease to be charming. *Oscar Wilde Discovers America* (*HBC*, pp153–4)

203. If the English girl ever met him [the American man], she would marry him; and if she married him, she would be happy. For, though he may be rough in manner and deficient in the picturesque insincerity of romance, yet he is invariably kind and thoughtful, and has succeeded in making his own country the Paradise of women. This, however, is perhaps why, like Eve, the women are always so anxious to get out of it. *Oscar Wilde Discovers America* (*HBC*, p154)

204. THE CANTERVILLE GHOST: I don't think I should like America.

VIRGINIA: I suppose because we have no ruins and no curiosities. *The Canterville Ghost* (*Works*, p197)

205. LADY CAROLINE: There are a great many things you haven't got in America, I am told, Miss Worsley. They say you have no ruins and no curiosities.

MRS. ALLONBY: What nonsense! They have their mothers and their manners.

HESTER: The English aristocracy supplies us with our curiosities, Lady Caroline. They are sent over to us every summer, regularly, in the steamers, and propose to us the day after they land. *A Woman of No Importance* (*Plays*, pp159–60) and similar quotation in *The Canterville Ghost* (*Works*, p197)

206. LORD FERMOR: Who are her people?.... Has she got any?

LORD HENRY: American girls are as clever at concealing their parents, as English women are at concealing their past. *The Picture of Dorian Gray* (*SC*, p51)

207. Warned by the example of her mother that American women do not grow old gracefully, she tries not to grow old at all, and often succeeds. *The American Invasion, Court and Society Review* (*Uncollected*, p39)

208. American girls have a wonderful charm and, perhaps, the chief secret of their charm is that they never talk seriously except about amusements. They have, however, one grave fault — their mothers. Dreary as were those old pilgrim fathers who left our shores more than two centuries ago to found a New England beyond seas, the Pilgrim Mothers who have returned to us in the nineteenth century are drearier still. *The American Invasion, Court and Society Review* (*Uncollected,* p38)

209. ... the fact remains that the American mother is a tedious person. The American father is far better, for he is never seen in London. He passes his life entirely in Wall Street and communicates with his family once a month by means of a telegram in cipher. *The American Invasion, Court and Society Review* (*Uncollected,* p39)

210. In fact, it may be truly said that no American child is ever blind to the deficiencies of its parents, no matter how much it may love them. *The American Invasion, Court and Society Review* (*Uncollected,* p39)

211. In America the young are always ready to give to those who are older than themselves the full benefits of their experience. *The American Invasion, Court and Society Review* (*Uncollected,* p38)

212. The youth of America is their oldest tradition. It has been going on now for three hundred years. To hear them talk one would imagine they were in their first childhood. As far as civilisation goes they are in their second. *A Woman of No Importance* (*Plays,* p136)

213. From its earliest years every American child spends most of its time correcting the faults of its father and mother. *The American Invasion, Court and Society Review* (*Uncollected,* p38)

214. I was disappointed with Niagara — most people must be disappointed with Niagara. Every American bride is taken there, and the sight of the stupendous waterfall must be one of the earliest, if not the keenest, disappointments in American married life. One sees it under bad conditions, very far away, the point of view not showing the splendour of the water. To appreciate it really one has to see it from underneath the fall, and to do that it is necessary to be dressed in a yellow oilskin, which is as ugly as a mackintosh — and I hope none of you ever wears one. It is a consolation to know, however, that such an artist as Madame Bernhardt has not only worn that yellow, ugly dress, but has been photographed

in it. *Personal Impressions of America lecture* (*Works,* p939)

215. [Niagara Falls is] simply a vast unnecessary amount of water going the wrong way and then falling over unnecessary rocks. The wonder would be if the water did not fall. *Quoted in Oscar Wilde: His Life and Wit* (HBP, p59)

216. The cities of America are inexpressibly tedious. The Bostonians take their learning too sadly; culture with them is an accomplishment rather than an atmosphere; their "Hub," as they call it, is the paradise of prigs. Chicago is a sort of monster shop, full of bustles and bores. Political life at Washington is like political life in a suburban vestry. Baltimore is amusing for a week, but Philadelphia is dreadfully provincial; and though one can dine in New York one could not dwell there. Better the far West with its grizzly bears and its untamed cowboys, its free open-air life and its free open-air manners, its boundless prairie and its boundless mendacity! This is what Buffalo Bill is going to bring to London; and we have no doubt that London will fully appreciate his show. *The American Invasion, Court and Society Review* (*Uncollected,* p36)

217. We in England have no idea of the distances in your country. The impression there seems to be that all of the large cities are located in the suburbs of New York; then come the Rocky Mountains, next the Indians, then San Francisco and the ocean. We do not understand that large cities like Chicago and Cincinnati are located in the heart of the country.... Why, this is a world! But it looks so barren and rugged in winter.... *Oscar Wilde Discovers America* (HBC, p205)

218. When I landed in New York and read what the newspapers had to say about me, I thought I was about to travel in an extensive lunatic asylum, but when I went out in society there, I found the most charming cosmopolitan people I ever had the pleasure of meeting. The newspapers are far from representing the true public opinion of the American people on art questions. I have met as intelligent, appreciative, sympathetic people on my travels as in the highest art and social centers of England. *Oscar Wilde Discovers America* (*HBC*, p336)

219. ... I was quite charmed with New York and with its men and beautiful women. The city has a cosmopolitan air, quite like Paris or Vienna. *Oscar Wilde Discovers America* (*HBC*, p82)

220. Once in New York, you are sure to be a great success. I know lots of people there who would give a hundred thousand dollars to have a grandfather, and much more than that to have a family ghost. *The Canterville Ghost* (*Works*, p197)

221. Indeed, the two most remarkable bits of scenery in the States are undoubtedly Delmonico's and the Yosemite valley; and the former place has done more to promote a good feeling between England and America than anything else has in this century. *Dinner and Dishes, Pall Mall Gazette* (*Uncollected*, p194)

222. I hate to fly through a country at this rate. The only true way, you know, to see a country is to ride on horseback. *Oscar Wilde Discovers America* (*HBC*, p63)

223. Why build it [the Chicago water tower] like a castle where one expects to see knights peering out? *Oscar Wilde Discovers America* (*HBC*, p179)

224. I find New York brilliant and cosmopolitan; Philadelphia, literary; Baltimore, pleasant; Washington, intellectual; Boston, more like Oxford than any city you have. The people in Chicago I find simple and strong, and without any foolish prejudices that have influenced Eastern America. I find the audiences in Chicago very sympathetic, and it gives me a sense of power to sway such large multitudes. It is grand. In fact, the side of your American civilization those of us in Europe who are watching your young republics are most interested in, is not the East but the West. We want to see what civilization you are making for yourselves and by yourselves. *Oscar Wilde Discovers America* (*HBC*, p183)

225. The West has kept itself free and independent while the East has been caught and spoiled with many of the flirting follies of Europe. *Oscar Wilde Discovers America* (*HBC*, p308)

226. The further West one comes, the more there is to like. The Western people are much more genial than those of the East, and I fancy I shall be greatly pleased with California. *Oscar Wilde Discovers America* (*HBC*, p243)

227. No part of America has struck me so favorably as California, although I have yet to see Colorado. I intend to return to San Francisco and the West Coast next year with a party of friends in the capacity of a private gentleman traveling for his own amusement and not as a public lecturer condemned to go on the platform at every place I stop. *Oscar Wilde Discovers America* (*HBC*, p275)

228. You know I have just come from California, which is a garden of beauty. Oh, it is so lovely! The cities of the Atlantic Coast look bare and dreary at this time of year. *Oscar Wilde Discovers America* (*HBC*, p284)

229. In California I dined with a gentleman who had fired eleven shots at a predatory poet and could not be convinced that he had been guilty of want of respect for literature in doing so. *Quoted in Oscar Wilde: His Life and Wit* (*HBP*, p62)

230. California is an Italy without its art. *Oscar Wilde Discovers America* (*HBC*, p306)

231. There were 4,000 people waiting at the "depot" to see me, open carriage, four horses, an audience at my lecture of the most cultivated people in 'Frisco, charming folk. I lecture here again tonight, also twice next week; as you see I am really appreciated — by the cultured classes. *Letter to Norman Forbes-Robertson* (*Letters*, p158)

232. It is an odd thing, but everyone who disappears is said to be seen at San Francisco. It must be a delightful city, and possess all the attractions of the next world. *The Picture of Dorian Gray* (*SC*, p223)

233. This is where I belong [at the Bohemian Club in San Francisco]! This is my atmosphere! I didn't know such a place existed in the whole United States. *Quoted in Oscar Wilde: His Life and Wit* (*HBP*, p63)

234. San Francisco is really a beautiful city. China Town ... is the most artistic town I have ever come across. *Personal Impressions of America lecture* (*Works*, p939)

235. When I was in San Francisco, I used to visit the Chinese theatres for their rich dresses, and the Chinese restaurants on account of the beautiful tea they made there. I saw rough Chinese navies, who did work that the ordinary Californian rightly might be disgusted with and refuse to do, sitting there drinking their tea out of tiny porcelain cups, which might be mistaken for the petals of a white rose, and handling them with care, fully appreciating the influence of their beauty; whereas in all the grand hotels of the land, where thousands of dollars have been lavished on great gilt mirrors and gaudy columns, I have been given my chocolate in the morning and my coffee in the evening in common delft cups about an inch-and-a-half thick. I think I have deserved something nicer. If these men could use these cups with tenderness, your children will learn by the influence of beauty and example to act in a like manner. The great need in America is for good decoration; art is not given to the people by costly foreign paintings in private galleries; people can learn more by a well-shaped vessel for ordinary use. *The Decorative Arts lecture* (*Uncollected*, p935) and similar quotations in *The House Beautiful lecture* (*Uncollected*, p921) and *House Decoration lecture* (*Uncollected*, p189)

236. I was delighted with the Chinese quarters [in San Francisco] ... they fascinated me. I wish those people had a quarter in London. I should take pleasure in visiting it often. Their theatre was plain and the stage was devoid of ornamentation. *Oscar Wilde Discovers America* (*HBC*, p248)

237. I disliked to leave San Francisco, and I should love to visit it again. *Oscar Wilde Discovers America* (*HBC*, p284)

238. The women here are beautiful [in San Francisco]. *Letter to Norman Forbes-Robertson* (*Letters*, p159)

239. American women are very beautiful, and some of the finest types of beauty I have ever seen I found in the South. *Oscar Wilde Discovers America* (*HBC*, p389)

240. The South has produced the best poet of America — Edgar Allen Poe — and with all its splendid traditions it would be impossible not to believe that she will continue to per-

fect what she has begun so nobly. *Oscar Wilde Discovers America* (*HBC*, p373)

241. The very physique in the South is far finer than that of the North, and its temperament infinitely more susceptible to the influences of beauty. *Oscar Wilde Discovers America* (*HBC*, p373)

242. [Southerners are] more agreeable and courteous than Northerners. [In Chicago, people] pushed with a brusque sort of energy, in the South people are more quiet and polite. It may be the result of climatic effects. *Oscar Wilde Discovers America* (*HBC*, p362)

243. Among the more elderly inhabitants of the South I found a melancholy tendency to date every event of importance by the late war. "How beautiful the moon is to-night," I once remarked to a gentleman standing near me. "Yes," was his reply, "but you should have seen it before the war." *Personal Impressions of America lecture* (*Works*, pp940–1)

244. It is a popular superstition that a visitor to the more distant parts of the United States is spoken to as "Stranger." But when I went to Texas I was called "Captain"; when I got to the centre of the country I was addressed as "Colonel"; and, on arriving at the borders of Mexico, as "General." *Quoted in Oscar Wilde: His Life and Wit* (*HBP*, pp66–7)

245. I wonder that the criminals do not plead the ugliness of your city [Cincinnati] as an excuse for their crimes. *Oscar Wilde Discovers America* (*HBC*, p189)

246. CITIZEN OF GRIGGSVILLE: Will you lecture us on aesthetics?

OSCAR WILDE: Begin by changing the name of your town. *Quoted in Oscar Wilde: His Life and Wit* (*HBP*, p66)

247. Salt Lake City contains only two buildings of note, the chief being the Tabernacle, which is in the shape of a soup-kettle. *Personal Impressions of America lecture* (*Works*, p940)

248. ... the [Mormon] Tabernacle has the shape of a soup kettle and decorations suitable for a jail. It was the most purely dreadful building I ever saw. There was not even the honesty to tell the truth, because they painted sham pillars. There are no pillars in the building. In the House of God, I think, no lies should be told. *Oscar Wilde Discovers America* (*HBC*, p307)

249. ... Leadville, the richest city in the world. It has also got the reputation of being the roughest, and every man carries a revolver. I was told that if I went there they would be sure to shoot me or my traveling manager. I wrote and told them that nothing that they could do to my traveling manager would intimidate me. *Personal Impressions of America lecture* (*Works*, p940)

250. ... when I was in Leadville, the richest city for silver in the world, and heard of the most incredible quantity of silver taken from its mountains, I thought how sad it was that the silver should be made into flat, ugly dollars, useful perhaps to the artist—for dollars are very good in their way—but which should not be the end and aim of life. There should be some better record of it left in your history than the merchant's panic and the ruined home. *The Decorative Arts lecture* (*Works*, p934)

251. There is nothing in my mind more coarse in conception and more vulgar in execution than modern jewelry. This is something that can be easily corrected. Something better should be made out of the beautiful gold which is stored up in your mountain hollows and strewn along your river beds. When I was at Leadville and reflected that all the shining silver that I saw coming from the mines would be made into ugly dollars, it made me sad. It should be made into something more permanent. The golden gates at Florence are as beautiful to-day as when Michelangelo saw them. *House Decoration lecture* (*Uncollected*, p188)

252. Pennsylvania, with its rocky gorges and woodland scenery, reminded me of Switzerland. The prairie reminded me of a piece of blotting paper. *Personal Impressions of America lecture* (*Works*, p941)

253. If one wants to realise what English Puritanism is—not at its worst (when it is very bad), but at its best, and then it is not very good—I do not think one can find much of it in England, but much can be found about Boston and Massachusetts. We have got rid of it. America still preserves it, to be, I hope,

a short-lived curiosity. *Personal Impressions of America lecture* (*Works*, p939)

254. ... no well behaved river ought to act that way. (*Regarding the Mississippi River*). *Oscar Wilde Discovers America* (*HBC*, p202)

255. Washington has too many bronze generals. *Oscar Wilde Discovers America* (*HBC*, p84)

256. In America, you see, I have for the first time been face to face with people who have never seen any good art.... *Oscar Wilde Discovers America* (*HBC*, p349)

257. But, as in your cities so in your literature, it is a permanent canon and standard of taste, an increased sensibility to beauty (if I may say so) that is lacking. *The English Renaissance of Art lecture* (*Uncollected*, p21)

258. For him [the American] art has no marvel, and Beauty no meaning, and the Past no message. *Oscar Wilde Discovers America* (*HBC*, p445)

259. ... the fear of the [American] eagle that I have come to cut his barbaric claws with the scissors of culture. *Letter to the Hon. George Curzon* (*Letters*, p138)

260. Your people love art but do not significantly honor the handicraftsman. *House Decoration lecture* (*Uncollected*, p183)

261. If you expect to have art in this country, you must have good morals to back it. *Oscar Wilde Discovers America* (*HBC*, p82)

262. You can make as good a design out of an American turkey as a Japanese out of his native stork. *Oscar Wilde Discovers America* (*HBC*, p177)

263. [Pictures] should be hung upon the eye-line. The habit in America of hanging them up near the cornice struck me as irrational at first. It was not until I saw how bad the pictures were that I realized the advantage of the custom. *Oscar Wilde Discovers America* (*HBC*, p254)

264. In England, all society and all art is centered in one city, and to me the society of a large provincial city like Manchester is simply unbearable. In your country there is no such similar center, but all over the country I find an element appreciative and intellectual. *Oscar Wilde Discovers America* (*HBC*, pp336-7)

265. I am struck by the type of civilization definitely American created by yourselves and for yourselves. *Oscar Wilde Discovers America* (*HBC*, p167)

266. The pictures hung up in most of the houses I have visited in America were dull, commonplace and tawdry. Poor pictures are worse than none. *The House Beautiful lecture* (*Works*, p920)

267. But you [Americans], you do not care much for Greek gods and goddesses, and you are perfectly and entirely right; and you do not think much of kings either, and you are quite right. But what you do love are your own men and women, your own flowers and fields, your own hills and mountains, and these are what your art should represent to you. *Art and the Handicraftsman lecture* (*Uncollected*, p113)

268. And so, as I said, find your subjects in everyday life; your own men and women, your own flowers and fields, your own hills and mountains; these are what your art should represent to you, for every nation can represent with prudence or with success only those things in which it delights, what you have with you and before you daily, dearest to your sight and to your heart, by the magic of your hand and the music of your lips you can gloriously express to others. All these commend themselves to the thoughtful student and artist. *The Decorative Arts lecture* (*Works*, p933)

269. Let the Greek carve his lions and the Goth his dragons: buffalo and wild deer are the animals for you. *Art and the Handicraftsman lecture* (*Uncollected*, p113)

270. You in America need more noble architecture. The old red-brick houses which your Puritan forefathers built for you are more beautiful than the sham Greek porticos of Fifth Avenue. *Oscar Wilde Discovers America* (*HBC*, p168)

271. To you, more than perhaps to any other country, has nature been generous in furnishing material for art workers to work in. You have marble quarries where the stone is more beautiful in colour than any the Greek ever had for their beautiful work. *House Decoration lecture* (*Uncollected*, p188)

272. So do not mind what art Philadelphia or New York is having, but make by the hands of your own citizens beautiful art for the joy of your own citizens, for you have here primary elements of a great artistic movement. *Art and the Handicraftsman lecture* (*Uncollected*, p111)

273. The gold is ready for you [Americans] in unexhausted treasure, stored up in the mountain hollow or strewn on the river sand, and was not given to you merely for barren speculation. There should be some better record of it left in your history than the merchant's panic and the ruined home. *Art and the Handicraftsman lecture* (*Uncollected*, p113)

274. We have as yet nothing like it in England. We call a man rich over there when he owns a share of Scotland, or a country or so. But he doesn't have such a control of ready money as does an American capitalist. *Oscar Wilde Discovers America* (*HBC*, p41)

275. Art must differ with place and people. What would be quite right in England would be quite wrong here. *Oscar Wilde Discovers America* (*HBC*, p64)

276. America is a country that has no trappings, no pageants and no gorgeous ceremonies. I saw only two processions—one was the fire brigade preceded by the police, the other was the police preceded by the fire brigade. *Oscar Wilde Discovers America* (*HBC*, p210)

277. A terrible danger is hanging over the Americans in London. Their future and their reputation this season depends entirely on the success of Buffalo Bill and Mrs. Brown Potter. *The American Invasion, Court and Society Review* (*Uncollected*, p36)

278. ... he seems to have had experience of almost every kind of meal except the "square meal" of the Americans. This he should study at once; there is a great field for philosophic epicure in the United States. *Dinners and Dishes, Pall Mall Gazette* (*Uncollected*, p194)

279. ... one of the most delightful things I find in America is meeting a people without prejudice — everywhere open to the truth. We have nothing like it in England.... *Oscar Wilde Discovers America* (*HBC*, p65)

280. It is well worth one's while to go to a country which can teach us the beauty of the word FREEDOM and the value of the thing

LIBERTY. *Personal Impressions of America lecture* (*Works*, p941)

281. The personal control of capital, with the power it gives over labor and life, has only appeared in modern American life. *Oscar Wilde Discovers America* (*HBC*, p41)

282. I am told that pork-packing is the most lucrative profession in America, after politics. *The Picture of Dorian Gray* (*SC*, p51)

283. On the whole, the American invasion has done English society a great deal of good. *The American Invasion Court and Society Review* (*Uncollected*, p37)

284. Sir Thomas: They say that when good Americans die, they go to Paris.

Duchess of Harley: Really! And where do bad Americans go to when they die?

Lord Henry: They go to America. *The Picture of Dorian Gray* (*SC*, p55) and similar quotation in *A Woman of No Importance* (*Plays*, p136)

285. I would rather have discovered Mrs. [Lily] Langtry than have discovered America. (*Letters*, p137)

286. Perhaps, after all, America never has been discovered. I myself would say that it had merely been detected. *The Picture of Dorian Gray* (*SC*, p55)

4

Art

287. One should either be a work of art, or wear a work of art. *Phrases and Philosophies for the Use of the Young, The Chameleon* (*Works*, p1245)

288. ... there are only two things in the world of any importance, Love and Art; you have both; they must never leave you. *Letter to Arthur Fish* (*Letters*, p455)

289. Art is not something which you can take or leave. It is a necessity of human life. *House Decoration lecture* (*Uncollected*, p183)

290. Love art for its own sake, and then all things that you need will be added to you. *The English Renaissance of Art lecture* (*Uncollected*, p21) and *L'Envoi* (*Uncollected*, p198)

291. Art finds her own perfection within, and not outside of, herself. *The Decay of Lying* (*Works*, p1082)

292. Art can never have any other claim but her own perfection.... *The English Renaissance of Art lecture* (*Uncollected*, p17) and *The Relation of Art to Dress lecture* (*Uncollected*, p53)

293. Art has no other aim but her own perfection, and proceeds simply by her own laws.... *The Truth of Masks* (*Works*, p1169)

294. Only art must be asked of art, only the past of the past. *The Rise of Historical Criticism* (*Works*, p1207)

295. Art never expresses anything but itself. It has an independent life, just as Thought has, and develops purely on its own lines. *The Decay of Lying* (*Works*, p1091)

296. Everything matters in art except the subject. *Interview in The Sketch* (*Uncollected*, p.xix)

297. The object of art is to stir the most divine and remote of the cords which make music in our soul; and colour is, indeed, of itself a mystical presence on things, and tone a kind of sentinel. *Lecture to Art Students at the Royal Academy* (*Uncollected*, p130)

298. For he who does not love art in all things does not love it at all, and he who does not need art in all things does not need it at all. *The English Renaissance of Art lecture* (*Uncollected*, p25)

299. Make some sacrifice for your art, and you will be repaid; but ask Art to sacrifice herself for you, and a bitter disappointment may come to you. *Letter to an Unidentified Correspondent* (*Letters*, p265)

300. Psychology is in its infancy as a science. I hope, in the interests of art, it will always remain so. *Quoted in Oscar Wilde: His Life and Wit* (*HBP*, p37)

301. Where in the arts themselves are we to find that breadth of human sympathy which is the condition of all noble work.... *The English Renaissance of Art lecture* (*Uncollected*, p15)

302. There is nothing in common life too mean, in common things too trivial to be ennobled by your touch; nothing in life that art cannot sanctify. *Decorative Arts lecture* (*Works*, p93) and similar quotation in *The House Beautiful lecture* (*Works*, p913 and p925)

303. What we want is something spiritual added to life. Nothing is so ignoble that Art cannot sanctify it. *House Decoration lecture* (*Uncollected*, p190)

304. For if man cannot find the noblest motives for his art in such simple things as a woman drawing water from a well or a man leaning with his scythe, he will not find them anywhere at all. *Art and the Handicraftsman lecture* (*Uncollected*, p112)

305. We spend our days, each one of us, in looking for the secret of life. Well, the secret of life is in art. *The English Renaissance of Art lecture* (*Uncollected*, p28)

306. ... catastrophes in life bring about catastrophes in art. *Aspects of Wilde* (*CC*, p97)

307. The aim of art is simply to make life more joyous. *The House Beautiful lecture* (*Works*, p916)

308. For the arts are made for life, not life for the arts. *The Relation of Dress to Art lecture* (*Uncollected*, p52)

309. What is true about Art is true about Life. *The Soul of Man* (*OWC*, p32)

310. For art is very life itself and knows nothing of death.... *The English Renaissance of Art lecture* (*Uncollected*, p14)

311. If life is noble and beautiful, art will be noble and beautiful. *Oscar Wilde Discovers America* (*HBC*, p177)

312. ... Life imitates Art far more than Art imitates Life. This results not merely from Life's imitative instinct, but from the fact that the self-conscious aim of Life is to find expression, and that Art offers it certain beautiful forms through which it may realise that energy. It is a theory that has never been put forward before, but it is extremely fruitful, and throws an entirely new light upon the history of Art. *The Decay of Lying* (*Works*, p1091)

313. Were we at the mercy of such impressions as Art or Life chose to give us? It seemed to me to be so. *The Portrait of Mr. W.H.* (*Works*, p345)

314. For life remains eternally unchanged; it is art which, by presenting it to us under various forms, enables us to realise its many sided mysteries, and to catch the quality of its most fiery-coloured moments. *Olivia at the Lyceum* (*Works*, p955)

315. Great works of art are living things. *The Critic as Artist* (*Works*, p1132)

316. Life by its realism is always spoiling the subject-matter of art. The supreme pleasure in literature is to realise the non-existent. *Letter to the Editor of the St. James Gazette* (*Letters*, p430)

317. ... art, if we are to have it, should concern itself more with the living than the dead — should be rather a noble symbol for the guiding of life than an idle panegyric on those who are gone. *Letter to the Rev. J. Page Hopps* (*Letters*, p247)

318. ... Life is Art's best, Art's only pupil. *The Decay of Lying* (*Works*, p1083)

319. Perhaps there may come into my art also, no less than into my life, a still deeper note, one of greater unity of passion, and directness of impulse. Not width but intensity is the true aim of modern art. *De Profundis* (*OWC*, p128)

320. We spend our days, each one of us, in looking for the secret of life. Well, the secret of life is in art. *The English Renaissance of Art lecture* (*Uncollected*, p28)

321. It is Art, and Art only, that reveals us to ourselves. *The Portrait of Mr. W.H.* (*Works*, p343)

322. Art, as so often happens, had taken the place of personal experience. *The Portrait of Mr. W.H.* (*Works*, p343)

323. ... the aim of art is not to reveal personality but to please. *London Models, English Illustrated Magazine* (*Works*, p34)

324. A picture is finished when all traces of the work, and of the means employed to bring about the result, have disappeared. *Lecture to Art Students at the Royal Academy* (*Uncollected*, p130)

325. For there is no art where there is no style, and no style where there is no unity, and unity is of the individual. *The Critic as Artist* (*Works*, p1119)

326. For art comes to one professing primarily to give nothing but the highest quality to one's moments, and for those moments' sake. *The English Renaissance of Art lecture* (*Uncollected*, p26)

327. ... I have only now, too late perhaps, found out how all art requires solitude as its companion.... *Letter to Matthew Arnold* (*Letters*, p112)

328. For it is not enough that a work of art should conform to the aesthetic demands of its age: there must be also about it, if it is to affect us with any permanent delight, the impress of a distinct individuality, an individuality remote from that of ordinary men, and coming near to us only by virtue of a certain newness and wonder in the work, and whose channels whose very strangeness makes us more ready to give them welcome. *The English Renaissance of Art lecture* (*Uncollected*, p9)

329. It is the spectator, and not life, that art really mirrors. *The Picture of Dorian Gray* (*SC*, p18) and *Letter to the Editor of the Scots Observer* (*Letters*, p441)

330. A mirror will give back to one one's own sorrow. But Art is not a mirror, but a crystal. It creates its own shapes and forms. *Letter to More Adey* (*Letters*, p672)

331. ... the most perfect art is that which most fully mirrors man in all his infinite variety.... *The Critic as Artist* (*Works*, p1115)

332. The nineteenth century dislike of romanticism is the rage of Caliban seeing his own face in the glass. The nineteenth century dislike of romanticism is the rage of Caliban not seeing his face in a glass. *The Picture of Dorian Gray* (*SC*, p18)

333. Art is always more abstract than we fancy. Form and colour tell us form and colour — that is all. *The Picture of Dorian Gray* (*SC*, p129)

334. Art must differ with place and people. *Oscar Wilde Discovers America* (*HBC*, p64)

335. There are two worlds. The one exists and is never talked about: it is called the real world because there is no need to talk about it in order to see it. The other is the world of art: one must talk about it because otherwise it would not exist. *Quoted in Oscar Wilde: His Life and Wit* (*HBP*, p192)

336. The work of art is to dominate the spectator: the spectator is not to dominate the work of art. The spectator is to be receptive. He is to be the violin on which the master is to play. And the more completely he can suppress his own silly views, his own foolish prejudices, his own absurd ideas of what art should be, or should not be, the more likely he is to understand and appreciate the work of art in question. *The Soul of Man* (*OWC*, p26)

337. ... the temperament to which art appeals. And what is that temperament? It is the temperament of receptivity. That is all. *The Soul of Man* (*OWC*, p26)

338. A temperament capable of receiving, through an imaginative medium, under imag-

inative conditions, new and beautiful impressions, is the only temperament that can appreciate a work of art. *The Soul of Man* (*OWC*, pp26–7)

339. The appeal of art is simply to the artistic temperament. Art does not address herself to the specialist. Her claim is that she is universal, and that in all her manifestations she is one. *The Critic as Artist* (*Works*, pp1149–50)

340. Art is the only serious thing in the world. And the artist is the only person who is never serious. *A Few Maxims for the Instruction of the Over-Educated* (*Works*, p1242)

341. There is no mood of passion that Art cannot give us, and those of us who have discovered her secret can settle beforehand what our experiences are going to be. *The Critic as Artist* (*Works*, p1132)

342. The man who sees both sides of the question sees nothing at all. Art is a passion, and, in matters of art, Thought is inevitably coloured by emotion, and so is fluid rather than fixed, and, depending upon fine moods and exquisite moments, cannot be narrowed into the rigidity of a scientific formula or a theological dogma. *Mr. Pater's Appreciations* (*Uncollected*, pp146–7) and *The Critic as Artist* (*Works*, p1144)

343. Art never expresses anything but itself. It has an independent life, just as Thought has, and develops purely on its own lines. It is not necessarily realistic in an age of realism, nor spiritual in an age of faith. So far from being the creation of its, it is usually in direct opposition to it, and the only history it preserves for us is the history of its own progress. Sometimes it returns upon its footsteps, and revives some antique form, as happened in the archaistic movement of late Greek Art, and in the pre–Raphaelite movement of our own day. At other times it entirely anticipates the age, and produces in one century work that it takes another century to understand, appreciate, and to enjoy. In no case does it reproduce the age. To pass from the art of a time to the time itself is the great mistake that all historians commit. *The Decay of Lying* (*Works*, p1091)

344. ... Art is useless because its aim is simply to create a mood. It is not meant to instruct, or to influence action in any way. *Letter to R. Clegg* (*Letters*, p478)

345. The aim of art is simply to create a mood. Is such a mode of life impractical? *The Critic as Artist* (*Works*, p1139)

346. I am very sorry, but artistic work can't be done unless one is in the mood; certainly my work can't. Sometimes I spend months over a thing, and don't do any good; at other times I write a thing in a fortnight. *Letter to George Alexander* (*Letters*, p463)

347. Religion springs from religious feeling, art from artistic feeling: you never get one from the other; unless you have the right root you will not get the right flower.... *Lecture to Art Students at the Royal Academy* (*Uncollected*, p128)

348. ... the sorrow with which Art fills us both purifies and initiates. *The Critic as Artist* (*Works*, p1135)

349. It is through Art, and through Art only, that we can shield ourselves from the sordid perils of actual existence. *The Critic as Artist* (*Works*, p1135)

350. ... in modern art atmosphere counts for so much. Modern life is complex and relative. *De Profundis* (*OWC*, p87)

351. The egoistic note is, and always has been to me, the primal and ultimate note of modern art, but *to be an Egoist one must have an Ego*. It is not everyone who says "I, I who can enter the Kingdom of Art." *Letter to Lord Alfred Douglas* (*Letters*, p874)

352. The motives for art are still around about us as they were round about the ancients. *House Decoration lecture* (*Uncollected*, p188)

353. But this restless modern intellectual spirit of ours is not receptive enough of the sensuous element of art; and so the real influence of the arts is hidden away from many of us: only a few escaping from the tyranny of the soul, have learned the secret of those high hours when thought is not. *The English Renaissance of Art lecture,* (*Uncollected*, pp15–6)

354. And what, I think, you should do is to realise completely your age in order to completely abstract yourself from it; remembering that if you are an artist at all, you will be not the mouthpiece of a century, but the master of eternity; that all art rests on a principle, and that mere temporal considerations are no principle at all; and that those who advise you to make your art representative of the nineteenth century are advising you to produce an art which your children, when you have them, will think old-fashioned. *Lecture to Art Students at the Royal Academy* (*Uncollected*, p124)

355. ... the essence of art is to produce the modern idea under an antique form. *Letter to Mary Anderson* (*Letters*, p197)

356. I can see no better way of getting rid of the mediaeval discord between soul and body than by sculpture. *Letter to Charles Eliot Norton* (*Letters*, p177)

357. The best that one can say of most modern creative art is that it is just a little less vulgar than reality. *The Critic as Artist* (*Works*, p1125)

358. Modern pictures are, no doubt, delightful to look at. At least, some of them are. But they are quite impossible to live with; they are too clever, too assertive, too intellectual. Their meaning is too obvious, and their method too clearly defined. One exhausts what they have to say in a very short time, and then they become as one's relations. *The Critic as Artist* (*Works*, p1147)

359. ... those sordid and stupid limitations of absolute modernity of form which have proved the ruin of so many of the Impressionists. Still, the art that is frankly decorative is the art to live with. It is, of all our visible arts, the one art that creates in us both mood and temperament. *The Critic as Artist* (*Works*, p1148)

360. The moment Art surrenders its imaginative medium it surrenders everything, As a method Realism is a complete failure, an the two things every artist should avoid is modernity of form and modernity of subject matter. *The Decay of Lying* (*Works*, p1091)

361. All around you, I said, lie the conditions for a great artistic movement for every great art. *Art and the Handicraftsman* (*Uncollected*, p112)

362. One of the most striking facts of history is that art was never so fine, never so delicate as were women were highly honoured, while there has been no good decorative work done in any age or any country where women have not occupied a high social position. It has been from the desire of women to beautify their households that decorative art has always received its impulse and encouragement. Women have natural art instincts, which men usually acquire only after long special training and study; and it may be the mission of the women in this country to revive decorative arts into honest, healthy life. *The House Beautiful lecture* (*Works*, p913)

363. For the great eras in the history of the development of all the arts have been eras not of increased feeling or enthusiasm in feeling for art, but of new technical improvements primarily and specifically. *The English Renaissance of Art lecture* (*Uncollected*, p4)

364. We must always remember that art has only one sentence to utter: there is for her only one high law, the law of form or harmony.... *The English Renaissance of Art lecture* (*Uncollected*, p10)

365. Art if rightly used will pave the way for a sort of universal brotherhood of man. *Oscar Wilde Discovers America* (*HBC*, p324)

366. As regards their origin, in art as in politics there is but one origin for all revolutions, a desire on the part of man for a nobler form of life, for a freer method and opportunity for expression. *The English Renaissance of Art lecture* (*Uncollected*, p4)

367. For the great eras in the history of the development of all the arts have been eras not of increased feeling or enthusiasm in feeling for art, but of new technical improvements primarily and specially. *The English Renaissance of Art lecture* (*Uncollected*, p10)

368. Art never harms itself by keeping aloof from the social problems of the day: rather, by doing so, it more completely realises for us that which we desire. *The English Renaissance of Art lecture* (*Uncollected*, p12)

369. And art will do more than make our lives joyous and beautiful; it will become part of the new history of the world and a part of the brotherhood of man; for art, by creating a common intellectual atmosphere between all countries might, if it could not overshadow the world with the silvery wings of peace, at least make men such brothers that they would not go out to slay one another for the whim or folly of some king or minister as they do in Europe, for national hatreds are always strongest where culture is lowest. *The Decorative Arts lecture* (*Works*, p934) and *The House Beautiful lecture* (*Works*, p925)

370. Varnishing is the only artistic process with which the Royal Academicians are thoroughly familiar. *Quoted in Oscar Wilde: His Life and Wit* (*HBP*, p86)

371. The Academy is too large and too vulgar. Whenever I have gone there, there have been either so many people that I have not been able to see the pictures, which was dreadful or so many pictures that I have not been able to see the people, which was worse. *The Picture of Dorian Gray* (*SC*, p18)

372. ... an educated person's ideas of Art are drawn naturally from what Art has been, whereas the new work of art is beautiful by being what Art has never been; and to measure it by the standard of the past is to measure it by a standard on the rejection of which its real perfection depends. *The Soul of Man* (*OWC*, p26)

373. ... as regards histories of art, they are quite valueless to you unless you are seeking the ostentatious oblivion of an art professorship. It is of no use to you to know the date of Perugino or the birthplace of Salvator Rosa: all that you should learn about art is to know a good picture when you see it, and a bad picture when you see it. As regards the date of the artist, all good works looks perfectly modern: a piece of Greek sculpture, a portrait of Velazquez — they are always modern, always of our time. And as regards the nationality of the artist, art is not national but universal. *Lecture to Art Students at the Royal Academy* (*Uncollected*, p123)

374. And if you teach a boy art, the beauty of form and colour will find its way into his heart, and he will love nature more; for there is no better way to learn to love nature than to understand art — it dignifies every flower in the field. He will have more pleasure and joy in nature when he sees how no flower by the wayside is too lowly, no little blade of grass too common, but some great designer has seen it and made noble use of it in decoration. *The Decorative Arts lecture* (*Works*, p936)

375. ... a lad who learns any simple art learns honesty, and truth-telling, and simplicity.... *Letter to Charles Godfrey Leland* (*Letters*, p170)

376. From the point of view of style, a healthy work of art is one whose style recognises the beauty of the material it employs.... From the point of view of subject, a healthy work of art is one the choices of whose subject is conditioned by the temperament of the artist, and comes directly out of it.... An unhealthy work of art, on the other hand, is a work whose style is obvious, old-fashioned and common, and whose subject is deliberately chosen, not because the artist has any pleasure in it, but because he thinks that the public will pay him for it. *The Soul of Man* (*OWC*, p22)

377. The conditions of art should be simple. A great deal more depends upon the heart than upon the head. Appreciation of art is not secured by any elaborate scheme of learning. Art requires a good healthy atmosphere. *House Decoration lecture* (*Uncollected*, pp187–8)

378. In its primary aspect a painting has more spiritual message or meaning than an exquisite fragment of Venetian glass or a blue tile from the wall of Damascus: it is a beautifully coloured surface, nothing more. *The English Renaissance of Art lecture* (*Uncollected*, p16)

379. Every single work of art is the fulfillment of a prophecy. For every work of art is the conversion of an idea into an image. Every single human being should be the fulfillment of a prophecy. For every human being should be the realisation of some ideal, either in the mind of God or in the mind of man. *De Profundis* (*OWC*, p117)

380. To us, who live in the nineteenth century, any century is a suitable subject for art except our own. *The Decay of Lying* (*Works*, p1091)

381. For there never was an age that so much needed the spiritual ministry of art as the present. Today more than ever the artist and a love of the beautiful are needed to tem-

per and counteract the sordid materialism of the age. *The House Beautiful lecture* (*Works*, p925)

382. While the Western world has been laying on art the intolerable burden of its own intellectual doubts and the spiritual tragedy of its own sorrows, the East has always kept true to art's primary and pictorial conditions. *The English Renaissance of Art lecture* (*Uncollected*, p16)

383. Art, even the art of fullest scope and widest vision, can never really show us the external world. All that it shows us is our own soul, the one world of which we have any real cognizance. *The Portrait of Mr. W.H.* (*Works*, p343)

384. All art is at once surface and symbol. Those who go beneath the surface do so at their peril. Those who read the symbol do so at their peril. *The Picture of Dorian Gray* (*SC*, p18)

385. At every single moment of one's life one is what one is going to be no less than what one has been. Art is a symbol, because man is a symbol. *De Profundis* (*OWC*, p109)

386. ... the various spiritual forms of the imagination have a natural affinity with certain sensuous forms of art.... *The English Renaissance of Art lecture* (*Uncollected*, p20)

387. Nor, in its primary aspect, has a painting, for instance, any more spiritual message or meaning for us than a blue tile from the wall of Damascus, or a Hitzen vase. It is a beautifully coloured surface, nothing more. *L'Envoi* (*Uncollected*, p198)

388. Art is mind expressing itself under the conditions of matter, and thus, even in the lowliest of her manifestations, she speaks to both sense and soul alike. *The Critic as Artist* (*Works*, p1137)

389. You say that a work of art is a form of action. It is not. It is the highest mode of thought. *Letter to the Editor of The St. James Gazette* (*Letters*, p434)

390. Thought and language are to the artist instruments of an art. *The Picture of Dorian Gray* (*SC*, p18)

391. Truth in art is the unity of a thing with itself: the outward rendered expressive of the inward: the soul made incarnate: the body instinct with the spirit. *De Profundis* (*OWC*, p105)

392. ... art is very life itself and knows nothing about death; she is absolute truth and takes no care of fact.... *The English Renaissance of Art lecture* (*Uncollected*, p14)

393. ... in art there is no such thing as a universal truth. A Truth in art is that whose contradictory is also true. *The Truth of Masks* (*Works*, p1173)

394. ... the two things on which all good art is founded, truth and honesty. In the world of business it is possible for the liar and the cheat to escape detection during all their lives— not so in art. *Oscar Wilde Discovers America* (*HBC*, pp214–5)

395. And yet the truths of art cannot be taught: they are revealed only, revealed to natures which have made themselves receptive of all beautiful impressions by the study and worship of all beautiful things. *The English Renaissance of Art lecture* (*Uncollected*, p23)

396. Art itself is really a form of exaggeration; and selection, which is the very spirit of Art, is nothing more than an intensified mode of over-emphasis. *The Decay of Lying* (*Works*, p1079)

397. Lying, the telling of beautiful untrue things, is the proper aim of art. *The Decay of Lying* (*Works*, pp1091–2)

398. All art is immoral. *The Critic as Artist* (*Works*, p1136)

399. The moral life of man forms part of the subject-matter of the artist, but the morality of art consists in the perfect use of an imperfect medium. *The Picture of Dorian Gray* (*SC*, p18)

400. The sphere of art and the sphere of ethics are absolutely distinct and separate. *Quoted in Oscar Wilde: His Life and Wit* (*HBP*, p131)

401. Nor, in looking at a work of art, should we be dreaming of what it symbolizes, but rather loving it for what it is. *L'Envoi* (*Works*, p198)

402. ... preferences in art are very valueless, what is needed is to understand the conditions of each art.... *Letter to Frank Granger* (*Letters*, p335)

403. We want to create it [art], not to define it. The definition should follow the work: the work should not adapt itself to the definition. *Lecture to Art Students at the Royal Academy* (*Uncollected*, p123)

404. Anything approaching an explanation is always derogatory to a work of art. If the public cannot understand the line, well — they cannot understand it. *Letter to Violet Fane* (*Letters*, p330)

405. Now art should never try to be popular. The public should try to make itself artistic. *The Soul of Man* (*OWC*, p17)

406. Healthy art is that which realizes that beauty of the age in which we live, while art is unhealthy that is obliged to go back to old romantic ages for its themes. *The Decorative Arts lecture* (*Works*, p930)

407. Romantic art deals with the exception and with the individual. *Letter to the Editor of the St. James Gazette* (*Letters*, p430)

408. Instead of this servile imitation of romantic ages, we should strive to make our own age a romantic age, and art should reproduce for us the faces and forms we love and revere. *The Decorative Arts lecture* (*Works*, p930)

409. Art is the science of beauty, and Mathematics the science of truth.... *Lecture to Art Students at the Royal Academy* (*Uncollected*, p123)

410. Art is the mathematical result of the emotional desire for beauty. *Letter to Marie Prescott* (*Letters*, p204)

411. Nothing, indeed, is more dangerous to the young artist than any conception of ideal beauty. He is constantly led by it either into weak prettiness or lifeless abstraction: whereas to touch the ideal at all you must not strip it of vitality. You must find it in life and re-create it in art. *Lecture to Art Students at the Royal Academy* (*Uncollected*, p123)

412. ... that mingling of classic grace with absolute reality which is the secret of all beautiful art.... *Mrs. Langtry as Hester Grazebrook* (*Uncollected*, p67)

413. From the point of view of style, a healthy work of art is one whose style recognizes the beauty of the material it employs.... *The Soul of Man* (*OWC*, p22)

414. The one characteristic of a beautiful form is that one can put into it whatever one wishes, and see in it whatever one chooses to see.... *The Critic as Artist* (*Works*, p1128)

415. For all great art is delicate art, roughness having very little to do with strength, and harshness very little to do with power. *The English Renaissance of Art lecture* (*Uncollected*, p21)

416. Few people will deny that they are doing injury to themselves and their children by living outside the beauty of life, which we call art, for art is no mere accident of existence which men may take or leave, but a very necessity of human life.... *The Decorative Arts lecture* (*Works*, p926)

417. If you develop art culture by beautifying the things around you, you may be certain that other arts will in the course of time. *The Decorative Arts lecture* (*Works*, p926)

418. ... the good we get from art is not what we derive directly, but what improvement is made in us by being accustomed to the sight of all gracious and comely things. *The Decorative Arts lecture* (*Works*, p934)

419. The art which has fulfilled the conditions of beauty has fulfilled all conditions: it is for the critic to teach the people how to find in the calm of such art the highest expression of their own most stormy passions. *The English Renaissance of Art lecture* (*Uncollected*, p18)

420. Art should have no sentiment about it but its beauty, no technique except what you cannot observe. One should be able to say of a picture not that it is "well painted," but that it is "not painted." *Lecture to Art Students at the Royal Academy* (*Uncollected*, p130)

421. A picture has no meaning but its beauty, no message but its joy. That is the first truth about art that you must never lose sight of. A picture is a purely decorative thing. *Lecture to Art Students at the Royal Academy* (*Uncollected*, p131)

422. No one takes any pleasure in doing bad or fraudulent work; the craving for the artistic finds a place in every heart.... *The Decorative Arts lecture* (*Works*, p926)

423. There is one thing much worse than no art, and that is bad art. *The Decorative Arts lecture* (*Works*, p932)

424. No art is better than bad art. *Oscar Wilde Discovers America* (*HBC*, p243)

425. ... archaeology is merely the science of making excuses for bad art; it is the rock on which many a young artist founders and shipwrecks; it is the abyss from which no artist, old or young, ever returns. Or, if he does return, he is so covered with the dust of the ages and the mildew of time, that he is quite unrecognizable as an artist, and has to conceal himself for the rest of his days under the cap of a professor, or as a mere illustrator of ancient history. *Lecture to Art Students at the Royal Academy* (*Uncollected*, p124)

426. In art good intentions are not of the smallest value. All bad art is the result of good intentions. *De Profundis* (*OWC*, p135)

427. Bad art is a great deal worse than no art at all. *House Decoration lecture* (*Uncollected*, p186)

428. Let us have no machine-made ornaments at all; it is all bad and worthless and ugly. *Art and the Handicraftsman* (*Uncollected*, p108)

429. Mere colour, unspoiled by meaning, and unallied with definite form, can speak to the soul in a thousand different ways. *The Critic as Artist* (*Works*, p1148)

430. Colour, indeed, is of itself a mystical presence on things, and tone a kind of sentiment. *L'Envoi* (*Uncollected*, p198)

431. For all beautiful colours are graduated colours, the colours that seem about to pass into one another's realm — colour without tone being like music without harmony, mere discord. *Art and the Handicraftsman* (*Uncollected*, p109)

432. ... the exquisite graduation of colour, one tone answering another like the answering chords of a symphony. *Art and the Handicraftsman* (*Uncollected*, p109)

433. Art is always more abstract than we fancy. Form and colour tell us of form and colour — that is all. *The Picture of Dorian Gray* (*SC*, p129)

434. ... we should remember that all the arts are fine arts and all the arts decorative arts. *Art and the Handicraftsman lecture* (*Uncollected*, p113)

435. Things are because we see them, and what we see, and how we see it depends on the Arts that have influenced us. At present, people see fogs, not because there are fogs, but because poets and painters have taught them the mysterious loveliness of such effects. There may have been fogs for centuries in London. I dare say there were. But no one saw them, and so we do not know anything about them. They did not exist till Art had invented them. Now, it must be admitted, fogs are carried to excess. They have become the mere mannerism of a clique, and the exaggerated realism of their method gives dull people bronchitis. Where the cultured catch an effect, the uncultured catch a cold. *The Decay of Lying* (*Works*, p1086)

436. I do not see the wisdom of decorating dinner-plates with sunsets and soup-plates with moonlit scenes. I do not think it adds anything to the pleasure of the canvas-back duck to take it out of such glories. Besides, we do not want a soup-plate whose bottom seems to vanish in the distance. One feels neither safe nor comfortable under such conditions.

House Decoration lecture (*Uncollected*, p187) and similar quotation in *The Decorative Arts lecture* (*Works*, p932)

437. We can forgive a man for making a useful thing as long as he does not admire it. The only excuse for making a useless thing is that one admires it intensely. All art is quite useless. *The Picture of Dorian Gray* (*SC*, p18)

438. The state is to make what is useful, the individual is to make what is beautiful. *The Soul of Man* (*OWC*, p15)

439. For there are not many arts, but one art merely — poem, picture and Parthenon, sonnet and statue — are all in their essence the same, and he who knows one knows all. *Mr. Whistler's Ten o'clock* (*Uncollected*, 49)

440. It is only an auctioneer who should admire all schools of art. *Letter to the Editor of the Pall Mall Gazette* (*Letters*, p277)

441. Art only begins where imitation ends. *De Profundis* (*OWC*, p128)

5

Artists

442. Sometimes I think that the artistic life is a long and lovely suicide, and am not sorry that it is so. *Letter to H.C. Marillier* (*Letters*, p272)

443. An artist revolves in a cycle of masterpieces, the first of which is no less perfect than the last. *Letter to the Editor of the Pall Mall Gazette* (*Letters*, p615)

444. God and other artists are always a little obscure. *Letter to Ada Leverson* (*Letters*, p625)

445. If a man is an artist he can paint anything. *Lecture to Art Students at the Royal Academy* (*Uncollected*, p130)

446. The true artist is known by the use he makes of what he annexes, and he annexes everything. *Olivia at the Lyceum, Dramatic Review* (*Works*, p955)

447. No artist desires to prove anything. Even things that are true can be proved. *The Picture of Dorian Gray* (*OWC*, p18)

448. ... on the staircase stood several Royal Academicians, disguised as artists. *Lord Arthur Savile's Crime* (*SC*, p265)

449. Between my art and the world there is now a wide gulf, but between art and myself there is none. I hope at least there is none. *De Profundis* (*OWC*, p129)

450. A true artist is a man who believes absolutely in himself, because he is absolutely himself. *The Soul of Man* (*OWC*, p20)

451. The courage to give yourselves up to your impressions: yes, that is the secret of the artistic life.... *The English Renaissance of Art lecture* (*Uncollected*, p24)

452. ... it is only when he becomes an artist that the secret laws of artistic creation are revealed to him. *Mr. Whistler's Ten o'clock* (*Uncollected*, p49)

453. I need not remind you that mere expression is to an artist the supreme and only mode of life. *Letter to Robert Ross* (*Letters*, p782)

454. Creation for the joy of creation, is the aim of the artist, and that is why the artist is a more divine type than the saint. The artist arrives at his moment with his own mood. *Interview in The Sketch* (*Uncollected*, p. xxi)

455. The function of the artist is to invent, not to chronicle. *Letter to the Editor of the St. James Gazette* (*Letters*, p430)

456. It often seems to me that art conceals the artist far more completely than it ever reveals him. *The Picture of Dorian Gray* (*SC*, pp129–30)

457. To reveal art and conceal the artist is art's aim. *The Picture of Dorian Gray* (*SC*, p18)

458. ... an artist, be he portrait-painter or dramatist, always reveals himself in his manner.... *The "Jolly" Art Critic, Pall Mall Gazette* (*Uncollected*, p134)

459. ... every portrait that is painted with feeling is a portrait of the artist, not of the sitter. *The Picture of Dorian Gray* (*SC*, p23)

460. The lowliest subject treated with loving earnestness and sincerity will, if the artist is competent, give the best results, just as the plainest words are the most effective in the mouth of an actor. *Oscar Wilde Discovers America* (*HB*, p191)

461. ... the true artist does not wait for life to be made picturesque for him, but sees life under picturesque conditions always—under conditions, that is to say, which are at once new and delightful. *The Relation of Dress to Art* (*Uncollected*, p51) and similar quotation in *Lecture to Art Students at the Royal Academy* (*Uncollected*, p129)

462. I have little faith in a young man who chooses what are called heroic subjects for his early efforts. It looks as though he were depending on his subject and not on his own power for success. *Oscar Wilde Discovers America* (*HB*, p191)

463. The originality which we ask from the artist is the originality of treatment, not of subject. It is only the unimaginative who ever invent. The true artist is known by the use he makes of what he annexes, and he annexes everything. *Olivia at the Lyceum, Dramatic Review* (*Works*, p955)

464. The absolute distinction of the artist is not his capacity to feel nature so much as his power of rendering it. *The English Renaissance of Art lecture* (*Uncollected*, p12)

465. All artistic creation is absolutely subjective. *The Critic as Artist* (*Works*, p1142)

466. To the artist, expression is the only mode under which he can conceive life at all. *De Profundis* (*OWC*, p116)

467. If a man treats his life artistically, his brain is his heart. *The Picture of Dorian Gray* (*SC*, p226)

468. For the artist is not concerned primarily with any theory of life but with life itself, with the joy and loveliness that should come daily on eye and ear for a beautiful external world. *Art and the Handicraftsman lecture* (*Uncollected*, p109) and similar quotation in *The Decorative Arts lecture* (*Works*, p931)

469. The artist must live the complete life, must accept it as it comes and stands like an angel before him, with its drawn and two-edged sword. *Quoted in Oscar Wilde: His Life and Wit* (*HBP*, p321)

470. ... the constancy of the artist cannot be to any definite rule or system of living, but to that principle of beauty only through which the inconstant shadows of his life are in their most fleeting moment arrested and made permanent. *L'Envoi* (*Uncollected*, p201)

471. ... the artistic life is simple self development. Humility in the artist is his frank acceptance of all experiences, just as Love in the artist is simply that sense of Beauty that reveals to the world its body and its soul. *De Profundis* (*OWC*, p109)

472. A subject that is beautiful in itself gives no suggestion to the artist. It lacks imperfection. *A Few Maxims for the Education of the Over-Educated* (*Works*, p1242)

473. ... the artist, who accepts the facts of life, and yet transforms them into shapes of beauty, and makes them vehicles of pity or of awe, and shows their colour-element, and their wonder, and their true ethical import also, and builds out of them a world more real than reality itself, and of loftier and more noble import — who shall set limits to him? *The Critic as Artist* (*Works*, p1145)

474. The painter, Basil Hallward, worshipping physical beauty far too much, as most painters do, dies by the hand of one in whose soul he has created a monstrous and absurd vanity. *Letter to the Editor of the St. James Gazette* (*Letters*, p430)

475. I dwelt on the moral education that working in any art would give a man — the two things on which all good art is founded, truth and honesty. *Oscar Wilde Discovers America* (*HBC*, p214)

476. Indeed, a national school is a provincial school, merely. Nor is there any such thing as a school of art even. There are merely artists, that is all. *Lecture to Art Students at the Royal Academy* (*Uncollected*, p123)

477. The artist is the creator of beautiful things. *The Picture of Dorian Gray* (*SC*, p18)

478. ... an artist will find beauty in ugliness.... *Mr. Whistler's Ten o'clock, Pall Mall Gazette* (*Uncollected*, p49)

479. ... when the artist cannot feed his eye on beauty, beauty goes from his work. *Lecture to Art Students at the Royal Academy* (*Uncollected*, p127)

480. Into the secure and sacred house of Beauty the true artist will admit nothing that is harsh or disturbing, nothing that gives pain, nothing that is debatable, nothing about which men argue. *The English Renaissance of Art lecture* (*Uncollected*, p13)

481. No artist recognises any standard of beauty but that which is suggested by his own temperament. The artist seeks to realise in a certain material his immaterial idea of beauty, and thus to transform an idea into an ideal. *Letter to the Editor of the Pall Mall Gazette* (*Letters*, p503)

482. Indeed, to me the most inartistic thing in this age of ours is not the indifference of the public to beautiful things, but the indifference of the artist to the things that are called ugly. For, to the real artist, nothing is beautiful or ugly in itself at all. *Lecture to Art Students at the Royal Academy* (*Uncollected*, p128)

483. A work of art is the unique result of a unique temperament. Its beauty comes from the fact that the author is what he is. It has nothing to do with the fact that other people want what they want. Indeed the moment that an artist takes notice of what other people want, and tries to supply the demand, he ceases to be an artist, and becomes a dull or an amusing craftsman, an honest or dishonest tradesman. He has no further claim to be considered as an artist. Art is the most intense mode of Individualism that the world has known. *The Soul of Man* (*OWC*, p17)

484. If you ask nine-tenths of the British public about the Pre-Raphaelites you will hear something about an eccentric lot of young men to whom belong a sort of divine crookedness and holy awkwardness in drawing all the chief objects of art. To know nothing about these great men is one of the necessary elements of English education. The satire that was paid them is the homage mediocrity pays to genius. *Oscar Wilde Discovers America* (*HBC*, p58)

485. The artist is indeed the child of his own age.... *The English Renaissance of Art lecture* (*Uncollected*, p13)

486. An artist's heart is in his head, and besides our business is to realise the world as we see it, not to reform it as we know it. *The Model Millionaire* (*Works*, p211)

487. ... artists have sex but art has none.... *Letter to Wemyss Reid* (*Letters*, p298)

488. She is like most artists; she is all style without any sincerity. *The Nightingale and the Rose* (*Works*, p280)

489. I know simply that a life of definite and studied materialism, and a philosophy of appetite and cynicism, and a cult of sensual and senseless ease, are bad things for an artist: they narrow the imagination, and dull the more delicate sensibilities. *Letter to William Rothenstein* (*Letters*, p891)

490. ... to censure an artist for a forgery was to confuse an ethical with an aesthetical problem. *The Portrait of Mr. W.H.* (*Works*, p302)

491. Formerly we used to canonise our great men; nowadays we vulgarise them. The vulgarisation of Rosetti has been going on for some time past with really remarkable success. And there seems no probability at present of the process being discontinued. *A Cheap Edition of a Great Man, Pall Mall Gazette* (*Uncollected*, p96)

492. The artist's view of life is the only possible one, and should be applied to everything, most of all to religion and morality. Cavaliers and Puritans are interesting for their costumes and not for their convictions. *Oscar Wilde, by Frank Harris* (*CG*, p56)

493. No artist has ethical sympathies. An ethical sympathy in an artist is an unpardonable mannerism of style. *The Picture of Dorian Gray* (*SC*, p18)

494. A true artist takes no notice whatever of the public. The public are to him non-existent. He has no poppied or honeyed cakes through which to give the monster sleep or sustenance. He leaves that to the popular novelist. *The Soul of Man* (*OWC*, p28)

495. ... between the attitude of the painter towards the public and the attitude of people towards art, there is a wide difference. *The Relation of Dress to Art* (*Uncollected*, p51)

496. Indeed, so far from its being true that the artist is the best judge of art, a really great artist can never judge of other people's work at all, and can hardly, in fact, judge of his own. *The Critic as Artist* (*Works*, p1150)

497. The artist works with his eye on the object. Nothing else interests him. What people are likely to say does not even occur to him. *The Three Trials of Oscar Wilde* (*UB*, p157)

498. What the artist is always looking for is that mode of existence in which soul and body are one and indivisible: in which the outward is expressive of the inward: in which Form reveals. *De Profundis* (*OWC*, p105)

499. If an artist is not a mere sham, he cannot be disturbed by any caricature or exaggeration. He has the truth on his side and the opinion of the whole world should be of no consequence to him. *Oscar Wilde Discovers America* (*HB*, p46)

500. At present, he has perhaps just a little too much appreciation of other people's work to be able to realise his own creative energy, but admiration is the portal to all great things. *Letter to Georgina Weldon* (*Letters*, p1080)

501. No artist is ever morbid. The artist can express everything. *The Picture of Dorian Gray* (*SC*, p18)

502. To call an artist morbid because he deals with morbidity as his subject-matter is as silly as if one called Shakespeare mad because he wrote King Lear. *The Soul of Man* (*OWC*, p21)

503. They [Aubrey Beardsley's drawings] are cruel and evil, and so like dear Aubrey, who has a face like a silver hatchet, with grass green hair.... They are like the naughty scribbles a precocious schoolboy makes on the margin of his copybooks. *Quoted in Oscar Wilde: His Life and Wit* (*HB*, p204)

504. One production of Michelangelo is worth a hundred by Edison. *Oscar Wilde Discovers America* (*HBC*, p167)

505. The greatest artists are stupid and tiresome men as a rule. Flaubert was certainly a stupid man. But bad poets and novelists are romantic and delightful. *Aspects of Wilde* (*CC*, p222)

506. The only artists I have ever known, who are personally delightful, are bad artists, good artists exist simply in what they make and consequently are perfectly uninteresting in what they are. *The Picture of Dorian Gray* (*SC*, p72)

507. Bad artists always admire each other's work. They call it being large-minded and free from prejudice. But a truly great artist cannot conceive of life being shown, or beauty fashioned, under any conditions other than those he has selected. Creation employs all its critical faculty within its own sphere. It may not use it in the sphere that belongs to others. It is exactly because a man cannot do a thing that he is the proper judge of it. *The Critic as Artist* (*Works*, p1150)

508. ... the institution of pottery should not be a refuge for people who cannot draw nor asylum for the artistically afflicted. *Oscar Wilde Discovers America* (*HBC*, p200)

509. I saw some designs on your vases done by someone who, I should say, had only five minutes to catch a train.... *Oscar Wilde Discovers America* (*HBC*, p200)

510. Admirable as are Mr. Whistler's fire-works on canvas, his fire-works in prose are abrupt, violent and exaggerated. *The New President, Pall Mall Gazette* (*Uncollected*, p138)

511. James [Whistler] is developing, but he will never arrive at passion, I fear. *Letter to Robert Ross* (*Letters*, p1118)

512. For that he is indeed one of the very greatest masters of painting is my opinion. And I may add that in this opinion Mr. Whistler himself entirely concurs. *Mr. Whistler's Ten o'clock, Pall Mall Gazette* (*Uncollected*, p50)

513. Weary of being asked by gloomy reporters "which was the most beautiful colour" and what is the meaning of the word "aesthetic," on my last Chicago interview I turned the conversation on three of my heroes, Whistler, Labouchere, and Irving, and the adored and adorable Lily. I send them all to you. *Letter to Mrs. George Lewis* (*Letters*, p154)

514. Mr. Whistler always spelt art, and we believe still spells it, with a capital "I." However, he was never dull. His brilliant wit, his caustic satire, and his amusing epigrams, or, perhaps we should say epitaphs on his contemporaries, made his views on art as delightful as they were misleading, and as fascinating as they were unsound. *The New President, Pall Mall Gazette* (*Uncollected*, p137)

515. Mr. Whistler seems to me to stand almost alone. Indeed, among all our public speakers I know but a few who can combine so felicitously as he does the mirth and malice of Puck with the style of the minor prophets. *The Relation of Dress to Art lecture* (*Uncollected*, p54)

516. Last night, at Prince's Hall, Mr. Whistler made his first public appearance as a lecturer on art, and spoke for more than an hour with really marvelous eloquence on the absolute uselessness of all lectures of the kind. *Mr. Whistler's Ten o'clock* (*Uncollected*, p47)

517. ... the ultimate expression of our artistic movement in painting has been ... in the work of such men as Whistler and Albert Moore, who have raised design and colour to the ideal level of poetry and music. *L'Envoi* (*Uncollected*, p196)

518. You should have such men as James Whistler among you teach you the beauty of joy and colour. When he paints a picture, he paints by reference not to the subject, which is merely intellectual, but to colour. *The House Beautiful lecture* (*Uncollected*, p186)

519. MR. HUMPHREY WARD, ART CRITIC: That's good, first-rate, a lovely bit of colour, but that [indicating another painting], you know, that's bad, drawing all wrong ... bad!

JAMES WHISTLER: My dear fellow, you must never say that this painting's good or that bad, never! Good and bad are not terms to be used by you; but say I like this, and I dislike that, and you'll be within your right. And now come and have a whiskey for you're sure to like that.

OSCAR WILDE: I wish I had said that.

JAMES WHISTLER: You will, Oscar, you will. *Oscar Wilde, by Frank Harris* (*CG,* p38)

520. With our James, vulgarity begins at home; would that it might stay there. *Letter to the Editor of The World* (*Letters,* p288)

521. ... if you are an artist at all, you will be not the mouthpiece of a century, but the master of eternity.... *Lecture to Art Students at the Royal Academy* (*Uncollected,* p124)

522. Trouble is light when one is an artist. *Oscar Wilde Discovers America* (*HB,* p180)

6

Beauty and the Beast

524. Oh, she is better than good — she is beautiful. *The Picture of Dorian Gray* (*SC*, p89)

525. ... it was better to be good-looking than to be good. *The Portrait of Mr. W.H.* (*Works*, p304)

526. Why, she is worse than ugly, she is good. *The Duchess of Padua* (*Works*, p619)

527. The price of beauty is a price above rubies. *Quoted in Oscar Wilde: His Life and Wit* (*HBC*, p243)

528. She has her virtues as most women have,
But beauty is a gem she may not wear.
It is better so, perchance.
A Florentine Tragedy (*Works*, p728)

529. CECILY: Miss Prism says that all good looks are a snare.

ALGERNON: They are a snare that every sensible man would like to be caught in. *The Importance of Being Earnest* (*Plays*, p384)

530. The husbands of very beautiful women belong to the criminal classes. *The Picture of Dorian Gray* (*SC*, p190)

531. After all, what do they tell us about Shakespeare? Simply that he was the slave of beauty. *The Portrait of Mr. W.H.* (*Works*, p312)

532. Nay, it is rather the beholder who lends to the beautiful thing its myriad meanings. *The Critic as Artist* (*Works*, p1127)

533. People say sometimes that beauty is only superficial. To me, beauty is the wonder of wonders. It is only the shallow people who do not judge by appearances. *The Picture of Dorian Gray* (*SC*, p39)

534. Beauty is justified of all her children, and cares nothing for explanations. The *Relation of Dress to Art, Pall Mall Gazette* (*Uncollected*, p52)

535. Beauty has as many meanings as man has moods. Beauty is the symbol of symbols. Beauty reveals everything, because it expresses nothing. When it shows us itself, it shows us the whole fiery coloured world. *The Critic as Artist* (*Works*, p1127)

536. To discern the beauty of a thing is the finest point to which we can arrive. *The Critic as Artist* (*Works*, p1154)

537. Thy beauty has troubled me. Thy beauty has grievously troubled me, and I have looked at thee overmuch. *Salome* (*Plays*, p119)

538. But I don't like German. It isn't at all a becoming language. I know perfectly well that I look quite plain after my German lesson. *The Importance of Being Earnest* (*Plays*, p337)

539. MLLE. MARIE ANNE DE BOVET: It's true, Mr. Wilde, that I am the ugliest woman in France?

OSCAR WILDE: In the world, Madame, in the world. *Oscar Wilde, by Frank Harris* (*CG*, p244) and similar quotation in (*Letters*, p393)

540. ... Lady Ruxton, an overdressed woman of forty-seven, with a hooked nose, who was always trying to get herself compromised, but was so peculiarly plain that to her great disappointment no one would ever believe anything against her. *The Picture of Dorian Gray* (*SC*, p188)

541. It is only very ugly or very beautiful women who ever hide their faces. *The Duchess of Padua* (*Works*, p669)

542. Yes: she is a peacock in everything but beauty. *The Picture of Dorian Gray* (*SC*, p24)

543. Ugliness I consider a kind of malady, and illness and suffering always inspire me with repulsion. A man with a toothache, ought, I know, to have my sympathy, for it is a terrible pain. Well, he fills me with nothing but aversion. He is tedious. He is a bore. I cannot stand him. I cannot look at him. I must get away from him. *Oscar Wilde, by Robert Sherard* (*GC*, p57)

544. Those who find ugly meanings in beautiful things are corrupt without being charming. This is a fault. Those who find beautiful meanings in beautiful things are the cultivated. For these there is hope. They are elect to whom beautiful things mean only beauty. *The Picture of Dorian Gray* (*SC*, p18)

545. Ugliness that had once been hateful to him because it made things real, became dear to him now for that very reason. Ugliness was the one reality. The coarse brawl, the loathsome den, the crude violence of disordered life, the very vileness of thief and outcast, were more vivid, in their intense actuality of impression, than all the gracious shapes of art, the dreamy shadows of song. They were what he needed for forgetfulness. *The Picture of Dorian Gray* (*SC*, p198)

546. I never quarreled with him. But three weeks ago he wrote me a letter breaking off our friendship. Ugly things cannot be done prettily, in life at any rate. *Letter to Robert Ross* (*Letters*, p1086)

547. No object is so ugly that, under certain conditions of light and shade, or proximity to other things, it will not look beautiful; no object is so beautiful that, under certain conditions, it will not look ugly. I believe that in every twenty-four hours what is beautiful looks ugly, and what is ugly looks beautiful, once. *Lecture to Art Students at the Royal Academy* (*Uncollected*, p129) and similar quotation in *The Relation of Dress to Art lecture* (*Uncollected*, p51)

548. Ugliness is one of the seven deadly virtues.... *The Picture of Dorian Gray* (*SC*, p206)

549. If children grow up among all fair and lovely things, they will grow to love beauty and detest ugliness before they know the reason why. *House Decoration lecture* (*Uncollected*, p189)

550. Indeed, to me the most inartistic thing in this age of ours is not the indifference of the public to beautiful things, but the indifference of the artist to things that are called ugly. For, to the real artist, nothing is beautiful or ugly in itself at all. *Lecture to Art Students at the Royal Academy* (*Uncollected*, p128)

551. Appearance is, in fact, a matter of effect merely.... *Lecture to Art Students at the Royal Academy* (*Uncollected*, p128)

552. Under certain conditions of light and shade, what is ugly in fact may become beautiful.... *The Relation of Dress to Art* (*Uncollected*, p51)

553. The only people a painter should know are people who are *bete* and beautiful, people who are an artistic pleasure to look at and an intellectual repose to talk to. *The Model Millionaire* (*Works*, p209)

554. The one characteristic of a beautiful form is that one can put into it whatever one wishes, and see in it whatever one chooses to see; and the Beauty, that gives to creation its universal and aesthetic element, makes the critic creator in his turn, and whispers of a thousand different things which were not present in the mind of him who carved the statue or painted the panel or graved the gem. *The Critic as Artist* (*Works*, 1128)

555. For, we who are working in art cannot accept any theory of beauty in exchange for beauty itself.... *Lecture to Art Students at the Royal Academy* (*Uncollected*, p123)

556. The painter, Basil Hallward, worshipping physical beauty far too much, as most painters do, dies by the hand of one in whose soul he has created a monstrous and absurd vanity. *Letter to the Editor of the St. James Gazette* (*Letters*, p430)

557. He has nothing, but looks everything. What more can one desire? *The Importance of Being Earnest* (*Plays*, p422)

558. Dandyism is the assertion of the absolute modernity of Beauty. *A Few Maxims for the Instruction of the Over-Educated, Saturday Review* (*Works*, p1096)

559. They say he has sold himself to the devil for a pretty face. *The Picture of Dorian Gray* (*SC*, p204)

560. The beautiful are always beautiful. *Letter to Ada Leverson* (*Letters*, p845)

561. Remember, too, how soon Beauty forsakes itself. Its action is no stronger than a flower, and like a flower it lives and dies. *The Portrait of Mr. W.H.* (*Works*, p317)

562. LORD HENRY: Life has everything I store for you, Dorian. There is nothing that you, with your extraordinary good looks, will not be able to do.

DORIAN GRAY: But suppose, Harry, I become haggard, and old, and wrinkled? What then?

LORD HENRY: Ah, then ... then, my dear Dorian, you would have to fight for your victories. As it is, they are brought to you. No, you must keep your good looks. We live in an age that reads too much to be wise and thinks too much to be beautiful. We cannot spare you. *The Picture of Dorian Gray* (*SC*, p118)

563. ... Beauty, like Wisdom, loves the lonely worshipper. *The Young King* (*Works*, p214)

564. The love that he bore him—for it was really love—had nothing in it that was not noble and intellectual. It was not the mere physical admiration of beauty that is born of the sense and that dies when the senses tire. *The Picture of Dorian Gray* (*SC*, p133)

565. Behind every exquisite thing that existed, there was something tragic. *The Picture of Dorian Gray* (*SC*, p52)

566. ... beauty, real beauty, ends where intellectual expression begins. Intellect is in itself a mode of exaggeration, and destroys the harmony of any face. The moment one sits down to think, one becomes all nose, or all forehead, or something horrid. Look at the successful men in any of the learned professions. How perfectly hideous they are! Except, of course, in the Church. But then in the Church they don't think. A bishop keeps on saying at the age of eighty what he was told to say when he was a boy of eighteen, and as a natural consequence he always looks absolutely delightful. *The Picture of Dorian Gray* (*SC*, p20)

567. We try to improve the conditions of the race by means of good air, free sunlight, wholesome water, and hideous bare buildings for the better housing of the lower orders. But these things merely produce health, they do not produce beauty. *The Decay of Lying* (*Works*, p1083)

568. ... it is only countries which possess great beauty that can appreciate beauty at all.... *Oscar Wilde Discovers America* (*HBC*, p428)

569. This devotion to beauty and to the creation of beautiful things is the test of all great civilised nations. *The English Renaissance of Art lecture* (*Uncollected*, p21)

570. Whatever you have that is beautiful for use, then you should use it, or part with it to someone who will. *The House Beautiful lecture* (*Works*, p921)

571. Now, when a thing is useless it should be made beautiful, otherwise it has no reason for existing at all. *Letter to the Editor of the Daily Telegraph* (*Letters*, p464)

572. He is as beautiful as a weathercock, only not quite so useful. *The Happy Prince* (*SC*, p236)

573. The only beautiful things, as somebody once said, are the things that do not concern us. As long as a thing is useful or necessary to us, or affects us in any way, either for pain or for pleasure, or appeals strongly to our sympathies, or is a vital part of the environment in which we live, it is outside the proper sphere of Art. *The Decay of Lying* (*Works*, p1077)

574. You love the beauty that you can see and touch and handle, the beauty that you can destroy, and do destroy, but of the unseen beauty of a higher life, you know nothing. *A Woman of No Importance* (*Plays*, p160)

575. For myself, I look forward to the time when aesthetics will take the place of ethics, when the sense of beauty will be the dominant law of life: it will never be so, and so I look forward to it. *Letter to Mrs. Lathbury* (*Letters*, p437)

576. Beauty shall be confined no longer to the bric-a-brac of the collector and the dust of the museum, but shall be, as it should be, the natural and national inheritance of all.... *The Relation of Dress to Art lecture* (*Uncollected*, p53)

577. I suppose, Windermere, you would like me to retire into a convent or become a hospital nurse or something of that kind, as people do in silly modern novels. That is stupid of you, Arthur; in real life we don't do such things—not as long as we have any good looks left, at any rate. *Lady Windermere's Fan* (*Plays,* p75)

578. I remember what you had said to me on that wonderful evening when we first dined together, about the search for beauty being the real secret of life. *The Picture of Dorian Gray* (*SC,* p65)

579. Spirit of Beauty, tarry yet awhile! *The Garden of Eros* (*Works,* p849)

7

Boredom, or Ennui

580. I hate to know you are lonely, or in danger of *ennui*, that enemy of modern life. *Letter to Lord Alfred Douglas* (*Letters*, p910)

581. I am bored with life, Prince. Since the opera season ended I have been a perpetual martyr to *ennui*. *Vera, or the Nihilists* (*Works*, p698)

582. I suffer very much. *Ennui* is the enemy. *Letter to Frank Harris* (*Letters*, p1131)

583. I ... left the next morning for the Hicks-Beachs' in Hampshire, to kill time and pheasants and the *ennui* of not having set the world on fire as yet. *Letter to Reginald Harding* (*Letters*, p84)

584. Whatever I do is wrong: because my life is not on a right basis. In Paris I am bad: here I am bored: the last state is the worse. *Letter to Robert Ross* (*Letters*, p1142)

585. ... today I am bored and sick to death of imprisonment. *Letter to Ada Leverson* (*Letters*, p648)

586. I simply cannot stand Berneval. I nearly committed suicide there last Thursday—I was so bored. *Letter to Robert Ross* (*Letters*, p934)

587. What was it separated you? I suppose he bored you. If so, he never forgave you. It's a habit bores have. *The Picture of Dorian Gray* (*SC*, p225)

588. The only horrible thing in the world is *ennui*, Dorian. That is the sin for which there is no forgiveness. *The Picture of Dorian Gray* (*SC*, p214)

589. I have blown my trumpets against the gates of dullness. *Letter to Mrs. George Lewis* (*Letters*, p389)

8

Britain and the British

590. The English have a miraculous power of turning wine into water. *Quoted in Oscar Wilde: His Life and Wit (HBP, 170)*

591. Beer, the Bible, and the seven deadly virtues have made our England what she is. *The Picture of Dorian Gray (SC, p206)*

592. The English country gentleman galloping after a fox — the unspeakable in full pursuit of the uneatable. *A Woman of No Importance (Plays, p138)*

593. ... there are only two forms of writers in England, the unread and the unreadable. *Letter to Leonard Smithers (Letters, p1037)*

594. ... three things the English public never forgives: Youth, power, and enthusiasm. *The English Renaissance of Art lecture (Uncollected, p8)*

595. The English think that a cheque-book can solve every problem in life. *An Ideal Husband (Plays, p309)*

596. It was safe, sure, and quiet, and did away with any necessity for painful scenes, to which, like most Englishmen, he had a rooted objection. *Lord Arthur Savile's Crime (SC, p282)*

597. ... he is a typical Englishman, always dull and usually violent. *An Ideal Husband (Plays, p285)*

598. And thou whose wounds are never
    healed,
Whose weary race is never won,
Cromwell's England! must thou yield
For every inch of ground a son?
    Ave Imperatrix (Works, p853)

599. The inherited stupidity of the race — sound English common sense he jovially termed it — was shown to be the proper bulwark for society. *The Picture of Dorian Gray (SC, p192)*

600. ... the British public is not equal to the mental strain of having more than one topic every three months. *The Picture of Dorian Gray (SC, p223)*

601. Thinking is the most unhealthy thing in the world, and people die of it just as they die of any other disease. Fortunately, in England at any rate, thought is not catching. Our splendid physique as a people is entirely due to our national stupidity. *The Decay of Lying (Works, p1072)*

602. If one puts forward an idea to a true Englishman — always a rash thing to do — he never dreams of considering whether the idea is right or wrong. The only thing he considers of any importance is whether one believes it oneself. *The Picture of Dorian Gray (SC, p27)*

603. The English detectives are really our best friends, and I have always found that by relying on their stupidity, we can do exactly what we like. *Lord Arthur Savile's Crime (SC, p293)*

604. It is the lack of imagination in the Anglo-Saxon race that makes the race so stupidly, harshly cruel. Those who are bringing about Prison Reform in Parliament are Celtic to a man. For every Celt has inborn imagination. *Letter to Georgina Weldon (Letters, p1080)*

605. Byron's personality ... was terribly wasted in its battle with the stupidity, and hypocrisy, and Philistinism of the English. Such battles do not always intensify strength: they often exaggerate weakness. Byron was never able to give us what he might have given us. Shelley escaped better. Like Byron, he got out of England as soon as possible. *The Soul of Man (OWC, pp8–9)*

606. There is no country in the world so much in need of unpractical people as this country of ours. With us, thought is degraded by its constant association with practice. *The Critic as Artist* (*Works*, p1139)

607. The intellect is not a serious thing, and never has been. It is an instrument on which one plays, that is all. The only serious form of intellect I know is the British intellect. And on the British intellect the illiterates play the drum. *A Woman of No Importance* (*Plays*, pp138–9)

608. To disagree with three-fourths of England on all points is one of the first elements of sanity; a deep source of consolation in all moments of spiritual doubt. *The English Renaissance of Art lecture* (*Uncollected*, p8)

609. Bosie is over here, with his brother. They are in deep mourning and the highest spirits. The English are like that. *Letter to George Ives* (*Letters*, p1173)

610. There is a great deal of the schoolboy in all Englishmen, that is what makes them so lovable. *Oscar Wilde, by Frank Harris* (*CG*, p260)

611. In England people actually try to be brilliant at breakfast. That is so dreadful of them! Only dull people are brilliant at breakfast. And then the family skeleton is always reading family prayers. *An Ideal Husband* (*Plays*, pp239–40)

612. ... in England, a man who can't talk morality twice a week to a large, popular, immoral audience is quite over as a serious politician. There would be nothing left for him as a profession except Botany or the Church. *An Ideal Husband* (*Plays*, p265)

613. I know how people chatter in England. The middle classes air their moral prejudices over their dinner-tables, and whisper about what they call the profligacies of their betters in order to try and pretend that they are in smart society and on intimate terms with the people they slander. In this country, it is enough for a man to have distinction and brains for every common tongue to wag against him. And what sort of lives do these people, who pose as being moral, lead themselves? My dear fellow, you forget that we are

in the native land of the hypocrite. *The Picture of Dorian Gray* (*SC*, p164)

614. My resolution is deliberately taken. Since it is impossible to have a work of art performed in England, I shall transfer myself to another fatherland, of which I have long been enamoured.... Here people are essentially anti-artistic and narrow-minded.... Of course I do not deny that Englishmen possess certain practical qualities; but, as I am an artist, these qualities are not those which I admire. Moreover, I am not at present an Englishman. I am an Irishman, which is by no means the same thing. *Quoted in Oscar Wilde: His Life and Wit* (*HBP*, p203)

615. The Englishman abroad is in the main a man of good manners and an agreeable companion. I am a Celt, but I can tell the truth about him. At home, the average Englishman is arrogant, ill-tempered, and tied down by prejudice which nothing will induce him to lay aside. *Oscar Wilde Discovers America* (*HBC*, p389)

616. No doubt I have English friends to whom I am deeply attached; but as to the English, I do not love them. There is a great deal of hypocrisy in England which you in France very justly find fault with. The typical Briton is a Tartuffe seated in his shop behind the counter. There are numerous exceptions but they only prove the rule. *Quoted in Oscar Wilde: His Life and Wit* (*HBP*, p203)

617. If one could only teach the English how to talk, and the Irish how to listen, society here would be quite civilised. *An Ideal Husband* (*Plays*, p310)

618. I live in London for its artistic life and opportunities. There is no lack of culture in Ireland, but it is nearly all absorbed in politics. Had I remained there my career would have been a political one. *Oscar Wilde Discovers America* (*HBC*, p244)

619. ... his work was that curious mixture of bad painting and good intentions that always entitles a man to be called a representative British artist. *The Picture of Dorian Gray* (*SC*, p226)

620. To know nothing about these great men [the Pre-Raphaelites] is one of the necessary elements of English education. The satire that was paid them is the homage mediocrity pays to genius. *Oscar Wilde Discovers America* (HBC, 58)

621. *Robert Elsmere* is of course a masterpiece — a masterpiece of the *genre ennuyeux*, the one form of literature that the English people seems thoroughly to enjoy. A thoughtful young friend of ours once told us that it reminded him of the sort of conversation that goes on at meat tea in the house of a serious Non-conformist family, and we can quite believe it. Indeed it is only in England that such a book could be reproduced. England is the home of lost ideas. *The Decay of Lying* (*Works*, p1074)

622. ... one of those characteristic British faces that, once seen, are never remembered.... *The Picture of Dorian Gray* (SC, p188)

623. Freckles run in Scotch families just as gout does in English families. *The Portrait of Mr. W.H.* (*Works*, p304)

624. All over England there is a Renaissance of the decorative Arts. Ugliness has had its day. *The Critic as Artist* (*Works*, pp1146–7)

625. England has more subjects for art than any other country: I suppose that is the reason it has fewer artists. *Letter to Reginald Turner* (*Letters*, p962)

626. Both my dear friends would wish me to retire to a monastery.... Why not La Trappe?... or worse still, some dim country place in England. *Quoted in Oscar Wilde: His Life and Wit* (HBP, p293)

627. If one wants to realize what English Puritanism is — not at its worst, when it is very bad — but at its best, and then it is not very good — I do not think one can find much of it in England, but much can be found about Boston and Massachusetts. We have got rid of it. America still preserves it, to be, I hope, a short-lived curiosity. *Oscar Wilde Discovers America* (HBC, p122)

628. I ... explained that my English dress [in Rome] was a form of penance. *Quoted in Oscar Wilde: His Life and Wit* (HBP, p324)

629. England is the land of intellectual fogs but you [Bernard Shaw] have done much to clear the air. *Letter to George Bernard Shaw* (*Letters*, p554)

630. London is too full of fogs and — and serious people.... Whether the fogs produce the serious people or whether the serious people produce the fogs, I don't know, but the whole thing rather gets on my nerves, and so I'm leaving this afternoon on the Club Train. *Lady Windermere's Fan* (*Plays*, p70)

631. I don't desire to change anything in England except the weather. *The Picture of Dorian Gray* (SC, p57)

632. I guess the laws of nature are not going to be suspended for the British aristocracy. *The Canterville Ghost* (*Works*, p184)

633. But how to write anything these grey days? I hate our sunless, loveless winter.... *Letter to Violet Fane* (*Letters*, p278)

634. All the condition she makes is that we live out of England — a very good thing, too! Demmed clubs, demmed climate, demmed cooks, demmed everything! Sick of it all. *Lady Windermere's Fan* (*Plays*, p87)

635. What a monstrous climate! I guess the old country is so overpopulated that they have not enough decent weather for everybody. I have always been of the opinion that emigration is the only thing for England. *The Canterville Ghost* (*Works*, p186)

636. ... Tartuffe has emigrated to England and opened a shop. *The Picture of Dorian Gray* (SC, p207)

637. How strange to live in a land where the worship of beauty and the passion of love a considered infamous. I hate England: it is only bearable to me because you are here. *Letter to Lord Alfred Douglas* (*Letters*, p622)

638. You know, at home in England it is always green. The green was such a rest to my weary eyes. It is the most restful of all colors. *Oscar Wilde Discovers America* (HBC, p284)

9

Charity and Sympathy

639. Lord Illingworth says that all influence is bad, but that a good influence is the worst thing in the world. *A Woman of No Importance* (*Plays*, p199)

640. He was oppressed with the sense of the barrenness of good intentions, and the futility of trying to be fine. *Lord Arthur Savile's Crime* (*SC*, p297)

641. If you want to mar a nature, you have merely to reform it. *The Picture of Dorian Gray* (*SC*, p90)

642. It is always a silly thing to give advice, but to give good advice is absolutely fatal. *The Portrait of Mr. W.H.* (*Works*, p305)

643. You are always wise and prudent (about other people's affairs). *Letter to Leonard Smithers* (*Letters*, p1030)

644. Ah! It is so easy to convert others. It is so difficult to convert oneself. *The Critic as Artist* (*Works*, p1143)

645. Whatever happens to another happens to oneself. *De Profundis* (*OWC*, p110)

646. DORIAN GRAY: I don't want to see him alone. He gives me good advice.

LORD HENRY: People are very fond of giving away what they need most themselves. It is what I call the depth of generosity. *The Picture of Dorian Gray* (*SC*, p72)

647. One can always be kind to people about whom one cares nothing. *The Picture of Dorian Gray* (*SC*, p114)

648. It is always with the best intentions that the worst work is done. *The Critic as Artist* (*Works*, p1149)

649. ... in the present state of things in England, the people who do the most harm are the people who try to do the most good.... *The Soul of Man* (*OWC*, p2)

650. The majority of people spoil their lives by an unhealthy and exaggerated altruism.... *The Soul of Man* (*OWC*, p1)

651. It takes a thoroughly selfish age, like our own, to deify self-sacrifice. *The Critic as Artist* (*Works*, p1140)

652. Even in acts of charity there should be some sense of humour. *Letter to Robert Ross* (*Letters*, p816)

653. ... self sacrifice is a thing that should be put down by law. It is so demoralizing to the people for whom one sacrifices one self. They always go to the bad. *An Ideal Husband* (*Plays*, p312)

654. Charity, as even those of whose religion it makes a formal part have been compelled to acknowledge, creates a multitude of evils. *The Critic as Artist* (*Works*, p1122)

655. ... charity degrades and demoralizes.... Charity creates a multitude of sins. *The Soul of Man* (*OWC*, p2)

656. We are often told that the poor are grateful for charity. Some of them are, no doubt, but the best amongst the poor are never grateful. They are ungrateful, discontented, disobedient, and rebellious. They are quite right to be so. Charity they feel to be a ridiculously inadequate mode of partial restitution, or a sentimental dole, usually accompanied by some impertinent attempt on the part of the sentimentalist to tyrannise over their private lives. Why should they be grateful for the crumbs that fall from the rich man's table? They should be seated at the board and are beginning to know it. *The Soul of Man* (*OWC*, p4)

657. They make the harsh error of judging another person's life without understanding it. Do not you — of all people — commit the same error. Charity is not a sentimental emotion: it is the only method by which the soul can attain to any knowledge — to any wisdom. *Letter to Georgina Weldon* (*Letters*, p1081)

658. Influence is simply a transfer of personality, a mode of giving away what is most precious to one's self, and its exercise produces a sense, and, it may be, a reality of loss. Every disciple takes away something from his master. *The Portrait of Mr. W.H.* (*Works*, p345)

659. The reason we all like to think so well of others is that we are all afraid for ourselves. The basis of optimism is sheer terror. We think that we are generous because we credit our neighbor with the possession of those virtues that are likely to be a benefit to us. We praise the banker that we may overdraw our account, and find good qualities in the highwayman in the hope that he may spare our pockets. *The Picture of Dorian Gray* (*SC*, p90)

660. If we lived long enough to see the results of our actions it may be that those who call themselves good would be sickened with a dull remorse, and those whom the world calls evil stirred by a noble joy. Each little thing that we do passes into the great machine of life which may grind our virtues to powder and make them worthless, or transform our sins into elements of a new civilisation, more marvelous and more splendid than any that has gone before. *The Critic as Artist* (*Works*, p1121)

661. That the desire to do good to others produces a plentiful crop of prigs is the least of the evils of which it is the cause. The prig is a very interesting psychological study, and though of all poses a moral pose is the most offensive, still to have a pose is something. It is a formal recognition of the importance of treating life from a definite and reasoned standpoint. That Humanitarian Sympathy wars against Nature, by securing the survival of failure, may make the man of science loathe its facile virtues. *The Critic as Artist* (*Works* p1139)

662. They miss their aim, too, these philanthropists and sentimentalists of our day, who are always chattering about one's duty to one's neighbour. For the development of the race depends on the development of the individual.... *The Critic as Artist* (*Works*, p1140)

663. You are too charming to go in for philanthropy, Mr. Gray — far too charming. *The Picture of Dorian Gray* (*SC*, p33)

664. Philanthropic people lose all sense of humanity. It is their distinguishing characteristic. *The Picture of Dorian Gray* (*SC*, p52)

665. Harry told me about a certain philanthropist who spent twenty years of his life trying to get some grievance redressed, or some unjust law altered — I forget exactly what it was. Finally he succeeded, and nothing could exceed his disappointment. He had absolutely nothing to do, almost died of *ennui*, and became a confirmed misanthrope. *The Picture of Dorian Gray* (*SC*, p124)

666. ... to influence a person is to give him one's own soul. He does not think with his natural thoughts, or burn with his natural passions. His virtues are not real to him. His sins, if there are such things as sins, are borrowed. He becomes an echo of some one else's music, an actor of a part that has not been written for him. The aim of life is self-development. To realize one's own nature perfectly — that is what each of us is here for. People are afraid of themselves nowadays. They have forgotten the highest of all duties, the duty that one owes to one's self. Of course they are charitable. They feed the hungry and clothe the beggar. But their own souls starve, and are naked. *The Picture of Dorian Gray* (*SC*, pp34–5)

667. People are so fond of giving away what they do not want themselves, that charity is largely on the increase. *Quoted in Oscar Wilde: His Life and Wit* (*HBP*, p153)

668. Sympathy is sort of a religion to him; that's why we can meet without murder and separate without suicide.... *Oscar Wilde, by Frank Harris* (*CG*, p296)

669. It is easy for people to have sympathy with suffering. It is difficult for people to have sympathy with thought. *The Critic as Artist* (*Works*, p1141)

670. I can sympathise with everything, except suffering. I cannot sympathise with that. It is too ugly, too horrible, too distressing. There is something terribly morbid in the modern sympathy with pain. One should sympathise with the colour, the beauty, the joy of life. The less said about life's sores, the better. *The Picture of Dorian Gray* (*SC*, p56) and similar quotation in *A Woman of No Importance* (*Plays*, p137)

671. To know anything about oneself, one must know all about others. There must be no mood with which one cannot sympathise, no dead mode of life that one cannot make alive. *The Critic as Artist* (*Works*, p1137) and *Mr. Pater's Appreciations, The Speaker* (*Uncollected*, p145)

672. One's days were too brief to take the burden of another's errors on one's shoulders. Each man lived his own life and paid his own price for living it. *The Picture of Dorian Gray* (*SC*, p201)

673. LORD CAVERSHAM: Oh, damn sympathy. There is a great deal too much of that sort of thing going on nowadays.

LORD GORING: I quite agree with you father. If there were less sympathy in the world, there would be less trouble in the world. *An Ideal Husband* (*Plays*, p297)

674. ... the real harm that emotional sympathy does is that it limits knowledge, and so prevents us from solving any single social problem. *The Critic as Artist* (*Works*, p1140)

675. But it must be remembered that while sympathy with joy intensifies the sum of joy in the world, sympathy with pain does not really diminish the amount of pain. It may make man better able to endure evil, but the evil remains. Sympathy with consumption does not cure consumption; that is what science does. *The Soul of Man* (*OWC*, p34)

676. ... as the nineteenth century has gone bankrupt through an overexpenditure of sympathy, I would suggest that we should appeal to science to put us straight. The advantage of the emotions is that they lead us astray, and the advantage of science is that it is not emotional. *The Picture of Dorian Gray* (*SC*, p57)

677. Where in the arts themselves are we to find that breadth of human sympathy which is the condition of all noble work.... *The English Renaissance of Art lecture* (*Uncollected*, p15)

678. He had to choose between living for himself and living for others, and terrible though the task laid upon him undoubtedly was, yet he knew that he must not suffer selfishness to triumph over love. Sooner or later we are all called upon to decide on the same issue — of us all, the same question is asked. *Lord Arthur Savile's Crime* (*SC*, p281)

679. Up to the present man has hardly cultivated sympathy at all. He has merely sympathy with pain, and sympathy with pain is not the highest form of sympathy. All sympathy is fine, but sympathy with suffering is the least fine mode. It is tainted with egotism. It is apt to become morbid. There is in it a certain element of terror for our own safety. We become afraid that we ourselves might be as the leper or as the blind, and that no man would have care of us. It is curiously limiting, too. One should sympathise with the entirety of life, not with life's sores and maladies merely, but with life's joy and beauty and energy and health and freedom. The wider sympathy is, of course, the more difficult. It requires more unselfishness. Anybody can sympathise with the sufferings of a friend, but it requires a very fine nature — it requires, in fact, the nature of a true Individualist — to sympathise with a friend's success. *The Soul of Man* (*OWC*, p33)

680. "What is a sensitive person?" said the [Fire] Cracker to the Roman Candle.

"A person who, because he has corns himself, always treads on other people's toes," answered the Roman Candle in a low whisper; and the Cracker nearly exploded with laughter. "Pray, what are you laughing at?" inquired the Rocket; "I am not laughing." "I am laughing because I am happy," replied the Cracker. "That is a very selfish reason," said the Rocket angrily. "What right have you to be happy? You should always be thinking about others. In fact, you should be thinking about me. I am always thinking about myself, and I expect everybody else to do the same. That is what is called sympathy. It is a beautiful virtue, and I possess it in a high degree.' *The Remarkable Rocket* (*Works*, p296)

681. I am sorry you are ill. I am wretched, which makes me sympathetic. *Letter to Robert Ross* (*Letters*, p1142)

682. You wretched man, why do you beg when pity is dead? *Aspects of Wilde* (*CC*, p162)

683. The head may approve the success of the winners, but the heart is sure to be with the fallen. *Oscar Wilde Discovers America* (*HBC*, p366)

684. And alien tears will fill for him
Pity's long-broken urn,
For his mourners will be outcast men,
And outcasts always mourn.
The Ballad of Reading Gaol (*OWC*, p185)

685. I am delighted to hear of my photograph being sold again: it shows revival of strange sympathies. *Letter to Robert Ross* (*Letters*, p1105)

686. For to cultivate sympathy you must be among living things and thinking about them, and to cultivate admiration you must be among beautiful things and looking at them. *The English Renaissance of Art lecture* (*Uncollected*, p27)

687. In the strangely simple economy of the world people only get what they give, and to those who have not enough imagination to penetrate the mere outward of things and feel pity, what pity can be given save that of scorn? *De Profundis* (*OWC*, p130)

688. The hard heart is the evil thing of life and art. I have also learnt sympathy with suffering. To me, suffering seems now a sacramental thing, that makes those whom it touches holy. *Letter to Carlos Blacker* (*Letters*, p912)

689. The burden of this world is too great for one man to bear, and the world's sorrow too heavy for one heart to suffer. *The Young King* (*Works*, p221)

690. To gain anything good we must sacrifice something of our luxury — we must think more of others. *Mr. Morris on Tapestry, Pall Mall Gazette* (*Works*, p974)

691. All good impulses are right. *Letter to Robert Ross* (*Letters*, p864)

692. All I do know is that life cannot be lived without much charity. *An Ideal Husband* (*Plays*, p273)

10

Common Sense

693. He had that rarest of all things, common sense. *Lord Arthur Savile's Crime* (*SC*, p281)

694. ... Lady Windermere has that uncommon thing called common sense. *Lady Windermere's Fan* (*Plays*, p41)

695. ... yet wisdom is not always best; there are times when she sinks to the level of common sense. *The Relation of Dress to Art lecture* (*Uncollected*, p53)

696. LORD GORING: But women who have common sense are so curiously plain, father, aren't they? Of course I only speak from hearsay.

LORD CAVERSHAM: No women, plain or pretty, has any common sense at all, sir. Common sense is the privilege of our sex.

LORD GORING: Quite so. And we men are so self-sacrificing that we never use it, do we, father?

LORD CAVERSHAM: I use it, sir, and nothing else.

LORD GORING: So my mother tells me. *An Ideal Husband* (*Plays*, p301)

697. These great folks have not much sense, so Providence makes it up to them in fine clothes. *The Duchess of Padua* (*Works*, p654)

698. Common sense indeed! You forget that I am very uncommon, and very remarkable. Why, anybody can have common sense, provided that they have no imagination. But I have imagination for I never think of things as they really are; I always think of them as being quite different. *The Remarkable Rocket* (*Works*, p297)

699. The fatal errors of life are not due to man's being unreasonable; an unreasonable moment may be one's finest moment. They are due to man's being logical. There is a wide difference. *De Profundis* (*OWC*, p69)

700. A man who allows himself to be convinced by an argument is a thoroughly unreasonable person. *An Ideal Husband* (*Plays*, p1141)

701. ... one is tempted to define man as a rational animal who always loses his temper when he is called upon to act in accordance with the dictates of his reason. *The Critic as Artist*

702. A practical scheme is either a scheme that is already in existence, or a scheme that could be carried out under existing conditions. But it is exactly the existing conditions that one objects to; and any scheme that could accept these conditions is foolish and wrong. *The Soul of Man* (*OWC*, p31)

703. Nowadays most people die of a sort of creeping common sense, and discover when it is too late that the only things one never regrets are one's mistakes. *The Picture of Dorian Gray* (*SC*, p58)

11

Conversation and Language

704. Conversation should touch on everything, but concentrate itself on nothing. *The Critic as Artist* (*Works*, p1130)

705. After all, the only proper intoxication is conversation. *Letter to Robert Ross* (*Letters*, p1078)

706. You would sacrifice anybody, Harry, for the sake of an epigram. *The Picture of Dorian Gray* (*SC*, p216)

707. Between me and life there is a mist of words always. I throw probability out of the window for the sake of a phrase, and the chance of an epigram makes me desert the truth. *Letter to Arthur Conan Doyle* (*Letters*, p47)

708. I love talking about nothing.... It is the only thing I know anything about. *An Ideal Husband* (*Plays*, p234)

709. I can't listen to anyone unless he attracts me by a charming style or by beauty of theme. *Quoted in Oscar Wilde: His Life and Wit* (*HBP*, p56)

710. Ultimately the bond of all companionship, whether in marriage or in friendship, is conversation.... *De Profundis* (*OWC*, p49)

711. It is a great nuisance. I can't find anyone in this house to talk to. And I am full of interesting information. I feel like the latest edition of something or other. *An Ideal Husband* (*Plays*, p319)

712. But I like talking to a brick wall — it's the only thing in the world that never contradicts me! *Lady Windermere's Fan* (*Plays*, p62)

713. "How well you talk!" said the Miller's wife, pouring herself out a large glass of warm ale; "really I feel quite drowsy. It is just like being in church." *The Devoted Friend* (*Works*, p288)

714. But he spake not a word. For he who speaks a word loses a faith. *The Teacher of Wisdom* (*Works*, p905)

715. But men are the slaves of words. *The Critic as Artist* (*Works*, p1121)

716. I never met so eloquent a fool. *A Florentine Tragedy* (*Works*, p727)

717. Eloquence is a beautiful thing but rhetoric ruins many a critic.... *Ben Jonson, Pall Mall Gazette* (*Uncollected*, p159)

718. He is tripping of speech as if he were some young aristocrat; but for my own part I care not for the stops so that the sense be plain. *Vera, or the Nihilists* (*Works*, p688)

719. ... I always say clearly what I know to be true.... To say "perhaps" spoils the remark. *Letter to Keningale Cook* (*Letters*, p52)

720. What a nice speech! So simple and so sincere! Just the sort of speech I like. *Lady Windermere's Fan* (*Plays*, p34)

721. Never mind what I say, Robert. I am always saying what I shouldn't say. In fact, I usually say what I really think. A great mistake nowadays. It makes one so liable to be misunderstood. *An Ideal Husband* (*Plays*, p264)

722. No; Gilbert, don't play anymore. Turn round and talk to me. Talk to me till the white-horned day comes into the room. There is something in your voice that is wonderful. *The Critic as Artist* (*Works*, p1109)

723. To speak poetry so well is so rare an accomplishment that it was a delight to listen to your lovely voice, with its fine sense of music and cadence and rhythmical structure. *Letter to Otho Stuart* (*Letters*, p417)

724. There is something in what you say, but there is not everything in what you say. *The Decay of Lying* (*Works*, pp1111–12)

725. No, dear Lord Augustus, you can't explain anything. It is your chief charm. *Lady Windermere's Fan* (*Plays*, p32)

726. Talks more and says less than anybody I ever met. She is made to be a public speaker. *An Ideal Husband* (*Plays*, p285)

727. It is my last reception and one wants something that will encourage conversation, particularly at the end of the season when everyone has practically said whatever they had to say, which, in most cases, was probably not much. *The Importance of Being Earnest* (*Plays*, p360)

728. ... still in these latter days when violent rhetoric does duty for eloquence and vulgarity usurps the name of nature, we should be grateful for a style that deliberately aims at perfection of form, that seeks to produce its effect by artistic means and sets before itself an ideal of grave and chastened beauty. *Mr. Pater's Imaginary Portraits* (*Uncollected*, pp142–3)

729. As for conversation, there are only five women in London worth talking to, and two of these can't be admitted into decent society. *The Picture of Dorian Gray* (*SC*, p64)

730. In society, says Mr. Mahaffy, every civilised man and woman ought to feel it their duty to say something, even when there is hardly anything to be said, and, in order to encourage this delightful art of brilliant chatter, he has published a social guide without which no *debutante* or dandy should ever dream of going out to dine ... the book can be warmly recommended to all who propose to substitute the vice of verbosity for the stupidity of silence. *Aristotle at Afternoon Tea, Pall Mall Gazette* (*Uncollected*, p83)

731. HESTER: I dislike London dinner parties.

MRS. ALLONBY: I adore them. The clever people never listen, and the stupid people never talk.

HESTER: I think the stupid people talk a great deal.

MRS. ALLONBY: Ah, I never listen. *A Woman of No Importance* (*Plays*, p144)

732. I remember we talked all the night through, or rather I talked and everyone else listened, for the great principle for the divi-sion of labour is beginning to be understood in English Society. The host gives excellent food, excellent wine, excellent cigarettes, and super-excellent coffee, that's his part, and all the men listen, that's theirs; while I talk and the stars twinkle their delight. *Oscar Wilde, by Frank Harris* (*CG*, p259)

733. One should never listen. To listen is a sign of indifference to one's hearers. *A Few Maxims for the Instruction of the Over-Educated, Saturday Review* (*Works*, p1242)

734. You see, it is a very dangerous thing to listen. If one listens, one may be convinced.... *An Ideal Husband* (*Plays*, p235)

735. LORD CAVERSHAM: Tell me, do you always really understand what you say, sir?

LORD GORING: Yes, father, if I listen attentively. *An Ideal Husband* (*Plays*, p297)

736. You are the only person in London I really like to have listen to me. *An Ideal Husband* (*Plays*, p323)

737. I have a perfect passion for listening through keyholes. One always hears such wonderful things through them. *An Ideal Husband* (*Plays*, p307)

738. WALTER PATER: I was rather afraid that people had not heard me.

OSCAR WILDE: We overheard you. *Aspects of Wilde* (*CC*, p68)

739. I am so sorry I was not here to listen to you, but I suppose I am too old now to learn. Except from you, dear Archdeacon, when you are in your nice pulpit. But then I always know what you are going to say, so I don't feel alarmed. *A Woman of No Importance* (*Plays*, p182)

740. ... what can be more detestable than the man, or woman, who insists on agreeing with everybody, and so makes "a discussion, which implies differences in opinion," absolutely impossible? Even the unselfish listener is apt to become a bore. *Aristotle at Afternoon Tea, Pall Mall Gazette* (*Uncollected*, pp84–5)

741. THE ROCKET: Conversation indeed! You have talked the whole time yourself. That is not conversation.

THE FROG: Somebody must listen, and I like to do all the talking myself. It saves time, and prevents arguments. *The Remarkable Rocket* (*Works*, p299)

742. I am not going to stop talking to him merely because he pays no attention. I like hearing myself talk. It is one of my greatest pleasures. I often have long conversations all by myself, and I am so clever that sometimes I don't understand a single word of what I am saying. *The Remarkable Rocket* (*Works*, pp299–300)

743. PRINCE PAUL: I find these Cabinet Councils extremely tiring.

PRINCE PETROVITCH: Naturally, you are always speaking.

PRINCE PAUL: No, I think it must be that I have to listen sometimes. It is so exhausting not to talk. *Vera, or the Nihilists* (*Works*, p696)

744. Here, in the interest of society, we feel bound to enter a formal protest. Nobody, even in the provinces, should ever be allowed to ask an intelligent question about pure mathematics across a dinner table. A question of this kind is quite as bad as enquiring suddenly about the state of a man's soul.... *Aristotle at Afternoon Tea, Pall Mall Gazette* (*Uncollected*, p84)

745. It is always worth while asking a question, though it is not always worth while answering one. *An Ideal Husband* (*Plays*, p267)

746. Questions are never indiscreet. Answers sometimes are. *An Ideal Husband* (*Plays*, p229)

747. You must not imagine that people in cafes listen to the conversations of others; nobody bothers to do anything of the kind. People in life listen primarily to their own conversation, then to the conversation of the person or persons with whom they are, if the latter are interesting. *Letter to George Ives* (*Letters*, p1172)

748. ... their conversation is most fascinating however as long as it is unintelligible, but when interpreted it is rather silly.... *Letter to Mrs. Bernard Beere* (*Letters*, p153)

749. Learned conversation is either the affectation of the ignorant or the profession of the mentally unemployed. And for what is called improving conversation, that is merely the foolish method by which the still more foolish philanthropist feebly tries to disarm the just rancour of the criminal classes. *The Critic as Artist* (*Works*, p1114)

750. Still, anybody can be made to talk, except the very obstinate, and even a commercial traveler may be drawn out and become quite interesting. *Aristotle at Afternoon Tea, Pall Mall Gazette* (*Uncollected*, p86)

751. Really domestic people are almost invariably bad talkers as their very virtues in home life have dulled their interest in outer things. *Aristotle at Afternoon Tea, Pall Mall Gazette* (*Uncollected*, p85)

752. Poor old Lord Mortlake, who had only two topics of conversation, his gout and his wife. I never could quite make out which of the two he was talking about. *An Ideal Husband* (*Plays*, p309)

753. But Mellor is tedious, and lacks conversation: also he gives me Swiss wine to drink: it is horrid. He occupies himself with small economies, and mean domestic interests. *Letter to Frank Harris* (*Letters*, p1131)

754. The brilliant phrase, like good wine, needs no bush. But just as the orator marks his good things by a dramatic pause, or by raising or lowering his voice, or by gesture, so the writer marks his epigrams with italics, setting the little gem, so to speak, like a jeweler — an excusable love of one's art, not all mere vanity, I like to think. *Oscar Wilde, by Frank Harris* (*CG*, p101)

755. ... in the case of those rare temperaments that are exquisitely susceptible to the influences of language, the use of certain phrases and modes of expression can stir the very pulse of passion, can send the red blood coursing through the veins, and can transform into a strange sensuous energy what in its origin had been mere aesthetic impulse, and desire of art. So, at least, it seems to have been with Shakespeare. *The Portrait of Mr. W.H.* (*Works*, p336)

756. ... something must come into my work, of fuller harmony of words, perhaps, of richer cadences, of more curious colour-effects, of simpler architectural-order, of some aesthetic quality at any rate. *De Profundis* (*OWC*, p128)

757. Words have their mystical power over the soul, and form can create the feeling from which it should have sprung. *The Portrait of Mr. W.H.* (*Works*, pp335–6)

758. Words have not merely music as sweet as that of viol and lute, colour as rich and vivid as any that makes lovely for us the canvas of the Venetian or the Spaniard, and plastic form no less sure and certain than that which reveals itself in marble or in bronze, but thought and passion and spirituality are theirs also, are theirs indeed alone. If the Greeks had criticised nothing but language, they would still have been the great art-critics of the world. *The Critic as Artist* (*Works,* p1117)

759. I never quarrel with actions. My one quarrel is with words. *The Picture of Dorian Gray* (*SC,* p206)

760. Lots of people act well, but very few people talk well, which shows that talking is much the more difficult thing of the two, and much the finer thing also. *The Devoted Friend* (*Works,* p288)

761. The only possible form of exercise is to talk, not walk. *Interview in The Sketch* (*Uncollected,* p. xxi)

762. Actions are the first tragedy in life, words are the second. Words are perhaps the worst. Words are merciless.... Oh! *Lady Windermere's Fan* (*Plays,* p66)

763. ... it is much more difficult to do a thing than to talk about it. *The Critic as Artist* (*Works,* p1121)

764. I have just finished my first long story [The Picture of Dorian Gray], and am tired out. I am afraid it is rather like my own life — all conversation and no action. I can't describe action: my people sit in chairs and chatter. *Letter to Beatrice Allhusen* (*Letters,* p425)

765. ... the real charm of the play, if it is to have charm, must be in the dialogue. The plot is slight, but, I think, adequate. *Letter to George Alexander* (*Letters,* p595)

766. Frank Harris is upstairs, thinking about Shakespeare at the top of his voice. I am earnestly idling. *Letter to Robert Ross* (*Letters,* p1121)

767. To converse with him is a physical no less than an intellectual recreation. *Letter to William Rothenstein* (*Letters,* p925)

768. Life goes on very pleasantly here. Frank Harris is of course exhausting. After our literary talk in the evening I stagger to my room, bathed in perspiration. I believe he talks the Rugby game. *Letter to Reginald Turner* (*Letters,* p1121)

769. Nichol, the son of a Glasgow professor, was there also — a nice fellow, but insane. He cannot think or talk, so he quotes Swinburne's *Poems and Ballads* always, instead of conversation — a capital idea, after all. *Letter to Robert Ross* (*Letters,* p1096)

770. You are a very irritating person ... and very ill-bred. I hate people who talk about themselves, as you do, when one wants to talk about oneself, as I do. It is what I call selfishness.... *The Remarkable Rocket* (*Works,* p299)

771. I am not going to stop talking to him merely because he pays no attention. I like hearing myself talk. It is one of my greatest pleasures. I often have long conversations with myself, and I am so clever that sometimes I don't understand a single word of what I am saying. *The Remarkable Rocket* (*Works,* pp299–300)

772. The two long years of silence kept my soul in bonds. It will all come back, I feel sure, and all will be well. *Letter to Carlos Blacker* (*Letters,* p912)

773. ... an old gentleman of considerable charm and culture, who had fallen, however, into bad habits of silence having ... said everything that he had to say before he was thirty. *The Picture of Dorian Gray* (*SC,* p54)

774. People who shout so loud, my lords, do nothing,
The only men I fear are silent men.
The Duchess of Padua (*Works,* p619)

775. Oh, I'm so glad you've come. There are a hundred things I want not to say to you. *Quoted in Oscar Wilde: His Life and Wit* (*HBP,* p176)

776. The postcard is the only mode of silence left to us. *Postcard to Robert Ross* (*Letters,* p902)

777. Your silence has been horrible. *De Profundis* (*OWC,* p92)

778. Sir Lewis Morris: There's a conspiracy against me, a conspiracy of silence [regarding his books being boycotted by the press]; but what can one do? What should I do?

Oscar Wilde: Join it. *Oscar Wilde, by Frank Harris* (*CG,* p246)

779. Every good storyteller nowadays starts with the end, and then goes on to the beginning and concludes with the middle. *The Devoted Friend* (*Works*, p288)

780. Of course when the moon is full I often return to Leon, to smoke a cigarette or to weave words about Life, but no one comes to see me. *Letter to Robert Ross* (*Letters*, p1074)

781. Whatever you have to say for yourself, say it without fear. *De Profundis* (*OWC*, p157)

782. We can talk afterwards, Frank, when all the stars come out to listen; now is the time to live and enjoy. *Oscar Wilde, by Frank Harris* (*CG*, p249)

783. But I must say that I no longer make *roulades* of phrases about the deep things I feel. When I write directly to you I speak directly. Violin-variations don't interest me. *Letter to Frank Harris* (*Letters*, p894)

784. I have grown tired of the inarticulate utterances of men and things. *De Profundis* (*OWC*, p155)

785. Ah! I have talked quite enough for to-day. All I want now is to look at life. You may come and look at it with me, if you care to. *The Picture of Dorian Gray* (*SC*, p60)

12

Craftsmen

786. It is impossible to have good workmanship unless the worker can see the beautiful things of Nature about him. *Oscar Wilde Discovers America* (*HBC*, p177)

787. All the teaching in the world is of no avail in art unless you surround your workmen with happy influences and with delightful things; it is impossible for him to have right ideas about colour unless he sees the lovely colours of Nature unspoiled about him, impossible for him to supply beautiful incident and action in the world about him unless he sees beautiful incident and action in the world about him, for to cultivate sympathy, you must be among living things and thinking about them, and to cultivate admiration you must be among beautiful things and looking at them. And so your houses and streets should be living schools of art where your workman may see beautiful forms as he goes to his work in the morning and returns to his home at eventide. *The Decorative Arts lecture* (*Works*, p929) and similar quotation in *The English Renaissance of Art lecture* (*Uncollected*, p27)

788. Give then, as I said, to your workmen of today the bright and noble surroundings that you can yourself create. Stately and simple architecture for your cities, bright and simple dress for your men and women: those are the conditions of a real artistic movement. *Art and the Handicraftsman lecture* (*Uncollected*, p109)

789. But one cannot get good work done unless the handicraftsman is furnished with rational and beautiful designs; if you have commonplace design, you must have commonplace work, and if you have commonplace work, you must have commonplace workmen; but really good design will produce thoroughly good workmen whose work is beautiful at the moment and for all time. *The Decorative Arts lecture* (*Works*, p927)

790. You must show your workmen specimens of good work so that they come to know what is simple and true and beautiful. *House Decoration Lecture* (*Uncollected*, p186)

791. How necessary, then, when the artist and the poet have supplied the handicraftsman with beautiful designs, thoughts and ideas, that in working them out he should be honoured with a loving encouragement and satisfied with fair surroundings. For the great difficulty that stands in the way of your artistic development is not a lack of interest in art, nor a lack of love for art, but that you do not honour the handicraftsman sufficiently, and do not recognise him as you should; all art must begin with the handicraftsman, and you must reinstate him into his rightful position. *The Decorative Arts lecture* (*Works*, p927) and similar quotation in *The House Beautiful lecture* (*Uncollected*, p913)

792. If you have poor and worthless designs in any craft or trade you will get poor and worthless workmen only, but the minute you have noble and beautiful designs, then you get men of power and intellect and feeling to work for you. By having good designs you have workmen who work not merely with their hands but with their hearts and heads too: otherwise you will get merely the fool or the loafer to work for you. *Art and the Handicraftsman lecture* (*Uncollected*, p107)

793. And so wherever good work and good decoration is found, it is a certain sign that the workman has laboured not only with his hands, but with his heart and head also. *The Decorative Arts lecture* (*Uncollected,* pp926–7)

794. Let it be for you to create an art that is made with the hands of the people, for the joy of the people, too, an art that will be an expression of your delight in life. *The Decorative Arts lecture* (*Works,* p926 and 937) and similar quotation in *House Decoration lecture* (*Uncollected,* p184)

13

Critique

795. It is criticism that makes us cosmopolitan. *The Critic as Artist* (*Works*, p1152)

796. Praise makes me humble, but when I am abused I know I have touched the stars. *Aspects of Wilde* (*CC*, p11)

797. Praise from anyone is very delightful. Praise from literary people is usually tainted with criticism. *The Three Trials of Oscar Wilde* (*UB*, p316)

798. There is a luxury in self-reproach. When we blame ourselves, we feel that no one else has a right to blame us. *The Picture of Dorian Gray* (*SC, 111*)

799. The highest as the lowest form of criticism is a mode of autobiography. *The Picture of Dorian Gray* (*SC*, p18)

800. That is what the highest criticism really is, the record of one's own soul. *The Critic as Artist* (*Works*, p1125)

801. I am concerned only with my view of art. I don't care twopence what other people think of it. *The Three Trials of Oscar Wilde* (*UB*, p124)

802. The moment criticism exercises any influence, it ceases to be criticism. The aim of the true critic is to try and chronicle his own moods, not to try and correct the masterpieces of others. *Interview in The Sketch* (*Uncollected*, p. xvii)

803. To the critic the work of art is simply a suggestion for a new work of his own, that need not necessarily bear any obvious resemblance to the thing that it criticises. *The Critic as Artist* (*Works*, p1128)

804. ... it is only by intensifying his own personality that the critic can interpret the personality and work of others, and the more strongly this personality enters into the interpretation, the more real the interpretation becomes, the more satisfying, the more convincing, and the more true. *The Critic as Artist* (*Works*, p1131)

805. The critic, then, considered as the interpreter, will give no less than he receives, and lend as much as he borrows.... *The Critic as Artist* (*Works*, p1132)

806. Indeed, so far from its being true that the artist is the best judge of art, a really great artist can never judge of other people's work at all, and can hardly, in fact, judge his own. That very concentration of vision that makes a man an artist, limits by its sheer intensity his faculty of fine appreciation. The energy of creation hurries him blindly on to his own goal. *The Critic as Artist* (*Works*, p1150)

807. ... it may be that the artist, desiring merely to contemplate and to create, is wise in not busying himself about change in others. *The Relation of Art the Dress lecture* (*Uncollected*, p53)

808. ... I would say that the highest Criticism, being the purest form of personal impression, is in its way more creative than creation, as it has least reference to any standard external to itself, and is, in fact, its own reason for existing, and, as the Greeks would put it, in itself, and to itself, and end. *The Critic as Artist* (*Works*, p1125)

809. The Greeks had no art critics. *The Critic as Artist* (*Works*, p1113)

810. In the best days of art there were no art critics. *The Critic as Artist* (*Works*, p1112)

811. Who would not be flippant when one is gravely told that the Greeks had no art critics? I can understand it being said that the constructive genius of the Greeks lost itself in criticism, but not that the race to whom we owe the critical spirit did not criticise. *The Critic as Artist* (*Works*, p1116)

812. Don't take your critic as any sure test of art, for artists, like the Greek gods, are only revealed to one another. *The English Renaissance of Art lecture* (*Uncollected*, p17)

813. And criticism — what place is that to have in our culture? Well, I think that the first duty of an art critic is to hold his tongue at all times, and upon all subjects.... *The English Renaissance of Art lecture* (*Uncollected*, p18)

814. I say that only an artist is a judge of art: there is a wide difference. As long as a painter is a painter merely, he should not be allowed to talk of anything but mediums and megilp, and on those subject should be compelled to hold his tongue; it is only when he becomes an artist that the secret laws of artistic creation are revealed to him. For there are not many arts, but one art merely — poem, picture and Parthenon, sonnet and statue — are all in their essence the same, and he who knows one knows all. *Mr. Whistler's Ten o'clock* (*Uncollected*, p49)

815. ... if a book is dull let us say nothing about it, if it is bright let us review it. *Letter to Wemyss Reid* (*Letters*, p298)

816. OSCAR WILDE: I shall always regard you as the best critic of my plays.

HERBERT BEERBOHM TREE: But I have never criticised your plays.

OSCAR WILDE: That's why. *Quoted in Oscar Wilde: His Life and Wit* (*HBP*, p210)

817. Literary criticism is not your forte, my dear fellow. Don't try it. You should leave that people who haven't been at a University. *An Ideal Husband* (*Plays*, p355)

818. I never approve, or disapprove, of anything now. It is an absurd attitude to take towards life. We are not sent into the world to air our moral prejudices. *The Picture of Dorian Gray* (*SC*, p89)

819. No work of art ever puts forward views. Views belong to people who are not artists. *The Three Trials of Oscar Wilde* (*UB*, p124)

820. People don't understand that criticism is prejudice, because to understand one must love, and to love one must have passion. *Letter to Leonard Smithers* (*Letters*, p1032)

821. Criticism will annihilate race-prejudices, by insisting upon the unity of the human mind in the variety of its forms. If we are tempted to make war upon another nation, we shall remember that we are seeking to destroy an element of our own culture, and possibly its most important element. *The Critic as Artist* (*Works*, p1153)

822. A critic should be taught to criticise a work of art without making any reference to the personality of the author. *Letter to the Editor of the St. James Gazette* (*Letters*, p432)

823. ... criticism of contemporary work should always be anonymous. *Letter to Wemyss Reid* (*Letters*, p363)

824. Your critic then, sir, commits the absolutely unpardonable crime of trying to confuse an artist with his subject-matter. For this, sir, there is no excuse at all. *Letter to the Editor of the Scots Observer* (*Letters*, p439)

825. The only thing that the artist cannot see is the obvious. The only thing that the public can see is the obvious. The result is the Criticism of the Journalist. *A Few Maxims for the Instruction of the Over-Educated, Saturday Review* (*Works*, p1242)

826. But, surely, the higher you place the creative artist, the lower must the critic rank. *The Critic as Artist* (*Works*, p1124)

827. ... the creative faculty is higher than the critical. There is really no comparison between them. *The Critic as Artist* (*Works*, p1118)

828. ... Criticism is itself an art. And just as artistic creation implies the working of the critical faculty, and, indeed, without it cannot be said to exist at all, so Criticism is really creative in the highest sense of the word. Criticism is, in fact, both creative and independent. *The Critic as Artist* (*Works*, p1124)

829. Indeed, I would call criticism a creation within a creation ... the critic deals with materials that others have, as it were purified for him, and to which imaginative form and colour have already been added. *The Critic as Artist* (*Works*, p1125)

830. The artistic critic, like the mystic, is an antinomian always. *The Critic as Artist* (*Works*, p1154)

831. Why should those who cannot create take upon themselves to estimate the value of creative work? What can they know about it? *The Critic as Artist* (*Works*, p1110)

832. The critic has to educate the public; the artist has to educate the critic. *Letter to the Editor of the Scots Observer* (*Letters*, p441)

833. ... I wish you would review my first volume of poems just about to appear: books so often fall into stupid and illiterate hands that I am anxious to be really *criticised:* ignorant praise or ignorant blame is so insulting. *Letter to Oscar Browning* (*Letters*, p111)

834. The true critic addresses not the artist ever but the public only. His work lies with them. Art can never have any other claim but her own perfection: it is for the critic to create for art the social aim, too, by teaching the people the spirit in which they are to approach all artistic work, the love they are to give it, the lesson they are to draw from it. *The English Renaissance of Art lecture* (*Uncollected*, p17)

835. I am always amused by the silly vanity of those writers and artists of our day who seem to imagine that the primary function of the critic is to chatter about their second-rate work. *The Critic as Artist* (*Works*, p1125)

836. A publisher is simply a useful middleman. It is not for him to anticipate the verdict of criticism. *Letter to the Editor of the St. James Gazette* (*Letters*, p433)

837. We are sorry, too, to find an English dramatic critic misquoting Shakespeare, as we had always been of the opinion that this was a privilege reserved specially for our English actors. *A Cheap Edition of Great Men, Pall Mall Gazette* (*Uncollected*, p98)

838. English dramatic criticism of our own day has never had a single success, in spite of the fact that it goes to all the first nights. *Interview in The Sketch* (*Uncollected*, p. xvii)

839. When criticism becomes in England a real art, as it should be, and when none but those of artistic instinct and artistic cultivation is allowed to write about works of art, artists will no doubt read criticisms with a certain amount of intellectual interest. *Letter to the Editor of the St. James Gazette* (*Letters*, p522)

840. Free criticism is as unknown as free trade. *The Rise of Historical Criticism* (*Works*, p1198)

841. Full of promise is an expression quite meaningless in even the most elementary art-criticism. *Letter to Stanley V. Makower* (*Letters*, pp960–1)

842. ... there has never been a creative age that has not been critical also. For it the critical faculty that invents fresh forms. The tendency of creation is to repeat itself. It is to the critical instinct that we owe each new school that springs up.... *The Critic as Artist* (*Works*, p1119)

843. ... it seems to me that most modern criticism is perfectly valueless.... So is most modern creative work also. Mediocrity weighing mediocrity in the balance, and incompetence applauding its brother. *The Critic as Artist* (*Works*, p1120)

844. There are two ways of disliking art.... One is to dislike it. The other is to dislike it rationally. *The Critic as Artist* (*Works*, p1144)

845. The critic is he who can translate in another manner or a new material his impression of beautiful things. *The Picture of Dorian Gray* (*SC*, p18)

846. Temperament is the primary requisite for the critic — a temperament exquisitely susceptible to beauty, and to the various impressions that beauty gives us. *The Critic as Artist* (*Works*, p1146)

847. The art which has fulfilled the conditions of beauty has fulfilled all conditions: it is for the critic to teach the people how to find in the calm of such art the highest expression of their own most stormy passions. *The English Renaissance of Art lecture* (*Uncollected*, p18)

848. As little should you judge of the strength and splendour of the sun and sea by the dust that dances in the beam, or the bubble that breaks on the wave, as take your critic for any sane test of art. *The English Renaissance of Art lecture* (*Uncollected*, p17)

849. ... if this new world has been made by the spirit and touch of a great artist, it will be a thing so complete and perfect that there will be nothing left for the critic to do. *The Critic as Artist* (*Works*, p1124)

850. For who is the true critic but he who bears within himself the dreams, and ideas, and feelings of myriad generations, and to whom no form of thought is alien, no emotional impulse obscure? *The Critic as Artist* (*Works,* p1138) and *Mr. Pater's Appreciations* (*Uncollected,* p145)

851. I have never collected the parodies of my works in poetry. Collecting contemporaneous things is like trying to hold froth in a sieve. *Letter to Walter Hamilton* (*Letters,* p390)

852. I never reply to my critics. I have far too much time. But I think someday I will give a general answer in the form of a lecture, which I shall call "Straight Talks to Old Men." ... *Quoted in Oscar Wilde: His Life and Wit* (*HBP,* p222)

853. They afterwards took me to a dancing saloon, where I saw the only rational method of art criticism I have ever come across. Over the piano was printed a notice: "Please do not shoot the pianist: he is doing his best." *Quoted in Oscar Wilde: His Life and Wit* (*HBP,* p65)

854. The richer the work of art the more diverse are the true interpretations. There is not one answer only, but many answers. I pity the book on which all critics agree. It must be a very obvious and shallow production. Congratulate yourself on the diversity of *contemporary* tongues. The worst of posterity is that it has but one voice. *Letter to W.E. Henley* (*Letters,* p373)

855. A critic cannot be fair in the ordinary sense of the word. It is only about things that do not interest one that one can give a really unbiased opinion, which is no doubt the reason why an unbiased opinion is always absolutely valueless. The man who sees both sides of a question is a man who sees absolutely nothing at all. *The Critic as Artist* (*Works,* p1144)

856. One can really ... be far more subjective in an *objective* form than in any other way. *Letter to Lord Alfred Douglas* (*Letters,* pp873–4)

857. When the critics disagree, the artist is in accord with himself. *Quoted in Oscar Wilde: His Life and Wit* (*HBC,* p132)

858. The critics have ceased to prophecy. That is something. It is in silence that the artist arrives. *Interview in The Sketch* (*Uncollected,* p. xxi)

859. Real critics? Ah! How perfectly charming they would be. I am always waiting for their arrival. An inaudible school would be nice. Why do you not found it? *Interview in The Sketch* (*Uncollected,* p. xvii)

14

Cynicism and Skepticism

860. You never say a moral thing, and you never do a wrong thing. Your cynicism is simply a pose. *The Picture of Dorian Gray* (*SC*, p22)

861. CECIL GRAHAM: What is a cynic?

LORD DARLINGTON: A man who knows the price of everything and the value of nothing.

CECIL GRAHAM: And a sentimentalist, my dear Darlington, is a man who sees the absurd value in everything and doesn't know the market price of a single thing. *Lady Windermere's Fan* (*Plays,* p61)

862. No, I am not at all cynical, I have merely got experience, which, however, is very much the same thing. *Lord Arthur Savile's Crime* (*SC*, p270)

863. To Lord Arthur it came early in life — before his nature had been spoiled by the calculating cynicism of middle-age, or his heart corroded by the shallow fashionable egotism of our day.... *Lord Arthur Savile's Crime* (*SC*, p281)

864. And remember that the sentimentalist is always a cynic at heart. Indeed sentimentality is merely the bank holiday of cynicism. And delightful as cynicism is from its intellectual side, now that it has left the Tub for the Club, it can never be more than the perfect philosophy for a man who has no soul. It has its social value, and to an artist all modes of expression are interesting, but in itself it is a poor affair, for to the true cynic nothing is ever revealed. *De Profundis* (*OWC*, p143)

865. ... for as every body has its shadow so every soul has its scepticism. *The English Renaissance of Art lecture* (*Uncollected,* pp24–5)

866. DUCHESS OF MONMOUTH: Religion?

LORD HENRY: The fashionable substitute for belief.

DUCHESS OF MONMOUTH: You are a sceptic.

LORD HENRY: Never! Scepticism is the beginning of faith. *The Picture of Dorian Gray* (*SC*, p207)

15

Death

867. To die for one's theological opinions is the worst use a man can make of his life.... *The Portrait of Mr. W.H.* (*Works*, p348)

868. A thing is not necessarily true because a man dies for it. *Quoted in Oscar Wilde: His Life and Wit* (*HBC*, p165)

869. Suicide is the greatest compliment that one can pay to society. *Oscar Wilde: The Story of an Unhappy Friendship* (*GC*, p41)

870. No man dies for what he knows to be true. Men die for what they want to be true, for what some terror in their hearts tells them is not true. *The Portrait of Mr. W.H.* (*Works*, p349)

871. Death is too rude, too obvious a key
To solve one single secret in a life's philosophy. *Humanitad* (*Works*, p819)

872. She had no right to kill herself. It was selfish of her. *The Picture of Dorian Gray* (*SC*, p114)

873. The girl never really lived, and so she never really died. *The Picture of Dorian Gray* (*SC*, p118)

874. For he who lives more lives than one
More deaths than one must die. *The Ballad of Reading Gaol* (*OWC*, p181)

875. If they know nothing of death, it is because they know little of life, for the secrets of life and death belong to those, and those only, whom the sequence of time affects, and who possess not merely the present but the future and can rise or fall from a past of glory or of shame. *The Critic as Artist* (*Works*, p1124)

876. ... I don't think I should play Quixote. To tilt with death is worse than to tilt with windmills. *Letter to Robert Ross* (*Letters*, p978)

877. To fight with the dead is either a vulgar farce or a revolting tragedy. *Letter to Lord Alfred Douglas* (*Letters*, p876)

878. Dead lips have their message for us, and hearts that have fallen to dust can communicate their joy. *The Critic as Artist* (*Works*, p1135)

879. Death and vulgarity are the only two facts in the nineteenth century that one cannot explain away. *The Picture of Dorian Gray* (*SC*, p223)

880. ... to see the statues of our departed statesmen in marble frock-coats and bronze. Double-breasted waistcoats adds a new horror to death. *The Decorative Arts lecture* (*Works*, p930)

881. I was obliged to call on dear Lady Harbury. I hadn't been there since her poor husband's death. I never saw a woman so altered; she looks quite twenty years younger. *The Importance of Being Earnest* (*Plays*, p358)

882. Rid of the world's injustice and pain,
He rests at last beneath God's veil of blue;
Taken from life while life and love were new.

The Tomb of Keats, The Irish Monthly (*Uncollected*, p46)

883. On the tomb of the dead thing he had most loved had he set this image of his own fashioning, that it might serve as a sign of the love of man that dieth not, and a symbol of the sorrow of man that endureth forever. *The Artist* (*Works*, p900)

884. Death must be so beautiful. To lie in the soft brown earth, with the grasses waving above one's head, and listen to silence. To have no yesterday and no to-morrow. To forget time, to forgive life, to be at peace. You can help me. You can open for me the portals of Death's house, for Love is always with you, and Love is stronger than Death is. *The Canterville Ghost* (*Works*, p198)

885. Did you say dead? O too swift runner, Death,

Couldst thou not wait for me a little space,
And I had done thy bidding!

The Duchess of Padua (*Works*, p609)

886. ... I was greatly shocked to read of poor Aubrey's death. Superbly premature as the flowering of his genius was, still he had immense development, and had not sounded his last stop. There were great possibilities always in the cavern of his soul, and there is something macabre and tragic in the fact that one who added another terror to life should have died at the age of a flower. *Letter to Leonard Smithers* (*Letters,* p1040)

887. Murder is always a mistake.... One should never do anything that one cannot talk about after dinner. *The Picture of Dorian Gray* (*SC,* p225)

888. Indeed everybody in the world should be either killed or kissed. *Letter to Aimee Lowther* (*Letters,* p583)

889. ROBERT SHERARD: If you saw a man throw himself into the river here, would you go after him?

OSCAR WILDE: I should consider it an act of gross impertinence to do so. His suicide would be a perfectly thought-out act, the definite result of a scientific process, with which I should have no right whatever to interfere. *Oscar Wilde: The Story of an Unhappy Friendship* (*GC,* p50)

890. There is here at Naples a garden where those who have determined to kill themselves go. A short time ago, after Bosie had gone away, I was so cast down by the boredom of leaving the villa at Posilipo, and by the annoyance that some absurd friends in England were giving me, that I felt I could bear no more. Really, I came to wish that I was back in my prisoner's cell picking oakum. I thought of suicide ... but one night when there were no stars I went down to that garden. As I sat there absolutely alone in the darkness, I heard a rustling noise, and sighing; and misty cloud-like things came round me. And I realized that they were the little souls of those who had killed themselves in that place, condemned to linger there ever after. They had killed themselves in vain. *Oscar Wilde: The Story of an Unhappy Friendship* (*GC,* pp69–70)

891. The world's a graveyard, and we each, like coffins,
Within us bear a skeleton.

The Duchess of Padua (*Works,* p636)

892. There are few things easier than to live badly and die well. *Vera, the Nihilist* (*Works,* p696)

893. Death is the common heritage of all, And death comes best when it comes suddenly. *The Duchess of Padua* (*Works,* p610)

894. And lastly, let us remember that art is the one thing which Death cannot harm. *Art and the Handicraftsman lecture* (*Uncollected,* p118)

895. Death is not a god. He is only the servant of the gods. *La Sainte Courtisane* (*Works,* p735)

896. ... death is but a newer life.... *Lotus Leaves* (*Works,* p764)

897. To leave life as one leaves a feast is not merely philosophy but romance. *Letter to Leonard Smithers* (*Letters,* p1003)

16

Domesticity

898. The General was essentially a man of peace, except in his domestic life. *The Importance of Being Earnest (Plays,* p431)

899. The home seems to me to be the proper sphere for the man. And certainly once a man begins to neglect his domestic duties he becomes painfully effeminate, does he not? And I don't like that. It makes men so very attractive. *The Importance of Being Earnest (Plays,* p400)

900. No letter from you today. I suspect that domesticity is dominating.... *Letter to Robert Ross (Letters,* p918)

901. I do protest, sirs, the domestic virtues Are often very beautiful in others. *The Duchess of Padua (Works,* p635)

902. The domestic virtues are not the true basis of art, though they may serve as an excellent advertisement for second-rate artists. *Pen, Pencil and Poison (Works,* p1106)

903. There is no peace except in one's own home. *Letter to Robert Ross (Letters,* p889)

17

Drama

904. Man is least himself when he talks in his own person. Give him a mask and he will tell you the truth. *The Critic as Artist* (*Works*, p1142)

905. ... I don't like scenes, except on the stage. *The Picture of Dorian Gray* (*SC*, p44)

906. ... when a play lasts too long, spectators tire. *Letter to Robert Ross* (*Letters*, p669)

907. It is the best play I ever slept through. *Quoted in Oscar Wilde: His Life and Wit* (*HBP*, p196)

908. In the case of the drama ... the theatre-going public like the obvious, it is true, but they do not like the tedious.... *The Soul of Man* (*OWC*, p19)

909. I think we must remember that no amount of advertising will make a bad play succeed, if it is not a good play well acted. *Letter to Marie Prescott* (*Letters*, p203)

910. The drama appeals to human nature, and must have as its ultimate basis the science of psychology and physiology. *Letter to Marie Prescott* (*Letters*, p204)

911. The drama is the meeting-place of art and life. *The English Renaissance of Art lecture* (*Uncollected*, p19)

912. For stage is not merely the meeting-place of all the arts, but is also the return of art to life. *The Truth of Masks* (*Works*, p1162)

913. The dream of the sculptor is cold and silent in the marble, the painter's vision immobile on the canvas. I want to see my work [writing plays] return again to life, my lines gain new splendour from your passion, new music from your lips. *Letter to Mary Anderson* (*Letters*, p179)

914. If I were asked of myself as a dramatist, I would say that my unique position was that I had taken the Drama, the most objec-tive form known to art, and made it as personal a mode of expression as the Lyric or the Sonnet, while enriching the characterization of the stage, and enlarging ... its artistic horizon. *Letter to Lord Alfred Douglas* (*Letters*, p874)

915. My "trivial comedy for serious people" [The Importance of Being Earnest] comes out in a few weeks.... *Letter to H.C. Pollitt* (*Letters*, p1103)

916. I hear London like some grey monster raging over the publication of Salome, but I am at peace for the moment.... *Letter to Oswald Yorke* (*Letters*, p558)

917. There are two ways of disliking my plays: one is to dislike them, the other is to prefer "Earnest." *Quoted in Oscar Wilde: His Life and Wit* (*HBP*, p229)

918. I am so glad, ladies and gentlemen, that you like my play ["Lady Windermere's Fan"]. I feel sure you estimate the merits of it almost as highly as I do myself. *Oscar Wilde, by Frank Harris* (*CG*, p83)

919. The play *is* a success. The only question is whether the first night's audience will be one. *Quoted in Oscar Wilde: His Life and Wit* (*HBP*, p227)

920. As for "success" on the stage, the public is a monster of strange appetites: it swallows, so it seems to me, honeycake and hellebore, with avidity: but there are many publics—and the artist belongs to none of them: if he is admired it is, a little, by chance. *Letter to an Unidentified Correspondent* (*Letters*, p626)

921. On the three first nights I have had in London, the public has been most successful, and, had the dimensions of the stage admitted of it, I would have called them before the curtain. Most managers, I believe, call them behind. *Interview in The Sketch* (*Uncollected*, p. xviii)

922. I am not nervous on the night that I am producing a new play. I am exquisitely indifferent. My nervousness ends at the last dress rehearsal; I know then what effect my play, as presented on the stage, has produced upon me. My interest in the play ends there, and I feel curiously envious of the public — they have such wonderfully fresh emotions in store for them. *Interview in The Sketch* (*Uncollected*, p. xviii)

923. The only inartistic incident of the evening was the hurling of a bouquet from a box at Mr. Irving while he was engaged in pourtraying the agony of Hamlet's death, and the pathos of his parting from Horatio. The Dramatic College might take up the education of spectators as well as that of players, and teach people that there is a proper moment for the throwing of flowers as well as a proper method. *Hamlet at the Lyceum Dramatic Review* (*Uncollected*, p75)

924. Now it is quite true that I hold that the stage is to a play no more than a picture-frame is to a painting, and that the actable value of a play has nothing whatsoever to do with its value as a work of art. *Letter to the Editor of The Daily Telegraph* (*Letters*, p519)

925. ... as a certain advance has been made in drama within the last ten or fifteen years, it is important to point out that this advance is entirely due to a few individual artists refusing to accept the popular want of taste as their standard, and refusing to regard Art as a mere matter of demand and supply. *The Soul of Man* (*OWC*, p25)

926. There is no passion in bronze, nor motion in marble. The sculptor must surrender colour, and the painter fullness of form. The epos changes into words, and music changes into tones. It is the Drama only that ... uses all means at once, and, appealing both to eye and ear, has at its disposal, and in its service, form and colour, tone, look, and word, the swiftness of motion, the intense realism of visible action. *The Portrait of Mr. W.H.* (*Works*, p324)

927. And, valuable as beauty of effect on the stage is, the highest beauty is not merely comparable with absolute accuracy of detail, but really dependent on it. *The Truth of Masks* (*Works*, p1170)

928. I like your superb confidence in the dramatic value of the mere facts of life. I admire the horrible flesh and blood of your creatures. *Letter to Bernard Shaw* (*Letters*, pp563–4)

929. All good plays are a combination of the dream of a poet and that practical knowledge of the actor which gives concentration to action, which intensifies situation, and for poetic effect, which is description, substitutes dramatic effect, which is Life. *Letter to Mary Anderson* (*Letters*, pp178–9)

930. Art, and art only, can make archeology beautiful; and the theatrical art can use it most directly and most vividly, for it can combine in one exquisite presentation the illusion of actual life with the wonder of the unreal world. *The Truth of Masks* (*Works*, p1163)

931. ... tragedy and comedy are so mixed in my life now that I lose the sense of difference. *Letter to Robert Ross* (*Letters*, p988)

932. Personally I like comedy to be intensely modern, and I like my tragedy to walk in purple and to be remote: but these are whims merely. *Letter to an Unidentified Correspondent* (*Letters*, p626)

933. Satire, always as sterile as it is shameful and as impotent as it is insolent, paid them that usual homage which mediocrity pays to genius.... *The English Renaissance of Art* (*Uncollected*, p8)

934. To write a comedy one requires comedy merely, but to write a tragedy, tragedy is not sufficient: the strain of emotion on the audience must be lightened: they will not weep if you have not made them laugh.... *Letter to Mary Anderson* (*Letters*, p196)

935. A laugh in an audience does not destroy terror, but, by relieving it, aids it. Never be afraid that by raising a laugh you destroy tragedy. On the contrary, you intensify it. *Letter to Marie Prescott* (*Letters*, p204)

936. The mimic spectacle of life that Tragedy affords cleanses the bosom of much "perilous stuff," and by presenting high and worthy objects for the exercise of the emotions purifies and spiritualises the man; nay, not merely does it spiritualise him, but it initiates him also into the noble feelings of which he might else have known nothing.... *The Critic as Artist* (*Works*, p1117)

937. We shall never have a real drama in England until it is recognized that a play is as personal and individual a form of self-expression as a poem or a picture. *Interview in The Sketch* (*Uncollected*, pp. xx-xxi)

938. It sometimes happens that at a *premiere* in London the least enjoyable part of the performance is the play. I have seen many audiences more interesting than the actors, and have often heard better dialogue in the *foyer* than I have onstage. *Hamlet at the Lyceum, Dramatic Review* (*Uncollected*, p75)

939. ... the drama is one of the artistic forms through which the genius of England of this century seeks in vain to find outlet and expression. He has had no worthy imitators. *The English Renaissance of Art lecture* (*Uncollected*, p19)

940. The only link between Literature and the Drama left to us in England at the present moment is the bill of the play. *A Few Maxims for the Instruction of the Over-Educated, Saturday Review* (*Works*, p1242)

941. I fancy that it is rarely that a theatrical dinner is presided over by a brilliant dramatist. *Letter to A.W. Pinero* (*Letters*, p563)

942. I am working at dramatic art because it's *the democratic* art and I want fame. (*Plays*, p. xxx)

943. An old gentleman lives here in the hotel [Hotel de la Plage at Berneval]. He dines alone in his room, and then sits in the sun. He came here for two days and has stayed two years. His sole sorrow is that there is no theatre. Monsieur Bonnet is a little heartless about this, and says that as the old gentleman goes to bed at 8 o'clock a theatre would be of no use to him. The old gentleman says that he only goes to bed at 8 o'clock because there is no theatre. They argued the point yesterday for an hour. I sided with the old gentleman, but Logic sides with Monsieur Bonnet, I believe. *Oscar Wilde, by Frank Harris* (*CG*, pp222-3)

944. As the inevitable result of this substitution of an imitative for a creative medium, this surrender of an imaginative form, we have the modern English melodrama. The characters in these plays talk on the stage exactly as they would talk off it; they have neither aspirations or aspirates; they are taken directly from life and reproduce its vulgarity down to the smallest detail; they present the gait, manner, costume and accent of real people, they would pass unnoticed in a third-class railway carriage. And yet how wearisome the plays are! They do not succeed in producing even the impression of reality at which they aim, and which is their only reason for existing. As a method, realism is a complete failure. *The Decay of Lying* (*Works*, pp1079-80)

945. With his marvelous and vivid personality, with a style that has really a true colour-element in it, with his extraordinary power, not over mere mimicry, but over imaginative and intellectual creation, Mr. [Henry] Irving, had his sole object been to give the public what they wanted, could have produced the commonest plays in the commonest manner, and made as much success and money as a man could possibly desire. But his object was not that. His object was to realise his own perfection as an artist, under certain circumstances, and in certain forms of Art. At first he appealed to the few; now he has educated the many. He has created in the public both taste and temperament. The public appreciate his artistic success immensely. I often wonder, however, whether the public understand that that success is entirely due to the fact that he did not accept their standard, but realised his own. *The Soul of Man* (*OWC*, p25-6)

946. A temperament capable of receiving, through an imaginative medium, and under imaginative conditions, new and beautiful impressions, is the only temperament that can appreciate a work of art. And true as this is in the case of the appreciation of sculpture and painting, it is still more true of the appreciation of such arts as the drama. For a picture and a statue are not at war with Time. They take no count of its succession. In one moment their unity may be apprehended. In the case of literature it is different. Time must be traversed before the unity of effect is realized. *The Soul of Man* (*OWC*, p27)

947. ... in Shakespeare, the most purely human of all the great artists, in the whole of Celtic myth and legend where the lovliness of the world is shown through a mist of tears.... *De Profundis* (*OWC*, p111)

948. Shakespeare is not by any means a flawless artist. He is too fond of going directly to life, and borrowing life's natural utterance. He forgets that when Art surrenders her imaginative medium she surrenders everything. *The Decay of Lying* (*Works*, p1079)

949. What would you say of a dramatist who would take nobody but beautiful people as characters in his play? Would you not say he was missing half of life? *Lecture to Art Students at the Royal Academy* (*Uncollected*, p129)

950. ... he [Shakespeare] more than once complains of the smallness of the stage on which he has to produce big historical plays and of the want of scenery which obliges him to cut out many effective open air incidents.... *The Truth of Masks* (*Works*, p1159)

951. It is worth noticing that Shakespeare's first and last plays were both historical plays. *The Truth of Masks* (*Works*, p1166)

952. In looking at Shakespeare's plays as a whole, however, what is really remarkable is their extraordinary fidelity as regards his personages and his plots. *The Truth of Masks* (*Works*, p1165)

953. Indeed to him the deformed figure of Richard was of as much value as Juliet's lovliness; he sets the surge of the radical beside the silks of the lord, and sees the stage effects to be got from each; he has as much delight in Caliban as he has in Ariel, in rags as he has in clothes of gold, and recognises the artistic beauty of ugliness. *The Critic as Artist* (*Works*, p1161)

954. Shakespeare might have met Rosencrantz and Guildenstern in the white streets of London, or seen the serving-men of rival houses bite their thumb at each other in the open square; but Hamlet came out of his soul, and Romeo out of his passion. *The Critic as Artist* (*Works*, p1142)

955. We become lovers when we see Romeo and Juliet, and Hamlet makes us students. The blood of Duncan is upon our hands, with Timon we rage against the world, and when Lear wanders upon the heath the terror of madness touches us. Ours is the sinlessness of Desdemona, and ours, also, the sin of Iago. *The Portrait of Mr. W.H.* (*Works*, p343)

956. We cannot tell, and Shakespeare himself does not tell us, why Iago is evil, why Regan and Goneril have hard hearts, or why Sir Andrew Aguecheek is a fool. It is sufficient that they are what they are, and that nature gives warrant for their existence. If a character in a play is lifelike, if we recognise it as true to nature, we have no right to insist on the author explaining its genesis to us. We must accept it as it is: and in the hands of a good dramatist mere presentation can take the place of analysis, and indeed is often a more dramatic method, because a more direct one. *Ben Jonson, Pall Mall Gazette* (*Uncollected*, p160)

957. [Shakespeare] is constantly protesting against the two special limitations of the Elizabethan stage — the lack of suitable scenery, and the fashion of men playing women's parts. ... *Shakespeare on Scenery, Dramatic Review* (*Uncollected*, p71)

958. ... instead of bemoaning the position of the playwright, it were better for the critics to exert whatever influence they might possess towards restoring the scene-painter to his proper position as an artist, and not allowing him to be built over by the property manager, or hammered to death by the carpenter. *Shakespeare on Scenery, Dramatic Review* (*Uncollected*, p74)

959. ... the background should always be kept as a background, and colour subordinated to effect. This, of course, can only be done when there is one single mind directing the whole production. The facts of art are diverse, but the essence of artistic effect is unity. Monarchy, Anarchy, and Republicanism may contend for the government of nations'; but a theatre should be in the power of a cultured despot. There may be division of labour, but there must be no division of mind. *The Truth of Masks* (*Works*, p1172)

960. A scene is primarily a decorative background for the actors, and should always be kept subordinate, first to the players, their dress, gesture and action; and secondly, to the fundamental principle of a decorative art, which is not to imitate but to suggest nature. *Mrs. Langtry as Hester Grazebrook, New York World* (*Uncollected,* p69)

961. ... I should like very much to see a good decorative landscape in scene-painting; for I have seen no open-air scene in any theatre which did not really mar the value of the actors. One must either, like Titian, make the landscape subordinate to the figures, or, like Claude, the figures subordinate to the landscape; for if we desire realistic acting we cannot have realistic scene-painting. *Mrs. Langtry as Hester Grazebrook, New York World* (*Uncollected,* p69)

962. There should only be two things consulted in building a theater; first the audience, then the actor. The trouble with too many theaters is, they have blue skies, red seats, green hangings, a great display of gilding, and then what is the actor to do? His costumes fall flat. The house, the scenery, and the stage should be only a setting; let the woods used be dark and rich looking. *Oscar Wilde Discovers America* (*HBC,* p248)

963. A painted door [on stage] is more like a real door than a real door itself, for the proper conditions of light and shade can be given to it.... *Shakespeare on Scenery, Dramatic Review* (*Uncollected,* p73)

964. ... My plays are difficult to produce well: they require artistic setting on the stage, a good company that knows something of the style essential to high comedy, beautiful dresses, a sense of the luxury of modern life, and unless you are going out with a management that is able to pay well for things that are worth paying for, and to spend money in suitable presentation, it would be much better for you not to think of producing my plays. *Letter to Grace Hawthorne* (*Letters,* pp617–8)

965. And lastly, let those critics who hold up for our admiration the simplicity of the Elizabethan Stage, remember that they are lauding a condition of things against which Shakespeare himself, in the spirit of a true artist, always strongly protested. *Shakespeare on Scenery, Dramatic Review* (*Uncollected,* p74)

966. Theatrical audiences are far more impressed by what they look at than by what they listen to.... *Shakespeare on Scenery, Dramatic Review* (*Uncollected,* p72)

967. Still, the quality of the drama is action. It is always dangerous to pause for picturesqueness. *Shakespeare on Scenery, Dramatic Review* (*Uncollected,* p73)

968. A noble play, nobly mounted gives us double artistic pleasure. The eye as well as the ear is gratified, and the whole nature is made exquisitely receptive of the influence of imaginative work. *Shakespeare on Scenery, Dramatic Review* (*Uncollected,* p73)

18

Education

969. Education is an admirable thing. But it is well to remember that nothing that is worth knowing can be taught. *A Few Maxims for the Instruction of the Over-Educated, Saturday Review* (*Works*, p1242) and similar quotation in *The Critic as Artist* (p1114)

970. Most of you will agree that there is an education independent of books that is of far greater service in life. *The Decorative Arts lecture* (*Works*, p935)

971. It is a very sad thing that nowadays there is so little useless information. *A Few Maxims for the Instruction of the Over-Educated, Saturday Review* (*Works*, p1242)

972. Learning is a sad handicap, Frank, an appalling handicap. *Oscar Wilde, by Frank Harris* (*CG*, p24)

973. To believe is very dull; to doubt is intensely engrossing. *Quoted in Oscar Wilde: His Life and Wit* (*HBP*, p166)

974. I always pass on good advice. It is the only thing to do with it. It is never of any use to oneself. *An Ideal Husband* (*Plays*, pp249–50)

975. The only way to atone for being occasionally a little over-dressed is by being always absolutely over-educated. *Phrases and Philosophies for the Use of the Young, The Chameleon* (*Works*, p1245) and similar quotation in *The Picture of Dorian Gray* (*SC*, p193)

976. I haven't a word to say.... Too much care was taken with our education, I am afraid. To have been well brought up is a great drawback nowadays. It shuts one out from so much. *A Woman of No Importance* (*Plays*, p184)

977. Dogma without literature is bad for boys. *Letter to Robert Ross* (*Letters*, p1102)

978. He had been to school where naturally he had not learned much. *Quoted in Oscar Wilde: His Life and Wit* (*HBP*, p257)

979. The higher education of men is what I should like to see. Men need it so sadly. *An Ideal Husband* (*Plays*, p281)

980. It usually takes ten years living with a man to complete a woman's education. *Oscar Wilde, by Frank Harris* (*CG*, p247)

981. The world is perfectly packed with good women. To know them is a middle-class education. *Lady Windermere's Fan* (*Plays*, pp59–60)

982. ... mamma, whose views on education are remarkably strict, has brought me up to be extremely short-sighted; it is part of her system; so do you mind my looking at you through my glasses? *The Importance of Being Earnest* (*Plays*, p400)

983. I am still conducting the establishment on the old lines and really think I have succeeded in combining the advantages of a public school with those of a private lunatic asylum, which, as you know, was my aim. *Letter to Campbell Dodgson* (*Letters*, p555)

984. Indeed, if it be really necessary that the School Board children should know about the Wars of the Roses, they could learn their lessons just as well out of Shakespeare as out of shilling primer, and learn them, I need not say, far more pleasurably. *The Truth of Masks* (*Works*, p1166)

985. A school should be the most beautiful place in every town and village — so beautiful that the punishment for undutiful children should be that they should be debarred from going to school the following day. *Quoted in Oscar Wilde: His Life and Wit* (*HBP*, p106)

986. I would have a workshop attached to every school, and one hour a day given up to the teaching of simple decorative arts. It would be a golden hour to the children. *House Decoration lecture* (*Uncollected,* p189) and similar quotation in *The Decorative Arts lecture* (*Works,* p935)

987. A good museum would teach your artisans more in one year than they would learn by means of books or lectures in ten years. *The House Beautiful lecture* (*Works,* p920)

988. ... I spoke of the necessity of art as the factor of a child's education, and how all knowledge comes in doing something not in thinking about it.... *Letter to Charles Godfrey Leland* (*Letters,* p170)

989. ... the true aim of education was the love of beauty, and that the methods by which education should work were the development of temperament, the cultivation of taste, and the creation of the critical spirit. *The Critic as Artist* (*Works,* p1146)

990. The most practical school of morals in the world, the best educator, is true art: it never lies, never misleads, never corrupts, for all good art, all high art, is founded on honesty, sincerity, and truth. *The Decorative Arts lecture* (*Works,* p936)

991. We teach people how to remember, we never teach them how to grow. *The Critic as Artist* (*Works,* p1152)

992. ... I am afraid that we are beginning to be over-educated; at least everybody who is incapable of learning has taken to teaching — that is really what our enthusiasm for education has come to. *The Decay of Lying* (*Works,* p1072)

993. ... the nuisance of the intellectual sphere is the man who is so occupied in trying to educate others, that he has never any time to educate himself. *The Critic as Artist* (*Works,* 1140)

994. [Professors] show a want of knowledge that must be the result of years of study. *Quoted in Oscar Wilde: His Life and Wit* (*HBP,* p115)

995. If you meet at dinner a man who has spent his life in educating himself — a rare type in our time, I admit, but still one occasionally to be met with — you rise from the table richer, and conscious that a high ideal has for a moment touched and sanctified your

days. But oh!... to sit next to a man who has spent his life in trying to educate others! What a dreadful experience that is! How appalling is that ignorance which is the inevitable result of the fatal habit of imparting opinions! How limited in range the creature's mind proves to be! How it wearies us, and must weary himself, with its endless repetitions and sickly reiteration! How lacking it is in any element of intellectual growth! In what a vicious circle it always moves! *The Critic as Artist* (*Works,* p1140)

996. The whole theory of modern education is radically unsound. Fortunately, in England at any rate, education produces no effect whatsoever. If it did, it would prove a serious danger to the upper classes, and probably lead to acts of violence in Grosvenor Square. *The Importance of Being Earnest* (*Plays,* p366)

997. LADY BASILDON: Ah! I hate being educated!

MRS. MARCHMONT: So do I. It puts one almost on a level with the commercial classes. *An Ideal Husband* (*Plays,* p222)

998. It is better for the country to have a good general standard of education than to have, as we have in England, a few desperately overeducated, and the remainder ignorant. One of the things that delighted me most in America was that the universities reached a class that we, in Oxford, have never been able to reach, the sons of farmers and people of moderate means. *Oscar Wilde Discovers America* (*HBC,* p349)

999. At times, being morbid, I am bored by the lack of intellect: but that is a grave fault: I attribute it to Oxford. None of us survive culture. *Letter to H.C. Pollitt* (*Letters,* p1116)

1000. Oxford still remains the most beautiful thing in England, and nowhere else are life and art so exquisitely blended, so perfectly made one. *Henry the Fourth at Oxford, Dramatic Review* (*Uncollected,* p79)

1001. ... Oxford —"that sweet city with her dreaming spires," lovely as Venice in its splendour.... *Art and the Handicraftsman lecture* (*Uncollected,* p117)

1002. I was the happiest man in the world when I entered Magdalen for the first time.

Oxford — the mere word to me is full of an inexpressible, an incommunicable charm. Oxford — the home of lost causes and impossible ideals.... *Oscar Wilde, by Frank Harris* (*CG*, p26)

1003. Oxford was paradise to me. My very soul seemed to expand within me to peace and joy. Oxford — the enchanted valley, holding in its flowerlet cup all the idealism of the middle-ages. Oxford is the capital of romance ... in its own way as memorable as Athens, and to me it was even more entrancing. In Oxford, as in Athens, the realities of sordid life were kept at a distance. *Oscar Wilde, by Frank Harris* (*CG*, pp26–7)

1004. It was during my undergraduate days at Oxford; days of lyrical ardour and of studious sonnet-writing; days when one loved the exquisite intricacy and musical repetitions of the ballad, and the villanelle with its linked long-drawn echoes and its curious completeness; days when one solemnly sought to discover the proper temper in which a triolet should be written; delightful days, in which, I am glad to say, there was far more rhyme than reason. *Mr. Pater's Appreciations, Speaker* (*Uncollected*, p144)

1005. Yes, I am aware that Cambridge is a sort of educational institute. I am glad I was not there. *The Portrait of Mr. W.H.* (*Works*, p347)

1006. Whatever people may say against Cambridge it is certainly the best preparatory school for Oxford that I know. *Letter to Robert Ross* (*Letters*, p377)

1007. He and I were in the same house at Eton. I was a year or two older than he was, but we were immense friends, and did all our work and all our play together. There was, of course, a good deal more play than work, but I cannot say that I am sorry for that. It is always an advantage not to have received a sound commercial education, and what I learned in the playing fields at Eton has been quite as useful to me as anything I was taught at Cambridge. *The Portrait of Mr. W.H* (*Works*, p304)

1008. The Oxford theatre opens tomorrow and I am going to see our "young barbarians at play." Young Oxfordians are very delightful, so Greek, and graceful, and uneducated. They have profiles but no philosophy. *Letter to Violet Fane* (*Letters*, p278)

1009. The only schools worth founding are schools without disciples. *Quoted in Oscar Wilde: His Life and Wit* (*HBP*, p167)

1010. One's disciples can parody one — nobody else. *Letter to Walter Hamilton* (*Letters*, p390)

1011. As I look about me, I am impelled for the first time to breathe a fervent prayer, "Save me from my disciples." *Oscar Wilde Discovers America* (*HBC*, p125)

19

Emotions

1012. ... of what an evanescent substance are our emotions made. *Letter to Robert Ross* (*Letters*, p781)

1013. I never change, except in my affections. *The Importance of Being Earnest* (*Plays*, p430)

1014. Emotional forces ... are as limited in extent and duration as the forces of physical energy. *De Profundis* (*OWC*, p147)

1015. ... one can never repeat exactly the same emotion. *The Critic as Artist* (*Works*, p1132)

1016. The secret of life is never to have an emotion that is unbecoming. *A Woman of No Importance* (*Plays*, p187) and similar quotation in *The Picture of Dorian Gray* (*SC*, p100)

1017. Her capacity for family affection is extraordinary. When her third husband died, her hair turned quite gold from grief. *The Picture of Dorian Gray* (*SC*, pp 189–90) and similar quotation in *The Importance of Being Earnest* (*Plays*, p359)

1018. There is always something ridiculous about the emotions of people whom one has ceased to love. *The Picture of Dorian Gray* (*SC*, p103)

1019. One can always be kind to people about whom one cares nothing. *The Picture of Dorian Gray* (*SC*, p114)

1020. It was foolish of me but, my dear boy, gentlemanly feelings linger in the most improbable places. It is one of the paradoxes of life. If I could have the feelings appropriate to my position — or rather lack of position — it would be better for me; but while natures alter, what is artificial is permanent always. *Letter to Robert Ross* (*Letters*, p1088)

1021. Find expression for a sorrow and it will become dear to you. Find expression for a joy, and you intensify its ecstasy. *The Critic as Artist* (*Works*, p1149)

1022. ... a sentimentalist is simply one who desires to have the luxury of an emotion without paying for it. *De Profundis* (*OWC*, p143)

1023. I suffered immensely. Then it passed away. I cannot repeat an emotion. No one can, except sentimentalists. *The Picture of Dorian Gray* (*SC*, p124)

1024. It is only shallow people who require years to get rid of an emotion. A man who is master of himself can end a sorrow as easily as he can invent a pleasure. I don't want to be at the mercy of my emotions. I want to use them, to enjoy them, and to dominate them. *The Picture of Dorian Gray* (*SC*, p123)

1025. ... women were better suited to sorrow than men. They lived on their emotions. They only thought of their emotions. When they took lovers, it was merely to have some one with whom they could have scenes. *The Picture of Dorian Gray* (*SC*, p106)

1026. What a typical woman you are! You talk sentimentally, and you are thoroughly selfish the whole time. *A Woman of No Importance* (*Plays*, pp172–3)

1027. Ernest is invariably calm. That is one of the reasons he always gets on my nerves. Nothing is so aggravating as calmness. There is something positively brutal about the good temper of most modern men. I wonder we women stand it as well as we do. *A Woman of No Importance* (*Plays*, pp153–4)

1028. ... in the questions of the emotions and their romantic qualities, unpunctuality is fatal. *Letter to Leonard Smithers* (*Letters*, p952)

1029. Shall Joy wear what Grief has fashioned? *The Young King* (*Works*, p221)

1030. The loves and sorrows that are great are destroyed by their own plentitude. *The Picture of Dorian Gray* (*SC*, p212)

1031. I believe that if one man were to live out his life fully and completely, were to give form to every feeling, expression to every thought, reality to every dream — I believe that the world would gain such a fresh impulse of joy that we would forget all the maladies of mediaevalism, and return to the Hellenic ideal, it may be. But the bravest man amongst us is afraid of himself. *The Picture of Dorian Gray* (*SC*, p35)

1032. For emotion for the sake of emotion is the aim of art, and emotion for the sake of action is the aim of life, and of that practical organisation of life that we call society. *The Critic as Artist* (*Works*, p1136)

1033. Mediaeval art is charming, but mediaeval emotions are out of date. One can use them in fiction of course. But then the only things that one can use in fiction are the things that one has ceased to use in fact. *The Picture of Dorian Gray* (*SC*, p94)

1034. LORD ILLINGWORTH: She is more than a mystery — she is a mood.

MRS. ALLONBY: Moods don't last.

LORD ILLINGWORTH: That is their chief charm. *A Woman of No Importance* (*Plays*, p144)

1035. Only one thing remains infinitely fascinating to me, the mystery of moods. To be master of these moods is exquisite, to be mastered by them more exquisite still. *Letter to H.C. Marillier* (*Letters*, p272)

1036. For what is morbidity but a mood of emotion or a mode of thought that one cannot express? *The Soul of Man* (*OWC*, p21)

1037. Nay, without thought or conscious desire, might not things external to ourselves vibrate in unison with our moods and passions, atom calling to atom in secret love or strange affinity? *The Picture of Dorian Gray* (*SC*, p120)

1038. ... the senses, like fire, can purify as well as destroy. *Lord Arthur Savile's Crime* (*SC*, p279)

1039. Because to influence a person is to give him one's own soul. He does not think with his natural thoughts, or burn with his natural pas-

sions. His virtues are not real to him. His sins, if there are such things as sins, are borrowed. He becomes an echo of some one else's music, an actor of a part that has not been written for him. The aim of life is self-development. To realize one's own nature perfectly — that is what each of us is here for. People are afraid of themselves nowadays. They have forgotten the highest of all duties, the duty that one owes to one's self. Of course they are charitable. They feed the hungry and clothe the beggar. But their own souls starve, and are naked. *The Picture of Dorian Gray* (*SC*, pp34–5)

1040. Science can never grapple with the irrational. That is why it has no future before it, in this world. *Quoted in Oscar Wilde: His Life and Wit* (*HBP*, p178)

1041. The advantage of the emotions is that they lead us astray, and the advantage of science is that it is not emotional. *The Picture of Dorian Gray* (*SC*, p57)

1042. One is tempted to define man as a rational animal who always loses his temper when he is called upon to act in accordance with the dictates of his reason. *Quoted in Oscar Wilde: His Life and Wit* (*HBP*, p125)

1043. I wonder who it was defined man as a rational animal. It was the most premature definition ever given. Man is many things, but he is not rational. *The Picture of Dorian Gray* (*SC*, p44)

1044. ... Frank Harris has no feelings. It is the secret of his success. Just as the fact that he thinks that other people have none either is the secret of the failure that lies in wait for him somewhere on the way of Life. *Letter to More Adey* (*Letters*, p813)

1045. No, Tuppy, you've lost your figure and you've lost your character. Don't lose your temper; you have only got one. *Lady Windermere's Fan* (*Plays*, p57)

1046. We lose our chances, we lose our figures, we even lose our characters; but we must never lose our tempers. That is our duty to our neighbor ... but sometimes we mislay it, don't we? *Oscar Wilde, by Frank Harris* (*CG*, p81)

1047. ... there are no real emotions left — only extraordinary adjectives. *Quoted in Oscar Wilde: His Life and Wit* (*HBP*, p71)

20

Enemies

1048. Great antipathy shews secret affinity. *Aspects of Wilde* (*CC*, p216)

1049. He and I are closer than friends. We are enemies linked together. The same sin binds us. *An Ideal Husband* (*Plays*, p287)

1050. ... wherever there is hatred between two people there is bond or brotherhood of some kind. I suppose that, by some strange law of the antipathy of similars, you loathed eachother, not because in so many points you were different, but because in some you were so like. *De Profundis* (*OWC*, p133)

1051. Next to having a staunch friend is the pleasure of having a brilliant enemy. *Oscar Wilde Discovers America* (*HBC*, p215)

1052. I would sooner lose my best friend than my worst enemy. To have friends, you know, one need only be good-natured; but when a man has no enemy left there must be something mean about him. *Vera, or the Nihilists* (*Works*, p698)

1053. Be careful to choose your enemies well. Friends don't much matter. But the choice of enemies is very important. *Aspects of Wilde* (*CC*, p93)

1054. I choose my friends for their good looks, my acquaintances for their good characters, and my enemies for their good intellects. A man cannot be too careful in the choice of his enemies. I have not got one who is a fool. *The Picture of Dorian Gray* (*SC*, p26)

1055. Why should he have been murdered? He was not clever enough to have enemies. *The Picture of Dorian Gray* (*SC*, p224)

1056. Not being a genius, he had no enemies.... *Lord Arthur Savile's Crime* (*SC*, p281)

1057. ... Ernest Harrowden, one of those middle-aged mediocrities so common in London clubs who have no enemies, but are thoroughly disliked by their friends.... *The Picture of Dorian Gray* (*SC*, p188)

1058. Every effect that one produces gives one an enemy. *The Picture of Dorian Gray* (*SC*, p208)

1059. If to have enemies is a measure of greatness, then you must be a Colossus, indeed, Prince. *Vera, or the Nihilists* (*Works*, p698)

1060. When the prurient and the impotent attack you, be sure you are right. *Letter to George Ives* (*Letters*, p619)

1061. He is never forgotten by his enemies, and often forgiven by his friends. *Letter to William Rothenstein* (*Letters*, p925)

1062. I find that forgiving one's enemies is a most curious pleasure; perhaps I should check it. *Letter to Lord Alfred Douglas* (*Letters*, p598)

1063. "Forgive your enemies," ... is not for the sake of the enemy but for one's own sake ... and because Love is more beautiful than Hate. *De Profundis* (*OWC*, p115)

1064. ... I turned all my friends into foes. I had the divinest evening.... *Oscar Wilde, by Frank Harris* (*CG*, p26)

1065. ... treachery is inseparable from faith. I often betray myself with a kiss. *Letter to Ada Leverson* (*Letters*, p615)

1066. It was of course my soul in its ultimate essence that I had reached. In many ways I had been its enemy, but I found it waiting for me as a friend. *De Profundis* (*OWC*, p114)

Fashion, Costumes and Style

1067. Fashion is what one wears oneself. What is unfashionable is what other people wear. *An Ideal Husband* (*Plays,* p292)

1068. Ah! my dear, you need not be nervous. You will always be as pretty as possible. That is the best fashion there is, and the only fashion that England succeeds in setting. *An Ideal Husband* (*Plays,* p279)

1069. No—what consoles one now-a-days is not repentance, but pleasure. Repentance is quite out of date and besides, if a woman really repents, she has to go to a bad dressmaker, otherwise no one believes in her. *Lady Windermere's Fan* (*Plays,* p75)

1070. DUCHESS OF MONMOUTH: All good hats are made out of nothing.

LORD HENRY: Like all good reputations.... *The Picture of Dorian Gray* (*SC,* p208)

1071. LORD GORING: I am glad you have called. I am going to give you some good advice.

MRS. CHEVELEY: Oh! Pray don't. One should never give a woman anything that she can't wear in the evening. *An Ideal Husband* (*Plays,* p308)

1072. ... if one is to behave badly, it is better to be bad in a becoming dress than in one that is unbecoming. *Letter to the Editor of The Daily Telegraph* (*Letters,* p467)

1073. Yes, you've got wonderfully good taste, Ernest. It's the excuse I've always given for your leading such a bad life. *The Importance of Being Earnest* (*Plays,* p396)

1074. You know we poor painters have to show ourselves in society from time to time, just to remind the public that we are not savages. With an evening coat and a white tie ... anybody, even a stockbroker, can gain a reputation for being civilised. *The Picture of Dorian Gray* (*SC,* p24)

1075. She was a curious woman, whose dresses always looked as if they had been designed in a rage and put on in a tempest. *The Picture of Dorian Gray* (*SC,* p62)

1076. She wore far too much rouge last night, and not quite enough clothes. That is always a sign of despair in a woman. *An Ideal Husband* (*Plays,* p267)

1077. She is still *décolleté,* and when she is in a very smart gown she looks like an *edition de luxe* of a bad French novel. She is really wonderful, and full of surprises. *The Picture of Dorian Gray* (*SC,* p189)

1078. LADY PLYMDALE: Who is that well-dressed woman talking to Windermere?

DUMBY: Haven't got the slightest idea. Looks like an *edition de luxe* of a wicked French novel, meant especially for the English market. *Lady Windermere's Fan* (*Plays,* p33)

1079. Never go anywhere now. Sick of London society. Shouldn't mind being introduced to my own tailor; he always votes on the right side. But object strongly to being sent down to dinner with my wife's milliner. Never could stand Lady Caversham's bonnets. *An Ideal Husband* (*Plays,* pp223–4)

1080. If I am late he is sure to be furious, and I couldn't have a scene in this bonnet. It is far too fragile. A harsh word would ruin it. *The Picture of Dorian Gray* (*SC,* p58)

1081. ... the modern bonnet is an irrational monstrosity not affording the wearer the slightest use: it does not keep the sun off in summer nor rain off in winter. The large hat of the last century was more sensible and useful, and nothing is more graceful in the world than a broad brimmed hat. *The House Beautiful lecture* (*Works,* p924)

1082. The broad-brimmed hat of 1640 kept the rain of winter and the glare of summer from the face; the same cannot be said of the hat of one hundred years ago, which, with its comparatively narrow brim and high crown, was the precursor of the modern "chimney-pot": a wide turned down collar is a healthier thing than a strangling stock, and a short cloak is much more comfortable than a sleeved overcoat, even though the latter may have had "three capes"; a cloak is easier to put on and off, lies lightly on the shoulders in summer, and wrapped round one in winter keeps one perfectly warm. A doublet, again, is simpler than a coat and waistcoat; instead of two garments one has one; by not being open it also protects the chest better. *Women's Dress, Pall Mall Gazette* (*Uncollected*, p57)

1083. Sentiment is all very well for the buttonhole. But the essential thing for a necktie is style. A well-tied tie is the first serious step in life. *A Woman of No Importance* (*Plays*, p179)

1084. A really well-made buttonhole is the only link between Art and Nature. *Phrases and Philosophies for the Use of the Young, The Chameleon* (*Works*, p1244)

1085. One should either be a work of art, or wear a work of art. *Phrases and Philosophies for the Use of the Young, The Chameleon* (*Works*, p1245)

1086. True art in dress will make our attire an instructor, an educator. *The Decorative Arts lecture* (*Works*, p931)

1087. When you can bend fashion to the service of anything good or beautiful, it is of immense importance. *Oscar Wilde Discovers America* (*HBC*, p349)

1088. Pretty child! Your dress is sadly simple, and your hair seems almost as Nature might have left it. But we can soon alter that. *The Importance of Being Earnest* (*Plays*, p420)

1089. CECILY: You dear romantic boy. I hope your hair curls naturally, does it?

ALGERNON: Yes, darling, with a little help from others. *The Importance of Being Earnest* (*Plays*, p397)

1090. Of course there are fashions in art just as there are fashions in dress, and perhaps none of us can ever quite free ourselves from the influence of custom and the influence of novelty. *Pen, Pencil and Poison* (*Works*, p1096)

1091. The new age is the age of style. *The Rise of Historical Criticism* (*Works*, p1224)

1092. ... behind the perfection of a man's style, must lie the passion of a man's soul. *Mr. Pater's Appreciations* (*Uncollected*, p146)

1093. Nineteenth-century dress is the result of our horror of the style. The tall hat will last as long as people dislike it. *Letter to Robert Ross* (*Letters*, p868)

1094. One of the chief faults of modern dress is that it is composed of far too many articles of clothing, most of which are the wrong substance.... *Women's Dress, Pall Mall Gazette* (*Uncollected*, p56)

1095. One should have nothing on one's dress that has not some meaning or that is not useful; beauty in dress consists in its simplicity — all useless and encumbering bows, flounces, knots, and other such meaningless things so fashionable today are nothing but the foolish invention of the milliner. All the evil of modern dressing has come from the failure to recognise that the right people to construct our apparel are artists, and not modern milliners, whose chief aim is to swell their bills. *The House Beautiful lecture* (*Works*, p923)

1096. Every nation seems suddenly to have become interested in the dress of its neighbors. Europe began to investigate its own clothes, and the amount of books being published on national costumes is quite extraordinary. *The Truth of Masks* (*Works*, pp1163–4)

1097. There is nothing to my mind more course in conception and more vulgar in execution than modern jewellery. This is something that can be easily corrected. Something better should be made out of the beautiful gold which is stored up in your mountain hollows and strewn along your river beds. *House Decoration lecture* (*Uncollected*, p188)

1098. Pure modernity of form is always somewhat vulgarising. It cannot help being so. *The Decay of Lying* (*Works*, p1077)

1099. ... in all my journeys through the country [America], the only well-dressed men that I saw — and in saying this I earnestly deprecate the polished indignation of your Fifth Avenue dandies— were the Western miners ... they wore only what was comfortable and therefore beautiful. *House Decoration lecture* (*Uncollected*, pp185–6)

1100. Waistcoats will show whether a man can admire poetry or not. *Letter to the Editor of The Daily Telegraph* (*Letters*, p466)

1101. Short loose trousers are in every way to be preferred to the tight knee breeches which often impede the proper circulation of the blood.... *Women's Dress, Pall Mall Gazette* (*Uncollected*, pp57–8)

1102. EDWARD CARSON: Were you fond of this boy?

OSCAR WILDE: Naturally. He had been my companion for six weeks.

EDWARD CARSON: Did you take the lad to Brighton?

OSCAR WILDE: Yes

EDWARD CARSON: And provided him with a suit of blue serge?

OSCAR WILDE: Yes

EDWARD CARSON: And a straw hat with a band of red and blue?

OSCAR WILDE: That, I think, was his unfortunate selection. *The Three Trials of Oscar Wilde* (*UB*, p138)

1103. ... the laws of Greek dress may be perfectly realised, even in moderately tight gowns with sleeves: I mean the principle of suspending all apparel from the shoulders, and of relying for the beauty of effect not on the stiff ready-made ornaments of the modern milliner—the bows where there should be no bows, and the flounces where there should be no flounces—but on the exquisite play of light and line that one gets from rich and rippling folds. I am not proposing an antiquarian revival of an ancient costume, but trying merely to point out the right laws of dress, laws which are dictated by art and not by archeology, by science and not by fashion; and just as the best work of art in our days is that which combines classic grace with absolute reality, so from a continuation of the Greek principles of beauty with the German principles of health will come, I feel certain, the costume of the future. *Women's Dress, Pall Mall Gazette* (*Uncollected*, p57)

1104. And as regards high heels, I quite admit that some additional height to the shoe or boot is necessary if long gowns are to be worn in the street; but what I object to is that the height should be given to the heel only, and not to the sole of the foot also. The modern high-heeled boot is, in fact, merely a clog of the time of Henry VI, with the front prop left out, and its most inevitable effect is to throw the body forward and consequently to produce that want of grace which always follows want of freedom. Why should clogs be despised?... A clog may be a dream of beauty, and, if not too high or too heavy, not comfortable also. *Women's Dress, Pall Mall Gazette* (*Uncollected*, pp55–6)

1105. ... it is from the shoulders, and from the shoulders only, that all garments should be hung. *Women's Dress, Pall Mall Gazette* (*Uncollected*, p55)

1106. Now it is quite true that as long as the lower garments are suspended from the hips, a corset is an absolute necessity; the mistake lies in not suspending all apparel from the shoulders. In the latter case a corset becomes useless, the body is left free and unconfined for respiration and motion, there is more health, and consequently more beauty. Indeed all the most ungainly and uncomfortable articles of dress that fashion has ever in her folly prescribed. Not the tight corset merely, but the farthingale, the vertugadin, the hoop, the crinoline, and that modern monstrosity the so-called "dress-improver" also, all of them have owed their origin to the same error of not seeing that it is from the shoulders only, that all garments should be hung. *Women's Dress, Pall Mall Gazette* (*Uncollected*, p55) and *Letter to the Editor of The Pall Mall Gazette* (*Letters*, p233)

1107. Nothing is beautiful, such as tight corsets, which is destructive of health; all dress follows out the lines of the figure—it should be free to move about in, showing the figure. Anything that disfigures the form or blots out the beauty of the natural lines is ugly, and so a knowledge of anatomy as well as art is necessary in correct dressmaking. If one could fancy the Medicean Venus taken from her pedestal in the Louvre to Mr. Worth's establishment in the Parlays Royal to be dressed in modern French millinery, every single beautiful line would be destroyed, and no one would look at her a second time. *The House Beautiful lecture* (*Works*, p923)

1108. No one appreciates more fully than I do the importance of Dress, in its relation to good taste and good health.... *Letter to Wemyss Reid* (*Letters*, p297)

1109. People should not mar beautiful surroundings by gloomy dress; dress nowadays is altogether too sombre, and we should accustom ourselves to the use of more colour and brightness; there should always be a beautifully arranged composition of well-balanced light and shade. There would be more joy in life if we would accustom ourselves to use all the beautiful colours we can in fashioning our own clothes. The dress of the future, I think, will use drapery to a great extent and will abound with joyous colour. *The House Beautiful lecture* (*Works*, p923)

1110. There would be more joy in life if we were to accustom ourselves to use all the beautiful colours we can in fashioning our own clothes. The dress of the future, I think, will use drapery to a great extent and will abound with joyous colour. *House Decoration lecture* (*Uncollected*, p185)

1111. The coat, then, of next season, will be an exquisite colour-note, and have also a great psychological value. It will emphasize the serious and thoughtful side of a man's character. One will be able to discern a man's views of life by the colour he selects. The colour of the coat will be symbolic. The imagination will concentrate itself on the waistcoat. Waistcoats will show whether a man can admire poetry or not. That will be very valuable. Over the shirt-front Fancy will preside. By a single glance one will be able to detect the tedious. *Letter to the Editor of The Daily Telegraph* (*Letters*, p466)

1112. Freedom in such selection of colour is a necessary condition of variety and individualism of costume, and the uniform black that is worn now, though valuable at a dinner party, where it serves to isolate and separate women's dress, to frame them as it were, still is dull and tedious and depressing in itself, and makes the aspect of club-life and men's dinners monotonous and uninteresting. The little note of individualism that makes dress delightful can only be attained nowadays by the colour and treatment of the flower one wears. This is a great pity. The colour of the coat should be entirely for the good taste of the wearer to decide. This would give pleasure, and produce charming variety of colour effects in modern life. *Letter to the Editor of The Daily Telegraph* (*Letters*, p465)

1113. Yes, the costume of the nineteenth century is detestable. It is so sombre, so depressing. *The Picture of Dorian Gray* (*SC*, p45)

1114. ... the dresses of one age do not artistically harmonise with the dresses of another; and, as far as dramatic value goes, to confuse the costumes is to confuse the play. *The Truth of Masks* (*Works*, p1169)

1115. Go through a book of costumes, and you will find that when dress was most simple, it was most beautiful.... *The House Beautiful lecture* (*Works*, p923)

1116. ... until an actor is at home in his dress, he is not at home in his part. *The Truth of Masks* (*Works*, p1173)

1117. Costumes, of course, they are to the designer; but dresses they should be to those that wear them. *The Truth of Masks* (*Works*, p1172)

1118. ... unless a dress is archeologically correct, and artistically appropriate, it always looks unreal, unnatural, and theatrical in the sense of artificial. *The Truth of Masks* (*Works*, p1171)

1119. But it is not enough that a dress should be accurate; it must also be appropriate to the stature and appearance of the actor and to his supposed condition, as well as to his necessary action in the play. *The Critic as Artist* (*Works*, p1170)

1120. To invent an entirely new costume is almost impossible except in burlesque or extravaganza, and as for combining the dress of different centuries into one, the experiment would be dangerous.... *The Truth of Masks* (*Works*, p1170)

1121. At Cambridge, for instance, during his day, a play of Richard the Third was performed, in which the actors were attired in real dresses of the time, procured from the great collection of historical costume in the Tower, which was always open to the inspection of managers, and sometimes placed at their disposal. *The Truth of Masks* (*Works*, p1164)

1122. The point, however, which I wish to emphasis is, not that Shakespeare appreciated the value of lovely costumes in adding picturesqueness to poetry, but that he saw how important costume is as a means of producing certain dramatic effects. Many of his plays ... depend for their illusion on the character of the various dresses worn by the hero or the heroine.... *The Truth of Masks* (*Works,* p1156)

1123. Indeed, to put any play of Shakespeare's on the stage, absolutely as he himself wished it to be done, requires the services of a good property-man, a clever wig-maker, a costumier with a sense of colour and a knowledge of textures, a master of the methods of making-up, a fencing master, a dancing master, and an artist to personally direct the whole production. For he is most careful to tell us the dress and appearance of each character. *The Truth of Masks* (*Works,* pp1159–60)

1124. Shakespeare was very much interested in costume ... he saw that costume could be made at once impressive of a certain effect on the audience and expressive of different types of character, and is one of the essential factors of the means which a true illusionist has at his disposal. *The Truth of Masks* (*Works,* p1161)

1125. ... anybody who cares to study Shakespeare's method will see that there is absolutely no dramatist of the French, English, or Athenian stage who relies so much for his illusionist effects on the dress of his actors as Shakespeare does himself. *The Truth of Masks* (*Works,* p1156)

1126. ... a really artistic production should bear the impress of one master, and one master only, who not merely should design and arrange everything, but should have complete control over the way in which each dress is to be worn. *The Truth of Masks* (*Works,* p1172)

1127. [I] am more than ever in disaccord with Carlyle on the question of the relation of clothes and Soul. A hole in the trousers may make one as melancholy as Hamlet, and out of bad boots a Timon may be made. *Letter to Frank Harris* (*Letters*, p1162)

1128. ... it is only fair to add that at the end of the play Mr. Wyndam accepts his lecture with a dignity and courtesy of manner that can only result from the habit of wearing delightful clothes. *Letter to the Editor of The Daily Telegraph* (*Letters*, p467)

1129. ... costume is a means of displaying character without description, and of producing dramatic situations and dramatic effects. *The Critic as Artist* (*Works*, p1173)

1130. For all costumes are caricatures. The basis of Art is not the Fancy Ball. Where there is lovliness of dress, there is no dressing up. *The Relation of Dress to Art lecture* (*Uncollected*, p52)

1131. ... the artistic temperament is always fascinated by the beauty of costume. *The Truth of Masks* (*Works*, p1156)

1132. Dear Colonel Morse, Will you kindly go to a good costumier (theatrical) for me and get them to make (you will not mention my name) two coats, to wear at matinees and perhaps in the evening. They should be beautiful; tight velvet doublet, with large flowered sleeves and little ruffs of cambric coming up from under collar. I send you design and measurements. They should be ready at Chicago on Saturday for matinee there — at any rate the black one. Any good costumier would know what I want — sort of Francis I dress: only knee-breeches instead of long hose. Also get me two pair of grey silk stockings to suit grey mouse-coloured velvet. The sleeves are to be flowered — if not velvet then plush -stamped with large pattern. They will excite a great sensation. I leave the matter to you. They were dreadfully disappointed at Cincinnati at my not wearing knee-breeches. Truly yours, Oscar Wilde. *Letter to Colonel W. F. Morse* (*Letters*, p141)

1133. If I were alone, marooned on some desert island, and had my things with me, I should dress for dinner every evening. *Quoted in Oscar Wilde: His Life and Wit* (*HBP*, p75)

1134. At present we have lost all nobility of dress and, in doing so, have almost annihilated the modern sculptor. And, in looking around at the figures which adorn our parks, one could almost wish that we had completely killed the noble art. To see the frockcoat of the drawing-room done in bronze, or the double waistcoat perpetuated in marble, adds a new horror to death. *House Decoration lecture* (*Uncollected*, p185)

1135. But he looks splendid in [rags]. I wouldn't paint him in a frock coat for any-thing. What you call rags I call romance. What seems poverty to you is picturesqueness to me. *The Model Millionaire* (*Works*, p211)

1136. To undress is romance, to dress, philanthropy. *Letter to Robert Ross* (*Letters*, p1100)

22

Fidelity

1137. Her trust makes me faithful, her belief makes me good. *The Picture of Dorian Gray* (*SC*, p92)

1138. Men should be careful; this very celibacy leads weaker vessels astray. *The Importance of Being Earnest* (*Plays*, p385)

1139. Those who are faithful know only the trivial side of love: it is only the faithless who know love's tragedies. *The Picture of Dorian Gray* (*SC*, p30)

1140. Well, there's nothing in the world like the devotion of a married woman. It's a thing no married man knows anything about. *Lady Windermere's Fan* (*Plays*, p59)

1141. London is full of women who trust their husbands. One can always recognize them. They look so thoroughly unhappy. *Lady Windermere's Fan* (*Plays*, p30)

1142. Certainly, more women grow old nowadays through the faithfulness of their admirers than through anything else! At least that is the only way I can account for the terribly haggard look of most of your pretty women in London. *An Ideal Husband* (*Plays*, p228)

1143. What a fuss people make about fidelity! Why, even in love it is purely a question for physiology. It has nothing to do with our own will. Young men want to be faithful, and are not; old men want to be faithless, and cannot. *The Picture of Dorian Gray* (*SC*, p46)

1144. Why should *you* be any different from me? I am told that there is hardly a husband in London who does not waste his life over *some* shameful passion. *Lady Windermere's Fan* (*Plays*, p22)

1145. ... the one charm of marriage is that it makes a life of deception absolutely neces-sary for both parties. I never know where my wife is, and my wife never knows what I am doing. *The Picture of Dorian Gray* (*SC*, p22)

1146. Secrets from other people's wives are a necessary luxury in modern life. So, at least, I am told at the club by people who are bald enough to know better. But no man should have a secret from his own wife. She invari-ably finds it out. *An Ideal Husband* (*Plays*, p258)

1147. ... in married life, three is company and two is none. *The Importance of Being Earnest* (*Plays*, p357)

1148. ... the romance of life is that one can love so many people and marry but one. *Oscar Wilde Discovers America* (*HBC*, p308)

1149. The happiness of a married man ... depends on the people he has not married. *A Woman of No Importance* (*Plays*, p181)

1150. Our husbands never appreciate any-thing in us. We have to go to others for that! *An Ideal Husband* (*Plays*, p235)

1151. ... nowadays everybody is jealous of everyone else, except, of course, husband and wife. *Letter to Robert Ross* (*Letters*, p867)

1152. My dear boy, the people who love only once in their lives are really the shallow people. What they call their loyalty, and their fidelity, I call either lethargy of custom or their lack of imagination. Faithfulness is to the emotional life what consistency is to the life of the intellect — simply a confession of fail-ure. Faithfulness! I must analyse it someday. The passion for property is in it. There are many things we would throw away if we were not afraid that others might pick them up. *The Picture of Dorian Gray* (*SC*, p66)

23

Flowers

1153. I can't afford orchids, but I spare no expense in foreigners. *The Picture of Dorian Gray* (SC, p63)

1154. GWENDOLEN: I had no idea there were any flowers in the country.

CECILY: Oh, flowers are as common here, Miss Fairfax, as people are in London. *The Importance of Being Earnest* (*Plays*, p404)

1155. ... as long as I can enjoy talk nonsense to flowers and children I am not afraid of the depraved luxury of a hat-box. *Letter to Julia Ward Howe* (*Letters*, p175)

1156. I quite agree with you that poor children *wonder* at flowers more than the children of the rich. *Letter to Phoebe Allen* (*Letters*, p306)

1157. I have many beautiful flowers, but children are the most beautiful flowers of all. *The Selfish Giant* (*Works*, p285)

1158. Gardenias and the peerage were his only weaknesses. Otherwise he was extremely sensible. *The Canterville Ghost* (*Works*, p185)

1159. My sweet rose, my delicate flower, my lily of lilies, it is perhaps in prison that I am going to test the power of love. *Letter to Lord Alfred Douglas* (*Letters*, p651)

1160. The season with its red roses of pleasure has absorbed me quite and I have almost forgotten how to write a letter. *Quoted in Oscar Wilde: His Life and Wit* (HBP, p1456)

1161. A red rose is not selfish because it wants to be a red rose. It would be horribly selfish if it wanted all the other flowers in the garden to be both red and roses. *The Soul of Man* (OWC, p33)

1162. A critic who posed as an authority on field sports assured me that no one ever went out hunting when roses were in full bloom. Personally, that is exactly the season I would select for the chase, but then I know more about flowers than I do about foxes, and like them much better. *Olivia at the Lyceum Court and Society Review* (*Works*, p956)

1163. Sir, I am deeply distressed to hear that the tuberose is so called from its being a "lumpy flower." It is not at all lumpy, and, even if it were, no poet should be heartless enough to say so. Henceforth there really must be two derivations for every word, one for the poet and one for the scientist. And in the present case the poet will dwell on the tiny trumpets of ivory into which the white flower breaks, and leave to the man of science horrid allusions to its supposed lumpiness and indiscreet revelations of its private life below ground. In fact, tuber as a derivation is disgraceful. On the roots of verbs Philology may be allowed to speak, but on the roots of flowers she must keep silence. *Letter to the Editor of the Pall Mall Gazette* (*Letters*, pp255–6)

1164. Better to take pleasure in a rose than to put its roots under a microscope. *The Truth of Masks* (*Works*, p1169)

1165. ... unless you have the right root you will not get the right flower.... *Lecture to Art Students at the Royal Academy* (*Uncollected*, p128)

1166. ... I know that for me, for whom flowers are part of desire, there are tears waiting in the petals of some rose. It has always been so with me from my boyhood. There is not a single colour hidden away in the chalice of a flower, or the curve of a shell, to which, by some subtle sympathy with the very soul of things, my nature does not answer. *De Profundis* (OWC, p155)

1167. All depends on the graduation of colour; look at the rose and see how all its beauty depends upon its exquisite graduations of colour, one answering to the other. *The House Beautiful lecture* (*Works*, p916)

1168. Flowers you will have, of course, about your room, but don't have all kinds of flowers vaguely arranged or crowded together in great bouquets. Some flowers, such as roses or violets whose greatest beauty is their colour, are made to be seen in masses, but flowers which are perfect in form, like the narcissus, daffodil, or lily, should be placed singly in a small Venetian glass so that they can hang naturally as they are seen upon their stem. *The House Beautiful lecture* (*Works*, p921)

1169. ... violets that woke the memory of dead romances. *The Picture of Dorian Gray* (*SC*, p147)

1170. The flowers which Ophelia carries with her in her madness are as pathetic as the violets that blossom on a grave. *The Critic as Artist* (*Works*, p1158)

1171. To buds of sheathed emerald; violets
Peered from their nooks of hiding, half afraid
Of their own lovliness; the vermeil rose
Opened its heart, and the bright star-flower
The Artist's Dream or Sen Artysty (*Works*, p856)

1172. Close at thy heals to taint the delicate air;
No sullen-blooming poppies to stain thy hair,
Those scarlet heralds of eternal sleep.
Lily of love, pure and inviolate!
Tower of ivory! Red rose of fire!
The New Helen (*Works*, p830)

1173. Love could I make the lily-petals part
And filch the treasures of its golden seed,
Or swoon for passion in the rose's heart
Till its red leaves with redder pain did bleed.
La Belle Gabrielle (*Works*, p815)

1174. She stands with eyes marred by the mists of pain,
Like some wan lily overdrenched with rain....
"Queen Henrietta Maria" for Ellen Terry (*Works*, p835)

1175. The feet of his love as she walked in the garden were like lilies set upon lilies. Softer than sleep-laden poppy petals were her lips, softer than violets and as scented. *The Critic as Artist* (*Works*, p1135)

1176. For Southwell's arch, and carved the House of One
Who loved the lilies of the field with all
Our dearest English flowers? the same sun
Rises for us: the seasons natural
Weave the same tapestry of green and grey:
The unchanged hills are with us: but that spirit hath passed away.
Humanitad (*Works*, p824)

1177. Perhaps you will not mind my coming a little late, lilies and languors and all! *Letter to Miss Boughton* (*Letters*, p106)

1178. Well, let me tell you that the reason we love the lily and the sunflower, in spite of what Mr. Gilbert may tell you, is not for any vegetable fashion at all. It is because these two lovely flowers are in England the two most perfect models of design, the most naturally adapted for decorative art — the gaudy leonine beauty of the one and the precious lovliness of the other giving to the artist the most entire and perfect joy. And so with you: let there be no flower in your meadows that does not wreathe its tendrils around your pillows ... no curving spray of wild rose or brier that does not live for ever in carven arch or window or marble.... *The English Renaissance of Art lecture* (*Uncollected*, p27)

1179. A work of art is useless as a flower is useless. A flower blossoms for its own joy. We gain a moment of joy by looking at it. That is all that is to be said about our relations to flowers. Of course man may sell flowers, and so make it useful to him, but this has nothing to do with the flower. It is not part of its essence. It is accidental. It is a misuse. *Letter to R. Clegg* (*Letters*, pp478–9)

1180. ... whenever a beautiful flower grows in a meadow or lawn, some other flower, so like it that it is differently beautiful, is sure to grow up beside it; all flowers and all works of art having a curious sympathy for each other. *Letter to Max Beerbohm* (*Letters*, p856)

1181. Your flowers are so lovely that they have made me well again. *Telegram to Ada Leverson* (*Letters*, p628)

1182. She is like a wonderful little flower, and if flowers could talk so sweetly as she does who would not be a gardener! *Letter to Mary Blakeney* (*Letters*, p160)

1183. The flower is a work of art. The book [*The Green Carnation*] is not. *Letter to the Editor of the Pall Mall Gazette* (*Letters*, p617)

1184. After the chill virginity of Swiss Alps and snow, I long for the red flowers of life that stain the feet of summer in Italy. *Letter to Robert Ross* (*Letters*, p1140)

1185. London is a desert without your dainty feet, and all the buttonholes have turned to weeds: nettles and hemlock are "the only wear." Write me a line, and take all my love — now and for ever. *Letter to Lord Alfred Douglas* (*Letters*, p594)

1186. I long to ride through New Mexico and Colorado and California. There are such beautiful flowers there, such quantities of lilies and, I am told, whole fields of sunflowers. Your climate is so much finer than that of England, so bright, so sunny, that your flowers are luxuriant. *Oscar Wilde Discovers America* (*HBC*, p63)

1187. The fact is that I picked a primrose in the wood yesterday, and it was so ill that I have been sitting up with it all night. *Quoted in Oscar Wilde: His Life and Wit* (*HBP*, p44)

1188. The weather is lovely, and the mimosa in flower — such powdered gold-dust dancing in the sun, the dainty feather-like leaves always tremulous with joy. *Letter to Reginald Turner* (*Letters*, p1119)

1189. I thank you so much for the flowers, they take these winds of March with beauty. I am glad that there is something in the world that the world cannot harm, nor the reporter interview. *Letter to Marion Meatyard* (*Letters*, p150)

1190. The habit of bringing flowers to the grave is now almost universal, and is a custom beautiful in its symbolism; but I cannot help thinking that the elaborate and expensive designs made by the florist are often far less lovely than a few flowers held loose in the hand. *Letter to the Reverend J. Page Hopps* (*Letters*, p247)

1191. ... the lips of Longfellow are still musical for us though his dust be turning into the flowers which he loved. *Art and the Handicraftsman lecture* (*Uncollected*, p119)

1192. There is an unknown land full of strange flowers and subtle perfumes, a land of which it is joy of all joys to dream, a land where all things are perfect and poisonous. *Letter to H.C Marillier* (*Letters*, p272)

1193. But neither milk-white rose nor red
May bloom in prison air;
The shard, the pebble, and the flint,
Are what they give us there:
For flowers have been known to heal
A common man's despair.
The Ballad of Reading Gaol (*OWC*, p184)

1194. For there is such a little time that that your youth will last — such a little time. The common hill-flowers wither, but they blossom again. The laburnum will be as yellow next June as it is now. In a month there will be purple stars on the clematis, and year after year the green night of its leaves will hold its purple stars. But we never get back our youth. *The Picture of Dorian Gray* (*SC*, pp39–40)

1195. ... the life of a man is no more than the life of a flower.... *De Profundis* (*OWC*, p111)

1196. If I do live again I would like it to be as a flower — no soul but perfectly beautiful. Perhaps for my sins I shall be made a red geranium!! *Letter to H.C. Marillier* (*Letters*, p267)

24

Food and Drink

1197. Culture depends on cookery. *Vera, or the Nihilists* (*Works*, p696)

1198. ... after a good dinner one can forgive anybody, even one's own relations. *A Woman of No Importance* (*Plays*, p163)

1199. ... a good lunch is better than a bad one for any living man. *Oscar Wilde, by Frank Harris* (*CG*, p255)

1200. There is always luncheon at 1 o'clock at the Café Royal. *Quoted in Oscar Wilde: His Life and Wit* (*HBP*, p154)

1201. Going out to breakfast is fatal to work. *Letter to Leonard Smithers* (*Letters*, p1069)

1202. To make a good salad is to be a brilliant diplomatist — the problem is entirely the same in both cases. To know exactly how much oil one must put with one's vinegar. *Vera, or the Nihilists* (*Works*, p696)

1203. A cook and a diplomist! An excellent parallel. If I had a son who was a fool I'd make him one or the other. *Vera, or the Nihilists* (*Works*, p696)

1204. Moderation is a fatal thing. Enough is as bad as a meal. More than enough is as good as a feast. *The Picture of Dorian Gray* (*SC*, p192)

1205. ... the highest respectability is of much less value than the possession of a good chef. And, after all, it is a very poor consolation to be told that the man who has given one a bad dinner, or poor wine, is irreproachable in his private life. *The Picture of Dorian Gray* (*SC*, p155)

1206. You haven't quarreled with your cook, I hope? What a tragedy that would be for you; you would lose all your friends. *Vera, or the Nihilists* (*Works*, p697)

1207. ... it is well that the laws of cookery should be explained: for were the national meal burned, or badly seasoned, or served up with the wrong sauce, a dreadful revolution might follow. *Dinners and Dishes, Pall Mall Gazette* (*Uncollected*, p193)

1208. ... cookery is an art; are not its principles the subject of South Kensington lectures, and does not the Royal Academy give a banquet once a year? *Dinners and Dishes, Pall Mall Gazette* (*Uncollected*, p193)

1209. EDWARD CARSON: Did he [Taylor] used to do his own cooking?

OSCAR WILDE: I don't know. I don't think he did anything wrong.

EDWARD CARSON: I have not suggested that he did?

OSCAR WILDE: Well, cooking is an art. *The Three Trials of Oscar Wilde* (*UB*, p140)

1210. His father made a fortune by selling some kind of food in circular tins — most palatable, I believe — I fancy it is the thing servants always refuse to eat. *Lady Windermere's Fan* (*Plays*, pp16–7)

1211. People are told not to buy pig in a poke — that may or may not be true. I don't think people should buy pigs at all. *Letter to Leonard Smithers* (*Letters*, p968)

1212. I had no notion that Lady Clementina liked sweets. I thought she was far too intellectual. *Lord Arthur Savile's Crime* (*SC*, p289)

1213. It is very kind of you, but Mrs. Daubeny never touches solids now. Lives entirely on jellies. But she is wonderfully cheerful, wonderfully cheerful. She has nothing to complain of. *A Woman of No Importance* (*Plays*, p189)

1214. MR. MONTFORD: I don't know that I like being watched when I'm eating!

MRS. MARCHMONT: Then I will watch someone else.

MR. MONTFORD: I don't know that I should like that either. *An Ideal Husband* (*Plays,* p239)

1215. JACK: How can you sit there, calmly eating muffins, when we are in this horrible trouble, I can't make out. You seem to me to be perfectly heartless.

ALGERNON: Well, I can't eat muffins in an agitated manner. The butter would probably get on my cuffs. One should always eat muffins quite calmly. It is the only way to eat them.

JACK: I say it's perfectly heartless your eating muffins at all, under the circumstances.

ALGERNON: When I am in trouble, eating is the only thing that consoles me. Indeed, when I am in really great trouble, as anyone who knows me intimately will tell you, I refuse everything except food and drink. At the present moment I am eating muffins because I am unhappy. Besides, I am particularly fond of muffins. *The Importance of Being Earnest* (*Plays,* pp410–11)

1216. Crime in England is rarely the result of sin. It is nearly always the result of starvation. *Pen, Pencil, and Poison* (*Works,* p1105)

1217. Well, I really am not going to be imprisoned in the suburbs for having dined in the West End. It is perfectly ridiculous. *The Importance of Being Earnest* (*Plays,* p438)

1218. Prison soup is very good and wholesome. *Letter to the Editor of The Daily Chronicle* (*Works,* p1064)

1219. The real difficulty we all have to face in life is not so much the science of cookery as the stupidity of cooks. And in this little handbook to practical Epicureanism the tyrant of the English kitchen is shown in her proper light. Her entire ignorance of herbs, her passion for extracts and essences, her total inability to make a soup which is anything more than a combination of pepper and gravy, her inveterate habit of sending up bread and poultices with pheasants—all these sins and many others are ruthlessly unmasked by the author. Ruthlessly and rightly. For the British cook is a foolish woman who should be turned for her iniquities into a pillar of salt which she never knows how to use. *Dinners and Dishes, Pall Mall Gazette* (*Uncollected,* p194)

1220. There are twenty ways of cooking a potato and three hundred and sixty-five ways of cooking an egg, yet the British cook, up to the present moment, knows only three methods of sending up either one or the other. *Dinners and Dishes, Pall Mall Gazette* (*Uncollected,* pp194–5)

1221. Who, indeed, in these degenerate days would hesitate between an ode and an omelette, a sonnet and a salami? *Dinners and Dishes, Pall Mall Gazette* (*Uncollected,* p193)

1222. You can't possibly ask me to go without having some dinner. It's absurd. I never go without my dinner. No one ever does, except vegetarians and people like that. *The Importance of Being Earnest* (*Plays,* p411)

1223. I am charmed to think I may have the chance of publishing some of your dainty, witty, fascinating prose, and if you abandon "the harmless necessary cauliflower" for a diet of roast snipe and burgundy I feel sure that you will not regret it. However, even vegetarianism, in your hands, would make a capital article—its connection with philosophy is very curious—dating form the earliest Greek days, and taken by the Greeks from the East—and so its connection with modern socialism, atheism, nihilism, anarchy, and other political creeds. It is strange that the most violent republicans I know are all vegetarians: Brussel sprouts seem to make people bloodthirsty, and those who live on lentils and artichokes are always calling for the gore of the aristocracy, and for the severed heads of kings. Your vegetarianism has given you a wise apathy—so at least you told me once—but in the political sphere a diet of green herbs seems dangerous. *Letter to Violet Fane* (*Letters,* p334)

1224. Indeed, the two most remarkable bits of scenery in the States are undoubtedly Delmonico's and the Yosemite valley; and the former place has done more to promote a good feeling between England and America than anything else has in this century. *Dinners and Dishes, Pall Mall Gazette* (*Uncollected,* p194)

1225. Englishmen always get romantic after a meal, and that bores me dreadfully. *An Ideal Husband* (*Plays,* p247)

1226. ... he seems to have had experience of almost every kind of meal except the "square meal" of the Americans. This he should study at once; there is a great field for philosophic epicure in the United States. *Dinners and Dishes, Pall Mall Gazette* (*Uncollected*, p194)

1227. What curious things people will sometimes eat!... I suppose they must be hungry. *Quoted in Oscar Wilde: His Life and Wit* (*HBP*, p250)

1228. I get now quite sufficient food — but simply in order that nothing should be wasted of what is given me. So one should look on love. *De Profundis* (*OWC*, p120)

1229. I have dined, so I don't dawnce. Those who dawnce don't dine. *Oscar Wilde Discovers America* (*HBC*, p89)

1230. I have made an important discovery ... that alcohol, taken in sufficient quantities, produces all the effects of intoxication. *Quoted in Oscar Wilde: His Life and Wit* (*HBP*, p329)

1231. After the first glass of absinthe you see things as you wish they were. After the second you see them as they are not. Finally you see things as they really are, and that is the most horrible thing in the world. *Quoted in Oscar Wilde: His Life and Wit* (*HBP*, p274)

1232. ... I had supper, the first course being whiskey, the second whiskey and the third whiskey. *Personal Impressions of America lecture* (*Works*, p940)

1233. If a man gets drunk, whether he does so on white wine or red matter little, and if a man has perversities of passion there is no use his denying particular details in a civil court.... *Letter to More Adey* (*Letters*, p794)

1234. EDWARD CARSON: Do you drink champagne yourself?

OSCAR WILDE: Yes; iced champagne is a favourite drink of mine — strongly against my doctor's orders.

EDWARD CARSON: Never mind your doctor's orders, sir?

OSCAR WILDE: I never do. *The Three Trials of Oscar Wilde* (*UB*, p144)

1235. I only care to see doctors when I am in perfect health; then they comfort one, but when one is ill they are most depressing. *Letter to Reginald Turner* (*Letters*, p1066)

1236. When you can refuse bread to the hungry, Reggie [Turner] and drink to the thirsty, you can apply for your diploma [as a doctor]. *Oscar Wilde, by Frank Harris* (*CG*, p315)

1237. I have had a cocktail of water and will now have my breakfast of fresh air. *Oscar Wilde Discovers America* (*HBC*, p37)

1238. I don't know if you know Smithers: he is usually in a large straw hat, has a blue tie delicately fastened with a diamond brooch of the impurest water — or perhaps wine, as he never touches water. *Letter to Reginald Turner* (*Letters*, p924)

1239. ... he never touches water: it goes to his head at once. *Letter to Reginald Turner* (*Letters*, p924)

1240. My dear Reggie, I hope you are in better spirits. Poor dear Sir John was always in the best spirits (and water): the most good-hearted of the alcoholic. *Letter to Reginald Turner* (*Letters*, p1121)

1241. Oh, he [Willy Wilde, Oscar's brother] occasionally takes an alcoholiday. *Quoted in Oscar Wilde: His Life and Wit* (*HBP*, p98)

25

France and the French

1242. When one is content one is silent, and nowhere is one more content than at Paris. *Quoted in Oscar Wilde: His Life and Wit* (*HBP*, p215)

1243. [Paris is] the most wonderful city in the world, the only civilised capital; the only place on earth where you find absolute toleration for all human frailties, with passionate admiration for all human virtues and capacities. *Oscar Wilde, by Frank Harris* (*CG*, p250)

1244. Paris is very purple and starred with gilt spangles. *Letter to an Unidentified Correspondent* (*Letters*, p1102)

1245. The intellectual atmosphere of Paris has done me good, and now I have ideas, not merely passions. *Letter to More Adey* (*Letters*, p1023)

1246. The French can treat any subject with wit, and where one laughs there is no immorality; immorality and seriousness begin together. *Letter to Leonard Smithers* (*Letters*, p1073)

1247. That France hath kissed the mouth of Liberty,
And found it sweeter than his honied
     bees.... *Louis Napoleon* (*Works*, p836)

1248. ... the French have not yet realised that the basis of all civilization is unlimited credit. Empires only fall when they have to pay their bills: at that moment the Barbarians arrive. *Letter to W. Morton Fullerton* (*Letters*, p1155)

1249. We will not war with France because her prose is perfect. *Quoted in Oscar Wilde: His Life and Wit* (*HBP*, p176)

1250. French prose, even in the hands of the most ordinary writers, is always readable, but English prose is detestable. *English Poetesses, Queen* (*Uncollected*, p63)

1251. In France they are wiser. The French painter uses the model simply for study; for the finished picture he goes direct to life. *London Models* (*Uncollected*, p35)

1252. The French were charming to me all the time, and produced my play *Salome*, and wrote about me as a living artist, but the English denied me even the barren recognition one gives to the dead. *Letter to Edward Rose* (*Letters*, p863)

1253. ... French people subscribe to nothing but sonnets when one is alive, and statues when one is dead. *Letter to Leonard Smithers* (*Letters*, p989)

1254. I was thinking in bed this morning that the great superiority of France over England is that in France every bourgeois wants to be an artist, whereas in England every artist wants to be a bourgeois. *Aspects of Wilde* (*CC*, pp73–4)

1255. Paris is terrible in the heat. I walk in streets of brass, and there is no one here. *Letter to Frank Harris* (*CG*, p224)

1256. Paris is hot and empty. Even the charming people of bad character have gone away. Perspiring English families are all that can be seen. *Letter to Leonard Smithers* (*Letters*, p1092)

1257. The weather in Paris is quite awful — real snow and other horrors. *Letter to Leonard Smithers* (*Letters*, p1034)

1258. Paris is quite wintry. I have not returned to the Moulin Rouge. *Letter to Leonard Smithers* (*Letters*, p1104)

1259. In shall go to Genoa. Paris is too dear. *Letter to Frank Harris* (*Letters*, p1137)

1260. I won't go to Paris, because I should spend all my money in no time. *Letter to Robert Ross* (*Letters*, p1138)

1261. If I live in Paris I may be doomed to things I don't desire.... I am frightened of Paris. *Oscar Wilde, by Frank Harris* (*CG*, p224)

1262. They want me to go to Paris with them on Thursday: they say one wears flannels and straw hats and dines in the Bois, but, of course, I have no money, as usual, and can't go. Besides, I want to see you. *Letter to Lord Alfred Douglas* (*Letters,* p594)

1263. Surely you have not left Paris? It seems impossible, as the city wears its wonted air of joy. *Letter to Leonard Smithers* (*Letters,* p1025)

1264. I wish I was back in Paris, where I did such good work. *Oscar Wilde: The Story of an Unhappy Friendship* (*GC*, p83)

1265. Paris is so charming that I think of becoming a French poet! *Letter to W. H. Grenfell* (*Letters,* p492)

26

Friends

1266. She is without one good quality, she lacks the finest spark of decency, and is quite the wickedest woman in London. I haven't a word to say in her favour ... and she is one of my greatest friends. *Quoted in Oscar Wilde: His Life and Wit* (*HBP*, p176)

1267. But what is the good of friendship if one cannot say exactly what one means? Anybody can say charming things and try to please and to flatter, but a true friend always says unpleasant things, and does not mind giving pain. *The Devoted Friend* (*Works*, p290)

1268. Anybody can sympathise with the suffering of a friend, but it requires a very fine nature — it requires, in fact, the nature of a true Individualist — to sympathise with a friend's success. *The Soul of Man* (*HBP*, p33)

1269. Robert gave Harry a terrible black eye, or Harry gave him one; I forget which one, but I know that they were great friends. *Quoted in Oscar Wilde: His Life and Wit* (*HBP*, p176)

1270. Robert, you are defending me at the risk of my life. *Quoted in Oscar Wilde: His Life and Wit* (*HBP*, p74)

1271. I must advertise for some new friends. *Letter to Leonard Smithers* (*Letters*, p1135)

1272. The basis of literary friendship is mixing the poisoned bowl. *Quoted in Oscar Wilde: His Life and Wit* (*HBP*, p216)

1273. All association must be quite voluntary. It is only in voluntary associations that man is fine. *The Soul of Man* (*OWC*, p6)

1274. One cannot demand friendship as a right. One cannot extort affection with a knife. *Letter to Robert Ross* (*Letters*, p1086)

1275. You don't understand what friendship is, Harry — or what enmity is, for that matter. You like everyone; that is to say, you

are indifferent to everyone. *The Picture of Dorian Gray* (*SC*, p26)

1276. Friends always share. *Quoted in Oscar Wilde: His Life and Wit* (*HBP*, p79)

1277. I think that generosity is the essence of friendship.... *The Devoted Friend* (*Works*, p289)

1278. ... one's friends are always a gift-god-given. *Letter to H.C. Marillier* (*Letters*, p269)

1279. I used to estimate friends by their number: now I know that to everyone who has even *one* friend, God has given *two* worlds. And I have really many — far more than I deserve — and it is always nice to have a little more than one deserves. *Letter to Selwyn Image* (*Letters*, p879) and similar quotation in *Letter to Dalhousie Young* (*Letters*, p881)

1280. ... your friendship — your fine chivalrous friendship — is worth more than all the money in the world. *Oscar Wilde: The Story of an Unhappy Friendship* (*GC*, p144)

1281. ... friendship is a fire where what is not flawless shrinks into gray ashes, and where what is imperfect is not purified but consumed. *Letter to Robert Sherard* (*Letters*, p210)

1282. Friendship is far more tragic than love. It lasts longer. *A Few Maxims for the Instruction of the Over-Educated, Saturday Review* (*Works*, p1242)

1283. Love is all very well in its way, but friendship is much higher. Indeed I know nothing in the world that is either nobler or rarer than a devoted friendship. *The Devoted Friend* (*Works*, p286)

1284. Friendship and love like ours need not meetings, but they are delightful. *Letter to Richard Le Gallienne* (*Letters*, p457)

1285. It is always painful to part from people whom one has known for a very brief space of time. The absence of old friends one can endure with equanimity. But even a momentary separation from anyone to whom one has just been introduced is almost unbearable. *The Importance of Being Earnest* (*Plays*, p393)

1286. I know him [George Moore] so well that I haven't spoken to him in ten years. *Aspects of Wilde* (*CC*, p98)

1287. I always like the last person who is introduced to me; but, as a rule, as soon as I know people I get tired of them. *Lord Arthur Savile's Crime* (*SC*, p301)

1288. I always like to know everything about my new friends, and nothing about my old ones. *The Picture of Dorian Gray* (*SC*, pp51–2)

1289. No doubt he will perform his task with all the added bitterness of an old friend. *The Three Trials of Oscar Wilde* (*UB*, p8)

1290. One has a right to judge a man by the effect he has over his friends. *The Picture of Dorian Gray* (*SC*, p164)

1291. I am utterly ashamed of my friendship with him. For by their friendships men can be judged. It is a test of every man. *Letter to Robert Ross* (*Letters*, p670)

1292. To me the mirror of perfect friendship can never be dulled by any treachery, however mean, or disloyalty, however base. Individuals come and go like shadows but the ideal remains untarnished always: the ideal of lives linked together not by affection merely, or the pleasantness of companionship, but by the capacity of being stirred by the same noble things in art and song. *Letter to Robert Sherard* (*Letters*, p210)

1293. When you and he ceased to be great friends, he ceased to be a great artist. *The Picture of Dorian Gray* (*SC*, p225)

1294. I hope to be at least a month with my friends, and to gain, in their healthful and affectionate company, peace, and balance, and a less troubled heart, and a sweeter mood. *De Profundis* (*OWC*, p154)

1295. No other friend have I now in this beautiful world. I want no other. Yet I am distressed to think that I will be looked on as careless of your own welfare, and indifferent of your good. You are made to help me. I weep with sorrow when I think how much I need help, but I weep with joy when I think I have you to give it to me. *Letter to Robert Ross* (*Letters*, pp858–9)

1296. ... friendship is a fire where what is flawless shrinks into grey ashes, and where what is imperfect is not purified but consumed. *Letter to Robert Sherard* (*Letters*, p210)

1297. It was a great joy to see you the other day, looking so beautiful, and improbable, and your friendship is a blossom on the crown of thorns that my life has become. *Letter to Aimee Lowther* (*Letters*, p1164)

1298. ... nothing can help or heal like the hand of a friend, and I seem to have far more now than I ever had, I suppose because I have, of course, far less, but know the wonderful beauty of friendship from a new standpoint and see it with changed eyes. *Letter to Dalhousie Young* (*Letters*, p882)

1299. These charges are founded on sand. Our friendship is founded on rock. *The Three Trials of Oscar Wilde* (*UB*, p312)

1300. Who are you? (what a difficult question for any one of us to answer!) I, at any rate, am your friend. *Letter to Philip Houghton* (*Letters*, p586)

1301. I dare say that if I knew him I should not be his friend at all. It is a very dangerous thing to know one's friends. *The Remarkable Rocket* (*Works*, p297)

1302. Remember also I have yet to know you. Perhaps we have yet to know each other. *De Profundis* (*OWC*, p157)

1303. Laughter is not at all a bad beginning for a friendship, and it is far the best ending for one. *The Picture of Dorian Gray* (*SC*, p25)

Gossip and Scandal

1304. LORD WINDERMERE: What is the difference between scandal and gossip?

CECIL GRAHAM: Oh, gossip is charming! History is merely gossip. But scandal is gossip made tedious by morality. *Lady Windermere's Fan* (*Plays,* p58)

1305. ... I like to know how I am spoken of. To be spoken of, and not to be spoken to, is delightful. *Letter to Ada Leverson* (*Letters,* p872)

1306. Anything is better than virtuous obscurity. (*Plays,* p. viii)

1307. ... there is only one thing in the world worse than being talked about, and that is not being talked about. *The Picture of Dorian Gray* (*SC,* p20)

1308. It is perfectly monstrous the way people go about, nowadays, saying things against one behind one's back that are absolutely and entirely true. *A Woman of No Importance* (*Plays,* p135) and *The Picture of Dorian Gray* (*SC,* p190)

1309. I don't at all like knowing what people say of me behind my back. It makes me far too conceited. *An Ideal Husband* (*Plays,* p324)

1310. Of course a man who is much talked about is always very attractive. One feels there must be something in him after all. *The Importance of Being Earnest* (*Plays,* p395)

1311. He must be quite respectable. One has never heard his name before in the whole course of one's life, which speaks volumes for a man nowadays. *A Woman of No Importance* (*Plays,* p128)

1312. ... I am dining with some very dull people who won't talk scandal, and I know that if I don't get my sleep now I shall never be able to keep awake during dinner. *Lord Arthur Savile's Crime* (*SC,* p285)

1313. Things like that make a man fashionable in Paris. But in London people are so prejudiced. One should never make one's *debut* with a scandal. One should reserve that to give an interest to one's old age. *The Picture of Dorian Gray* (*SC,* p113)

1314. LADY WINDERMERE: I will have no one in my house about whom there is any scandal.

LORD DARLINGTON: Oh, don't say that, Lady Windermere. I should never be admitted! *Lady Windermere's Fan* (*Plays,* pp10–11)

1315. Mrs. Cheveley is one of those very modern women of our time who find a new scandal as becoming as a new bonnet, and air them both in the Park every afternoon at five-thirty. I am sure she adores scandals, and that the sorrow of her life at present is that she can't manage to have enough of them. *An Ideal Husband* (*Plays,* p267)

1316. Early in life she had discovered the important truth that nothing looks so like innocence as an indiscretion, and by a series of reckless escapades, half of them quite harmless, she had acquired all the privileges of a personality. She had more than once changed her husband — indeed, Debrett credits her with three marriages — but as she had never changed her love, the world had long ago ceased to talk scandal about her. *Lord Arthur Savile's Crime* (*SC,* p266)

1317. The basis of every scandal is an immoral certainty. *The Picture of Dorian Gray* (*SC,* p216) and *A Woman of No Importance* (*Plays,* p140)

1318. I know how people chatter in England. The middle classes air their moral prejudices over their dinner-tables, and whisper about what they call the profligacies of their betters in order to try and pretend that they are in smart society and on intimate terms with the people they slander. In this country, it is enough for a man to have distinction and brains for every common tongue to wag against him. And what sort of lives do these people, who pose as being moral, lead themselves? My dear fellow, you forget that we are in the native land of the hypocrite. *The Picture of Dorian Gray* (*SC*, p164)

1319. Scandals and slander are related to the hatred of the people who invent them and are not, in any shadowy sense even, effigies or images of the person attacked. *Oscar Wilde, by Frank Harris* (*CG*, p105)

1320. That is the reason [people] are pleased to find out other people's secrets. It distracts public attention from their own. *An Ideal Husband* (*Plays*, p259)

1321. LORD WINDERMERE: Well, it is no business of yours, is it, Cecil?

CECIL GRAHAM: None. That is why it interests me. My own business always bores me to death. I prefer other people's. *Lady Windermere's Fan* (*Plays*, p55)

1322. I love scandals about other people, but scandals about myself don't interest me. They have not got the charm of novelty. *The Picture of Dorian Gray* (*SC*, p162)

1323. ... what is said of a man is nothing. The point is, who says it. *De Profundis* (*OWC*, p145)

1324. The things people say about a man do not alter a man. He is what he is. *The Soul of Man* (*OWC*, p11)

1325. Slander and folly have their way for a season, but for a season only. *Letter to Joaquin Miller* (*Letters*, p142) and similar quotation in *Art and the Handicraftsman* lecture (*Uncollected*, p116)

28

Gratitude

1326. To awaken gratitude in the ungrateful were as vain as to try to wake the dead by cries. *Letter to Robert Ross (Letters, p1086)*

1327. I used to think gratitude a great burden to carry. Now I know that bit is something that makes the heart lighter. The ungrateful man is one who walks slowly with feet and heart of lead. But when one knows the strange joy of gratitude to God and man the earth becomes lovlier to one, and it is a pleasure to count up, not one's wealth but one's debts, not the little that one possesses, but he much that one owes. *Letter to Max Beerbohm (Letters, p856)* and similar quotations in *Letter to Major J. O. Nelson (Letters, p862)* and *Letter to Frank Harris (Letters, p894)*

1328. I learnt gratitude: and though, in the eyes of the world, I am of course a disgraced and ruined man, still every day I am filled with wonder at all the beautiful things that are left to me: loyal and loving friends: good health: books: one of the greatest of the many worlds God has given to each man: the pageant of the seasons: the lovliness of leaf and flower: the nights hung with silver and the dawns dim with gold. I often find myself strangely happy. *Letter to Carlos Blacker (Letters, pp911–2)*

1329. Of course I have lost much, but still ... when I reckon up all that is *left* to me, the sun and the sea of this beautiful world; its dawn dim with gold and its nights hung with silver; many books, and all flowers, and a few good friends; and a brain and body to which health and power are not denied — really I am rich when I count up what I still have: and as for money, my money did me horrible harm. It wrecked me. I hope just to have enough to enable me to live simple and write well. *Letter to William Rothenstein (Letters, 892)*

1330. I am glad to say I am not an embittered man: on the contrary, I am very happy. I have learnt gratitude — a new lesson for me — and a certain amount of humility as regards myself, and I don't desire riches or wild profligacy anymore. I want peace and have found it, and perhaps someday may do a work of art that you may take pleasure in. *Letter to Arthur Humphreys (Letters, p880)*

29

Greece and the Greeks

1331. ... the Greek spirit is essentially modern. *The Rise of Historical Criticism* (*Works*, p1240)

1332. The old fable that the Greek gods took service with a new religion under assumed names has more truth in it than the many care to discover. *The Rise of Historical Criticism* (*Works*, p1202)

1333. The sovereignty of Greece and Rome is not yet passed away, though the gods of one be dead and the eagles of the other tired. *The English Renaissance of Art lecture* (*Uncollected*, p22)

1334. Greek philosophy began and ended in scepticism: the first and the last word of Greek history was Faith. Splendid thus in its death, like winter sunsets, the Greek religion passed away into the horror of night. *The Rise of Historical Criticism* (*Works*, p1237)

1335. For the artists, like the Greek gods, are revealed only to one another ... their real value and place time only can show. *The English Renaissance of Art lecture* (*Uncollected*, p17)

1336. The Greeks were a nation of art critics, because they were spared a sense of the infinite. *The Critic as Artist* (*Works*, p1137)

1337. The Greeks had no art critics. *The Critic as Artist* (*Works*, p1113)

1338. Who would not be flippant when he is gravely told that the Greeks had no art-critics? I can understand it being said that the constructive genius of the Greeks lost itself in criticism, but not that the race to whom we owe the critical spirit did not criticise. *The Critic as Artist* (*Works*, p1116)

1339. ... the tired spirit broods with that calm and certain joy that one gets when one has found something that the ages never dull

and the world cannot harm; and with it comes that desire of Greek things which is often an artistic method of expressing one's desire for perfection.... *L'Envoi* (*Uncollected*, p201)

1340. To the Greeks this problem of the conditions of poetic production, and the places occupied by either spontaneity or self-consciousness in any artistic work, had a peculiar fascination. *The English Renaissance of Art lecture* (*Uncollected*, p11)

1341. ... to the Greek, pure artist, that work is most instinct with spiritual life which conforms most closely to the perfect facts of physical life also. *The English Renaissance of Art lecture* (*Uncollected*, p7)

1342. The fragile clay vases of the Greeks still keep for us pictures of Sappho, delicately painted in black and red and white; but of her song we have only the echo of an echo. *English Poetesses* (*Uncollected*, p60)

1343. Phidias and the achievements of Greek art are foreshadowed in Homer. *The English Renaissance of Art lecture* ((*Uncollected*, p7)

1344. A workman is given a design stolen from a Greek temple and does it because he is paid for doing it — the worst reason for doing anything; no modern stonecutter could leave the stamp of this age upon his work as the ancient workmen did. *The Decorative Arts lecture* (*Works*, pp930–1)

1345. Let the Greek carve his lions ... buffalo and wild deer are the animals for you [Americans]. *Art and the Handicraftsman lecture* (*Uncollected*, p113)

1346. To say that Ford is like a glittering Corinthian colonnade adds nothing to our knowledge of either Ford or Greek architecture. *Ben Jonson, Pall Mall Gazette* (*Uncollected*, p161)

1347. There is not ... a single delicate line, or delightful proportion, in the dress of the Greeks, which is not echoed exquisitely in their architecture. A nation [England] arrayed in stove-pipe hats and dress-improvers might have built Pantechnichon possibly, but the Parthenon never. *The Relation of Dress to Art, Pall Mall Gazette* (*Uncollected*, p53)

1348. Greek dress was in its essence inartistic. Nothing should reveal the body but the body. *Phrases and Philosophies for the Use of the Young, The Chameleon* (*Works*, p1245)

1349. The Greek dress was the lovliest dress the world has ever seen, and the English dress of the last century one of the most monstrous. *The Critic as Artist* (*Works*, p1170)

1350. To be really mediaeval one should have no body. To be really modern one should have no soul. To be really Greek one should have no clothes. *A Few Maxims for the Instruction of the Over-Educated, Saturday Review* (*Works*, p1242)

1351. ... seeing Greece is really a great education for anyone and will I think benefit me greatly. *Letter to the Rev. H.R. Bramley* (*Letters*, p45)

1352. It is in the Theban market-place not on the hillside of Parnassus that men become lunatic. *Letter to More Adey* (*Letters*, p804)

1353. Let us live like Spartans, but let us talk like Athenians. *Letter to H.C. Marillier* (*Letters*, p274)

1354. ... I am a Greek born out of due time. *Oscar Wilde, by Frank Harris* (*CG*, p199)

Happiness and Pleasure

1355. When we are happy, we are always good, but when we are good, we are not always happy. *The Picture of Dorian Gray* (*SC*, p93)

1356. My duty as a gentleman has never interfered with my pleasure in the smallest degree. *The Importance of Being Earnest* (*Plays*, p392)

1357. My courtiers called me the Happy Prince, and happy indeed I was, if pleasure be happiness. *The Happy Prince* (*SC*, p238)

1358. ... what consoles one now-a-days is not repentance, but pleasure. *Lady Windermere's Fan* (*Plays*, p75)

1359. She ultimately was so broken-hearted that she went into a convent, or onto the operatic stage, I forget which. No; I think it was decorative art-needlework she took up. I know she had lost all sense of pleasure in life. *An Ideal Husband* (*Plays*, p284)

1360. Pleasure is the only thing one should live for. Nothing ages like happiness. *Phrases and Philosophies for the Use of the Young, The Chameleon* (*Works*, p1244)

1361. What else is there to live for, father? Nothing ages like happiness. *An Ideal Husband* (*Plays*, p235)

1362. Let us get what pleasure we may in the fleeting days; for night cometh, and the silence that can never by broken. *Oscar Wilde, by Frank Harris* (*CG*, p240)

1363. Life without desire would not be worth living to me. As one gets older one is more difficult to please; but the sting of pleasure is ever keener than in youth and far more egotistic. *Oscar Wilde, by Frank Harris* (*CG*, p300)

1364. ... he wore the sweet smile of those who are always looking for the moon at midday. *Letter to Frances Forbes-Robertson* (*Letters*, p1144)

1365. I do not interest myself in that British view of morals that sets Messalina above Sporus: both pleasures are matters of temperament, and like all sensual pleasures lack nobility and slay the soul.... *Letter to Arthur Humphreys* (*Letters*, p880)

1366. Man has sought to live intensely, fully, perfectly. When he can do so without exercising restraint on others, or suffering it ever, and his activities are all pleasurable to him, he will be saner, healthier, more civilised, more himself. Pleasure is Nature's test, her sign of approval. When a man is happy, he is in harmony with himself and his environment. *The Soul of Man* (*OWC*, p36)

1367. Pleasure is the only thing worth having a theory about. But I am afraid I cannot claim my theory as my own. It belongs to Nature, not to me. Pleasure is Nature's test, her sign of approval. *The Picture of Dorian Gray* (*SC*, p93)

1368. I don't regret for a single moment having lived for pleasure. I did it to the full, as one should do everything that one does to the full. There was no pleasure I did not experience. I threw the pearl of my soul into a cup of wine. I went down the primrose path to the sound of flutes. I lived on honeycomb. But to have continued the same life would have been wrong because it would have been limiting. I had to pass it on. The other half of the garden had its secrets for me also. *De Profundis* (*OWC*, p108)

1369. ... to realise oneself through pleasure is finer than to do so through pain. *The Three Trials of Oscar Wilde* (*UB*, p123)

1370. I want my pleasure unbittered by any drop of pain. *Oscar Wilde, by Frank Harris* (*CG*, p300)

1371. You came to me to learn the Pleasure of Life and the Pleasure of Art. Perhaps I am chosen to teach you something much more wonderful, the meaning of Sorrow, and its beauty. *De Profundis* (*OWC*, p158)

1372. I myself feel happier with Bosie than I could be if all my laurels were given back to me. *Letter to Reginald Turner* (*Letters*, p961)

1373. ... the only thing for me was to accept everything. Since then —curious as it will no doubt sound to you — I have been happier. *De Profundis* (*OWC*, p114)

1374. It is joy alone which appeals to my soul; the joy of life and beauty and love.... *Oscar Wilde, by Frank Harris* (*CG*, p256)

1375. I can be perfectly happy by myself. With freedom, books, flowers, and the moon, who could not be happy? *De Profundis* (*OWC*, pp127–8)

1376. I adore simple pleasures. They are the last refuge of the complex. *The Picture of Dorian Gray* (*SC*, p44) and A Woman of No Importance (*Plays*, p148)

31

Hate

1377. Hate granted you every single thing you wished for. It was an indulgent Master to you. It is so, indeed, to all who serve it. *De Profundis* (*OWC*, p72)

1378. Hate, you have yet to learn, is, intellectually considered, the Eternal Negation. Considered from the point of view of the emotions it is a form of Atrophy, and kills everything but itself. *De Profundis* (*OWC*, p73)

1379. Hate blinds people. You were not aware of that. Love can read the writing on the remotest star, but Hate so blinded you that you could see no further than the narrow, walled-in, and already lust-withered garden of your common desires. *De Profundis* (*OWC*, p68)

1380. In you Hate was always stronger than Love.... You did not realise that there is not room for both passions in the same soul. They cannot live together in that fair carven house. Love is fed by the imagination, by which we become wiser than we know, better than we feel, nobler than we are: by which we can see Life as a whole: by which, and by which alone, we can understand others in their real as in their ideal relations. Only what is fine, and finely conceived, can feed Love. But anything will feed Hate.... *De Profundis* (*OWC*, p68)

1381. In your hideous game of hate together, you had both thrown dice for my soul, and you happened to have lost. That was all. *De Profundis* (*OWC*, p72)

1382. Yet each man kills the thing he loves,
By each let this be heard,
Some do it with a bitter look,
Some with a flattering word,
The coward does it with a kiss,
The brave man with a sword! *The Ballad of Reading Goal* (*OWC*, p170)

1383. Am I right in saying that Hate blinds people? Do you see it now? If you don't, try to see it. *De Profundis* (*OWC*, p75)

32

History

1384. The one duty we owe to history is to rewrite it. *The Critic as Artist* (*Works*, p1121)

1385. ... the details of history ... are always wearisome and usually inaccurate. *The Critic as Artist* (*Works*, p1119)

1386. We cannot re-write the whole of history for the purpose of gratifying our moral sense of what should be. *Pen, Pencil, and Poison* (*Works*, p1106)

1387. Raleigh, writes a whole history of the world, without knowing anything whatsoever about the past. *The Decay of Lying* (*Works*, p1082)

1388. The ancient historians gave us delightful fiction in the form of fact; the modern novelist presents us with dull facts under the guise of fiction. *The Decay of Lying* (*Works*, p1073)

1389. ... in the works of our own Carlyle, whose *French Revolution* is one of the most fascinating historical novels ever written, facts are either kept in their proper subordinate position, or else entirely excluded on the general ground of dullness. *The Decay of Lying* (*Works*, p1080)

1390. But even men of the noblest possible moral character are extremely susceptible to the influence of the physical charms of others. Modern, no less than Ancient History, supplies us with many most painful examples of what I refer to. If it were not so, indeed, History would be quite unreadable. *The Importance of Being Earnest* (*Plays*, p401)

1391. When you are present, the air is cosmopolitan and the room seems to be full of brilliant people. You are one of those rare persons who give one the sense of creating history as they live. *Letter to Julia Ward Howe* (*Letters*, p176)

1392. The longer one studies life and literature, the more strongly one feels that behind everything that is wonderful stands the individual, and that it is not the moment that makes the man, but the man who creates the age. *The Critic as Artist* (*Works*, p1119)

1393. I mean that intellectual curiosity of the nineteenth century which is always looking for the secret of the life that still lingers round old and bygone forms of culture. It takes from each what is serviceable for the modern spirit. *The English Renaissance of Art lecture* (*Uncollected*, p22)

1394. ... the dreadful thing about modernity was that it put Tragedy into the raiment of Comedy, so that the great realities seemed commonplace or grotesque or lacking in style. It is quite true about modernity. It has probably always been true about actual life. It is said that all martyrdoms seemed mean to the looker-on. The nineteenth century is no exception to the general rule. *De Profundis* (*OWC*, p129)

1395. ... could anything be less impressive than the unfortunate hero gravely heralding a dawn that rose long ago, and so completely missing its true significance that he proposes to carry on the business of the old firm under a new name. *The Decay of Lying* (*Works*, p1076)

1396. The ages live in history through their anachronisms. *Phrases and Philosophies for the Use of the Young, The Chameleon* (*Works*, p1245)

1397. ... that dreadful record of crime known as history.... Give children beauty, not the record of bloody slaughters and barbarous brawls, as they call history.... You give the criminal calendar of Europe to your children under the name of history. *Oscar Wilde Discovers America* (*HBC*, p127)

1398. In the false education of our present system, minds too young to grapple with the subjects in the right sense are burdened with those bloody slaughters and barbarous brawls of the French and English wars that calendar of infamy, European history. *The Decorative Arts lecture* (*Works*, p935)

1399. [The ideal historian] is to be free from all bias towards friend and country; he is to be courteous and gentle in criticism; he is not to regard history as a mere opportunity for splendid and tragic writing; nor is he to falsify truth for the sake of a paradox or an epigram.... While acknowledging the importance of particular facts as samples of higher truths, he is to take a broad and general view of humanity. He is to deal with the whole race and with the world, not with particular tribes or separate countries. He is to bear in mind that the world is really an organism wherein no one part can be moved without the others being affected also. He is to distinguish between cause and occasion between the influence of general laws and particular fancies, and he is to remember that the greatest lessons of the world are contained in history and that it is the historians duty to manifest them so as to save nations from following those unwise policies which always lead to dishonour and ruin, and to teach individuals to apprehend by the intellectual culture of history those truths which else they would have to learn in the bitter school of experience. *The Rise of Historical Criticism* (*Works*, p1234)

1400. The appeal to antiquity is fatal to those of us who are romanticists. *The Picture of Dorian Gray* (*SC*, p209)

1401. ... longing for the old dead days ... is so modern.... *L'Envoi* (*Uncollected*, p201)

1402. I know that there are many historians, or at least writers on historical subjects, who still think it necessary to apply moral judgments to history, and who distribute their praise or blame with the solemn complacency of a successful schoolmaster. This, however, is a foolish habit, and merely shows that the moral instinct can be brought to such a pitch of perfection that it will make its appearance wherever it is not required. Nobody with the true historical sense ever dreams of blaming Nero, or scolding Tiberius, or censuring Caesar Borgia. These personages have become like the puppets of a play. They may fill us with terror, or horror or wonder, but they do not harm us. They are not in immediate relation to us. We have nothing to fear from them. They have passed into the sphere of art and science, and neither art nor science knows anything of moral approval or disapproval. *Pen, Pencil and Poison* (*Works*, pp1106–7)

1403. There were times when it appeared to Dorian Gray that the whole of history was merely the record of his own life, not as he had lived it in act and circumstance, but as his imagination had created it for him, as it had been in his brain and in his passions. He felt that he had known them all, those strange terrible figures that had passed across the stage of the world and made sin so marvelous an evil so full of subtlety. It seemed that in some mysterious way their lives had been his own. *The Picture of Dorian Gray* (*SC*, p157)

1404. The ancient world wakes from its sleep, and history moves as a pageant before our eyes, without obliging us to have recourse to a dictionary or an encyclopaedia for the perfection of our enjoyment. *The Truth of Masks* (*Works*, p1163)

1405. The spirit of an age is not born and does not die on a definite day. *The Rise of Historical Criticism* (*Works*, p1198)

1406. History, no doubt, has splendid lessons for our instruction, just as all good art comes to us as the herald of the noblest truth. *The Rise of Historical Criticism* (*Works*, p1207)

1407. Humanity takes itself too seriously. It is the world's original sin. If the caveman had known how to laugh, history would have been different. *The Picture of Dorian Gray* (*SC*, p57)

33

Home Decor

1408. Have nothing in your house that has not given pleasure to the man who made it and is not a pleasure to those who use it. *The House Beautiful lecture* (*Works*, p914) and similar quotation in *Art and the Handicraftsman* lecture (*Uncollected*, p116)

1409. ... the decorations of a house should express the feeling of those who live in it. *The House Beautiful lecture* (*Works*, p914)

1410. ... ornament should represent the feeling in a man's life.... *The House Beautiful lecture* (*Works*, p914)

1411. Comfort is the only thing our civilization can give us. *Lord Arthur Savile's Crime* (*SC*, p268)

1412. Have nothing in your house that is not useful or beautiful; if such a rule were followed out, you would be astonished at the amount of rubbish you would get rid of. In the question of decoration the first necessity is that any system of art should bear the impress of a distinct individuality; it is difficult to lay down rules as to the decoration of dwellings because every home should wear an individual air in all its furnishings and decorations. *The House Beautiful lecture* (*Works*, p914)

1413. There can be no nobler influence in a room than a marble Venus of Milo: in the presence of an image so pure, no tongue would dare to talk scandal. There should be casts of good men in the library. *The House Beautiful lecture* (*Works*, p922)

1414. Those of you who have old china use it I hope. There is nothing so absurd as having good china stuck up in a cabinet merely for show while the family drink from delft; if you can't use good old china without breaking it, then you don't deserve to have it. Whatever you have that is beautiful for use, then you should use it, or part with it to someone who will. *The House Beautiful lecture* (*Works*, p921)

1415. As regards style of furniture: avoid the "early English" or Gothic furniture ... it is very well for those who lived in castles and who needed occasionally to use it as a means of defense or as a weapon of war. A lighter and more graceful style of furniture is more suitable for our peaceful times. *The House Beautiful lecture* (*Works*, p918)

1416. Embroidery you will have, of course, but don't, I pray you, have everything covered with embroidery as if it were washing day. *The House Beautiful lecture* (*Works*, p920)

1417. One must have a piano I suppose, but it is a melancholy thing, and more like a dreadful, funereal packing-case in form than anything else.... *The House Beautiful lecture* (*Works*, p920)

1418. The grand piano is a funeral case. I prefer the upright. *Oscar Wilde Discovers America* (*HBC*, p351)

1419. The revolving stool should be sent to the museum of horrors, and a seat large enough for two players should be substituted. *The House Beautiful lecture* (*Works*, p921)

1420. Hat racks are, I suppose, necessary. I have never seen a really nice hat rack; the ordinary one is more like some horrible instrument of torture than anything useful or graceful, and it is perhaps the ugliest thing in the house. *The House Beautiful lecture* (*Works*, p915)

1421. About the ceiling: the ceiling is a great problem always—what to do with the great expanse of white plaster. Don't paper it; that gives one the sensation of living in a paper box, which is not pleasant. *The House Beautiful lecture* (*Works*, p917)

1422. I have seen far more rooms spoiled by wallpapers than by anything else: when everything is covered with a design the room is restless and the eye disturbed. *Letter to W.A.S. Benson* (*Letters*, p259)

1423. As regards the floor: don't carpet it all over, as nothing is more unhealthy or inartistic than modern carpets; carpets absorb the dust, and it is impossible to keep them as perfectly clean as anything about us should be. In this, as in all things, art and sanitary regulations go hand in hand. *The House Beautiful lecture* (*Works*, p918)

1424. About pictures: I have to see the ruining of so many fine pictures in the framing, by reason of the frame being out of all keeping with the picture. *The House Beautiful lecture* (*Work*, p921)

1425. Two pictures should not be hung side by side — they will either kill one another, or else commit artistic suicide. *The House Beautiful lecture* (*Works*, p922)

1426. Put no photographs of paintings on your walls — they are libels on great masters; there is no way to get a worse idea of a painter than by a photograph of his work.... *The House Beautiful lecture* (*Works*, p922)

1427. There should be no pictures in the hall, for it is no place for a good picture, and a poor one should be put nowhere ... and no picture should be placed where you have not time to sit down and reverence and admire and study it. *The House Beautiful lecture* (*Works*, p915)

1428. A good picture is always improved by being hung on a coloured surface that suits it, or by being placed in surroundings which are harmonious to it, but the delicacy of line in an etching for instance is often spoiled by the necessarily broad, if not course, pattern on a block-printed wallpaper. *Letter to W.A.S. Benson* (*Letters*, p258)

1429. As regards rooms generally: in America the great fault in decoration is the entire want of harmony or a definite scheme in colour; there is generally a collection of a great many things individually pretty but which do not combine to make a harmonious whole. Colours resemble musical notes: a single false colour or false note destroys the whole. Therefore, in decorating a room one keynote of colour should predominate; it must be decided before hand what scheme of colour is desired and have all else adapted to it, like the answering calls in a symphony of music; otherwise, your room will be a museum of colours. *The House Beautiful lecture* (*Works*, p915)

1430. There is one article of furniture which has confronted me wherever I have gone on this continent [America], and that for absolutely horrid ugliness surpasses anything I have seen — the cast-iron American stove. If it had been left in its natural ugliness it might be endured as a necessary nuisance, like a dull relation or a rainy day, but manufacturers persist in decorating it with wreaths of black-leaded and grimy roses at the base and surmounting it with a dismal funeral urn — or, where they are more extravagant than usual, with two. *The Decorative Arts lecture* (*Works*, p928)

1431. ... what place can I ascribe to art in our education? Consider how susceptible children are to the influence of beauty, for they are easily impressed and are pretty much what their surroundings make them. How can you expect them, then, to tell the truth if everything about them is telling lies, like the paper in the hall declaring itself marble? Why I have seen wallpaper which must lead a boy brought up under its influence to a career of crime; you should not have such incentives to sin lying about your drawing-rooms. *The Decorative Arts lecture* (*Works*, p934)

1432. If you go into a house where everything is course and you find the common cups chipped and the saucers cracked, it will often be because the children have an utter contempt for them, but if everything is dainty and delicate, you teach them practically what beauty is, and gentleness and refinement of manner are unconsciously acquired. *The Decorative Arts* (*Works*, p935) and similar quotation in *House Decoration lecture* (*Uncollected*, p189)

1433. So, in years to come there will be nothing in any man's house that has not given delight to its maker and does not give delight to it user. *The English Renaissance of Art lecture* (*Uncollected*, p23)

1434. If you can't use it, you don't deserve it. *Oscar Wilde Discovers America* (HBC, p254)

Individualism

1435. I think that the realisation of oneself is the prime aim of life.... *Three Trials of Oscar Wilde* (*UB*, p123)

1436. Now, nothing should be able to harm a man except himself. What a man really has, is what is in him. What is outside of him should be a matter of no importance. *The Soul of Man* (*OWC*, p8)

1437. "Know thyself" was written over the portal of the antique world. Over the portal of the new world, "Be thyself" shall be written. *The Soul of Man* (*OWC*, p9)

1438. Be brave! Be yourself! *Lady Windermere's Fan* (*Plays*, p37)

1439. Very few among us have the courage openly to set up our own standard of values and abide by it. *Quoted in Oscar Wilde: His Life and Wit* (*HBP*, p167)

1440. At every single moment of one's life one is what one is going to be no less than what one has been. *De Profundis* (*OWC*, p109)

1441. But for the full development of Life to its highest mode of perfection, something more is needed. What is needed is Individualism. *The Soul of Man* (*OWC*, p3)

1442. Man is complete in himself. *The Soul of Man* (*OWC*, p11)

1443. They miss their aim, too, these philanthropists and sentimentalists of our day, who are always chattering about one's duty to one's neighbour. For the development of the race depends on the development of the individual.... *The Critic as Artist* (*Works*, p1140)

1444. If you wish to understand others you must intensify your own individualism. *The Critic as Artist* (*Works*, p1131)

1445. When a man has realised Individualism, he will also realise sympathy and exercise it freely and spontaneously. *The Soul of Man* (*OWC*, p33)

1446. As it was, we always misunderstood ourselves and rarely understood others. *The Picture of Dorian Gray* (*SC*, p74)

1447. ... you should absorb but imitate never, copy never. *Art and the Handicraftsman lecture* (*Uncollected*, p113)

1448. ... imitation can be made the sincerest form of insult.... *The Decay of Lying* (*Works*, p1086)

1449. In this world like meets with like. *An Ideal Husband* (*Plays*, p287)

1450. It often happened that when we thought we were experimenting on others we were really experimenting on ourselves. *The Picture of Dorian Gray* (*SC*, p75)

1451. A man whose desire is to be something separate from himself, to be a member of Parliament, or a successful grocer, or a prominent solicitor, or a judge, or something equally tedious, invariably succeeds in being what he wants to be. That is his punishment. Those who want a mask have to wear it. *De Profundis* (*OWC*, p125)

1452. Most people are other people. Their thoughts are someone else's opinions, their life a mimicry, their passions a quotation. *De Profundis* (*OWC*, p114)

1453. The moment I met you I saw that you were quite unconscious of what you really are, of what you really might be. There was so much in you that charmed me that I felt I must tell you something about yourself. I thought how tragic it would be if you were wasted. *The Picture of Dorian Gray* (*SC*, p39)

1454. And while to the claims of charity a man may yield and yet be free, to the claims of conformity no man may yield and remain free at all. *The Soul of Man* (*OWC*, p13)

1455. And of all men we are most wretched who

must live each other's lives and not our own
Humanitad (*Works*, p825)

1456. When each member of the community has sufficient for his wants, and is not interfered with by his neighbor, it will not be an object of interest to him to interfere with anyone else. *The Soul of Man* (*OWC*, p14)

1457. People ... go through their lives in a sort of coarse comfort, like petted animals, without ever realising that they are probably thinking other people's thoughts, living by other people's standards, wearing practically what one may call other people's second-hand clothes, and never being themselves for a single moment. *The Soul of Man* (*OWC*, p13)

1458. I do not think that one person influences another, nor do I think there is any bad influence in the world. *Quoted in Oscar Wilde: His Life and Wit* (*HBP*, p137)

1459. It is only by realising what I am that I have found comfort of any kind. *De Profundis* (*OWC*, p100)

1460. Everything must come to one out of one's own nature. There is no use in telling a person a thing that they don't feel and can't understand. *De Profundis* (*OWC*, p73)

1461. If my nature had been made to suit your comprehension rather than my own requirements, I am afraid I would have made a very poor figure in the world. *Vera, or the Nihilists* (*Works*, p698)

1462. I always say I and not "we." We belongs to the days of anonymous articles, not to signed articles like mine. To say "we have seen at Argos" either implies that I am a Royal Personage, or that the whole staff of the DUM visited Argos. *Letter to Keningale Cook* (*Letters*, p52)

1463. My ruin came not from too great individualism of life, but from too little. To one disgraceful, unpardonable, and to all time contemptible action of my life, was to allow myself to appeal to society for help and protection. *Quoted in Oscar Wilde: His Life and Wit* (*HBP*, p289)

1464. There is no general rule of health; it is all personal, individual.... I only demand that freedom which I willingly concede to others. No one condemns another for preferring green to gold. Why should any taste be ostracised? Liking and disliking are not under our control. I want to choose the nourishment which suits *my* body and *my* soul. *Oscar Wilde, by Frank Harris* (*CG*, pp56–7)

1465. Yes; there are suggestive things in Individualism. Socialism annihilates family life, for instance. With the abolition of private property, marriage in its present form must disappear. This is part of the programme. Individualism accepts this and makes it fine. It converts the abolition of legal restraint into a form of freedom that will help the full development of personality, and make the love of man and woman more wonderful, more beautiful, and more ennobling. *The Soul of Man* (*OWC*, p12)

1466. You know what beautiful, wise, sensible schemes of life people bring to one: there is nothing to be said against them: except that they are not for oneself. *Letter to Robert Ross* (*Letters*, p980)

1467. ... I know that there is no such thing as changing one's life: one merely wanders round and round within the circle of one's own personality. *Letter to Robert Ross* (*Letters*, p978)

1468. Man makes his end for himself out of himself: no end is imposed by external conditions, he must realise his true nature; must be what *nature* orders. (*SC*, p. xxiii)

1469. ... to influence a person is to give him one's own soul. He does not think his natural thoughts, or burn with his natural passions. His virtues are not real to him. His sins, if there are such thing as sins, are borrowed. He becomes an echo of someone else's music, an actor of a part that has not been written for him. The aim of life is self-development. To realise one's own nature perfectly — that is what each of us is here for. *The Picture of Dorian Gray* (*SC*, pp34–5)

1470. What are the incredible things, but the things that one has faithfully believed? What are the improbable things? The things that one has done oneself. *The Critic as Artist* (*Works*, p1132)

1471. ... a man is called selfish if he lives in the manner that seems to him most suitable for the full realization of his own personality; if, in fact, the primary aim of his life is self-development. *The Soul of Man* (*OWC*, p32)

1472. It is not selfish to think for oneself. A man who does not think for himself does not think at all. It is grossly selfish to require of one's neighbor that he should think in the same way, and hold the same opinions. *The Soul of Man* (*OWC*, p33)

1473. Selfishness is not living as one wishes to live, it is asking others to live as one wishes to live. Unselfishness is letting other people's lives alone, not interfering with them. *The Soul of Man* (*OWC*, pp32–3)

1474. Selfishness always aims at creating around it an absolute uniformity of type. Unselfishness recognizes infinite variety of type as a delightful thing, accepts it, acquiesces in it, enjoys it. *The Soul of Man* (*OWC*, p33)

1475. DUMBY: What a mystery you are!

LADY PLYMDALE: I wish *you* were!

DUMBY: I am — to myself. I am the only person in the world I should like to know thoroughly; but I don't see any chance of it just at present. *Lady Windermere's Fan* (*Plays*, p35)

1476. I like you to regard *all* things from *my* point of view. In *other* matters I like my friends to be free from my tyrannous personality. *Letter to Reginald Turner* (*Letters*, p878)

1477. I used to rely on my personality: now I know that my personality really rested on the fiction of *position*. Having lost position, I find my personality of no avail. *Letter to Robert Ross* (*Letters*, p1138)

1478. ... by selecting its own mode of expression, a personality might make itself perfect. *The Soul of Man* (*OWC*, p12)

1479. Technique is really personality. That is the reason why an artist cannot teach it, why the pupil cannot learn it, and why the critic cannot understand it. *The Critic as Artist* (*Works*, p1150)

1480. Most personalities have been obliged to be rebels. Half their strength has been wasted in friction. *The Soul of Man* (*OWC*, p8)

1481. ... personality does not require intellect to help it: it is a dynamic force of its own, and is often as superbly unintelligent as the great forces of nature.... *Letter to Lord Alfred Douglas* (*Letters*, p871)

1482. It will be a marvelous thing — the true personality of man — when we see it. It will grow naturally and simply, flower-like or as a tree grows. It will not be at discord. It will never argue or dispute. It will not prove things. It will know everything. And yet it will not busy itself about knowledge. It will have wisdom. Its value will not be measured by material things. It will have nothing. And yet it will have everything, and whatever one takes from it, it will still have, so rich will it be. It will not be always meddling with others, or asking them to be like itself. It will love them because they will be different. And yet while it will not meddle with others it will help all, as a beautiful thing helps us, by being what it is. The personality of man will be very wonderful. It will be as wonderful as the personality of a child ... it will not worry about the past, nor care whether things happened or did not happen. Nor will it admit any laws but its on laws; nor any authority but its own authority. *The Soul of Man* (*OWC*, p9)

1483. Art is the most intense mode of Individualism that the world has known. I am inclined to say that it is the only real mode of Individualism that the world has known. *The Soul of Man* (*OWC*, p17)

1484. ... you [must] require a sense of individualism about each man and women, for this is the essence of art — a desire on the part of man to express himself in the noblest way possible. *Art and the Handicraftsman lecture* (*Uncollected*, p111)

1485. For what is decoration but the worker's expression of joy in his work? And not joy merely — that is a great thing yet not enough — but that opportunity of expressing his own individuality which, as it is the essence of all life, is the source of all art. *The English Renaissance of Art lecture* (*Uncollected*, p26)

1486. For it is not enough that a work of art should conform to the aesthetic demands of its age: there must be also about it, if it is to affect us with any permanent delight, the impress of a distinct individuality.... *The English Renaissance of Art lecture* (*Uncollected*, p9) and similar quotations in *L'Envoi* (*Uncollected*, pp199–200) and The Decorative Arts lecture (*Works*, p932)

1487. On the whole, an artist in England gains something by being attacked. His individuality is intensified. He becomes more completely himself. *The Soul of Man* (*OWC*, p21)

1488. ... the English dislike individualism. *Letter to the Editor of The Daily Telegraph* (*Letters*, p466)

1489. Of course, nations and individuals, with that healthy natural vanity which is the secret of existence, are always under the impression that is it of them that the Muses are talking.... *The Decay of Lying* (*Works*, p1087)

1490. The note of the perfect personality is not rebellion, but peace. *The Soul of Man* (*OWC*, p9)

1491. I don't defend my conduct, I explain it. *Letter to Robert Ross* (*Letters*, p780)

1492. The longer one studies life and literature the more strongly one feels that behind everything that is wonderful stands the individual, and that it is not the moment that makes the man but the man who creates the age. *The Critic as Artist* (*Works*, p1119)

1493. To reject one's own experiences is to arrest one's own development. To deny one's own experiences is to put a lie onto the lips of one's own life. It is no less than a denial of the soul. *De Profundis* (*OWC*, p100)

1494. Strange, that we knew so little about ourselves, and that our most intimate personality was concealed from us! Were we to look in tombs for our real life, and in art for the legend of our days? *The Portrait of Mr. W.H.* (*Works*, p345)

1495. It is to be noted also that Individualism does not come to man with any sickly cant about duty, which merely means doing what other people want because they want it; or any hideous cant about self-sacrifice, which is merely a survival of savage mutilation. In fact, it does not come to man with any claims upon him at all. It comes naturally and inevitably

out of man. It is the point to which all development tends. It is the differentiation to which all organisms grow. It is the perfection that is inherent in every mode of life, and towards which every mode of life quickens. And so individualism exercises no compulsion over man. On the contrary it says to man that he should suffer no compulsion to be exercised over him. It does not try to force people to be good. It knows that people are good when they are let alone. Man will develop Individualism out of himself. Man is now so developing Individualism. To ask whether Individualism is practical is like asking whether Evolution is practical. Evolution is the law of life, and there is no Evolution except towards Individualism. Where this tendency is not expressed, it is a case of artificially arrested growth, or of disease, or of death. *The Soul of Man* (*OWC*, p32)

1496. I believe most of all in personal liberty for every human soul. Each man ought to do what he likes, to develop as he will. *Oscar Wilde, by Frank Harris* (*CG*, p281)

1497. It is a humiliating confession, but we are all made out of the same stuff. In Falstaff there is something of Hamlet, in Hamlet there is not a little of Falstaff. The fat knight has his moods of melancholy, and the young prince his moments of course humour. Where we differ from eachother is purely in accidentals, tricks of habit and the like. The more one analyses, the more all reasons for analyses disappear. Sooner or later one comes to that dreadful universal thing called human nature. Indeed, as anyone who has ever worked among the poor knows only too well, the brotherhood of man is no mere poet's dream, it is a most depressing and humiliating reality. *The Decay of Lying* (*Works*, pp1075–6)

1498. For out of ourselves we can never pass, nor can there be in creation what in the creator was not. *The Critic as Artist* (*Works*, p1142)

1499. People whose desire is solely for self-realisation never know where they are going. They can't know. In one sense of the word it is, of course, necessary, as the Greek oracle said, to know oneself. That is the first achievement of knowledge. But to recognize that the soul of man is unknowable is the ultimate achievement of Wisdom. The final mystery is oneself. When one has weighed the sun in a balance, and measured the steps of the moon, and mapped out the seven heavens star by star, there still remains oneself. Who can calculate the orbit of his own soul? *De Profundis* (*OWC*, p126)

1500. Still I believe that at the beginning God made a world for each separate man, and in that world which is within us one should seek to live. *Letter to Robert Ross* (*Letters*, p781)

1501. To be good is to be in harmony with one's self.... Discord is to be forced to be in harmony with others. One's own life — that is the important thing. *The Picture of Dorian Gray* (*SC*, p93)

1502. When you have chosen your own part, abide by it, and do not weakly try and reconcile yourself with the world. The heroic cannot be the common nor the common heroic. Congratulate yourself if you have done something strange and extravagant and broken the monotony of a decorous age. *Art and the Handicraftsman lecture* (*Uncollected*, p118)

1503. ... we are never more true to ourselves as when we are inconsistent. *The Critic as Artist* (*Works*, p1142)

1504. One should always be a little improbable. *Phrases and Philosophies for the Use of the Young* (*Works*, p1245)

1505. ... the aim of life is to realise one's own personality — one's *own* nature. *Letter to Georgina Weldon* (*Letters*, p1080)

1506. You have a wonderful personality. Develop it. Be yourself. Don't imagine that your perfection lies in accumulating or possessing external things. Your perfection is inside of you. *The Soul of Man* (*OWC*, p10)

Intelligence and Ignorance

1507. ... he is complex without being interesting. *Letter to Reginald Turner* (*Letters*, p1132)

1508. He had no curiosity. It was his chief defect. *The Picture of Dorian Gray* (*SC*, p224)

1509. There are only two kinds of people who are really fascinating — people who know absolutely everything, and people who know absolutely nothing. *The Picture of Dorian Gray* (*SC*, p100)

1510. They did not understand a single word of what he was saying, but that made no matter, for they put their heads on one side and looked wise, which is quite as good as understanding a thing and very much easier. *The Birthday of the Infanta* (*SC*, p256)

1511. Seriousness is the only refuge of the shallow. *Quoted in Oscar Wilde: His Life and Wit* (*HBP*, p171)

1512. It is only the superficial qualities that last. Man's deeper nature is soon found out. *Phrases and Philosophies for the Use of the Young, The Chameleon* (*Works*, p1245)

1513. Only the shallow know themselves. *Phrases and Philosophies for the Use of the Young, The Chameleon* (*Works*, p1244)

1514. The supreme vice is shallowness. Whatever is realised is right. *De Profundis* (*OWC*, p72)

1515. I am but too conscious of the fact that we are born in an age when only the dull are treated seriously, and I live in terror of not being misunderstood. *The Critic as Artist* (*Works*, p1114)

1516. Dullness is the coming of age of seriousness. *Phrases and Philosophies for the Use of the Young, The Chameleon* (*Works*, p1244)

1517. Who are the people the world takes seriously? All the dull people one can think of, from the Bishops down to the bores. *Lady Windermere's Fan* (*Plays*, p6)

1518. I confess not to be a worshipper at the Temple of Reason. *Letter to William Ward* (*Letters*, p25)

1519. Dullness is always an irresistible temptation for brilliancy, and stupidity is the permanent Bestia Trionfans that calls wisdom from its cave. *The Critic as Artist* (*Works*, p1125)

1520. Although, in this dull stupid age of
ours,
The most eccentric thing a man can do
Is to have brains, then the mob mocks at
him....
The Duchess of Padua (*Works*, p614)

1521. Whenever a man does a thoroughly stupid thing, it is always from the noblest motives. *The Picture of Dorian Gray* (*SC*, p18)

1522. ... in the soul of one who is ignorant there is always room for a great idea. *De Profundis* (*OWC*, p122)

1523. Dorian is far too wise not to do foolish things now and then, my dear Basil. *The Picture of Dorian Gray* (*SC*, p88)

1524. The method by which the fool arrives at his folly was as dear to him as the ultimate wisdom of the wise. *The Critic as Artist* (*Works*, p1111)

1525. Remember that the fool in the eyes of the gods and the fool in the eyes of man are very different. *De Profundis* (*OWC*, p39)

1526. But it really takes a saint to suffer such fools gladly. *Oscar Wilde, by Frank Harris* (*CG*, p105)

1527. ... even dogmatism is no excuse for ignorance. *Great Writers by Little Men, Pall Mall Gazette* (*Uncollected*, p93)

1528. The real fool, such as the gods mock or mar, is he who does not know himself. *De Profundis* (*OWC*, p39)

1529. Of what use is it to a man to travel sixty miles an hour? Is he any the better for it? Why, a fool can buy a railway ticket and travel sixty miles an hour. Is he any less a fool? *Oscar Wilde Discovers America* (*HBC*, p186)

1530. ... as seriousness of manner is the disguise of the fool, folly in its exquisite modes of triviality and indifference and lack of care is the robe of the wise man. In so vulgar an age as this we all need masks. *Letter to Philip Houghton* (*Letters*, p586)

1531. JACK: I am sick to death of cleverness. Everybody is clever now-a-days. You can't go anywhere without meeting clever people. The thing has become an absolute public nuisance. I wish to goodness we had a few fools left.

ALGERNON: We have.

JACK: I should extremely like to meet them. What do they talk about?

ALGERNON: The fools? Oh! About the clever people, of course.

JACK: What fools! *The Importance of Being Earnest* (*Plays*, pp370–1)

1532. I think you are wrong, Basil, but I won't argue with you. It is only the intellectually lost who ever argue. *The Picture of Dorian Gray* (*SC*, p29)

1533. Ordinary cruelty is simply stupidity. It is the entire want of imagination. *Letters to the Editor of The Daily Chronicle* (*Letters*, p848)

1534. There is no sin except stupidity. *The Critic as Artist* (*Works*, p1153)

1535. Nothing pains me except stupidity and morality. *Telegram to Ada Leverson* (*Letters*, p130)

1536. Vulgarity and stupidity are two very vivid facts of modern life. One regrets them, naturally. But there they are. They are subjects for study like everything else. *The Soul of Man* (*OWC*, p21)

1537. I do not approve of anything that tampers with natural ignorance. Ignorance is like a delicate exotic fruit: touch it and the bloom is gone. *The Importance of Being Earnest* (*Plays*, pp365–6)

1538. She thought that, because he was stupid, he would be kindly, when, of course, kindliness requires imagination and intellect. *Quoted in Oscar Wilde: His Life and Wit* (*HBP*, p155)

1539. SIR ROBERT CHILTERN: ... he was a man of a most subtle and refined intellect. A man of culture, charm, and distinction. One of the most intellectual men I ever met.

LORD GORING: Ah! I prefer a gentlemanly fool any day. There is more to be said for stupidity than people imagine. Personally I have a great admiration for stupidity. It is a sort of fellow-feeling, I suppose. *An Ideal Husband* (*Plays*, p261)

1540. ... there is always more brass than brains in an aristocracy. *Vera, or the Nihilists* (*Works*, p709)

1541. The security of society lies in custom and unconscious instinct, and the basis of the stability of society, as a healthy organism, is the complete absence of any intelligence among its members. *The Critic as Artist* (*Works*, p1141)

1542. The well-bred contradict other people. The wise contradict themselves. *Phrases and Philosophies for the Use of the Young, The Chameleon* (*Works*, p1244)

1543. Lord Henry had the charm of being very dangerous. But that was all. He was too clever and too cynical to be really fond of. *The Picture of Dorian Gray* (*SC*, p130)

1544. In the wild struggle for existence, we want to have something that endures, and so we fill our minds with rubbish and facts, in the silly hope of keeping our place. The thoroughly well-informed man — that is the modern ideal. And the mind of the thoroughly well-informed man is a dreadful thing. It is like a bric-a-brac shop, all monsters and dust, with everything priced above its proper value. *The Picture of Dorian Gray* (*SC*, p29)

1545. We live in an age that reads too much to be wise, and thinks too much to be beautiful. *The Picture of Dorian Gray* (*SC*, p118) and similar quotation in *London Models English Illustrated Magazine* (*Uncollected*, p34)

1546. Intellectually, we must admit, he was not of much importance. He never said a brilliant or even an ill-natured thing in his life.

But then he was wonderfully good-looking, with his crisp, brown hair, his clear-cut profile, and his grey eyes. *A Model Millionaire* (*Works*, p209)

1547. However, I think anything is better then high intellectual pressure. That is the most unbecoming thing there is. It makes the noses of the young girls so particularly large. And there is nothing so difficult to marry as a large nose, men don't like them. *An Ideal Husband* (*Plays*, p248)

1548. I like looking at geniuses and listening to beautiful people. *An Ideal Husband* (*Plays*, p237)

1549. I know so many men in London whose only talent is for washing. I suppose that is why men of genius so seldom wash; they are afraid of being mistaken for men of talent only! *Quoted in Oscar Wilde: His Life and Wit* (*HBP*, p175)

1550. ACQUAINTANCE: Genius is born, not made.

OSCAR WILDE: Not "paid," my dear fellow, not "paid." *Oscar Wilde, by Frank Harris* (*CG*, p242)

1551. He was not clever enough to have enemies. Of course, he had a wonderful genius for painting. But a man can paint like Velasquez and yet be as dull as possible. *The Picture of Dorian Gray* (*SC*, p224)

1552. He had that dislike of being stared at, which comes on geniuses late in life and never leaves the commonplace. *The Picture of Dorian Gray* (*SC*, p81)

1553. ... there are times when wisdom becomes a burden and knowledge is one with sorrow: for as every body has its shadow so every soul has its scepticism. *The English Renaissance of Art lecture* (*Uncollected*, pp23–4)

1554. ... while knowledge is power, suffering is part of knowledge. *English Poetesses* (*Uncollected*, p62)

1555. Don't talk to me, Frank, about the hardships of the poor. The hardships of the poor are necessities, but talk to me of the hardships of men of genius, and I could weep tears of blood. *Oscar Wilde, by Frank Harris* (*CG*, p57)

1556. Frank [Harris] insists on my always being at high intellectual pressure; it is most exhausting; but when we arrive at Napoule I am going to break the news to him — now an open secret — that I have softening of the brain, and cannot always be a genius. *Letter to Robert Ross* (*Letters*, p1110)

1557. I don't think I am equal to the intellectual architectures of thought: I have moods and moments; and Love, or Passion with the mask of Love, is my only consolation. *Letter to Robert Ross* (*Letters*, p1105)

1558. The demand of the intellect is merely to feel itself alive; that nothing which has ever interested men or women can cease to be a fit subject for culture. *The English Renaissance of Art lecture* (*Uncollected*, p20)

1559. I can stand brute force, but brute reason is quite unbearable. There is something unfair about its use. It is hitting below the intellect. *Quoted in Oscar Wilde: His Life and Wit* (*HBP*, p67)

1560. The contest between Athena and Ares was that eternal contest between rational thought and the brute force of ignorance... . *The Rise of Historical Criticism* (*Works*, p1200)

1561. EDWARD CARSON: What was the age of Mr. Shelley?

OSCAR WILDE: I should think about twenty. I first met him in October when arranging for the publication of my books. I asked him to dine with me at the Albemarle Hotel.

EDWARD CARSON: Was that for the purpose of having an intellectual treat?

OSCAR WILDE: Well, for him, yes. *The Three Trials of Oscar Wilde* (*UB*, p137)

1562. I know no one who has a more intellectual influence than yourself: to be ranked amongst your friends is, for anyone, a liberal education. *Letter to Oscar Browning* (*Letters*, p360)

1563. Anything is good that stimulates thought in whatever age. *The Three Trials of Oscar Wilde* (*UB*, p123)

1564. An idea that is not dangerous is unworthy of being called an idea at all. *The Critic as Artist* (*Works*, p1141)

1565. All great ideas *are* dangerous. *De Profundis* (*OWC*, p124)

1566. All thought is immoral. Its very essence is destruction. If you think of anything, you kill it. Nothing survives being thought of. *A Woman of No Importance* (*Plays*, p187)

1567. Nothing refines but the intellect. *A Woman of No Importance* (*Plays*, p181)

1568. ... Thought is degraded by its constant association with practice. *The Critic as Artist* (*Works*, p1139)

1569. From the high tower of Thought we can look out at the world. Calm, and self-centered, and complete, the aesthetic critic contemplates life, and no arrow drawn at a venture can pierce between the joints of his harness. He at least is safe. He has discovered how to live. *The Critic as Artist* (*Works*, p1139)

1570. It has been said that the great events of the world take place in the brain. It is in the brain, and the brain only, that the great sins of the world take place also. *The Picture of Dorian Gray* (*SC*, p35)

1571. But strange that I was not told
That the brain can hold
In a tiny ivory cell,
God's heaven and hell.
Roses and Rue (*Works*, p838)

1572. Of course I need not remind *you* how fluid a thing thought is with me — with us all. *Letter to Robert Ross* (*Letters*, p781)

1573. How thoughtful of him! To expect the unexpected shows a thoroughly modern intellect. *An Ideal Husband* (*Plays*, p299)

1574. You know more than you think you know, just as you know less than you want to know. *The Picture of Dorian Gray* (*SC*, p38)

1575. Nowadays to be intelligible is to be found out. *Lady Windermere's Fan* (*Plays*, p12)

1576. Knowledge would be fatal. It is the uncertainty that charms one. A mist makes things wonderful. *The Picture of Dorian Gray* (*SC*, p217)

1577. Let us go down to Covent Garden and look at the roses. Come! I am tired of thought. *The Critic as Artist*, (*Works*, p1155)

Journalism

1578. Journalism is a terrible cave where the divine become tainted —for a moment only. *Letter to Richard Le Gallienne* (*Letters,* p552)

1579. They talk about yellow fever but I think that one who has survived the newspapers is impregnable. *Letter to Mrs. George Lewis* (*Letters,* p173)

1580. Journalism is unreadable and literature is not read. *The Critic as Artist* (*Works,* p1114)

1581. What is behind the leading article but prejudice, stupidity, cant and twaddle? *The Soul of Man* (*OWC,* p23)

1582. In the old days men had the rack. Now they have the press. *The Soul of Man* (*OWC,* p23)

1583. Instead of monopolising the seat of judgment, journalism should be apologising in the dock. *Quoted in Oscar Wilde: His Life and Wit* (*HBP,* p152)

1584. In centuries before ours the public nailed the ears of journalists to the pump. That was quite hideous. In this century journalists have nailed their own ears to the keyhole. That is much worse. *The Soul of Man* (*OWC,* p24)

1585. VICOMTE DE NANJAC: I read all your English newspapers. I find them so amusing.

LORD GORING: Then, my dear Nanjac, you must certainly read between the lines. *An Ideal Husband* (*Plays,* p234)

1586. In England, Journalism, not, except in a few well-known instances, having been carried to such excesses of brutality, is still a great factor, a really remarkable power.... *The Soul of Man* (*OWC,* pp23–4)

1587. In France, in fact, they limit the journalist, and allow the artist almost perfect freedom. Here we allow absolute freedom to the journalist, and entirely limit the artist. *The Soul of Man* (*OWC,* p24)

1588. English public opinion ... tries to constrain and impede and warp the man who makes things that are beautiful in effect, and compels the journalist to retail things that are ugly, or disgusting, or revolting in fact, so that we have the most serious journalists in the world, and the most indecent newspapers. *The Soul of Man* (*OWC,* pp24–5)

1589. ... journalists in England are never gentlemen and nobody, consequently, expects them to act as such, or to possess any sense of honour. *Oscar Wilde: The Story of an Unhappy Friendship* (*GC,* p224)

1590. Bad manners make a journalist. *Oscar Wilde Discovers America* (*HBC,* p32)

1591. And it is only fair to state, with regard to modern journalists, that they always apologize to one in private for what they have written against one in public. *The Soul of Man* (*OWC,* p21)

1592. A reporter called me from Washington and wanted to get details of my private life. I told him I wished I had one. *Oscar Wilde Discovers America* (*HBC,* p205)

1593. Oh! Spies are of no use nowadays. Their profession is over. The newspapers do their work instead. *An Ideal Husband* (*Plays,* p303)

1594. ... at present the newspapers are trying hard to induce the public to judge a sculptor, for instance, never by his statues but by the way he treats his wife; a painter by the amount of his income and a poet by the colour of his necktie. *Art and the Handicraftsman lecture* (*Uncollected,* p116)

1595. The journalist is always reminding the public of the existence of the artist. That is unnecessary of him. He is always reminding the artist of the existence of the public. That is indecent of him. *Interview in The Sketch* (*Uncollected*, p. xxi)

1596. As for modern newspapers with their dreary records of politics, police-courts, and personalities, I have long ago ceased to care what they write about me — my time being all given up to the gods and the Greeks. *Letter to an Unidentified Correspondent* (*Letters*, p115)

1597. EDWARD CARSON: Did you ever hear that he was employed as a newspaper boy?

OSCAR WILDE: No, I never heard that he was connected with literature in any form. *The Three Trials of Oscar Wilde* (*UB*, p160)

1598. There should be a law that no ordinary newspaper should be allowed to write about art. The harm they do by their foolish and random writing it would be impossible to overestimate.... *Art and the Handicraftsman lecture* (*Uncollected*, p116)

1599. The fact is that the public have an insatiable curiosity to know everything, except what is worth knowing. Journalism, conscious of this, and having tradesmanlike habits, supplies their demands. *The Soul of Man* (*OWC*, 24)

1600. ... there is much to be said in favour of modern journalism. By giving us the opinions of the uneducated, it keeps us in touch with the ignorance of the community. By carefully chronicling the current events of contemporary life, it shows us of what very little importance such events really are. *The Critic as Artist* (*Works*, p1145)

1601. Newspapers even have degenerated, they may now be absolutely relied upon. One feels it as one wades through their columns. It is always the unreadable that occurs. *The Decay of Lying* (*Works*, p1072)

1602. LADY HUNSTANTON: But do you believe all that is written in the newspapers?

LORD ILLINGWORTH: I do. Nowadays it is only the unreadable that occurs. *A Woman of No Importance* (*Plays*, p139)

1603. The newspapers chronicle with increasing avidity the sins of the second-rate, and with the conscientiousness of the illiterate give us the accurate and prosaic details of the doings of people of absolutely no interest

whatever. *Quoted in Oscar Wilde: His Life and Wit* (*HBC*, p152)

1604. There are possibly some journalists who take a real pleasure in publishing horrible things, or who, being poor, look to scandals as forming a sort of permanent basis for an income. But there are other journalists, I feel certain, men of cultivation, who really dislike publishing these things, who know that it is wrong to do so, and only do it because the unhealthy conditions under which their occupation is carried on oblige them to supply the public with what the public wants, and to compete with other journalists in making that supply as full and satisfying to the gross popular appetite as possible. It is a very degrading position for any body of educated men to be placed in, and I have no doubt that most of them feel it acutely. *The Soul of Man* (*OWC*, p25)

1605. As for modern journalism, it is not my business to defend it. It justifies its own existence by the great Darwinian principle of the survival of the vulgarist. I have merely to do with literature. *The Critic as Artist* (*Works*, p1114)

1606. The poor reviewers are apparently reduced to be the reporters of the police-court of literature, the chroniclers of the doing of the habitual criminals of art. It is sometimes said of them that they do not read all through the works they are called upon to criticise. They do not. Or at least they should not. If they did so, they would become confirmed misanthropes.... *The Critic as Artist* (*Works*, p1120)

1607. To disagree on all points with the modern newspaper is one of the chief indications of sanity. *Oscar Wilde Discovers America* (*HBC*, p208)

1608. I have been influenced by all the books I have read, and by none of the newspapers. *Letter to an Unidentified Correspondent* (*Letters*, p480)

1609. It was a fatal day when the public discovered that the pen is mightier than the paving-stone, and can be made as offensive as the brickbat. They at once sought for the journalist, found him, developed him, and made him their industrious well-paid servant. It is greatly to be regretted, for both their sakes. *The Soul of Man (OWC,* p23)

1610. In America the President reigns for four years, and Journalism governs for ever and ever. *The Soul of Man (OWC, 23)*

1611. ... to fight with the common interviewer is to fight with the dead. *Letter to Robert Ross (Letters,* p877)

1612. If a journalist is run over by a four-wheeler in the Strand, an incident I regret to say I have never witnessed, it suggests nothing to me from a dramatic point of view. Perhaps I am wrong; but the artist must have his limitations. *Quoted in Oscar Wilde: His Life and Wit (HBC,* p226)

1613. OSCAR WILDE: I am sure that you must have a great future in literature before you.

GILBERT BURGESS: What makes you think so?

OSCAR WILDE: Because you seem to be such a very bad interviewer. I feel sure that you must write poetry. I certainly like the colour of your necktie very much. Goodbye. *Interview in The Sketch (Uncollected,* pp. xxi–xxii) and (*Letters,* pp790–1)

Labor and Leisure

1614. I am hard at work being idle; late midnights and famishing morrows follow one another. *Oscar Wilde: The Story of an Unhappy Friendship* (*GC*, p83)

1615. I never put off till to-morrow what I can possibly do ... the day after. *Quoted in Oscar Wilde: His Life and Wit* (*HBP*, p173)

1616. When are you coming down? I am lazy and languid, doing no work. I need stirring up. *Letter to Robert Ross* (*Letters*, p542)

1617. There is something tragic about the enormous number of young men there are in England at the present moment who start life with perfect profiles, and end by adopting some useful profession. *Phrases and Philosophies for the Use of the Young, The Chameleon* (*Works*, p1245)

1618. Cultivated idleness seems to me to be the proper occupation for man. *Letter to the Editor of the Scots Observer* (*Letters*, p447)

1619. The condition of perfection is idleness; the aim of perfection is youth. *Phrases and Philosophies for the Use of the Young, The Chameleon* (*Works*, p1245)

1620. In my young days, one never met anyone in society who worked for their living. It was not considered the thing. *A Woman of No Importance* (*Plays*, p128)

1621. LADY BRACKNELL: Do you smoke?

JACK: Well, yes, I must admit I smoke.

LADY BRACKNELL: I am glad to hear it. A man should always have an occupation of some kind. There are far too many idle men in London as it is. *The Importance of Being Earnest* (*Plays*, p365)

1622. MABEL CHILTERN: Why do you call Lord Goring good-for-nothing?

LORD CAVERSHAM: Because he leads such an idle life.

MABEL CHILTERN: How can you say such a thing? Why, he rides in the Row at ten o'clock in the morning, goes to the opera three times a week, changes his clothes at least five times a day, and dines out every night of the season. You don't call that leading an idle life, do you? *An Ideal Husband* (*Plays*, p223)

1623. Nobody else's work gives me any suggestion. It is only by entire isolation from everything that one can do any work. Idleness gives one the mood in which to write, isolation the conditions. Concentration on oneself recalls the new and wonderful world that one presents in the colour and cadence of words in movement. *Interview in The Sketch* (*Uncollected*, p. xx)

1624. Work is man's great prerogative and the real essence of art; it is only the loafer and the idle saunterer who is as useless and uninteresting to the artist as he is to himself. *The Decorative Arts lecture* (*Works*, p932)

1625. Nothing is more picturesque and graceful than a man at work. *House Decoration lecture* (*Uncollected*, p188)

1626. I have never watched a man do anything useful who has not been graceful at some moment of his labour: it is only the loafer and the idle saunterer who is as useless and uninteresting to the artist as he is to himself. *Art and the Handicraftsman lecture* (*Uncollected*, p112)

1627. The best people of all classes should be given to the pursuits of artistic industry, and everyone should be taught to use his hands; the human hand is the most beautiful and delicate piece of mechanism in the world, although many people seem to have no other use for their hands than to squeeze them into gloves that are far too small for them. *The Decorative Arts lecture* (*Works*, p936)

1628. It is to do nothing that the elect exist. *The Critic as Artist* (*Works*, p1136)

1629. Let me say to you now that to do nothing is the most difficult thing in the world, the most difficult and the most intellectual. *The Critic as Artist* (*Works*, p1136)

1630. 'Tis a great advantage, I admit, to have done nothing, but one must not abuse even that advantage. *Oscar Wilde Discovers America* (*HBC*, p159)

1631. I consider no one too good to do his own work. *Quoted in Oscar Wilde: His Life and Wit* (*HBP*, p287)

1632. ... work is the curse of the drinking classes of this country. *Oscar Wilde: by Frank Harris* (*CG*, p98)

1633. It is a curious fact that the worst work is done with the best intentions, and that people are never so trivial as when they take themselves very seriously. *Quoted in Oscar Wilde: His Life and Wit* (*HBP*, p110)

1634. ... business-worries are the worst enemies of sanity. *Letter to More Adey* (*Letters*, p804)

1635. Each of the professions means a prejudice. The necessity for a career forces everyone to take sides. We live in an age of the overworked, and the undereducated; the age in which people are so industrious that they become absolutely stupid. And, harsh though it may sound, I cannot help saying that such people deserve their doom. The sure way of knowing nothing about life is to try to make oneself useful. *The Critic as Artist* (*Works*, p1139)

1636. Basil, my dear boy, puts everything that is charming in him into his work. The consequence is that he has nothing left for life but his prejudices, his principle, and his common sense. *The Picture of Dorian Gray* (*SC*, p72)

1637. Men of thought should have nothing to do with action. *Vera, or the Nihilists* (*Works*, p716)

1638. I never quarrel with actions. My one quarrel is with words. *The Picture of Dorian Gray* (*SC*, p206)

1639. We have been deluded by the name of action: to think is to act. *Quoted in Oscar Wilde: His Life and Wit* (*HBP*, p124)

1640. We might make ourselves spiritual by detaching ourselves from action, and become perfect by the rejection of energy. *The Critic as Artist* (*Works*, p1139)

1641. Action is limited and relative. Unlimited and absolute is the vision of him who sits at ease and watches, who walks in loneliness and dreams. *The Critic as Artist* (*Works*, p1136)

1642. There are two kinds of men in the world, two great creeds, two different forms of natures: men to whom the end of life is action, and men to whom the end of life is thought. *The English Renaissance of Art lecture* (*Uncollected*, p25)

1643. ... people who live in the world of action don't understand that there is another world in which they who are not free live: a world in which nothing happens but emotions, and in which consequently emotions have a power, a proportion, a permanence that is beyond the possibility of description. *Letter to More Adey* (*Letters*, p680)

1644. ... don't talk about action. It is a blind thing dependent on external influences, and moved by an impulse of whose nature it is unconscious. It is a thing incomplete in its essence, because limited by accident, and ignorant of its direction, being always at variance with its aim. Its basis is the lack of imagination. It is the last resource of those who do not know how to dream. *The Critic as Artist* (*Works*, p1121)

1645. When we have fully discovered the scientific laws which govern life, we shall realise that the one person who has more illusions than the dreamer is the man of action. He, indeed, knows neither the origin of his deeds nor their results. *The Critic as Artist* (*Works*, p1121)

1646. Action! What is action? It dies at the moment of its energy. It is a base concession to fact. The world is made by the singer for the dreamer. *Quoted in Oscar Wilde: His Life and Wit* (*HBP*, p124)

1647. Action, indeed, is always easy, and when presented to us in its most aggravated, because most continuous form, which I take to be that of real industry, becomes simply the refuge of people who have nothing whatever to do. *The Critic as Artist* (*Works*, p1121)

1648. Exercise! Good God! No gentleman ever takes exercise. You don't seem to understand what a gentleman is. *The Importance of Being Earnest* (*Plays*, p438)

1649. I am afraid I play no outdoor games at all, except dominoes.... I have sometimes played dominoes outside French cafes. *Quoted in Oscar Wilde: His Life and Wit* (*HBP*, p147)

1650. Football is all very well as a game for rough girls, but it is hardly suitable for delicate boys. *Quoted in Oscar Wilde: His Life and Wit* (*HBP*, p147)

1651. ... the attitudes assumed [in Cricket] were so indecent. *Oscar Wilde Discovers America* (*HBC*, p8)

1652. ... but he was very languid in his manner, and not a little vain of his good looks, and had a strong objection to football, which he used to say was a game only suitable for the sons of the middle classes. *The Portrait of Mr. W.H.* (*Works*, p304)

1653. Dear Mrs. Smithers, Thank you so much for your charming card: I wish I could come to your party, but I am a wretched walker and would probably not arrive till midsummer. *Letter to Mrs. Leonard Smithers* (*Letters*, p1114)

1654. OSCAR WILDE: At Portura nine out of ten boys only thought of football or cricket or rowing. Nearly every one went in for athletics—running and jumping and so forth; no one appeared to care for sex. We were healthy young barbarians and that was all.

FRANK HARRIS: Did you go in for games?

OSCAR WILDE (smiling): No, I never liked to kick or be kicked. *Oscar Wilde, by Frank Harris* (*CG*, p18)

1655. Industry is the root of all ugliness. *Phrases and Philosophies for the Use of the Young, The Chameleon* (*Works*, p1245)

1656. I have no sympathy myself with industry of any kind, least of all with such industries as you seem to recommend. Indeed, I have always been of the opinion that hard work is simply the refuge of people who have nothing whatever to do. *The Remarkable Rocket* (*Works*, p300)

1657. ... if our days are barren without industry, industry without art is barbarism. *The English Renaissance of Art lecture* (*Uncollected*, p26)

1658. ... . when a child grows up he learns that industrious we must be, but industry without art is simply barbarism. *The House Beautiful lecture* (*Works*, p925)

1659. The best people of all classes should be given to the pursuits of artistic industry, and everyone should be taught to use his hands; the human hand is the most beautiful and delicate piece of mechanism in the world, although many people seem to have no other use for their hands than to squeeze them into gloves that are far too small for them. *The Decorative Arts lecture* (*Works*, 936)

1660. I have nothing to do with commerce and what is called progress. I am a student of art. I see that in the rush and crash of business the native and characteristic picturesqueness of people is being rapidly destroyed, and I desire to do what I can to rescue from oblivion the truly artistic peculiarities that still survive. *Oscar Wilde Discovers America* (*HBC*, p362)

1661. For producing your best work also you will require some leisure and freedom from sordid care. *Letter to an Unidentified Correspondent* (*Letters*, p265)

1662. The extreme beauty of Italy may ruin you, as I think it has done me, for hard work again.... *Letter to William Ward* (*Letters*, p36)

1663. I assure you that there are moments when art almost attains to the dignity of manual labour. *The Model Millionaire* (*Works*, p210)

1664. All unintellectual labour, all monotonous, dull labour, all labour that deals with dreadful things, and involves unpleasant conditions, must be done by machinery. *The Soul of Man* (*OWC*, p15)

1665. I cannot help saying that a great deal of nonsense is being written and talked nowadays about the dignity of manual labour. There is nothing necessarily dignified about manual labour at all, and most of it is absolutely degrading. It is mentally and morally injurious to a man to do anything in which he does not find pleasure, and many forms of labour are pleasureless activities, and should be regarded as such. To sweep a slushy crossing for eight hours on a day when the east wind is blowing is a disgusting occupation. To sweep it with mental, moral, or physical dignity seems to me to be impossible. To sweep it with joy would be appalling. Man is made for something better than disturbing dirt. All work of that kind should be done by a machine. *The Soul of Man* (*OWC*, p15)

1666. ... in a free country one cannot live without a slave.... *Letter to Norman Forbes-Robertson* (*Letters*, p127)

1667. ... at the close of the war the slaves found themselves free, found themselves indeed so absolutely free that they were free to starve. *The Soul of Man* (*OWC*, p5)

1668. The fact is, that civilisation requires slaves. The Greeks were quite right there. Unless there are slaves to do the ugly, horrible, uninteresting work, culture and contemplation become almost impossible. Human slavery is wrong, insecure, and demoralising. On mechanical slavery, on the slavery of the machine, the future of the world depends. *The Soul of Man* (*OWC*, p16)

1669. Just as the worst slave owners were those who were kind to their slaves, and so prevented the horror of the system being realized by those who suffered from it, and understood by those who contemplated it, so, in the present state of things in England, the people who do the most harm are the people who try to do the most good. *The Soul of Man* (*OWC*, p2)

1670. Every man must be left quite free to choose his own work. No form of compulsion must be exercised over him. If there is, his work will not be good for him, will not be good in itself, and will not be good for others. *The Soul of Man* (*OWC*, p6)

1671. Oh, duty is what one expects from others, it is not what one does oneself. *A Woman of No Importance* (*Plays*, p172)

1672. ... every action has its consequence. *Letter to Carlos Blacker* (*Letters*, p947)

38

Life and Living

1673. To live is the rarest thing in the world. Most people exist, that is all. *The Soul of Man* (*OWC*, p8)

1674. Nothing should be out of the reach of hope. Life is a hope. *A Woman of No Importance* (*Plays*, p130)

1675. Life is not complex. We are complex. Life is simple, and the simple thing is the right thing. *Letter to Robert Ross* (*Letters*, p783)

1676. Complex people waste half their strength in trying to conceal what they do. Is it any wonder they should always come to grief? *Letter to Robert Ross* (*Letters*, p788)

1677. There is no secret of life. Life's aim, if it has one, is simply to be always looking for temptations. There are not nearly enough. I sometimes pass a whole day without coming across a single one. It is quite dreadful. It makes one so nervous about the future. *A Woman of No Importance* (*Plays*, p187)

1678. Live without desire would not be worth living to me. *Oscar Wilde, by Frank Harris* (*CG*, p300)

1679. ... what man has sought for is, indeed, neither pain nor pleasure, but simply Life. *The Soul of Man* (*OWC*, p36)

1680. Ah! you had no motives in life. You had appetites merely. A motive is an intellectual aim. *De Profundis* (*OWC*, p39)

1681. And if Life be, as it surely is, a problem to me, I am no less a problem to Life. *De Profundis* (*OWC*, p102)

1682. Never had life seemed lovelier to him; never had the things of evil seemed more remote. *Lord Arthur Savile's Crime* (*SC*, p279)

1683. Everything is dangerous, my dear fellow. If it wasn't so, life wouldn't be worth living. *An Ideal Husband* (*Plays*, p259)

1684. I am leading a very good life, and it does not agree with me. *Letter to Leonard Smithers* (*Letters*, p1117)

1685. Experience is a question about instinct about life.... *Quoted in Oscar Wilde: His Life and Wit* (*HBP*, p176)

1686. ... no theory of life seemed to him to be of any importance compared with life itself. *The Picture of Dorian Gray* (*SC*, p147)

1687. ... I think life is far too important a thing ever to talk seriously about it. *Lady Windermere's Fan* (*Plays*, p11) and Vera, or the Nihilists (*Works*, p698)

1688. That we should treat all the trivial things of life seriously, and all the serious things of life with sincere and studied triviality. *Quoted in Oscar Wilde: His Life and Wit* (*HBP*, p226)

1689. ... public and private life are different things. They have different laws, and move on different lines. *An Ideal Husband* (*Plays*, p253)

1690. How strange it is, the most real parts of one's life always seem to be a dream! *Vera, or the Nihilists* (*Works*, p717)

1691. For most of us the real life is the life we do not lead, and thus, remaining more true to the essence of its own perfection, more jealous of its own unattainable beauty, is less likely to forget form in feeling or to accept the passion of creation as any substitute for the beauty of the created thing. *The English Renaissance of Art lecture* (*Uncollected*, pp12–3) and similar quotation in L'Envoi (*Uncollected*, p202)

1692. We can have in life but one great experience at best, and the secret of life is to reproduce that experience as often as possible. *The Picture of Dorian Gray* (*SC*, p208)

1693. One can live for years sometimes without living at all, and then all life comes crowding into one single hour. *Vera, or the Nihilists* (*Works*, p717)

1694. Life is simply a *mauvais quart d'heure* made up of exquisite moments. *A Woman of No Importance* (*Plays*, p153)

1695. ... teach man to concentrate himself upon the moments of a life that is itself but a moment. *The Picture of Dorian Gray* (*SC*, p145)

1696. To stake all one's life on a single moment, to risk everything on one throw, whether the stake be power or pleasure, I care not — there is no weakness in that. There is a horrible, terrible courage. I had that courage. *An Ideal Husband* (*Plays*, p263)

1697. In that wild throb when all existences

Seemed narrowed to one single ecstasy.
     Charmides (*Works*, p813)

1698. We have lived our lives in a land of dreams!

How sad it seems.
     Her Voice (*Works*, p842)

1699. Life has at last become as real to me as a dream. *Letter to an Unidentified Correspondent* (*Letters*, p644)

1700. Life is not governed by will or intention. Life is a question of nerves, and fibres, and slowly built-up cells in which thought hides itself and passion has its dreams. *The Picture of Dorian Gray* (*SC*, p228)

1701. In point of fact the natural life is the unconscious life. *Letter to Robert Ross* (*Letters*, pp789–90)

1702. The art of living. The only really Fine Art we have produced in modern times. *An Ideal Husband* (*Plays*, p284)

1703. ... life itself was the first, the greatest, of all the arts, and for it all the other arts seemed to be but a preparation. *The Picture of Dorian Gray* (*SC*, p143)

1704. Life itself is an art, and has its modes of style no less than the arts that seek to express it. *Pen, Pencil and Poison* (*Works*, p1095)

1705. Later on in life, humour goes, but laughter is the primaeval attitude towards life — a mode of approach that survives only in artists and criminals! *Letter to Robert Ross* (*Letters*, p1106)

1706. ... it is not easy to recapture the artistic mood of detachment from the accidents of life. *Letter to Robert Ross* (*Letters*, p1242)

1707. Life holds the mirror up to Art, and either reproduces some strange type imagined by painter or sculptor, or realises in fact what has been dreamed in fiction. Scientifically speaking, the basis of life — the energy of life, as Aristotle would call it — is simply the desire for expression, and Art is always presenting various forms through which the expression can be attained. *The Decay of Lying* (*Works*, p1085)

1708. ... the spectacle of life contains its own secret. *Balzac in English* (*Uncollected*, p163)

1709. ... he looks on life rather as a picture to be painted than as a problem to be solved. *Olivia at the Lyceum Dramatic Review* (*Works*, p955)

1710. To become the spectator of one's own life ... is to escape the suffering of life. *The Picture of Dorian Gray* (*SC*, p125)

1711. Dorian Gray, having led a life of mere sensation and pleasure, tries to kill conscience, and at that moment kills himself. Lord Henry Wotten seeks to be a mere spectator of life. He finds that those who reject battle are more deeply wounded than those who take part in it. *Letter to the Editor of The St. James Gazette* (*Letters*, p428)

1712. ... life is terribly deficient in form. Its catastrophes happen in the wrong way and to he wrong people. There is a grotesque horror about its comedies, and its tragedies seem to culminate in farce. One is always wounded when one approaches it. Things last either too long or not long enough. *The Critic as Artist* (*Works*, p1132)

1713. There is at least this beautiful mystery in life, that at the moment it feels most complete it finds some secret sacred niche in its shrine empty and waiting.... Then comes a time of exquisite expectancy. *Letter to H.C. Marillier* (*Letters*, p282)

1714. The great events of life often leave one unmoved; they pass out of consciousness, and, when one thinks of them, become unreal. Even the scarlet flowers of passion seam to grow in the same meadow as the poppies of oblivion. We regret the burden of their memory, and have anodynes against them. But the little things, the things of no moment, remain with us. In some tiny ivory cell the brain stores the most delicate, and the most fleeting impressions. *The Portrait of Mr. W.H. (Works,* p313)

1715. For he who lives more lives than one
More deaths than one must die.
The Ballad of Reading Gaol (OWC, p181)

1716. In life there is really no small or great thing. All things are of equal value and of equal size. *De Profundis (OWC,* p46)

1717. The great things of life are what they seem to be, and for that reason, strange as it may sound to you, are often difficult to interpret. But the little things of life are symbols. We receive our bitter lessons most easily through them. *De Profundis (OWC,* p79)

1718. The girl never really lived, and so she has never really died ... the moment she touched actual life, she marred it, and it marred her, and so she passed away. *The Picture of Dorian Gray (SC,* p118)

1719. What a pity that in life we only get our lessons when they are of no use to us! *Lady Windermere's Fan (Plays,* p66)

1720. ..."too late now" are in art and life the most tragical words. *Letter to Mary Anderson (Letters,* p202)

1721. I was deeply affected — with a sense, also, of the uselessness of all regrets. Nothing could have been otherwise, and Life is a very terrible thing. *Letter to Robert Ross (Letters,* p1128)

1722. It's an old story, I'm afraid, the story of man's cruelty to man. *Oscar Wilde, by Frank Harris (CG,* p197)

1723. For the secret of life is suffering. It is what is hidden behind everything. *De Profundis (OWC,* p106)

1724. Ah, my dear, don't tell me that you have exhausted life. When a man says that one knows that life has exhausted him. *The Picture of Dorian Gray (SC,* p191)

1725. As for a spoiled life, no life is spoiled but one whose growth is arrested. *The Picture of Dorian Gray (SC,* p90)

1726. Now-a-days people seem to look on life as a speculation. It is not a speculation. It is a sacrament. Its ideal is Love. Its purification is sacrifice. *Lady Windermere's Fan (Plays,* p7)

1727. All this self-sacrifice is wrong, we are meant to live. That is the meaning of life. *Letter to George Alexander (Letters,* p600)

1728. Live! Live the wonderful life that is in you! Let nothing be lost upon you. Be always searching for new sensations. Be afraid of nothing... *The Picture of Dorian Gray (SC,* p39)

1729. But there are moments when one has to choose between living one's own life, fully, entirely, completely — or dragging out some false, shallow, degrading existence that the world in its hypocrisy demands. You have that moment now. Choose! Oh, my love, choose! *Lady Windermere's Fan (Plays,* p37)

39

Love and Romance

1730. Each time one loves is the only time that one has ever loved. *The Picture of Dorian Gray* (*SC*, p208)

1731. I'm afraid it's the old, old story, dear. Love — well, not love at first sight, but love at the end of the season, which is so much more satisfactory. *Lady Windermere's Fan* (*Plays*, p40)

1732. When one is in love, one begins by deceiving one's self. And one ends by deceiving others. That is what the world calls a romance. *A Woman of No Importance* (*Plays*, p182) and similar quotation in *The Picture of Dorian Gray* (*SC*, p68)

1733. To be in love is to surpass one's self. *The Picture of Dorian Gray* (*SC*, p83)

1734. Are you in love? If not, why not? *Letter to Reginald Turner* (*Letters*, p1133)

1735. You will always be loved, and you will always be in love with love. *The Picture of Dorian Gray* (*SC*, p65)

1736. We are of course desperately in love. I have been obliged to be away nearly all the time since our engagement, civilizing the provinces by my remarkable lectures, but we telegraph to eachother twice a day, and the telegraph clerks have become quite romantic in consequence. I hand in my messages, however, very sternly, and try to look as if "love" was a cryptogram for "buy Grand Trunks" and "darling" a cypher for "sell out at par." I am sure it succeeds. *Letter to Waldo Story* (*Letters*, p225)

1737. I am hard at work lecturing and getting quite rich, tho' it is horrid being so much away from her, but we telegraph to each other twice a day, and I rush back suddenly from the uttermost parts of the earth to see her for an hour, and do all the foolish things which wise lovers do. *Letter to Lillie Langtry* (*Letters*, pp224–5)

1738. ... Love does not traffic in a market-place, nor use a huckster's scales. Its joy, like the joy of the intellect, is to feel itself alive. The aim of Love is to love: no more, and no less. *De Profundis* (*OWC*, p76)

1739. Love is better than wisdom, and more precious than riches.... *The Fisherman and His Soul* (*Works*, p257)

1740. Surely love is a wonderful thing. It is more precious than emeralds, and dearer than fine opals. Pearls and pomegranates cannot buy it, nor is it set forth in the market-place. It may not be purchased of the merchants, nor can it be weighed out in the balance for gold. *The Nightingale and the Rose* (*Works*, p278)

1741. How evil it is to buy Love, and how evil to sell it! *Letter to Robert Ross* (*Letters*, p1187)

1742. ... what does money matter? Love is more than money. *The Picture of Dorian Gray* (*SC*, p76)

1743. I cannot live without an atmosphere of Love: I must love and be loved, whatever price I pay for it. *Letter to Robert Ross* (*Letters*, p942)

1744. But you have to let love in, and with its gold
Gilded all life. Do you not think that love
Fills up the sum of life?
  The Duchess of Padua (*Works*, p629)

1745. A heart may be broken and yet fulfill its natural functions. The soul may sit in the shadow of death, and yet the body walk in the ways of life, and breathe and eat and know the sun and rain. *Letter to More Adey* (*Letters*, p680)

1746. Peace, Peace O breaking heart, Love comes apace,

And surely great delight and gladness brings,
Now look at last upon his shining face,
And listen to the flying of his wings
And the sweet voice of Love that sings.
Heart's Yearnings (*Works*, p759)

1747. Into a house where a heart is hard cometh there not always a bitter wind? *The Star Child* (*Works*, p262)

1748. I lost one illusion last night. I thought I had no heart. I find I have, and a heart doesn't suit me, Windermere. Somehow it doesn't go with modern dress. *Lady Windermere's Fan* (*Plays*, p74)

1749. What a silly thing Love is! It is not half as useful as Logic, for it does not prove anything, and it is always telling one of things that are not going to happen, and making one believe things that are not true. In fact, it is quite unpractical, and, as in this age to be practical is everything, I shall go back to Philosophy and study Metaphysics. *The Nightingale and the Rose* (*Works*, p282)

1750. Where there is no exaggeration there is no love, and where there is no love there is no understanding. It is only about things that do not interest one, that one can give a really unbiased opinion; and this is no doubt the reason why an unbiased opinion is always valueless. *Mr. Pater's Appreciations, Speaker* (*Uncollected*, pp144–5)

1751. ... the imagination itself is the world-light ... the world is made by it, and yet the world cannot understand it: that is because the imagination is simply a manifestation of Love, and it is Love and the capacity for it , that distinguishes one human from another. *De Profundis* (*OWC*, p123)

1752. Most people live *for* love and admiration. But it is *by* love and admiration that we should live. *De Profundis* (*OWC*, p120)

1753. I did love you. And you loved me. You know you loved me; and love is a very wonderful thing. I suppose that when a man has once loved a woman, he will do anything for her, except continue to love her? *An Ideal Husband* (*Plays*, p310)

1754. I know now how much greater love is than everything else. You have taught me the divine secret of the world. *Letter to Lord Alfred Douglas* (*Letters*, p651)

1755. Only love can keep anyone alive. *A Woman of No Importance* (*Works*, p207)

1756. Love can translate the very meanest thing
Into a sign of sweet remembrances.
A Florentine Tragedy (*Works*, p729)

1757. I would sit alone and sing no song
But listen for the coming of Love's feet.
Love is a pleasant messenger to greet.
Heart's Yearnings (*Works*, p758)

1758. ... what is romance but humanity? *The English Renaissance of Art lecture* (*Uncollected*, p5)

1759. ... the worst of having a romance of any kind is that it leaves one so unromantic. *The Picture of Dorian Gray* (*SC*, p30)

1760. How silly to write on pink paper! It looks like the beginning of a middle-class romance. Romance should never begin with a sentiment. It should begin with science and end with a settlement. *An Ideal Husband* (*Plays*, p299)

1761. Romance is the privilege of the rich, not the profession of the unemployed. *The Model Millionaire* (*Works*, p209)

1762. You were the prettiest of playthings, the most fascinating of small romances. *A Woman of No Importance* (*Plays*, p217)

1763. There was romance in every place. But Venice, like Oxford, has kept the background for romance, and, to the true romantic nature, background was everything. *The Picture of Dorian Gray* (*SC*, p177)

1764. Yes: even at Napoule there is romance: it comes in boats and takes the form of fisher-lads, who draw great nets, and are bare limbed: they are strangely perfect. I was at Nice lately: romance there is a profession pled beneath the moon. *Letter to Leonard Smithers* (*Letters*, p1119)

1765. The only difference between a caprice and a lifelong passion is that a caprice lasts a little longer. *The Picture of Dorian Gray* (*SC*, p40)

1766. Romance never dies. It is like the moon and lives forever. *The Remarkable Rocket* (*Works*, p295)

1767. "Romance is dead, Romance is dead, Romance is dead," she murmured. She was one of those people who think that, if you say the same thing over and over a great many times, it becomes true in the end. *The Remarkable Rocket* (*Works*, p295)

1768. ... there is no such thing as a romantic experience; there are romantic memories, and there is the desire of romance — that is all. Our most fiery moments of ecstasy are merely shadows of what somewhere else we have felt, or of what we long someday to feel. So at least it seems to me. *Letter to H.C. Marillier* (*Letters*, p272)

1769. He must have a truly romantic nature for he weeps when there is nothing at all to weep about. *The Remarkable Rocket* (*Works*, p298)

1770. I am not at all romantic. I am not old enough. I leave romance to my seniors. *An Ideal Husband* (*Plays*, p232)

1771. My handwriting has gone to bits, because I am nervous and unhappy. I never could understand mathematics, and now life is a mathematical problem. When it was a romantic one, I solved it — too well. *Letter to Leonard Smithers* (*Letters*, p1039)

1772. Every romance one has in one's life is a romance lost to one's art. *Interview in The Sketch* (*Uncollected*, p. xix)

1773. All romances should end in a sonnet. I suppose all romances do. *Letter to Reginald Turner* (*Letters*, p1075)

1774. ... whatever my life may have been ethically, it has always been *romantic,* and Bosie is my romance. *Letter to Reginald Turner* (*Letters*, p948)

1775. LORD HENRY: Romanticists! You have all the methods of science.

DUCHESS OF MONMOUTH: Men have educated us.

LORD HENRY: But not explained you. *The Picture of Dorian Gray* (*SC*, p210)

1776. True love is but a woman's toy,
They never know the lover's pain,
And I who loved as loves a boy
Must love in vain, must love in vain.

   Serenade (*Works*, p860)

1777. A man can be happy with any woman, as long as he does not love her. *The Picture of Dorian Gray* (*SC*, p192)

1778. DORIAN GRAY: I like the duchess very much, but I don't love her.

LORD HENRY: And the duchess loves you very much, but she likes you less, so you are excellently matched. *The Picture of Dorian Gray* (*SC*, p215)

1779. I cannot love where I cannot trust. *The Sphinx without a Secret* (*Works*, p205)

1780. Love is easily killed. *Lady Windermere's Fan* (*Plays*, p78)

1781. ... it is only those we love who can betray us.... *Oscar Wilde, by Frank Harris* (*CG*, p308)

1782. A kiss may ruin a human life.... *I* know that, *I* know that too well. *A Woman of No Importance* (*Plays*, p212)

1783. It is difficult not to be unjust to what one loves. *The Critic as Artist* (*Works*, p1112)

1784. I have got to blame you, and I am far too fond of you to blame anyone else. *Letter to Robert Ross* (*Letters*, p783)

1785. There is no love where there is any guilt.... *The Duchess of Padua* (*Works*, p649)

1786. Oh modern miracles! Can it assuage One lover's breaking heart?

   The Garden of Eros (*Works*, p850)

1787. My heart is broken, heart's are made to be broken: that is why God sends sorrow into the world. The hard heart is the evil thing of life and art. *Letter to Carlos Blacker* (*Letters*, p912)

1788. Sure it is the guilty,
Who, being very wretched, need love most.

   The Duchess of Padua (*Works*, p649)

1789. Now it seems to me that Love of some kind is the only possible explanation of the extraordinary amount of suffering that there is in the world. I cannot conceive any other explanation. I am convinced that there is no other, and that if the worlds have indeed, as I have said, been built out of Sorrow, it has been by the hands of Love, because in no other way could the Soul of man for whom the worlds are made reach the full stature of its perfection. Pleasure for the beautiful body, but pain for the beautiful Soul. *De Profundis* (*OWC*, p107)

1790. Ah! Hadst thou liked me less and loved me more,
Through all those summer days of joy and rain,
I had not now been sorrow's heritor,

Or stood a lackey in the House of Pain
   Because I Have Loved Much (*Works,* p840)

1791. ... you may never meet again with such love again in your whole life ... if you throw it away, the day may come when you will starve for love and it will not be given to you.... *Lady Windermere's Fan* (*Plays,* p53)

1792. And we were vain and ignorant nor knew
That when we stabbed thy heart it was our own real hearts we slew.
   Athanasia (*Works,* p826)

1793. Why does Love tarry in his flight
And not come near for my heart's delight -
   Heart's Yearnings (*Works,* p759)

1794. ... the birth of Love, and all the wonder and the fear and the perilous delight of one on whose boyish brows the little wings of love have beaten for the first time. *L'Envoi* (*Uncollected,* p200)

1795. The shipman's needle is not set more sure
Than I am to the lodestone of your love.
   The Duchess of Padua (*Works,* p644)

1796. I think of you always, and love you always, but chasms of moonless night divide us. We cannot cross it without hideous and nameless peril. *Letter to Lord Alfred Douglas* (*Letters,* p902)

1797. He is witty, graceful, lovely to look at, loveable to be with. He has also ruined my life, so I can't help loving him — it is the only thing to do. *Letter to Leonard Smithers* (*Letter,* p952)

1798. I love him and have always loved him. He ruined my life, and for that very reason I seem forced to love him more. *Letter to Reginald Turner* (*Letters,* p948)

1799. I shall often be unhappy, but still I love him: the mere fact that he wrecked my life makes me love him. *Letter to Robert Ross* (*Letters,* p943)

1800. Everyone is furious at me for going back to you, but they don't understand us. I feel that it is only with you that I can do anything at all. Do remake my ruined life for me, and then our friendship and love will have a different meaning to the world. *Letter to Lord Alfred Douglas* (*Letters,* p933)

1801. If I hadn't rejoined him and lived with him for two months, I should never have gotten over the longing for him. *Quoted in Oscar Wilde: His Life and Wit* (*HBP,* p305)

1802. What is the "Love that dare not speak its name"?—"The love that dare not speak its name" in this century is such a great affection of an elder for a younger man as there was between David and Jonathan, such as Plato made the very basis of his philosophy, and such as you find in the sonnets of Michelangelo and Shakespeare. It is that deep, spiritual affection that is as pure as it is perfect. It dictates and pervades great works of art like those of Shakespeare and Michelangelo, and those two letters of mine, such as they are. It is in this century misunderstood, so much misunderstood that it may be described as the "Love that dare not speak its name" and on account of it I am placed where I am now. It is beautiful, it is fine, it is the noblest form of affection. There is nothing unnatural about it. It is intellectual, and it repeatedly exists between an elder and a younger man, when the elder man has intellect, and the younger man has all the joy, hope and glamour of life before him. That it should be so the world does not understand. The world mocks at it and sometimes puts one in the pillory for it. *The Three Trials of Oscar Wilde* (*UB,* p236)

1803. What is left to us is the knowledge that we love each other.... *Letter to Lord Alfred Douglas* (*Letters,* p880)

1804. ... one should love all things, not wisely but too well. *Quoted in Oscar Wilde: His Life and Wit* (*HBP,* p126)

1805. And Love! That noble madness, whose august
And inextinguishable might can slay
The soul with honeyed drugs, — alas! I must
From such sweet ruin play the runaway....
   Humanitad (*Works,* p819)

1806. One world was not enough for two
Like me and you.
   Her Voice (*Works,* p842)

1807. I would not have you either stay or go;
For if you stay you steal my love away from me,
And if you go you take my love away.
   The Duchess of Padua (*Works,* p628)

1808. I did but touch the honey of romance–
And must I lose a soul's inheritance?
   Helas (*Works,* p864)

1809. He made me see what Life is, and what Death signifies, and why Love is stronger than both. *The Canterville Ghost* (*Works*, p204)

1810. Love, you are strong, and young, and very brave,
Stand between me and the angel of death,
And wrestle with him for me.
   The Duchess of Padua (*Works*, p678)

1811. Love only knows no winter; never dies:
Nor cares for frowning storms or leaden skies,
And mine for thee shall never pass away,
Though my weak lips may falter in my lay.
   Ravenna (*Works*, p785)

1812. Without love, or love's holiest treasure,
I shall pass into Hades abhorred,
To the grave as my chamber of pleasure,
To death as my Lover and Lord.
   A Song of Lamentation (*Works*, p762)

1813. I do not care: Death has no power on love,
And so by Love's immortal sovereignty
I will die with you.
   The Duchess of Padua (*Works*, p678)

1814. ... the mystery of love is greater than the mystery of death. *Salome* (*Plays*, p124)

1815. Love can canonize people. The saints are those who have been most loved. *Letter to Robert Ross* (*Letters*, p859)

1816. He saw that love was that lost secret of the world for which the wise men had been looking, and that it was only through love that one could approach either the heart of the leper or the feet of God. *De Profundis* (*SC*, p113)

1817. There is no love but the love of God. *La Sainte Courtisane* (*Works*, p737)

1818. Ay! Without love
Life is no better than the unhewn stone
Which in no quarry lies, before the sculptor
Has set God within it. Without love
Life is as silent as the common reeds
That through the marshes or by rivers grow,
And have no music in them.
   The Duchess of Padua (*Works*, p629)

1819. I wish I had never laid eyes upon you! You have spoiled the romance of my life.

How little you can know of love, if you say it mars your art! Without your art, you are nothing. *The Picture of Dorian Gray* (*SC*, p102)

1820. ... there are only two things in the world of any importance, Love and Art. *Letter to Arthur Fish* (*Letters*, p455)

1821. Love is a more wonderful thing than art. *The Picture of Dorian Gray* (*SC*, p99)

1822. I used to think ambition the great thing in the world. It is not. Love is the great thing in the world. *An Ideal Husband* (*Plays*, p304)

1823. Love is the sacrament of life; it sets
Virtue where virtue was not; cleanses men
Of all the vile pollutions of this world;
It is the fire which purges gold from dross,
It is the fan which winnows wheat from chaff,
It is the spring which in some wintry soil
Makes innocence to blossom like a rose.
   The Duchess of Padua (*Works*, p641)

1824. ... a kind word to me now is as lovely to me as a flower is, and love can heal all wounds. *Letter to Mrs. Bernard Beere* (*Letters*, p846)

1825. Every day I said to myself, "I must keep Love in my heart today, else how shall I live through the day." *De Profundis* (*OWC*, p76)

1826. ... to Humility there is nothing that is impossible, and to Love all things are easy. *De Profundis* (*OWC*, p156)

1827. It is love, and not German philosophy, that is the true explanation of this world, whatever may be the explanation of the next. *An Ideal Husband* (*Plays*, p273)

1828. ... it is love, and the capacity for it, that distinguishes one human being from another. *De Profundis* (*OWC*, pp123–4)

1829. Sweet, there is nothing left to say
But this, that love is never lost....
   Her Voice (*Works*, p842)

1830. ... no one can possibly shut the doors against love forever. *De Profundis* (*OWC*, p157)

1831. The world shuts its gateway against me, and the door of Love lies open. *Letter to Robert Ross* (*Letters*, p942)

1832. To love oneself is the beginning of a life-long romance.... *An Ideal Husband* (*Plays*, p292) and *Phrases and Philosophies for the Use of the Young* (*Works*, p1245)

40

Marriage

1833. I don't care about the London season! It is too matrimonial. People are either hunting for husbands, or hiding from them. *An Ideal Husband* (*Plays*, p230)

1834. I have a theory that it is always the women who propose to us, and not we who propose to the women. *The Picture of Dorian Gray* (*SC*, p92)

1835. Women are wonderfully practical, much more practical than we are. In situations of that kind we often forget to say anything about marriage and they always remind us. *The Picture of Dorian Gray* (*SC*, p92)

1836. An engagement should come on a young girl as a surprise, pleasant or unpleasant, as the case may be. It is hardly a matter that she could be allowed to arrange herself. *The Importance of Being Earnest* (*Plays*, p364)

1837. Then he proposed to me in broad daylight this morning, in front of that dreadful statue of Achilles. Really, the things that go on in front of that work of art are quite appalling. *An Ideal Husband* (*Plays*, p276)

1838. MRS. CHEVELEY: ... you asked me to be your wife.

LORD GORING: That was the natural result of my loving you. *An Ideal Husband* (*Plays*, p309)

1839. I am not in favor of long engagements. They give people the opportunity of finding out each other's character before marriage which I think is never advisable. *The Importance of Being Earnest* (*Plays*, p422)

1840. I think to elope is cowardly. It's running away from danger. And danger has become so rare in modern life. *A Woman of No Importance* (*Plays*, p132)

1841. I am not punctual myself, I know, but I do like punctuality in others, and waiting, even to be married, is out of the question. *The Importance of Being Earnest* (*Plays*, p424)

1842. I really don't see anything romantic in proposing. It is very romantic to be in love. But there is nothing romantic about a definite proposal. Why, one may be accepted. One usually is, I believe. Then the excitement is all over. The very essence of romance is uncertainty. If I ever get married, I'll certainly try to forget the fact. *The Importance of Being Earnest* (*Plays*, p350)

1843. It's perfectly scandalous the amount of bachelors who are going about society. There should be a law passed to compel them all to marry within twelve months. *A Woman of No Importance* (*Plays*, p150)

1844. I don't think England should be represented abroad by an unmarried man.... It might lead to complications. *A Woman of No Importance* (*Plays*, p130)

1845. LORD HENRY: Women love us for our defects. If we have enough of them, they will forgive us everything, even our intellects. You will never ask me to dinner again after saying this, I am afraid, Lady Narborough, but it is quite true.

LADY NARBOROUGH: Of course it is true, Lord Henry. If we women did not love you for your defects, where would you all be? Not one of you would ever be married. You would be a set of unfortunate bachelors. Not, however, that that would alter you much. Nowadays all the married men live like bachelors, and all the bachelors like married men. *The Picture of Dorian Gray* (*SC*, p191) and similar quotation in *A Woman of No Importance* (*Plays*, p151)

1846. Bachelors are not fashionable anymore. They are a damaged lot. Too much is known about them. *An Ideal Husband* (*Plays*, p295)

1847. Lane's views on marriage seem somewhat lax. Really, if the lower orders don't set us a good example, what on earth is the use of them? They seem, as a class, to have no sense of moral responsibility. *The Importance of Being Earnest* (*Plays*, p348)

1848. I cannot understand why people make such a fuss about being married. In my day we never dreamed of billing and cooing in public, or in private for that matter. *Lord Arthur Savile's Crime* (*SC*, p284)

1849. ... girls never marry the men they flirt with. Girls don't think it right. *The Importance of Being Earnest* (*Plays*, p351)

1850. The amount of women in London who flirt with their husbands is perfectly scandalous. It looks so bad. It is simply washing one's clean laundry in public. *The Importance of Being Earnest* (*Plays*, p356)

1851. It's most dangerous now-a-days for a husband to pay any attention to his wife in public. It always makes people think that he beats her when they're alone. *Lady Windermere's Fan* (*Plays*, p30)

1852. ... I never had a flirtation with anybody. However, it was Narborough's fault. He was dreadfully shortsighted, and there is no pleasure in taking a husband who never sees anything. *The Picture of Dorian Gray* (*SC*, p188)

1853. Her sense of humour keeps her from the tragedy of a *grande passion*, and, as there is neither romance nor humility in her love, she makes an excellent wife. *The American Invasion, Court and Society Review* (*Uncollected*, p39)

1854. Ah, my husband is a sort of promissory note; I am tired of meeting him. *A Woman of No Importance* (*Plays*, p152)

1855. Egad! I might be married to her; she treats me with such demmed indifference. *Lady Windermere's Fan* (*Plays*, p28)

1856. Affection comes later on in married life. In married life affection comes when people thoroughly dislike each other. *An Ideal Husband* (*Plays*, p301)

1857. ... she would have soon found out that you were absolutely indifferent to her.

And when a woman finds that out about her husband, she either becomes dreadfully dowdy, or wears very smart bonnets that some other woman's husband has to pay for. *The Picture of Dorian Gray* (*SC*, p114)

1858. Our husbands would really forget our existence if we didn't nag at them from time to time, just to remind them that we have a perfect legal right to do so. *Lady Windermere's Fan* (*Plays*, p11)

1859. All men are married women's property. That is the only true definition of what married women's property really is. *A Woman of No Importance* (*Plays*, p11)

1860. Loveless marriages are horrible. But there is one thing worse than an absolutely loveless marriage. A marriage in which there is love, but on one side only; faith, but on one side only; devotion, but on one side only, and in which of the two hearts one is sure to be broken. *An Ideal Husband* (*Plays*, p340)

1861. Ah, I forgot, your husband is the exception. Mine is the general rule, and nothing ages a woman so rapidly as having married the general rule. *An Ideal Husband* (*Plays*, p285)

1862. Twenty years of romance make a woman look like a ruin; but twenty years of marriage make her something like a public building. *A Woman of No Importance* (*Plays*, p143)

1863. So much marriage is certainly not becoming. *A Woman of No Importance* (*Plays*, p143)

1864. I have often observed that in married households the champagne is rarely of a first rate brand. *The Importance of Being Earnest* (*Plays*, p348)

1865. It is the growth of the moral sense in women that makes marriage such a hopeless, one-sided institution. *An Ideal Husband* (*Plays*, p294)

1866. ... none of us men may be good enough for the women we marry.... *Lady Windermere's Fan* (*Plays*, p21)

1867. ... if we men married the women we deserved, we should have a very bad time of it. *An Ideal Husband* (*Plays*, p322)

1868. Really, this horrid House of Commons quite ruins our husbands for us. I think the Lower House by far the greatest blow to a happy married life that there has been since that terrible thing called Higher Education for Women was invented. *An Ideal Husband* (*Plays*, pp280–1)

1869. Oh, women have become so highly educated, Jane, that nothing should surprise us now-a-days, except happy marriages. They apparently are getting remarkably rare. *A Woman of No Importance* (*Plays*, p155)

1870. LADY MARKBY: In my time, of course, we were taught not to understand anything.... But modern women understand everything, I am told.

MRS. CHEVELEY: Except their husbands. That is the one thing the modern woman never understands.

LADY MARKBY: And a very good thing, too, dear, I dare say. It might break up many a happy home if they did. *An Ideal Husband* (*Plays*, p281)

1871. MISS PRISM: No married man is ever attractive except to his wife.

CHASUBLE: And often, I am told, not even to her.

MISS PRISM: That depends on the intellectual sympathies of the woman. Maturity can always be depended on. Ripeness can be trusted. Young women are green. I spoke horticulturally. My metaphor was drawn from fruits. *The Importance of Being Earnest* (*Plays*, p385)

1872. How merry is that husband by whose hearth
Sits an uncomely wife.
The Duchess of Padua (*Works*, p615)

1873. In our day it is best for a man to be married, and men must give up the tyranny in married life which was once so dear to them, and which, we are afraid, lingers still, here and there. *A Handbook to Marriage, Pall Mall Gazette* (*Uncollected*, p192)

1874. I saw Stuart [Merrill] in the street the other day. He looked fat and married. *Aspects of Wilde* (*CC*, p167)

1875. I believe that you are really a very good husband, but that you are thoroughly ashamed of your own virtues. *The Picture of Dorian Gray* (*SC*, p22)

1876. Ah, all that I have noticed is that they are horribly tedious when they are good hus-

bands, and abominably conceited when they are not. *A Woman of No Importance* (*Plays*, p152)

1877. The real drawback to marriage is that it makes one unselfish. And unselfish people are colourless. They lack individuality. *The Picture of Dorian Gray* (*SC*, p89)

1878. I don't think a husband should be too fascinating. It is so dangerous. *Lord Arthur Savile's Crime* (*SC*, p272)

1879. LORD DARLINGTON: It's a curious thing, Duchess, about the game of marriage — a game, by the way, that is going out of fashion — the wives hold all the honours and invariably lose the odd trick.

DUCHESS OF BERWICK: The odd trick? Is that the husband, Lord Darlington?

LORD DARLINGTON: It would be rather a good name for the modern husband. *Lady Windermere's Fan* (*Plays*, p11)

1880. Because the husband is vile — should the wife be vile also? *Lady Windermere's Fan* (*Plays*, p8)

1881. Let me see — you have been married twice already; suppose you try — falling in love for once. *Vera, or the Nihilists* (*Works*, p698)

1882. Ah, nowadays people marry as often as they can, don't they? It is most fashionable. *An Ideal Husband* (*Plays*, p225)

1883. Of course, married life is merely a habit, a bad habit. *The Picture of Dorian Gray* (*SC*, p224)

1884. PRINCE PETROVITCH: My dear General, your nephew must be a perfect Turk. He seems to get married three times a week regularly.

GENERAL KOTEMKIN: Well, he wants a dowry to console him. *Vera, or the Nihilists* (*Works*, p715)

1885. ... the sultan does not know how much he is married, but he unquestionably is so to a very large extent; on the principle that you cannot have too much of a good thing a woman is valued in proportion to her stoutness, and so far from there being any reduction made in the marriage-market for taking a quantity, you must pay so much per pound.... *A Ride Through Morocco, Pall Mall Gazette* (*Works*, p962)

1886. He was eccentric, I admit. But only in later years. And that was the result of the

Indian climate, and marriage, and indigestion, and other things of that kind. *The Importance of Being Earnest* (*Plays*, p431)

1887. You will never marry again, Lady Narborough. You were far too happy. When a woman marries again it is because she detested her first husband. When a man marries again, it is because he adored his first wife. Women try their luck; men risk theirs. *The Picture of Dorian Gray* (*SC*, p191)

1888. She had more than once changed her husband — indeed, Debrett credits her with three marriages but as she had never changed her love, the world had long ago ceased to talk scandal about her. *Lord Arthur Savile's Crime* (*SC*, p266)

1889. I have only been married once. That was in consequence of a misunderstanding between myself and a young woman. *The Importance of Being Earnest* (*Plays*, p348)

1890. I have always been of the opinion that a man who desires to get married should know either everything or nothing. Which do you know? *The Importance of Being Earnest* (*Plays*, p365)

1891. The proper basis for marriage is a mutual misunderstanding. *Lord Arthur Savile's Crime* (*SC*, p270)

1892. And, indeed, marriage is the one subject on which all women agree and all men disagree. *A Handbook to Marriage Pall Mall Gazette* (*Uncollected*, p191)

1893. Men marry because they are tired; women because they are curious. Both are disappointed. *A Woman of No Importance* (*Plays*, p181) and similar quotation in *The Picture of Dorian Gray* (*SC*, p63)

41

Mediocrity

1894. Mediocrity always detests ability, and loathes genius. *Oscar Wilde, by Frank Harris* (*CG,* p259)

1895. Caricature is the tribute that mediocrity pays to genius. *Quoted in Oscar Wilde: His Life and Wit* (*HBP,* p55)

1896. Only mediocrities progress. An artist revolves in a cycle of masterpieces, the first of which is no less perfect than the last. *Letter to the Editor of the Pall Mall Gazette* (*Letters,* p615)

1897. Indifference is the revenge the world takes on mediocrities. *Vera, or the Nihilists* (*Works,* p698)

1898. Mediocrity weighing mediocrity in the balance, and incompetence applauding its brother — that is the spectacle which the artistic activity of England affords us from time to time. *The Critic as Artist* (*Works,* p1120)

1899. To be popular, one must be a mediocrity. *The Picture of Dorian Gray* (*SC,* p208)

1900. So mediocre is Mr. Caine's book that even accuracy could not make it better. *Great Writers by Little Men, Pall Mall Gazette* (*Uncollected,* p94)

Men

1901. If a man is a gentleman, he knows quite enough, and if he is not a gentleman, whatever he knows is bad for him. *The Picture of Dorian Gray* (*SC*, p49) and *A Woman of No Importance* (*Plays*, p177)

1902. A gentleman never looks out of the window. *Oscar Wilde: The Story of an Unhappy Friendship* (*GC*, p26)

1903. When men give up saying what is charming, they give up thinking what is charming. *Lady Windermere's Fan* (*Plays*, p43)

1904. Believe me, you are better than most other men, and I sometimes think you pretend to be worse. *Lady Windermere's Fan* (*Plays*, p5)

1905. LADY WINDERMERE: Are *all* men bad?

DUCHESS OF BERWICK: Oh, all of them, my dear, all of them, without any exception. And they never grow any better. Men become old, but they never become good. *Lady Windermere's Fan* (*Plays*, p15)

1906. Men are such cowards. They outrage every law of the world, and are afraid of the world's tongue. *Lady Windermere's Fan* (*Plays*, p49)

1907. We practical men like to see things, not to read about them. *The Picture of Dorian Gray* (*SC*, p56)

1908. The Ideal Man. Oh, the Ideal Man should talk to us as if we were goddesses, and treat us as if we were children. He should refuse all our serious requests, and gratify every one of our whims. He should encourage us to have caprices, and forbid us to have missions. He should always say much more than he means, and always mean much more than he says. *A Woman of No Importance* (*Plays*, p156)

Men and Women

1909. LORD ILLINGWORTH: The Book of Life begins with a man and a woman in a garden. MRS. ALLONBY: It ends with the revelations. *A Woman of No Importance* (*Plays*, p148)

1910. Men who are dandies and women who are darlings rule the world, at least they should do so. *The Model Millionaire* (*Works*, p209)

1911. I don't like compliments, and I don't see why a man should think he is pleasing a woman enormously when he says to her a whole heap of things that he doesn't mean. *Lady Windermere's Fan* (*Plays*, p5)

1912. ... women are never disarmed by compliments. Men always are. That is the difference between the two sexes. *An Ideal Husband* (*Plays*, p311)

1913. Between men and women there is no friendship possible. There is passion, enmity, worship, love, but no friendship. *Lady Windermere's Fan* (*Plays*, p36)

1914. The annoying thing is that the wretches can be perfectly happy without us. That is why I think it is every woman's duty to never leave them alone for a single moment, except during this short breathing after dinner; without which, I believe, we poor women would be absolutely worn to shadows. *A Woman of No Importance* (*Plays*, p150)

1915. The only way a woman can ever reform a man is by boring him so completely that he loses all possible interest in life. *The Picture of Dorian Gray* (*SC*, p114)

1916. MRS. ALLONBY: Earnest is invariably calm. That is one of the reasons he gets on my nerves. Nothing is so aggravating as calmness. There is something positively brutal about the good temper of most modern men. I wonder we women stand it as well as we do.

LADY STUTFIELD: Yes; men's good temper shows that they are not so sensitive as we are, not so finely strung. It makes a great barrier often between husband and wife, does it not? *A Woman of No Importance* (*Plays*, pp153–4)

1917. MRS. CHEVELEY: How you men stand up for eachother!

LORD GORING: How you women war against eachother! *An Ideal Husband* (*Plays*, p311)

1918. LORD WINDERMERE: How hard good women are!

LADY WINDERMERE: How weak bad men are! *Lady Windermere's Fan* (*Plays*, p21)

1919. A bad man is the sort of man who admires innocence, and a bad woman is the sort of woman a man never gets tired of. *A Woman of No Importance* (*Plays*, p180)

1920. If a woman wants to hold a man, she merely has to appeal to what is worst in him. We make gods of men and they leave us. Others make brutes of them and they fawn and are faithful. How hideous life is! *Lady Windermere's Fan* (*Plays*, p47)

1921. Women represent the triumph of matter over mind, just as men represent the triumph of mind over morals. *The Picture of Dorian Gray* (*SC*, p64) and similar quotation in *A Woman of No Importance* (*Plays*, p180)

1922. LADY STUTFIELD: Ah! The world was made for men and not for women.

MRS. ALLONBY: Oh, don't say that, Lady Stutfield. We have a much better time than they have. There are far more things forbidden to us than are forbidden to them. *A Woman of No Importance* (*Plays*, p133)

1923. You know what a woman's curiosity is. Almost as great as a man's! *An Ideal Husband* (*Plays*, p230)

1924. A woman's life revolves in curves of emotions. It is upon lines of intellect that a man's life progresses. *An Ideal Husband* (*Plays*, p337)

1925. I think man's reason the most misleading and thwarting guide that the sun looks upon, except perhaps the reason of a woman. *Letter to William Ward* (*Letters*, p25)

1926. Ah! the strength of women comes from the fact that psychology cannot explain us. Men can be analyzed, women ... merely adored. *An Ideal Husband* (*Plays*, p229)

1927. How can a woman be expected to be happy with a man who insists on treating her as if she were a perfectly rational being? *A Woman of No Importance* (*Plays*, p155)

1928. Man, poor, awkward, reliable, necessary man belongs to a sex that has been rational for millions of years. He can't help himself. It is in his race. The History of Women is quite different. We have always been picturesque and protest against the mere existence of common sense. We saw its dangers form the first. *A Woman of No Importance* (*Plays*, p155)

1929. How dull men are! They should listen to brilliant women, and look at beautiful ones, and when, as in the present case, a woman is both beautiful and brilliant, they might have the ordinary common sense to admit that she is verbally inspired. *Letter to Lady Randolph Churchill* (*Letters*, pp566–7)

1930. Oh, it is indeed a burning shame that there should be one law for men and another law for women. I think.... I think that there should be no law for anybody. *Interview in The Sketch* (*Uncollected*, p. xix) and similar quotation in *The Importance of Being Earnest* (*Plays*, p429)

1931. Don't have one law for men and another for women. You are unjust to women in England. And till you count what is a shame in a woman to be an infamy in a man, you will always be unjust, and Right, that pillar of fire, and Wrong, that pillar of cloud, will be made dim to your eyes, or be not seen at all, or if seen, not regarded. *A Woman of No Importance* (*Plays*, p161)

1932. Most women are so artificial that they have no sense of Art. Most men are so natural that they have no sense of Beauty. *A Few Maxims for the Instruction of the Over-Educated, Saturday Review* (*Works*, p1242)

1933. He should never run down other pretty women. That would show he had no taste, or make one suspect he had too much. *A Woman of No Importance* (*Plays*, p156)

1934. A man's face is his autobiography. A woman's face is her work of fiction. (*Letters*, p1055)

1935. Men do not know what women do for love. *The Duchess of Padua* (*Works*, p646)

1936. I see when men love women
They give them but little of their lives,
But women when they love give everything.
  The Duchess of Padua (*Works*, p650)

1937. Do you remember saying that women's love
Turns men to angels? Well, the love of man
Turns women into martyrs; for its sake
We do or suffer anything.
  The Duchess of Padua (*Works*, 645)

1938. How little pity
We women get in this untimely world;
Men lure us to some dreadful precipice,
And, when we fall, they leave us.
  The Duchess of Padua (*Works*, p650)

1939. The real Don Juan is not the vulgar person who goes about making love to all the women he meets, and what novelists call "seducing" them. The real Don Juan is the man who says to women: "Go away! I don't want you. You interfere with my life. I can do without you." Swift was the real Don Juan. Two women died for him. *Aspects of Wilde* (*CC*, p57)

1940. DUCHESS OF MONMOUTH: We women, as some one says, love with our ears, just as you men love with your eyes, if you ever love at all.

DORIAN GRAY: It seems to me that we never do anything else. *The Picture of Dorian Gray* (*SC*, p208)

1941. When a man loves a woman, then he knows
God's secret, and the secret of the world.
  The Duchess of Padua (*Works*, p641)

1942. Men always want to be a woman's first love. That is their clumsy vanity. We women have a more subtle instinct about things. What we like is to be a man's last romance. *A Woman of No Importance* (*Plays*, p154)

1943. LORD ILLINGWORTH: I was very young at the time. We men know life too early.

MRS. ARBUTHNOT: And we women know life too late. That is the difference between men and women. *A Woman of No Importance* (*Plays,* p214)

1944. I am disgraced: he is not. That is all. It is the usual history of a man and a woman as it usually happens, as it always happens. And the ending is the ordinary ending. The woman suffers. The man goes free. *A Woman of No Importance* (*Plays,* p204)

1945. A woman who can keep a man's love, and love him in return, has done all the world wants of women, or should want of them. *An Ideal Husband* (*Plays,* p337)

1946. Women are not meant to judge us, but to forgive us when we need forgiveness. Pardon, not punishment, is their mission. *An Ideal Husband* (*Plays,* p337)

1947. Being adored is a nuisance. Women treat us just as humanity treats its gods. They worship us, and are always bothering us to do something for them. *The Picture of Dorian Gray* (*SC,* p94)

1948. Ouida loved Lord Litton with a love that made his life a burden. *Quoted in Oscar Wilde: His Life and Wit* (*HBP,* p170)

1949. ... men can love what is beneath them — things unworthy, stained, dishonoured. We women worship when we love; and when we lose our worship, we lose everything. *An Ideal Husband* (*Plays,* p255)

1950. ... the difference in a way in which a man loves a woman from that in which a woman loves a man; the passion that women have for making ideals, which is their weakness, and the weakness of a man who dares not show his imperfections to the thing he loves. *Interview in The Sketch* (*Uncollected,* pp. xix–xx)

1951. MRS. ALLONBY: We women adore failures. They lean on us.

LORD ILLINGWORTH: You worship success. You cling to them.

MRS. ALLONBY: We are the laurels to hide their baldness.

LORD ILLINGWORTH: And they need you always, except at the moment of triumph. *A Woman of No Importance* (*Plays,* pp146–7)

1952. Why can't you women love us, faults and all? Why do you place us on monstrous pedestals? We have all feet of clay, women as well as men; but when we men love women, we love them knowing their weaknesses, their follies, their imperfections, love them all the more, it may be, for that reason. It is not the perfect, but the imperfect, who have need of love. It is when we are wounded by our own hands, or by the hands of others, that love should come to cure us — else what use is love at all? All sins, except a sin against itself, Love should forgive. All lives, save loveless lives, true Love should pardon. A man's love is like that. It is wider, larger, more human than a woman's. Women think that they are making ideals of men. What they are making of us are false idols merely ... let women make no more idols of men! *An Ideal Husband* (*Plays,* pp289–90)

1953. DORIAN GRAY: ... women give to men the very gold of their lives.

LORD HENRY: Possibly, but they invariably want it back in such very small change. *The Picture of Dorian Gray* (*SC,* p94)

1954. Women, as some witty Frenchman once put it, inspire us with the desire to do masterpieces, and always prevent us from carrying them out. *The Picture of Dorian Gray* (*SC,* p94)

1955. All women become like their mothers. That is their tragedy. No man does. That's his. *The Importance of Being Earnest* (*Plays,* p370) and similar quotation in *A Woman of no Importance* (*Plays,* p168)

44

Models and Modeling

1956. For an artist to marry his model is as fatal for a *gourmet* to marry his cook: the one gets no sittings, and the other gets no dinners. *London Models, English Illustrated Magazine* (*Uncollected*, p31)

1957. Professional models are a purely modern invention. To the Greeks, for instance, they were quite unknown. *London Models, English Illustrated Magazine* (*Uncollected*, p29)

1958. Millionaire models are rare enough; but, by Jove, model millionaires are rarer still. *The Model Millionaire* (*Works*, p212)

1959. Model-painting, in a word, while it may be the condition of art, is not by any means its aim. *London Models, English Illustrated Magazine* (*Uncollected*, p34)

1960. If the modern sculptor were to ask me where he should go for a model, I would tell him that he might, if he would, find in everyday life subjects in the nobility of labour entirely worthy of his attention — the depicting of men in their daily work; there is not a worker in mine or ditch, in the shop or at the furnace, who is not at some moment of his work in graceful attitude. *The Decorative Arts lecture* (*Works*, p932)

1961. It is really of very little use to dress up a London girl in Greek draperies and to paint her as a goddess. The robe may be the robe of Athens, but the face is usually the face of Brompton. *London Models, English Illustrated Magazine* (*Uncollected*, p35)

1962. Now and then, it is true, one comes across a model whose face is an exquisite anachronism, and who looks lovely and natural in the dress of any century but her own. *London Models, English Illustrated Magazine* (*Uncollected*, p35)

1963. They careen gaily through all centuries and through all costumes, and, like actors, are interesting only when they are not themselves. *London Models, English Illustrated Magazine* (*Uncollected*, p30)

1964. Then there is the true Academy model. He is usually a man of thirty, rarely good-looking, but a perfect miracle of muscles. In fact he is the apotheosis of anatomy, and is so conscious of his own splendour that he tells you of his tibia and his thorax, as if no one else had anything of the kind. *London Models, English Illustrated Magazine* (*Uncollected*, p32)

1965. Are we not all weary of him, that venerable imposter fresh from the steps of the Piazza di Spagna, who, in the leisure moments that he can spare from his customary organ, makes the rounds of the studios and is waited for in Holland Park? *The Relation of Dress to Art lecture* (*Uncollected*, p52)

1966. Now and then some old veteran knocks at a studio door, and proposes to sit as Ajax defying the lightning, or as King Lear upon the blasted heath. *London Models, English Illustrated Magazine* (*Uncollected*, p30)

1967. Very well, but where can one find subjects for sculpture out of men who wear frock-coats and chimney-pot hats? *Art and the Handicraftsman lecture* (*Uncollected*, p112)

1968. And so, as I said, find your subjects in everyday life: your own men and women, your own flowers and fields, your own hills and mountains: these are what your art should represent to you, for every nation can represent with prudence or with success only those things in which it delights, what you have with you and before you daily, dearest to your sight and to your heart, by the magic of your hand or the music of your lips you can gloriously express to others. All these commend themselves to the thoughtful student and artist. *The Decorative Arts lecture* (*Works,* p933)

1969. English models rarely look at a picture, and never venture on any aesthetic theories. In fact, they realise very completely Mr. Whistler's idea of the function of an art critic, for they pass no criticisms at all. *London Models, English Illustrated Magazine* (*Uncollected,* p30)

1970. On the whole the English female models are very naïve, very natural and very good-humoured. The virtues which the artist values most in them are prettiness and punctuality. *London Models, English Illustrated Magazine* (*Uncollected,* p31)

1971. As a rule the model, nowadays, is a pretty girl from about twelve to twenty-five years of age, who knows nothing about art, cares less, and is merely anxious to earn seven or eight shillings a day without much trouble. *London Models, English Illustrated Magazine* (*Uncollected,* p30)

1972. However, we must not blame the sitters for the shortcomings of the artists. The English models are a well-behaved and hardworking class, and if they are more interested in artists than in art, a large section of the public is in the same condition, and most of our modern exhibitions seems to justify its choice. *London Models, English Illustrated Magazine* (*Uncollected,* p35)

1973. However, though they cannot appreciate the artist as artist, they are quite ready to appreciate the artist as a man. *London Models, English Illustrated Magazine* (*Uncollected,* p31)

45

Music

1974. I never talk during music — at least, during good music. If one hears bad music, it is one's duty to drown it in conversation. *The Picture of Dorian Gray* (*SC*, p62)

1975. I like Wagner's music better than anybody's. It is so loud that one can talk the whole time without other people hearing what one says. *The Picture of Dorian Gray* (*SC*, p62)

1976. You see, if one plays good music, people don't listen, and if one plays bad music people don't talk. *The Importance of Being Earnest* (*Plays*, p360)

1977. Musical people are so absurdly unreasonable. They always want one to be perfectly dumb at the very moment when one is longing to be perfectly deaf. *An Ideal Husband* (*Plays*, p276)

1978. ... she insisted on discussing music as if it were actually written in the German language. Now, whatever music sounds like, I am glad to say that it does not sound in the smallest degree like German. *The Critic as Artist* (*Works*, p1109)

1979. ... she did not care a bit for music, but was extremely fond of musicians.... *Lord Arthur Savile's Crime* (*SC*, p270)

1980. [George] Moore conducts his musical education in public. *Quoted in Oscar Wilde: His Life and Wit* (*HBP*, p163)

1981. How we should smile if it were to be announced that B flat would for some months be the fashionable note! *Quoted in Oscar Wilde: His Life and Wit* (*HBP*, p106)

1982. After playing Chopin, I feel as if I had been weeping over sins that I had never committed, and mourning over tragedies that were not my own. Music always seems to me to produce that effect. It creates for one a past of which one has been ignorant, and fills one with a sense of sorrows that have been hidden from one's tears. I fancy a man who had led a perfectly commonplace life, hearing by chance some curious piece of music, and suddenly discovering that his soul, without his being conscious of it, had passed through terrible experiences, and known fearful joys, or wild romantic loves, or great renunciations. *The Critic as Artist* (*Works*, p1110)

1983. When Rubenstein plays to us the "Sonata Appassionata" of Beethoven he gives us not merely Beethoven, but also himself, and so gives us Beethoven absolutely — Beethoven reinterpreted through a rich artistic nature, and made vivid and wonderful to us by a new intense personality. When a great actor plays Shakespeare we have the same experience. His own individuality becomes a vital part of the interpretation. *The Critic as Artist* (*Works*, p1131)

1984. The progress in modern music has been due to the invention of new instruments entirely, and in no way to an increased consciousness on the part of the musician of any wider social aim. *The English Renaissance of Art lecture* (*Uncollected*, p10)

1985. The typewriting machine, when played with expression, is not more annoying than the piano when played by a sister or near relation. Indeed, many among those most devoted to domesticity prefer it. *Quoted in Oscar Wilde: His Life and Wit* (*HBP*, p292)

1986. All my pianists look exactly like poets; and all my poets look exactly like pianists. *Lord Arthur Savile's Crime* (*SC*, p267)

1987. ... you must not think I don't like good music. I adore it, but I am afraid of it. It makes me too romantic. I have simply worshipped pianists — two at a time, sometimes....

I don't know what it is about them. Perhaps it is that they are foreigners. They all are, ain't they? *The Picture of Dorian Gray* (*SC*, p62)

1988. LADY HUNSTANTON: Music makes one feel so romantic — at least it always gets on one's nerves.

MRS. ALLONBY: It's the same thing, nowadays. *A Woman of No Importance* (*Plays*, p198)

1989. Your own sweet bright singing — so Celtic in its careless joy, its informal wind-like music, and its pathos of things I delight in: pathos of us who are Celts comes from our quickened sense of the beauty of life: the pathos of the English from their sense of life's ugliness: so at least it seems to me. Do keep on making music: and don't add any stops to your flute. *Letter to Katharine Tynan Hinkson* (*Letters*, p627)

1990. ... when the ideal is realised, it is robbed of its wonder and its mystery, and becomes simply a new starting-point for an ideal that is other than itself. That is the reason why music is the perfect type of art. Music can never reveal its ultimate secret. *The Critic as Artist* (*Works*, p1129)

1991. ... music is the art in which form and matter are always one, the art whose subject cannot be separated from the methods of its expression, the art which most completely realizes the artistic ideal, and is the condition to which all other arts are constantly aspiring. *The English Renaissance of Art lecture* (*Uncollected*, p17) and *L'Envoi* (*Uncollected*, p197)

1992. That fellow Rigo (*sic*) who ran away with the Princess de Chimay, Clara Ward, was then the leader of the orchestra of Tziganes in the Grand Café. I called him over to my table and said to him: "I am writing a play about a woman dancing with her bare feet in the blood of a man she has craved for and slain. I want you to play something in harmony with my thoughts." And Rigo played such wild and terrible music that those who were there ceased their talk and looked at eachother with blanched faces. Then I went back and finished *Salome. Aspects of Wilde* (*CC*, p33)

1993. I don't play accurately — anyone can play accurately — but I play with wonderful expression. As far as the piano is concerned, sentiment is my forte. I keep science for life. *The Importance of Being Earnest* (*Plays*, p347)

1994. From the point of view of form, the type of all the arts is the art of the musician. *The Picture of Dorian Gray* (*SC*, p18)

Names

1995. She certainly has a wonderful faculty of remembering people's names, and forgetting their faces. *A Woman of No Importance* (*Plays*, p131)

1996. They actually succeed in spelling his name right in the newspapers. That in itself is fame, on the continent. *An Ideal Husband* (*Plays*, p225)

1997. He must be quite respectable. One has never heard his name before in the whole course of one's life, which speaks volumes for a man, nowadays. *A Woman of No Importance* (*Plays*, p128)

1998. When I like people immensely, I never tell their names to any one. It is like surrendering a part of them. I have grown to love secrecy. *The Picture of Dorian Gray* (*SC*, p22)

1999. I always call by their Christian names people whom I like. People I dislike I call something else. *The Three Trials of Oscar Wilde* (*UB*, p142)

2000. You mustn't call me Wilde. If I am your friend, my name to you is Oscar. If we are only strangers, I am Mr. Wilde. *Oscar Wilde: The Story of an Unhappy Friendship* (*GC*, p59)

2001. Dear Reggie, I was only in Cambridge for the night with Oscar Browning (I wish he was *not* called Oscar) and left the next morning for the Hicks-Beachs' in Hampshire, to kill time and pheasants and the *ennui* of not having set the world on fire as yet. *Letter to Reginald Harding* (*Letters*, p84)

2002. You forget: there is O'Connell and O. Wilde. *Quoted in Oscar Wilde: His Life and Wit* (*HBP*, p167)

2003. O. Wilde! Who is O. Wilde? Nobody knows O. Wilde. But Oscar Wilde is a household word. *Quoted in Oscar Wilde: His Life and Wit* (*HBP*, p167)

2004. I like signing my name as if it was to some document of great importance as "Send two bags of gold by bearer" or "Let the Duke be slain tomorrow and the Duchess await me at the hostelry." *Letter to William Ward* (*Letters*, p32)

2005. I don't wish to sign my name, though I am afraid everyone will know who the writer is: one's style is one's signature. *Letter to Edward Lawson* (*Letters*, p464)

2006. Now this was silly of you. I changed my name [to Sebastian Melmouth] so as not to be bothered, and then you go and write to me as Oscar Wilde. You must be careful and thoughtful about things. Just as much trouble is caused by carelessness as by crime, my friend. *Letter to Thomas Martin* (*Letters*, p871)

2007. I am in the Public Press sometimes "the ex-convict, which is too obvious: sometimes I am Mr. Oscar Wilde," a phrase I remember: sometimes "the man Wilde, a phrase I don't. So I like to know how I am spoken of. To be spoken of, and not to be spoken to, is delightful." *Letter to Ada Leverson* (*Letters*, p870)

2008. His calling you Ernest was awful. It is the effect of vegetables on the mind. *Letter to Ernest Dowson* (*Letters*, p909)

2009. JACK: Personally, darling, to speak quite candidly, I don't much care about the name of Ernest.... I don't think the name suits me at all.

GWENDOLYN: It suits you perfectly. It is a divine name. It has a music of its own. It produces vibrations. *The Importance of Being Earnest* (*Plays*, p362)

2010. JACK: Algy! Can't you recollect what our father's Christian name was?

ALGERNON: My dear boy, we were never on

speaking terms. He died before I was a year old. *The Importance of Being Earnest (Plays,* p431)

2011. Pinker seems an absurdity. It was simply the fatal attraction of his name that made me pin my faith to him. *Letter to Reginald Turner (Letters,* p976)

2012. Your title pleases me little, but everyone has some secret reason for christening a child: some day you must tell me yours. *Letter to Laurence Housman (Letters,* p923)

2013. Your handwriting in your last letter was quite beautiful, but are you sure that you spell your name right? *Letter to H.C. Pollitt (Letters,* p1120)

2014. How can you be so childish? It is perfectly clear that Simons doesn't know how to pronounce his own name. *Aspects of Wilde (CC,* p77)

2015. I have known several Jacks, and they all, without exception, were more than usually plain. Besides, Jack is a notorious domesticity for John. And I pity any woman who is married to a man called John. She would probably never be allowed to know the entrancing pleasure of a single moment's solitude. *The Importance of Being Earnest (Plays,* p363)

2016. How dangerous it is to be called "John" is the moral. Anything may happen to a person called John. *Letter to Robert Ross (Letters,* p1177)

2017. It is difficult to understand why Mr. Cyrus Thornton should have called his volume *Voices of the Street.* However, poets have a perfect right to christen their own children, and if the wine is good no one should quarrel with the bush. *From the Poet's Corner, Pall Mall Gazette (Uncollected,* p170)

2018. What a pretty name you have! It is worthy of fiction. Would you mind if I wrote a book called *The Story of Aubrey Richardson?* I won't, but I should like to. There is music in its long syllables, and a memory of romance, and a suggestion of wonder. Names fascinate me terribly. *Letter to Aubrey Richardson (Letters,* p418)

2019. I love even historic names, Frank, as Shakespeare did. Surely everyone prefers Norfolk, Hamilton and Buckingham to Jones or Smith or Robinson. *Oscar Wilde, by Frank Harris (CG,* p67)

2020. Our aesthetes and those of the last century were content to live in the midst of the most dreadful surroundings, provided they could call beauty long names. *Oscar Wilde Discovers America (HBC,* p349)

2021. Territorial names have always a *cachet* of distinction; they fall on the ear full toned with secular dignity. That's how I get all the names of my personages, Frank. I take up a map of the English counties, and there they are. Our English villages have often exquisitely beautiful names. Windermere, for instance, or Hunstanton. *Oscar Wilde, by Frank Harris (CG,* p82)

2022. My dear Smithers, I am very glad you went to Margate, which, I believe, is the *nom-de-plume* of Ramsgate. *Letter to Leonard Smithers (Letters,* p1032)

2023. People are sometimes christened Tertius and Decimus, as being the third and tenth sons. Why not call the boy Sexagesimus? Thus the sixtieth year of her Majesty's reign would be commemorated. Still that is an awkward name, and would not make the youthful owner popular at school. *Interview in The Sketch (Uncollected,* p. xvi)

2024. It is a sad truth, but we have lost the faculty of giving lovely names to things. Names are everything. *The Picture of Dorian Gray (SC,* p206)

Nature and the Country

2025. Man is hungry for beauty and must be filled. There is a void: Nature will fill it. *Oscar Wilde Discovers America* (*HBC*, p35)

2026. You are so rich in other things. Leave me the little vineyard of my life; leave me the walled-in garden and the well of water.... *A Woman of No Importance* (*Plays*, p174)

2027. I have a strange longing for the great simple primaeval things, such as the Sea, to me no less of a mother than the Earth. It seems to me that we all look on Nature too much, and live with her too little. *De Profundis* (*OWC*, p154)

2028. When I get up in the morning and look out the window, the first thing I see is a miracle going on in the back garden. *Aspects of Wilde* (*CC*, p67)

2029. Nature is a foolish place to look for inspiration, but a charming one in which to forget one ever had any. *Letter to E.W. Godwin* (*Letters*, p257)

2030. Like most artificial people he had a love of nature. *Pen, Pencil and Poison* (*Works*, p1101)

2031. He felt that they had lived with Nature, and that she had taught them peace. *Lord Arthur Savile's Crime* (*SC*, p278)

2032. Nothing is more evident than that Nature hates Mind. Thinking is the most unhealthy thing in the world, and people die of it just as they die of any other disease. *The Decay of Lying* (*Works*, pp1071–2)

2033. The worst use that a man can make of Nature is to turn her into a mirror for his own vices, nor are Nature's secrets ever disclosed to those who approach her in this spirit. *From the Poet's Corner, Pall Mall Gazette* (*Uncollected*, p169)

2034. ... anybody can be good in the country. There are no temptations there. *The Picture of Dorian Gray* (*SC*, p221)

2035. Let us go and lie on the grass and smoke cigarettes and enjoy Nature. *The Decay of Lying* (*Works*, p1071)

2036. You don't know what an existence they lead down there. It is pure unadulterated country life. They get up early because they have so much to do, and go to bed early, because they have so little to think about. There had not been a scandal in the neighbourhood since the time of Queen Elizabeth, and consequently they all fall asleep after dinner. *The Picture of Dorian Gray* (*SC*, p188)

2037. Personally I cannot understand how anybody manages to exist in the country, if anybody who is anybody does. The country always bores me to death. *The Importance of Being Earnest* (*Plays*, p404)

2038. But somehow, I feel sure that if I lived in the country for six months, I should become so unsophisticated that no one would take the slightest notice of me. *A Woman of No Importance* (*Plays*, p132)

2039. When one is in town one amuses oneself. When one is in the country one amuses other people. *The Importance of Being Earnest* (*Plays*, p349)

2040. If Nature had been comfortable, mankind would never have invented architecture, and I prefer houses to the open air. In a house we all feel of the proper proportions. Everything is subordinated to us, fashioned for our use and our pleasure. Egotism itself, which is so necessary to a proper sense of human dignity, is entirely the result of indoor life. Out of doors one becomes abstract and impersonal. One's individuality absolutely leaves one. *The Decay of Lying* (*Works*, p1071)

2041. Glory of sun and moon, let them be wrought for us by our landscape artist and be on the walls of the rooms we sit in to remind us of the undying beauty of the sunsets that fade and die, but do not let us eat our soup off them and send them down to the kitchen twice a day to be washed and scrubbed by the handmaid. *Art and the Handicraftsman lecture* (*Uncollected*, p111)

2042. A thing in Nature becomes much lovelier if it reminds us of a thing in Art, but a thing in Art gains no real beauty through reminding us of a thing in Nature. *Letter to the Editor of the Speaker* (*Letters*, p302)

2043. No better way is there to learn to love Nature than to understand Art. It dignifies every flower of the field. *House Decoration lecture* (*Uncollected*, p190)

2044. Nature is always behind the age. It takes a great artist to be thoroughly modern. *Quoted in Oscar Wilde: His Life and Wit* (*HBP*, p86)

2045. Nature is elbowing her way into the charmed circle of art. *Quoted in Oscar Wilde: His Life and Wit* (*HBP*, p82)

2046. Art is our spirited protest, our gallant attempt to teach Nature her proper place. As for the infinite variety of Nature, that is a pure myth. It is not to be found in Nature herself. It resides in the imagination, or fancy, or cultivated blindness of the man who looks at her. *The Decay of Lying* (*Works*, p1071)

2047. We call ourselves a utilitarian age, and we do not know the uses of a single thing. We have forgotten that Water can cleanse, and Fire purify, and that the Earth is mother to us all. As a consequence our Art is of the Moon and plays with shadows, while Greek art is of the sun and deals directly with things. I feel sure that in elemental forces there is purification, and I want to go back to them and live in their presence. *De Profundis* (*OWC*, p155)

2048. Society, as we have constituted it, will have no place for me, has none to offer; but Nature, whose sweet rains fall on unjust and just alike, will have clefts in the rocks where I may hide, and secret valleys in whose silence I may weep undisturbed. She will hang the night with stars so that I may walk abroad in the darkness without stumbling, and send the wind over my footprints so that none may track me to my hurt: she will cleanse me in great waters, and with bitter herbs make me whole. *De Profundis* (*OWC*, p156)

2049. I tremble with pleasure when I think that on the very day of my leaving prison both the laburnum and the lilac will be blooming in the gardens, and that I shall see the wind stir into restless beauty the swaying gold of one, and make the other toss the pale purple of its plumes so that all the air shall be Arabia for me. *De Profundis* (*OWC*, p155)

2050. I feel that water purifies, and that in nature there is, for me at any rate, healing power. *Letter to Ernest Dowson* (*Letters*, p883)

2051. I am on the Riviera, in blue and gold weather, the sun warm as wine, and apricot-coloured. The little hotel where I am staying is right on the Golf-de Juan, and all round are pine-woods with their pungent breath: the wind growing aromatic as it moves through the branches: one's feet crushing sweetness out of the fallen needles: I wish you were here. *Letter to Louis Wilkinson* (*Letters*, p1113) and similar quotation in *Letter to H.C. Pollitt* (*Letters*, p1115)

2052. He did not wring his hands nor
    weep,
Nor did he peek or pine,
But he drank the air as though it held
Some healthful anodyne;
With open mouth he drank the sun,
And drank the morning air.
The Ballad of Reading Gaol (*OWC*, p172)

2053. The high sapphire wall of sea, the gold dust of the sun, the petals and perfumes of southern flowers— perhaps these may tune my soul to some note of beauty. *Letter to Laurence Housman* (*Letters*, p1111)

2054. ... tonight on my return I will look at your wonderful productions by starlight: the moon just at present is not to be relied on: indeed she never is. *Letter to Leonard Smithers* (*Letters*, p922)

2055. Sweet girl! So devoted to sunsets! Shows such refinement of feeling, does it not? After all, there is nothing like nature, is there? *Lady Windermere's Fan* (*Plays*, p13)

2056. For the voices that have their dwelling in sea and mountain are not alone the chosen music of liberty only; other messages are there in the wonder of windswept height and the majesty of silent deep, messages that, if you listen to them, will give you the wonder of all new imagination, the treasure of all new beauty. *The Decorative Arts lecture* (*Works*, p937) and similar quotation in *The English Renaissance of Art lecture* (*Uncollected*, pp19–20)

2057. ... these woods change the air to aromatic: the wind that makes their branches restless is pungent with keen odours: when one walks in their dappled shadows one's feet crush sweetness out of the fallen needles: and the still sweeter sun is as warm as wine, and coloured like an apricot. *Letter to Laurence Housman* (*Letters*, p1113)

2058. Let us return to Life and Nature; they will recreate Art for us, and send the red blood coursing through her veins.... *The Decay of Lying* (*Works*, p1078)

2059. The things of nature do not really belong to us; we should leave them to our children as we have received them. *Oscar Wilde Discovers America* (*HBC*, p350)

Pain, Sorrow and Suffering

2060. The evolution of man is slow. The injustice of man is great. It was necessary that pain should be put forward as a mode of self-realization. *The Soul of Man* (*OWC*, p35)

2061. For the secret of life is suffering. It is what is hidden behind everything. *De Profundis* (*OWC*, p106)

2062. To become the spectator of one's own life is to escape the suffering of life. *The Picture of Dorian Gray* (*SC*, p125)

2063. Misfortunes one can endure — they come from outside, they are accidents. But to suffer for one's own faults— ah!- there is the sting of life! *Lady Windermere's Fan* (*Plays*, p19)

2064. Later on, one sees the Gorgon's head, and one suffers, because it does not turn one to stone. *Letter to Louis Wilkinson* (*Letters*, 1113)

2065. The world has always laughed at its own tragedies, that being the only way in which it has been able to bear them. *A Woman of No Importance* (*Plays*, p183)

2066. Pain is not the ultimate mode of perfection. It is merely provisional and a protest. It has reference to wrong, unhealthy, unjust surroundings. When the wrong, and the disease, and the injustice are removed, it will have no further place. It will have done its work. It is a great work, but it is almost over. Its sphere lessons every day. Nor will man miss it. For what man has sought for is, indeed, neither pain nor pleasure, but simply Life. *The Soul of Man* (*OWC*, p36)

2067. It is something that at a time of disgrace and shame I should still be regarded as an artist: I wish I could feel more pleasure: but I seem dead to all emotion except those of anguish and despair. *Quoted in Oscar Wilde: His Life and Wit* (*HBP*, p284)

2068. I quite hold with you on all you say about the relation of human suffering to art; as art is the most intense mode of expression, so suffering is the most real mode of life, the one for which we are all ultimately created. *Letter to Leonard Housman* (*Letters*, p1027)

2069. The only people I would care to be with now are artists and people who have suffered: Those who know what Beauty is, and those who know what Sorrow is: nobody else interests me. *De Profundis* (*OWC*, p102)

2070. Sorrow, then, and all that it teaches one, is my new world. I used to live entirely for pleasure. I shunned sorrow and suffering of every kind. I hated both. *De Profundis* (*OWC*, p104)

2071. Truly, much is given to some, and little is given to others. Injustice has parceled out the world, nor is there equal division of aught save sorrow. *The Star Child* (*Works*, p261)

2072. Behind Joy and Laughter there may be a temperament, coarse, hard and callous. But behind Sorrow there is always Sorrow. Pain, unlike Pleasure, wears no mask. *De Profundis* (*OWC*, p105)

2073. I have said that behind Sorrow there is always Sorrow. It were still wiser to say that behind sorrow, there is always a soul. And to mock at a soul in pain is a dreadful thing. Unbeautiful are their lives who do it. *De Profundis* (*OWC*, p130)

2074. ... my heart is broken, hearts are made to be broken: that is why God sends sorrow into the world. *Letter to Carlos Blacker* (*Letters*, p912)

2075. Where there is Sorrow there is holy ground ... sorrow is the most sensitive of all created things. *Letter to More Adey* (*Letters*, p814)

2076. Where there is sorrow there is holy ground. Some day you will realize what this means. You will know nothing of life till you do. *De Profundis* (*OWC*, p86)

2077. But well for him whose foot hath trod
The weary road of toil and strife,
Yet from the sorrows of his life
Build ladders to be nearer God.
  Tristitiae (*Works*, p757)

2078. ... if, after I go out [of prison], a friend of mine had a sorrow, and refused to allow me to share it, I should feel it most bitterly. *De Profundis* (*OWC*, p128)

2079. I have a right to share in Sorrow, and he who can look at the lovliness of the world, and share its sorrow, and realise something of the wonder of both, is in immediate contact with divine things, and has got as near to God's secret as anyone can get. *De Profundis* (*OWC*, p128)

2080. You have yet to learn that Prosperity, Pleasure and Success may be rough of grain and common in fibre, but that Sorrow is the most sensitive of all created things. There is nothing that stirs in the whole world of thought or motion to which Sorrow does not vibrate in terrible if exquisite pulsation. *De Profundis* (*OWC*, p58)

2081. Had our life together been as the world fancied it to be, one simply of pleasure, profligacy and laughter, I would not be able to recall a single passage in it. It is because it was full of moments and days tragic, bitter, sinister in their warnings, dull or dreadful in their monotonous scenes and unseemly violences, that I can see or hear each separate incident in detail, can indeed see or hear little else. *De Profundis* (*OWC*, p54)

2082. But the life of man is a sorrow
And death a relief from pain,
For love only lasts till tomorrow
And life without love is vain.
  Ye Shall be Gods (*Works*, p745)

2083. ... my life, whatever it had seemed to myself and to others, had all the while been a real Symphony of Sorrow, passing through its rhythmically-linked movements to its certain resolution, with that inevitableness that in Art characterises the treatment of every great theme. *De Profundis* (*OWC*, p55)

2084. So out of the reach of tears and sorrow
Under the wild-rose let us play,
And if death and severing come tomorrow,
I have your kisses, sweet heart, today.
  Love Song (*Works*, p757)

2085. ... out of Sorrow have the worlds been built, and at the birth of a child or a star there is pain. *De Profundis* (*OWC*, p106)

2086. There is always something infinitely mean about other people's tragedies. *The Picture of Dorian Gray* (*SC*, p70)

2087. Suffering is one long moment. We cannot divide it by seasons. We can only record its moods, and chronicle their return. With us [in prison] time itself does not progress. It revolves. It seems to circle round one centre of pain. *De Profundis* (*OWC*, p83)

2088. Suffering—curious as it may sound to you—is the means by which we exist, because it is the only means by which we become conscious of existing; and the remembrance of suffering in the past is necessary to us as the warrant, the evidence, of our continued identity. *De Profundis* (*OWC*, p54)

2089. To me, suffering seems now a sacramental thing, that makes those whom it touches holy. *Letter to Carlos Blacker* (*Letters*, p912)

2090. ... I find hidden away in my nature something that tells me that nothing in the whole world is meaningless, and suffering least of all. *De Profundis* (*OWC*, p96)

2091. But while to propose to be a better man is a piece of unscientific cant, to have become a *deeper* man is the privilege of those who have suffered. And such I think I have become. You can judge for yourself. *De Profundis* (*OWC*, p127)

2092. I am quite off balance with want and worries, and have also had to have an operation on my throat, unpaid for yet, except in pain. *Letter to Robert Ross* (*Letters*, p1061)

2093. Never even in the most perfect days of my development as an artist could I have found words fit to bear so august a burden [Lady Wilde's death], or to move with sufficient stateliness of music through the purple pageant of my incommunicable woe. *Quoted in Oscar Wilde: His Life and Wit* (*HBP*, p284)

2094. ... I have, after terrible struggles and difficulties, been able to comprehend some of the lessons hidden in the heart of pain. *De Profundis* (*OWC,* pp104–5)

2095. ... I am afraid I may have denied myself, and would weep bitterly, if I had not wept away all my tears. *Letter to Laurence Housman* (*Letters,* p928)

2096. My desire to live is as intense as ever, and though my heart is broken, hearts are made to be broken: that is why God sends sorrow into the world. The hard heart is the evil thing of life and art. *Letter to Carlos Blacker* (*Letters,* p912)

2097. I had forgiven him; but I did not want to see him. I had suffered too much by him and through him, far too much. *Oscar Wilde, by Frank Harris* (*CG,* p309)

2098. No man of my position can fall into the mire without getting a great deal of pity from his inferiors; and I know that when a play lasts too long, spectators tire. *My* tragedy has lasted far too long: its climax is over: its end is mean; and I am quite conscious of the fact that when the end *does* come I shall return an unwelcome visitant to a world that does not want me; a *revenant,* as the French say, as one whose face is grey with long imprisonment and crooked with pain. Horrible as are the dead when they rise from their tombs, the living who come out from tombs are more horrible still. Of all this I am only too conscious. When one has been for eighteen months in a prison cell, one sees things and people for what they really are. The sight turns one to stone. *Letter to Robert Ross* (*Letters,* pp669–70)

2099. Oh, Frank, you would turn all the tragedies into triumphs, you are a fighter. My life is done. *Oscar Wilde, by Frank Harris* (*CG,* p262)

2100. FELLOW INMATE: I am sorry for you; it is harder for the likes of you than it is for the likes of us.

OSCAR WILDE: No, my friend, we all suffer alike. *Quoted in Oscar Wilde: His Life and Wit* (*HBP,* p278)

2101. I am deeply sorry I gave him pain, but, like most people, he only realizes the pain he gets and not the pain he gives. *Letter to Leonard Smithers* (*Letters,* p1005)

2102. Here, indeed, is the true lover. What I sing of, he suffers; what is joy to me, to him is pain. Surely love is a wonderful thing. *The Nightingale and the Rose* (*Works,* p278)

2103. It often happens that the real tragedies of life occur in such an inartistic manner that they hurt us by their crude violence, their absolute incoherence, their absurd want of meaning, their entire lack of style. *The Picture of Dorian Gray* (*SC,* p115)

2104. For my own sake I must forgive you. One cannot always keep an adder in one's breast to feed on one, nor rise up every night to sow thorns in the garden of one's soul. *De Profundis* (*OWC,* p94)

2105. Suffering is a terrible fire; it either purifies or destroys. *Letter to Mrs. Bernard Beere* (*Letters,* p846)

2106. Pain, if it comes, cannot last forever.... *Letter to Lord Alfred Douglas* (*Letters,* p650)

2107. ... it is rarely in the world's history that its ideal has been one of joy and beauty. The worship of pain has far more often dominated the world. *The Soul of Man* (*OWC,* p34)

2108. The worship of sorrow must give place ... to the worship of the beautiful. *Oscar Wilde, by Frank Harris* (*CG,* p31)

49

Passion

2109. A *grande passion* is the privilege of people who have nothing to do. That is the one use of the idle classes of a country. *The Picture of Dorian Gray* (*SC*, p65) and *A Woman of No Importance* (*Plays*, p182)

2110. Great passions are for the great of soul, and great events can be seen only by those who are on a level with them. *De Profundis* (*OWC*, p148)

2111. Nothing is serious except passion. *A Woman of No Importance* (*Plays*, p138)

2112. It is said that passion makes one think in a circle. *The Picture of Dorian Gray* (*SC*, p197)

2113. It is no doubt true that to be filled with an absorbing passion is to surrender the security of one's lower life, and yet in such surrender there may be gain, certainly there was for Shakespeare. *The Portrait of Mr. W.H.* (*Works*, p327)

2114. The worship of the senses has often, and with much justice, been decried, men feeling a natural instinct of terror about passions and sensations that seem stronger than themselves, and that they are conscious of sharing with the less highly organized forms of existence. *The Picture of Dorian Gray* (*SC*, p144)

2115. He gains his inspiration from form, and from form purely, as an artist should. A real passion would ruin him. *The Critic as Artist* (*Works*, p1148)

2116. His own nature had revolted against the excess of anguish that had sought to maim and mar the perfection of its calm. With subtle and finely wrought temperaments it is always so. Their strong passions must either bruise or bend. They either slay the man, or themselves die. Shallow sorrows and shallow

loves live on. The loves and sorrows that are great are destroyed by their own plentitude. *The Picture of Dorian Gray* (*SC*, p212)

2117. It was the passions about whose origin we deceived ourselves that tyrannized most strongly over us. Our weakest motives were those of whose nature we were conscious. *The Picture of Dorian Gray* (*SC*, p75)

2118. Perhaps, by finding perfect expression for a passion, I had exhausted the passion itself. Emotional forces, like the forces of physical life, have their positive limitations. *The Portrait of Mr. W.H.* (*Works*, p345)

2119. ... if you limit passion, you impoverish life, you weaken the mainspring of art, and narrow the realm of beauty. *Oscar Wilde, by Frank Harris* (*CG*, p291)

2120. ... gladness that comes, not from the rejection, but from the absorption, of all passion.... *L'Envoi* (*Uncollected*, p201)

2121. For, sweet, to feel is better than to
> know,
And wisdom is a childless heritage,
One pulse of passion — youth's first fiery
> glow, -
Are worth the hoarded proverbs of the sage:
Vex not thy soul with deadly philosophy,
Have we not lips to kiss with, hearts to love
> and eyes to see!
Panthea (*Works*, p830)

2122. Mirror my wildest passions like the
> sea
And give my rage a brother —! Liberty!
Sacred Hunger for Liberty (*Works*, p859)

2123. For there are times when all existences
Seem narrowed to one single ecstasy,
And Passion sets a seal upon the lips.
The Duchess of Padua (*Works*, p631)

2124. Difference of object does not alter singleness of passion. It merely intensifies it. *The Picture of Dorian Gray* (*SC*, p208)

2125. Of course there's always someone else.... Change is the essence of passion. *Oscar Wilde, by Frank Harris* (*CG*, p300)

2126. And what a world it is! What a panorama of passions! What a pell-mell of men and women! *Balzac in English* (*Uncollected*, p163)

2127. ... to understand one must love, and to love one must have passion. *Letter to Leonard Smithers* (*Letters*, p1030)

2128. ... the birth of Love, and all the wonder and the fear and the perilous delight of one on whose boyish brows the little wings of love have beaten for the first time. *L'Envoi* (*Uncollected*, p200)

2129. Then comes Desire, with its many maladies, and Lust that makes one love all that one loathes, and Shame, with its ashen face and secret smile. *The Portrait of Mr. W.H.* (*Works*, p336)

2130. So me too stormy passions work my
    wrong,
And for excess of Love my Love is dumb.
Silentium Amoris or *The Silence of Love* (*Works*, p841)

2131. I want the sheer passion of love to dominate everything. No morbid self-sacrifice. No renunciation. A sheer flame of love between a man and a woman. *Letter to George Alexander* (*Letters*, p600)

2132. ... passions are False Gods that will have victims at all costs. *Letter to Robert Ross* (*Letters*, p671)

2133. How strange to live in a land where the worship of beauty and the passion of love are considered infamous. I hate England. It is only bearable to me because you are here. *Letter to Lord Alfred Douglas* (*Letters*, p622)

2134. ... I think I could prove that passion, the desire of the man for the woman and the woman for the man, has been enormously strengthened in modern times. Christianity has created, or at least cultivated, modesty, and modesty has sharpened desire. Christianity has helped to lift woman to an equality with man, and this modern intellectual development has again intensified passion out of all knowledge. The woman is not a slave but an equal, who gives herself according to her own feeling, is infinitely more desirable to a man than any submissive serf who is always waiting on his will. And this movement intensifying passion is every day gaining force. *Oscar Wilde, by Frank Harris* (*CG*, p292)

2135. We are animals at best, and love
Is merely passion with a holy name.
The Duchess of Padua (*Works*, p641)

2136. The only difference between a caprice and a life-long passion is that the caprice lasts a little longer. *The Picture of Dorian Gray* (*SC*, p40)

2137. For when one looks back upon the life that was so vivid in its emotional intensity, and filled with such fervent moments of ecstasy or of joy, it all seems to be a dream and an illusion. What are the unreal things, but the passions that once burned like fire? *The Critic as Artist* (*Works*, p1132)

2138. To have a capacity for a passion and not to realise it, is to make oneself incomplete and limited. *The Critic as Artist* (*Works*, p1117)

2139. There is no passion that we cannot feel, no pleasure that we may not gratify, and we can choose the time of our initiation and the time of our freedom also. Life! Life! *The Critic as Artist* (*Works*, p1135)

50

Past, Present and Future

2140. Time is a waste of money. *Phrases and Philosophies for the Use of the Young, The Chameleon* (*Works,* p1244)

2141. The worst of posterity is that it has but one voice. *Letter to W. E. Henley* (*Letters,* p372)

2142. I met you either too late or to soon, I don't know which. *De Profundis* (*OWC,* p41)

2143. To be premature is to be perfect. *Phrases and Philosophies for the Use of the Young, The Chameleon* (*Works,* p1245)

2144. He was always late on principle, his principle being that punctuality is the thief of time. *The Picture of Dorian Gray* (*SC,* p61)

2145. I feel we are both premature. People who count their chickens before they are hatched act very wisely: because chickens run about so absurdly that it is almost impossible to count them accurately.... *Letter to Robert Ross* (*Letters,* p1078)

2146. I like men who have a future and women who have a past. *The Picture of Dorian Gray* (*SC,* p192)

2147. She is not symbolic of any age. It is the ages that are her symbols. *The Decay of Lying* (*Works,* p1087)

2148. What, madam, do you think that that little clock knows of what the great golden sun is doing? *Oscar Wilde: The Story of an Unhappy Friendship* (*GC,* p72)

2149. Most modern calendars mar the sweet simplicity of our lives by reminding us that each day that passes is the anniversary of some perfectly uninteresting event. *Quoted in Oscar Wilde: His Life and Wit* (*HBP,* p114)

2150. You are remarkably modern, Mabel. A little too modern, perhaps. Nothing is so dangerous as being too modern. One is apt to grow old-fashioned quite suddenly. I have

known many instances of it. *An Ideal Husband* (*Plays,* p278)

2151. The one charm of the past is that it's the past. *The Picture of Dorian Gray* (*SC,* p116)

2152. You may fancy yourself safe and think yourself strong. But a chance tone of colour in a room or a morning sky, a particular perfume that you once loved and that brings subtle memories with it, a line from a forgotten poem that you had come across again, a cadence from a piece of music that you had ceased to play ... it is one these things that our lives depend. *The Picture of Dorian Gray* (*SC,* p228)

2153. I have had to look at my past face to face. *De Profundis* (*OWC,* p153)

2154. One's past is what one is. It is the only way which people should be judged. *An Ideal Husband* (*Plays,* p253)

2155. It is not his past, but his future, that people so much object to, I am afraid. *Letter to Robert Ross* (*Letters,* p1040)

2156. EDWARD CARSON: Did you ask what his previous occupation was?

OSCAR WILDE: I never inquire about people's pasts.

EDWARD CARSON: Nor their future?

OSCAR WILDE: Oh, that is problematical. *The Three Trials of Oscar Wilde* (*UB,* p143)

2157. What other people call one's past has, no doubt, everything to do with them, but absolutely nothing to do with oneself. The man who regards his past is a man who deserves to have no future to look forward to. *The Critic as Artist* (*Works,* p1142)

2158. The past could always be annihilated. Regret, denial, or forgetfulness could do that. But the future was inevitable. *The Picture of Dorian Gray* (*SC,* p133)

2159. The present was to him the key to the explanation of the past, as it was to the prediction of the future. *The Rise of Historical Criticism* (*Works*, p1206)

2160. ... that the future will in the course of human things resemble the past, if not reproduce it. *The Rise of Historical Criticism* (*Works*, p1215)

2161. What lies before me is my past. I have got to make myself look on that with different eyes, to make God look on it with different eyes. This I cannot do by ignoring it, or slighting it, or praising it, or denying it. It is only to be done by fully accepting it as an inevitable part of the evolution of my life and character: by bowing my head to everything that I have suffered. *De Profundis* (*OWC*, p158)

2162. ... the memory of our friendship is the shadow that walks with me here [in prison]: that never seems to leave me ... there is nothing that happened in those ill-starred years that I cannot recreate in that chamber of the brain which is set apart for grief and despair. *De Profundis* (*OWC*, p67)

2163. Could the passionate past that is fled
Call back its dead,
Could we live it all over again,
Were it worth the pain!
Roses and Rue (*Works*, p837)

2164. But the past is of no importance. The present is of no importance. It is with the future that we have to deal. For the past is what man should not have been. The present is what man ought not to be. The future is what artists are. *The Soul of Man* (*OWC*, p31)

2165. ... a picture and a statue are not at war with Time. They take no count of its succession. In one moment their unity may be apprehended. In the case of literature it is different. Time must be traversed before unity of effect is realized. *The Soul of Man* (*OWC*, p27)

2166. Only art must be asked of art, only the past of the past. *The Rise of Historical Criticism* (*Works*, p1207)

2167. Whatever begins must also end. *Oscar Wilde, by Frank Harris* (*CG*, p299)

2168. Do not be afraid of the past. If people tell you that it is irrevocable, do not believe them. The past, the present and the future are but one moment in the sight of God, in whose sight we should try to live. Time and space, succession and extension, are merely accidental conditions of Thought. The Imagination can transcend them, and move in a free sphere of ideal existences. Things, also, are in their essence what we choose to make them. A thing *is* according to the mode in which one looks at it. *De Profundis* (*OWC*, p158)

2169. For lo, what changes time can bring!
The cycles of revolving years
May free my heart from all its fears,
And teach my lips a song to sing.
Rome Unvisited (*Works*, p753)

2170. Oh, dust should never be removed; it is the bloom of time. *Oscar Wilde Discovers America* (*HBC*, p190)

2171. ... what purple hours one can snatch from that grey slowly-moving thing we call Time! *Letter to Robert Ross* (*Letters*, p1187)

2172. The tired spirit broods with that calm and certain joy that one gets when one has found something that the ages never dull and the world cannot harm.... *L'Envoi* (*Uncollected*, p201)

2173. For he to whom the present is the only thing that is present, knows nothing of the age in which he lives. To realize the nineteenth century one must realize every century that has preceded it, and that has contributed to its making. *Mr. Pater's Appreciations, Speaker* (*Uncollected*, p145) and *The Critic as Artist* (*Works*, p1137)

2174. And so it comes that he who seems to stand most remote from his age is he who mirrors it best, because he has stripped life of what is accidental and transitory.... *The English Renaissance of Art lecture* (*Uncollected*, p14)

2175. All beautiful things belong to the same age. *Pen, Pencil and Poison* (*Works*, p1096)

2176. For beauty is the only thing that time cannot harm. Philosophies fall away like sand, and creeds follow one another like the withered leaves of autumn; but what is beautiful is a joy for all seasons and a possession for all eternity. *The English Renaissance of Art lecture* (*Uncollected*, p21)

2177. We think in Eternity, but we move slowly through Time. *De Profundis* (*OWC*, p107)

2178. The spirit of an age is not born and does not die on a definite day. *The Rise of Historical Criticism* (*Works*, p1198)

Philosophy, Spirituality and Religion

2179. Oh, what a lesson! And what a pity that in life we only get our lessons when they are of no use to us! *Lady Windermere's Fan* (*Plays*, p66)

2180. ... there is a fatality about good resolutions—that they are always made too late. Mine certainly were. *The Picture of Dorian Gray* (*SC*, p115)

2181. The life of contemplation is the highest life, and so recognized by the philosopher. *The Three Trials of Oscar Wilde* (*UB*, p123)

2182. ... we are all in the gutter, but some of us are looking at the stars. *Lady Windermere's Fan* (*Plays*, p59)

2183. Experience is the name everyone gives to their mistakes. *Lady Windermere's Fan* (*Plays*, p61) and similar quotation in *Vera, or the Nihilists* (*Works*, p696)

2184. Experience was of no ethical value. It was merely the name men gave to their mistakes. *The Picture of Dorian Gray* (*SC*, p74)

2185. To regret one's own experiences is to arrest one's own development. *Quoted in Oscar Wilde: His Life and Wit* (*HBP*, p289)

2186. In this world there are only two tragedies. One is not getting what one wants, and the other is getting it. *Lady Windermere's Fan* (*Plays*, p60)

2187. Prayer must never be answered: if it is, it ceases to be prayer and becomes correspondence. *Quoted in Oscar Wilde: His Life and Wit* (*HBP*, p165)

2188. ... when the gods wish to punish us they answer our prayers. *An Ideal Husband* (*Plays*, p264)

2189. It does not matter what [man] is, as long as he realizes the perfection of the soul that is within him. *The Soul of Man* (*OWC*, p12)

2190. It is only shallow people who do not judge by appearances. The mystery of the world is the visible, not the invisible. *Letter to W.E. Combe* (*Letters*, p540)

2191. It is only through the mystery of creation that one can gain any knowledge of the quality of created things. *The English Renaissance of Art lecture* (*Uncollected*, p17)

2192. The tendency of creation is to repeat itself. *The Critic as Artist* (*Works*, p1119)

2193. For secrets are always smaller than their manifestations. By the displacement of an atom a world may be shaken. *De Profundis* (*OWC*, p150)

2194. ... every little action of the common day makes or unmakes character. *De Profundis* (*OWC*, p96)

2195. Those who forget what honour is, forget all things. *The Duchess of Padua* (*Works*, p624)

2196. Each of us has heaven and hell in him.... *The Picture of Dorian Gray* (*SC*, p169)

2197. Heaven is a despotism. I shall be at home there. *Vera, or the Nihilists* (*Works*, p698)

2198. Ideals are dangerous things. Realities are better. They wound, but they are better. *Lady Windermere's Fan* (*Plays*, p77)

2199. Only the imagination of man is limitless. The appetite seems curiously bounded. *Letter to Reginald Turner* (*Letters*, p855)

2200. The only thing that one really knows about human nature is that it changes. Change is the one quality we can predicate of it. *The Soul of Man* (*OWC*, p31)

2201. ... nothing is worth doing except what the world says is impossible. *Lecture to Art Students at the Royal Academy* (*Uncollected*, p127)

2202. Man can believe the impossible, but man can never believe the improbable. *Quoted in Oscar Wilde: His Life and Wit* (*HBP*, p125)

2203. It is enough that our fathers have believed. They have exhausted the faith-faculty of the species. Their legacy to us is the scepticism of which they were afraid. *The Critic as Artist* (*Works*, p1137)

2204. Religions die when they are proved to be true. Science is the record of dead religions. *Phrases and Philosophies for the Use of the Young, The Chameleon* (*Works*, p1244)

2205. Religions, however, may be absorbed, but they are never disproved.... *The Rise of Historical Criticism* (*Works*, p1202)

2206. As I don't believe in the theory, I am not likely to convert you to it. *The Portrait of Mr. W.H.* (*Works*, p303)

2207. As for the Church, I cannot conceive anything better for the culture of a country than the presence in it of a body of men whose duty it is to believe in the supernatural, to perform daily miracles, and to keep alive that mythopoeic faculty which is so essential for the imagination. But in the English Church a man succeeds, not through his capacity for belief, but through his capacity for disbelief. Ours is the only church where the sceptic stands at the altar, and where St Thomas is regarded as the ideal apostle. *The Decay of Lying* (*Works*, p1089)

2208. DUCHESS OF MONMOUTH: Religion?
LORD HENRY: The fashionable substitute for belief.
DUCHESS OF MONMOUTH: You are a sceptic.
LORD HENRY: Never! Scepticism is the beginning of faith. *The Picture of Dorian Gray* (*SC*, p207)

2209. SIR ROBERT CHILTERN: ... may I ask, at heart, are you an optimist or a pessimist? Those seem to be the only two fashionable religions left to us nowadays.
MRS. CHEVELEY: Oh, I'm neither. Optimism begins in a broad grin, and Pessimism ends with blue spectacles. Besides, they are both of them merely poses. *An Ideal Husband* (*Plays*, p228)

2210. His sermon and his beard want cutting both. *The Duchess of Padua* (*Works*, p615)

2211. ... the sermon of the divine is always humorous, and the writing of the humorous is depressing. *Oscar Wilde Discovers America* (*HBC*, p215)

2212. I am as hungry as a widow is for a husband, as tired as a young maid is of good advice, and as dry as a monk's sermon. *The Duchess of Padua* (*Works*, p607)

2213. A sermon is but a sorry sauce, when You have nothing to eat with it.
The Duchess of Padua (*Works*, p623)

2214. If I *could hope* that the church would wake in me some earnestness and purity I would go over *as a luxury*, if for no better reasons. But I can hardly hope it would, and to go over to Rome would be to sacrifice and give up my two great gods "Money and Ambition." *Letter to William Ward* (*Letters*, p39)

2215. Still I get so wretched and low and troubled that in some desperate mood I will seek the shelter of a Church which simply enthralls me by its fascination. *Letter to William Ward* (*Letters*, p39)

2216. I know you are keenly alive to beauty, and do try and see in the Church not man's hand only but also a little of God's. *Letter to William Ward* (*Letters*, p40)

2217. It is a curious, and therefore natural thing, but I cannot stand Christians because they are never Catholics, and I cannot stand Catholics because they are never Christians. Otherwise I am at one with the Indivisible Church. *Letter to Robert Ross* (*Letters*, p1191)

2218. Self-denial is the shining sore on the leprous body of Christianity. *Oscar Wilde, by Frank Harris* (*CG*, p287)

2219. ... I really must become a Catholic, though I fear that if I went before the Holy Father with a blossoming rod it would turn at once into an umbrella or something dreadful of that kind. It is absurd to say that the age of miracles is past. It has not yet begun. *Letter to Robert Ross* (*Letters*, p1177)

2220. To be either a Puritan, a prig, or a preacher is a bad thing. To be all three at once reminds one of the worst excesses of the French Revolution. *Letter to Robert Ross* (*Letters*, p1085)

2221. And when I saw the old white Pontiff, successor of the Apostles and Father of Christendom, pass, carried high above the throng, and in passing turn and bless me where I knelt, I felt my sickness of body and soul fall from me like a worn garment, and I was made whole. I wrote to Robbie Ross that I expected to see that my umbrella had blossomed. *Aspects of Wilde* (*CC*, p192)

2222. The Pope may be cultivated. Many Popes have been; the bad Popes have been. The bad Popes loved Beauty, almost as passionately, nay, with as much passion as the good Popes hated Thought. To the wickedness of the Papacy humanity owes much. The goodness of the Papacy owes a terrible debt to humanity. *The Soul of Man* (*OWC*, p30)

2223. Religion does not help me. The faith that others give to what is unseen, I give to what one can touch, and look at. My Gods dwell in temples made with hands, and within the circle of actual experience is my creed made perfect and complete: too complete it may be, for like many or all of those who have placed their Heaven in this earth, I have found in it not merely the beauty of Heaven, but the horror of Hell also. *De Profundis* (*OWC*, p98)

2224. It is the confession, not the priest, that gives us absolution. *The Picture of Dorian Gray* (*SC*, p111)

2225. Humanity will always love Rousseau for having confessed his sins, not to a priest, but to the world.... *The Critic as Artist* (*Works*, p1108)

2226. BASIL HALLWARD: Ah! you don't know what it cost me to tell you all that I have told you.

DORIAN GRAY: My dear Basil, what have you told me? Simply that you felt you admired me too much. That is not even a compliment.

BASIL HALLWARD: It was not intended as a compliment. It was a confession. Now that I have made it, something seems to have gone out of me. Perhaps one should never put one's worship into words. *The Picture of Dorian Gray* (*SC*, p130)

2227. No one should ever tell the name of his god. *La Sainte Courtisane* (*Works*, p735)

2228. Surely you know that nowadays the religion of a literary man is an affair strictly between himself ... and his public. *Quoted in Oscar Wilde: His Life and Wit* (*HBP*, p166)

2229. Ordinary theology has long since converted its gold into lead, and words and phrases that once touched the heart of the world have become wearisome and meaningless through repetition. If theology desires to move us, she must re-write her formulas. *Quoted in Oscar Wilde: His Life and Wit* (*HBP*, p112)

2230. CHARLES BROOKFIELD: Do you keep Christmas, Oscar?

OSCAR WILDE: No, Brookfield; the only festival of the Church I keep is Septuagesima. Do you keep Septuagesima, Brookfield?

BROOKFIELD: Not since I was a boy.

WILDE: Ah, to be a boy again! *Aspects of Wilde* (*CC*, p106)

2231. Being man's enemy am I not God's friend? *The Duchess of Padua* (*Works*, p639)

2232. We are all willing to ask God to make others good. *Oscar Wilde, by Frank Harris* (*CG*, p104)

2233. ... God made the world just as much for me as for anyone else. *De Profundis* (*OWC*, p127)

2234. LORD GORING: Mrs. Cheveley! Great heavens! ... May I ask what you were doing in my drawing room?

MRS. CHEVELEY: Merely listening. I have a perfect passion for listening through keyholes. One always hears such wonderful things through them.

LORD GORING: Doesn't that sound rather like tempting providence?

MRS. CHEVELEY: Oh! Surely Providence can resist temptation by this time.

An Ideal Husband (*Plays*, pp307–8) and similar quotation in *Lord Arthur Savile's Crime* (*SC*, p267)

2235. People fashion their God after their own understanding. They make their God first and worship him afterwards. *Quoted in Oscar Wilde: His Life and Wit* (*HBP*, p287)

2236. There is no god but that mirror that thou seest, for this is the Mirror of Wisdom. And it reflecteth all things that are in heaven and on earth. *The Fisherman and His Soul* (*Works*, p247)

2237. But strange that I was not told
That the brain can hold
In a tiny ivory cell,
God's heaven and hell.
  Roses and Rue (*Works*, 838)

2238. The gods are sometimes just and always humorous. *Letter to Robert Ross* (*Letters*, p1087)

2239. It was of course my soul in its ultimate essence that I had reached. In many ways I had been its enemy, but I found it waiting for me as a friend. When one comes in contact with the soul it makes one simple as a child.... *De Profundis* (*OWC*, p114)

2240. In sublimity of soul there is no contagion. High thoughts and high emotions are by their very existence isolated. *De Profundis* (*OWC*, p149)

2241. There was something within us that knew nothing of sequence and extension. And yet, like the philosopher of the Ideal City, was the spectator of all time and of all existence.... It was we who were unreal, and our conscious life was the least important part of our development. The soul, the secret soul, was the only reality. *The Portrait of Mr. W.H.* (*OWC*, p344)

2242. I came [to Naples] to realize the perfection of my temperament and my soul. We have all to choose our own methods. I have chosen mine. *Letter to Carlos Blacker* (*Letters*, p947)

2243. Nothing can cure the soul but the senses, just as nothing can cure the senses but the soul. *The Picture of Dorian Gray* (*SC*, p37 and p196)

2244. The harmony of soul and body — how much that is! We in our madness have separated the two, and have invented a realism that is vulgar, an identity that is void.... *The Picture of Dorian Gray* (*SC*, p28)

2245. Those who see any difference between body and soul have neither. *Phrases and Philosophies for the Use of the Young, The Chameleon* (*Works*, p1244)

2246. ... the senses, no less than the soul, have their spiritual mysteries to reveal. *The Picture of Dorian Gray* (*SC*, p147)

2247. ... the soul itself, the soul of each one of us, is to each one of us a mystery. It hides in the dark and broods, and consciousness cannot tell us of its workings. *The Portrait of Mr. W.H.* (*Works*, p343)

2248. ... the mood of rebellion closes up the channels of the soul, and shuts out the airs of heaven. *De Profundis* (*OWC*, p108)

2249. There is no thing more precious than a human soul, nor any earthly thing that can be weighed with it. It is worth all the gold that is in the world, and is more precious than the rubies of kings. *The Fisherman and His Soul* (*Works*, p238)

2250. The spirit alone is of importance. *De Profundis* (*OWC*, p127)

2251. Only that is spiritual which makes its own form. If I may not find its secret within myself, I shall never find it. If I have not got it already, it will never come to me. *De Profundis* (*OWC*, p99)

2252. ... while in the opinion of society, Contemplation is the gravest sin of which any citizen can be guilty, in the opinion of the highest culture it is the proper occupation of man. *The Critic as Artist* (*Works*, p1136)

2253. By contact with divine things, he will become divine. *The Critic as Artist* (*Works*, p1154)

2254. It is only the sacred things that are worth touching. *The Picture of Dorian Gray* (*SC*, p68)

2255. Conscience and cowardice are really the same things.... Conscience is the trade-name of the firm, that is all. *The Picture of Dorian Gray* (*SC*, p24)

2256. Conscience is but the name which cowardice
Fleeing from battle scrawls upon its shield.
  The Duchess of Padua (*Works*, p615)

2257. The mere existence of conscience, that faculty of which people prate so much nowadays, and are so ignorantly proud, is a sign of our imperfect development. *The Critic as Artist* (*Works*, p1122)

2258. I must confess that most modern mysticism seems to me to be simply a method of imparting useless knowledge in a form that no one can understand. *Quoted in Oscar Wilde: His Life and Wit* (*HBP*, p111)

2259. [Mystics possess] that quality of absolute unintelligibility that is the peculiar privilege of the verbally inspired. *Quoted in Oscar Wilde: His Life and Wit* (*HBP*, pp111–2)

2260. The truths of metaphysics are the truth of masks. *The Truth of Masks* (*Works*, p1173)

2261. GEORGE ALEXANDER: Do you really believe in palmists?

OSCAR WILDE: Always ... when they prophecy nice things.

GEORGE ALEXANDER: When do they ever prophecy anything else?

OSCAR WILDE: Never. If they did no one would believe in them, and the poor creatures must earn a living somehow.

GEORGE ALEXANDER: Oh, you're impossible!

OSCAR WILDE: No, not impossible, my dear fellow.... Improbable ... yes.... I grant you improbable. *Quoted in Oscar Wilde: His Life and Wit* (*HBP*, p255)

2262. I wish Olivia would take off her pretty mittens when her fortune is being told. Chiromancy is a science which deals almost entirely with the lines on the palm of the hand, and mittens would seriously interfere with its mysticism. *Olivia at the Lyceum, Dramatic Review* (*Works*, p956)

2263. The devil was once crossing the Libyan desert, and he came upon a spot where a number of small fiends were tormenting a holy hermit. The sainted man easily shook off their evil suggestions. The devil watched their failure, and then he stepped forward to give them a lesson. "What you do is too crude," he said. "Permit me for one moment." With that he whispered to the holy man. "Your brother has just been made Bishop of Alexandria." A scowl of malignant jealousy at once clouded the serene face of the hermit. "That," said the devil to his imps, "is the sort of thing which I should recommend." *Quoted in Oscar Wilde: His Life and Wit* (*HBP*, pp127–8)

2264. Wisdom comes with winters. *A Florentine Tragedy* (*Works*, p727)

2265. When Wisdom has been profitless to me, and Philosophy barren, and the proverbs and phrases of those who have sought to give me consolation as dust and ashes in my mouth, the memory of that little lowly silent act of Love has unsealed for me all the wells of pity, made the desert blossom like a rose, and brought me out of the bitterness of lonely exile into harmony with the wounded, broken and great heart of the world. *De Profundis* (*OWC*, p86)

2266. ... you can get along very well without philosophy if you surround yourselves with beautiful things.... *The Decorative Arts lecture* (*Works*, p926)

2267. Philosophy may teach us to bear with equanimity the misfortunes of our neighbors, and science resolve the moral sense into a secretion of sugar, but art is what makes the life of each citizen a sacrament and not a speculation, art is what makes the life of the whole race immortal. *The English Renaissance of Art lecture* (*Uncollected*, p21)

2268. Art and Liberty seem to me more vital and more religious than any Creed. The artists view of life is the only possible one and should be applied to everything, above all to religion. *Quoted in Oscar Wilde: His Life and Wit* (*HBP*, p166)

2269. WOMAN: What terrible weather we're having.

OSCAR WILDE: Yes, but if it wasn't for the snow, how could we believe in the immortality of the soul?

WOMAN: What an interesting question, Mr. Wilde! But tell me exactly what you mean.

OSCAR WILDE: I haven't the slightest idea. *Quoted in Oscar Wilde: His Life and Wit* (*HBP*, p176)

2270. The moment of repentance is the moment of initiation. More than that, it is the means by which one alters one's past. *De Profundis* (*OWC*, p124)

2271. The evolution of man is slow. The injustice of man is great. *The Soul of Man* (*OWC*, p35)

2272. Nothing that actually occurs is of the smallest importance. *Phrases and Philosophies for the Use of the Young, The Chameleon* (*Works*, p1244)

2273. To have survived at all — is a thing so marvelous to me, that it seems to me sometimes, not that the age of miracles is over, but that it is only just beginning; and that there are powers in God, and powers in man, of which the world has up to the present known little. *Letter to Frank Harris* (*Letters*, p895)

2274. ... it is only the impossible things that are worth doing nowadays! *Mrs. Langtry as Hester Grazebrook, New York World* (*Uncollected*, p70)

2275. Good resolutions are useless attempts to interfere with scientific laws. Their origin is pure vanity. Their result is absolutely *nil*. They give us, now and then, some of those luxurious sterile emotions that have a certain charm for the weak. That is all that can be said for them. They are simply cheques that men draw on a bank where they have no account. *The Picture of Dorian Gray* (*SC*, p115)

2276. ... you must always create your own plots. *Letter to Aimee Lowther* (*Letters*, p1164)

2277. ... look out on life in proper fashion: attitude is all. *Letter to H.C. Pollitt* (*Letters*, p1107)

52

Poets and Poetry

2278. ... beautiful poems, like threads of beautiful silks, may be woven into many patterns and to suit many designs, all wonderful and all different.... *L'Envoi* (*Uncollected*, p201)

2279. A poet can survive everything but a misprint. *Quoted in Oscar Wilde: His Life and Wit* (*HBP*, p111)

2280. All bad poetry springs from genuine feeling. *The Critic as Artist* (*Works*, p1148)

2281. I should say that one man's poetry is another man's poison! *The Three Trials of Oscar Wilde* (*UB*, p235)

2282. There are two ways of disliking poetry. One is not to like it, and the other is to read Pope. *Aspects of Wilde* (*CC*, p177)

2283. Little poets are an extremely interesting study. The best of them have often some new beauty to show us, and though the worst of them may bore yet they rarely brutalize. *From the Poet's Corner Pall Mall Gazette* (*Uncollected*, p166)

2284. A great poet, a really great poet, is the most unpoetical of all creatures. But inferior poets are absolutely fascinating. The worse their rhymes are, the more picturesque they look. The mere fact of having published a book of second-rate sonnets makes a man quite irresistible. He lives the poetry that he cannot write. The others write the poetry that they dare not realize. *The Picture of Dorian Gray* (*SC*, p72)

2285. Indeed, one should never talk of a moral poem or an immoral poem — poems are either well written or badly written, that is all. A good work aims at the purely artistic effect. *Oscar Wilde Discovers America* (*HBC*, p58) and similar quotation in *The English Renaissance of Art* lecture (*Uncollected*, pp20–1)

2286. As truly religious people are resigned to everything, even to mediocre poetry, there is no reason at all why Madame Guyun's verses should not be popular with a large section of the community. *Quoted in Oscar Wilde: His Life and Wit* (*HBP*, p112)

2287. There seems to be some curious connection between piety and poor rhymes. *Quoted in Oscar Wilde: His Life and Wit* (*HBP*, p112)

2288. Poets are not so scrupulous as you are. They know how useful passion is for publication. Nowadays a broken heart will run to many editions. *The Picture of Dorian Gray* (*SC*, pp28–9)

2289. The merchant's price. I think they love not art
Who break the crystal of a poet's heart....
On the Sale by Auction of Keats' Love Letters (*Works*, p871)

2290. The popularity of the poem will be largely increased by the author's painful death by starvation. The public love poets to die in that way. It seems to them dramatically right. Perhaps it is. *Letter to Leonard Smithers* (*Letters*, p996)

2291. Believe me that we value your American poets much more you're your American millionaires; and that we estimate you by the amount of great men you have produced, not by your hoarded wealth. *Oscar Wilde Discovers America* (*HBC*, p183)

2292. As for American poets, we in England think there are only two— Walt Whitman and Emerson. *Oscar Wilde Discovers America* (*HBC*, p76)

2293. There are good poets in England but none in Switzerland. There the mountains are too high. Art cannot add to nature. *Oscar Wilde Discovers America* (*HBC*, p306)

2294. We have been able to have fine poetry in England because the public do not read it, and consequently do not influence it. *The Soul of Man* (*OWC*, p18)

2295. But between a poet's deliberate creation and historical accuracy, there is a wide field of mythopoeic faculty. *The Rise of Historical Criticism* (*Works*, p1202)

2296. ... the great poet is always the great seer, seeing less with the eyes of the body than he does with the eyes of the soul. *The Critic as Artist* (*Works*, p1115)

2297. Poets, you know, are always ahead of science; all the great discoveries of science have been stated before in poetry. *Oscar Wilde Discovers America* (*HBC*, p65)

2298. I feel as if I had made a sonnet out of skilly! And that is something. *Letter to Frank Harris* (*Letters*, p1025) and *Letter to William Rothenstein* (*Letters*, p1024)

2299. I am a poet and can only sing in the sunshine when I am happy. *Oscar Wilde, by Frank Harris* (*CG*, p263)

2300. Since I have met you I have been re-reading your poems, seeing you, hearing you through them. How the finely woven veil of form reveals in all the arts! I can recognize a whole life in the choice of an adjective. *Letter to Richard Le Gallienne* (*Letters*, p351)

2301. All fine imaginative work is self-conscious and deliberate. No poet sings because he must sing. At least, no great poet does. A great poet sings because he chooses to sing. *The Critic as Artist* (*Works*, p1118)

2302. When a man acts he is a puppet. When he describes, he is a poet. *The Critic as Artist* (*Works*, p1122)

2303. I am afraid you are going to be a poet: How terribly tragic! *Letter to Louis Wilkinson* (*Letters*, p1168)

2304. The maker of a poem is a "poet," not an "author." ... *Letter to John Lane* (*Letters*, p533)

2305. His prose is the beautiful *prose* of a poet, and his poetry the beautiful *poetry* of a prose-writer. *Letter to William Rothenstein* (*Letters*, p925)

2306. ... it is not that I like poetical prose, but that I love the prose of the poets. *English Poetesses, Queen* (*Uncollected*, p66)

2307. Writers of poetical prose are rarely good poets. *Sir Edwin Arnold's Last Volume, Pall Mall Gazette* (*Uncollected*, p174)

2308. ... whoever is a poet grows not old; that is reserved for prose writers only. *Letter to A.P.T. Elder* (*Letters*, p249)

2309. My dear Henley, I am so sorry to hear about your trouble. All poets love their mothers, and as I worship mine I can understand how you feel. *Letter to W.E. Henley* (*Letters*, p367)

2310. We sicken with the same maladies as the poets, and the singer lends us his pain. *The Critic as Artist* (*Works*, p1135)

2311. The simple utterance of joy is not poetry any more than a mere personal cry of pain.... *The English Renaissance of Art lecture* (*Uncollected*, p12)

2312. I suppose you think that mental anxiety is good for poets. It is not the case, when pecuniary worries are concerned. *Letter to Leonard Smithers* (*Letters*, p977)

2313. The negotiations over my poem still drag on: as yet no offer, and no money in consequence. Still I keep on building castles of fairy gold in the air: we Celts always do. *Letter to Earnest Dowson* (*Letters*, p971)

2314. ... my work as a poet is separate from my life as a man–and as for my life, it is one ruined, unhappy, lonely and disgraced. *Letter to Leonard Smithers* (*Letters*, p1104)

2315. Dante was full of pity as are all great poets, for they know the weakness of human nature. *Oscar Wilde, by Frank Harris* (*CG*, p251)

2316. Longfellow himself was a beautiful poem, more beautiful than anything he ever wrote. *Oscar Wilde Discovers America* (*HBC*, p240)

2317. ... the lips of Longfellow are still musical for us though his dust be turning into the flowers which he loved. *Art and the Handicraftsman lecture* (*Uncollected*, p119)

2318. Wordsworth went to the lakes, but he was never a lake poet. He found in stones the sermons he had already hidden there. *The Decay of Lying* (*Works*, p1078)

2319. We need not say anything about the poets, for they, with the unfortunate exception of Mr. Wordsworth, have been really faithful to their high mission, and are universally recognised as being absolutely unreliable. *The Decay of Lying* (*Works,* p1080)

2320. ... romantic poetry ... is essentially the poetry of impressions, being like that latest school of painting, the school of Whistler and Albert Moore, in its choice of situation as opposed to subject; in its dealings with exceptions rather than with the types of life; in its brief intensity; in what one might call its fiery-coloured momentariness, it being indeed the momentary situations of life, the momentary aspects of nature, which poetry and painting now seek to render for us. *L'Envoi* (*Uncollected,* p201)

2321. Yes, Browning was great. And as what will he be remembered? As a poet? Ah, not as a poet! he will be remembered as a writer of fiction, as the most supreme writer of fiction, it may be, that we ever had. His sense of the dramatic situation was unrivalled, and, if he could not answer his own problems, he could at least put problems forth, and what more should an artist do? *The Critic as Artist* (*Works,* p1111)

2322. Meredith is a prose Browning. And so is Browning. *The Critic as Artist* (*Works,* p1111)

2323. To Morris we owe poetry whose perfect precision and clearness of word and vision has not been excelled in the literature of our country.... *The English Renaissance of Art lecture* (*Uncollected,* p9)

2324. How can a man [Tennyson] be a great poet and lead the life of an English country-gentleman? Think of a man going down to breakfast at eight o'clock with the family and writing *Idylls of the King* till lunchtime! *Aspects of Wilde* (*CC,* p214)

2325. The greatest artists are stupid and tiresome men as a rule. Flaubert was certainly a stupid man. But bad poets and novelists are romantic and delightful. *Aspects of Wilde* (*CC,* p222)

2326. Sir Edwin Arnold has a very picturesque or, perhaps we should say, a very pictorial style. He knows India better than any living Englishman knows it, and Hindustani better than any English writer should know it. If his descriptions lack distinction, they at least have the merit of being true, and when he does not interlard his pages with an interminable and intolerable series of foreign words he is pleasant enough. But he is not a poet. He is simply a poetical writer — that is all. *Sir Edwin Arnold's Last Volume, Pall Mall Gazette* (*Uncollected,* p174)

2327. Mrs. Browning is unapproachable by any woman who has ever touched lyre or blown through reed since the days of the great Aeolian poetess. But Sappho, who, to the antique world was a pillar of flame, is to us but a pillar of shadow.... The fragile clay vases of the Greeks still keep for us pictures of Sappho, delicately painted in black and red and white; but of her song we have only the echo of an echo.... Sappho was undoubtedly a far more flawless and perfect artist. She stirred the whole antique world more than Mrs. Browning ever stirred our modern age. Never had love such a singer. Even in the few lines that remain to us the passion seems to scorch and burn. *English Poetesses* (*Uncollected,* pp59–60)

2328. In the case of poetry, as in the case of the other arts, what may appear to be simple technicalities of method are in their essence spiritual, not mechanical. *On Keats' Sonnet on the Blue, Century Guild Hobby Horse* (*Uncollected,* p40)

2329. I do not believe poets and artists should live in solitude, but rather that they should associate with each other and mix freely in society. I have always done this myself, and I have preached my theories in every salon in London. *Oscar Wilde Discovers America* (*HBC,* p46)

2330. ... the most joyous poet is not he who sows the desolate highways of this world with the barren seed of laughter, but he who makes his sorrow most musical, this indeed being the meaning of joy in art.... *L'Envoi* (*Uncollected,* p196)

2331. Perhaps, as I want my poem to reach the poorer classes, we might give away a cake of Maypole soap with each copy: I hear it dies people the most lovely colours, and is also cleansing. *Letter to Leonard Smithers* (*Letters,* p1063)

2332. Rhyme, that exquisite echo which in the Muse's hollow hill creates and answers its own voice; rhyme, which in the hands of the real artist becomes not merely a material element of metrical beauty, but a spiritual element of thought and passion also, waking a new mood, it may be, or stirring a fresh train of ideas, or opening by mere sweetness and suggestion of sound some golden door at which the Imagination itself had knocked in vain; rhyme, which can turn man's utterance to the speech of gods; rhyme, the one chord we have added to the Greek lyre.... *The Critic as Artist* (*Works*, p1111)

2333. To speak poetry so well is so rare an accomplishment that it was a delight to listen to your lovely voice, with its fine sense of music and cadence and rhythmical structure. *Letter to Otho Stuart* (*Letters*, p417)

2334. And so in poetry ... the real poetical quality, the joy of poetry, comes never from the subject but from an inventive handling of rhythmical language.... *The English Renaissance of Art lecture* (*Uncollected*, p16)

2335. I am sorry you have rhymed "tears" to "ideas" in your envoy; rhymes of this kind are very wicked, but you certainly have a light touch and a pleasant fancy. *Letter to Graham Hill* (*Letters*, p380)

2336. ... as you, the poem of my days, are away, [I] am forced to write poetry. *Letter to Robert Ross* (*Letters*, p869)

2337. His poems seem to have music and colour—the best things possible that poetry can have. *Letter to Mrs. Birkbeck* (*Letters*, p507)

2338. I remember bright young faces, and grey misty quadrangles, Greek forms passing through Gothic cloisters, life playing among ruins, and, what I love best in the world, Poetry and Paradox dancing together! *Letter to H.C. Marillier* (*Letters*, p269)

2339. While all other forms of poetry may flourish in an ignoble age, the splendid individualism of the lyrist, fed by its own passion, and lit by its own power, may pass as a pillar of fire as well across the desert as across places that are pleasant. *The English Renaissance of Art lecture* (*Uncollected*, p18)

2340. There is indeed a poetical attitude to be adopted towards all things, but all things are not fit subjects for poetry. *The English Renaissance of Art lecture* (*Uncollected*, p13)

2341. ... love is not fashionable anymore, the poets have killed it. They wrote so much about it that nobody believed them, and I am not surprised. True love suffers and is silent. *The Remarkable Rocket* (*Works*, p295)

2342. Are you still enamoured of love and poetry? I hope so. They are the only two things in the world that remain. *Letter to Graham Hill* (*Letters*, p483)

2343. ... it is only for lovers that poets write. *Letter to Violet Fane* (*Letters*, p330)

2344. For to the poet all times and places are one; the stuff he deals with is eternal and eternally the same: no theme is inept, no past or present preferable. The steam whistle will not affright him nor the flutes of Arcadia weary him: for him there is but one time, the artistic moment; but one law; the law of form; but one land, the land of Beauty. *The English Renaissance of Art lecture* (*Uncollected*, p14)

2345. The poet is the spectator of all time and of all existence. For him no form is obsolete, no subject out of date; rather, whatever of life and passion the world has known.... *The English Renaissance of Art lecture* (*Uncollected*, p13)

2346. I suppose that the poet will sing and the artist will paint regardless whether the world praises or blames. He has his own world and is independent of his fellow men. *House Decoration lecture* (*Uncollected*, p183) and *The Decorative Arts lecture* (*Works*, p927)

2347. Poetry should be like a crystal, it should make life more beautiful and less real. *Letter to W. Graham Robertson* (*Letters*, p347)

2348. But the poet is the supreme artist, for he is the master of colour and form, and the real musician besides, and is lord over all life and all arts.... *Mr. Whistler's Ten o'clock* (*Uncollected*, p49)

2349. Create yourself. Be yourself your poem. *Aspects of Wilde* (*CC*, p223)

2350. No country has ever had so many poetesses at once. Indeed, when one remembers that the Greeks had only nine muses, one is sometimes apt to fancy that we have too many. And yet the work done by women in the sphere of poetry is really of a very high standard of excellence. *English Poetesses* (*Uncollected*, p63)

2351. ... England never appreciates a poet until he's dead. *Oscar Wilde Discovers America* (*HBC*, p65)

53

Politics, Government and Law

2352. I think little of pen and ink in revolutions. One dagger will do more than a hundred epigrams. *Vera, or the Nihilists* (*Works*, p688)

2353. I suspect a conspiracy with ramifications. I suppose ramifications are a sort of dagger? *Letter to Reginald Turner* (*Letters*, p921)

2354. It is true that our modern sense of the continuity of history has shown us that neither in politics nor in nature are there revolutions ever but evolutions only.... *The English Renaissance of Art lecture* (*Uncollected*, p5)

2355. ... pity seems to beat in vain at the doors of officialism; and power, no less than punishment, kills what else were good and gentle in man; the man without knowing it loses his natural kindliness, or grows afraid of its exercise. *Letter to More Adey* (*Letters*, p664)

2356. There is not there [at Tuileries Palace] one little blackened stone which is not to me a chapter in the Bible of Democracy. *Oscar Wilde: The Story of an Unhappy Friendship* (*GC*, p35)

2357. Nations may not have missions but they certainly have functions. *The Rise of Historical Criticism* (*Works*, p1239)

2358. ... the aim of culture is not rebellion but peace.... *The English Renaissance of Art lecture* (*Uncollected*, p7)

2359. Disobedience, in the eyes of any one who has read history, is man's original virtue. It is through disobedience that progress has been made, through disobedience and through rebellion. *The Soul of Man* (*OWC*, p4)

2360. Agitators are a set of interfering, meddling people, who come down to some perfectly contented class of the community,

and sow the seeds of discontent among them. That is the reason why agitators are so absolutely necessary. Without them, in our incomplete state, there would be no advance towards civilization. *The Soul of Man* (*OWC*, p5)

2361. ... the more a people has been interfered with, the more difficult it becomes to generalize the laws of its progress and to analyse the separate forces of its civilization.... *The Rise of Historical Criticism* (*Works*, p1228)

2362. I only know two terms—civilization and barbarism; and I am on the side of civilization. *Oscar Wilde Discovers America* (*HBC*, p41)

2363. ... the causal connection between political revolutions and the fertility of the soil ... goes a step farther and points out the psychological influences on a people's character exercised by the various extremes of climate — in both cases the first appearance of a most valuable form of historical criticism. *The Rise of Historical Criticism* (*Works*, p1220)

2364. I had thoughts of entering public life once myself. There are so many things that need reforming. Indeed, I took the chair at a meeting some time ago, and we passed resolutions condemning everything that we did not like. However, they did not seem to have much effect. Now I go in for domesticity, and look after my family. *The Remarkable Rocket* (*Works*, p300)

2365. Lord Goring: I adore political parties. They are the only place left to us where people don't talk politics.

Lady Basildon: I delight in talking politics. I talk them all day long. But I can't bear listening to them. I don't know how the unfortunate men in the House stand these long debates.

LORD GORING: By never listening. *An Ideal Husband* (*Plays*, p235)

2366. Politics are my only pleasure. You see nowadays it is not fashionable to flirt till one is forty, or to be romantic till one is forty-five, so we poor women who are under thirty, or say we are, have nothing open to us but politics or philanthropy. And philanthropy seems to me to have become simply the refuge of people who wish to annoy their fellow-creatures. I prefer politics. I think they are more ... becoming! *An Ideal Husband* (*Plays*, pp229–30)

2367. A man cannot always be estimated by what he does. He may keep the law, and yet be worthless. He may break the law, and yet be fine. He may be bad, without ever doing anything bad. He may commit a sin against society, and yet realise through that sin his true perfection. *The Soul of Man* (*OWC*, p11)

2368. It is supposed that because a thing is the rule it is right. *Letter to the Editor of The Daily Chronicle* (*Letters*, p160)

2369. Society takes upon itself the right to inflict appalling punishments on the individual, but it also has the supreme vice of shallowness, and fails to realise what it has done. *De Profundis* (*OWC*, p101)

2370. What right has society to punish us unless it can prove we have hurt or injured someone else against his will? *Oscar Wilde, by Frank Harris* (*CG*, p291)

2371. Were there no laws there'd be no law-
        breakers,
So all men would be virtuous.
        The Duchess of Padua (*Works*, p664)

2372. Of course there were many things of which I was convicted that I had not done, but then there are many things of which I was convicted that I had done, and a still greater number of things in my life for which I never was indicted at all. *De Profundis* (*OWC*, pp100–1)

2373. Morality does not help me. I am a born antinomian. I am one of those who are made for exceptions, not for laws. *De Profundis* (*OWC*, p98)

2374. Reason does not help me. It tells me that the laws under which I am convicted are wrong and unjust laws, and the system under

which I have suffered a wrong and unjust system. *De Profundis* (*OWC*, p99)

2375. Lady Colin has exhausted all her powers of imagination in the witness-box. *Quoted in Oscar Wilde: His Life and Wit* (*HBP*, p163)

2376. Truth may be found, I believe, at the bottom of a well. It is, apparently, difficult to find in a court of law. *The Three Trials of Oscar Wilde* (*UB*, p240)

2377. MICHAEL: Ay! But, Father Peter, they say a good lawyer can break the law as often as he likes, and no one can say him nay. If a man knows the law he knows his duty.

PETER: True, Michael, if a man knows the law there is nothing illegal he cannot do when he likes: that is why folks become lawyers. That is about all they are good for.... *Vera, or the Nihilists* (*Works*, p682)

2378. Just as much trouble is caused by carelessness as by crime, my friend. *Letter to Thomas Martin* (*Letters*, p871)

2379. Nobody ever commits a crime without doing something stupid. *The Picture of Dorian Gray* (*SC*, p181)

2380. The criminal classes have always had a wonderful attraction for me. *Oscar Wilde: The Story of an Unhappy Friendship* (*GC*, p95)

2381. The criminal classes are so close to us that even the policeman can see them. They are so far away from us that only the poet can understand them. *A Few Maxims for the Instruction of the Over-Educated, Saturday Review* (*Works*, p1243)

2382. No crime is vulgar, but all vulgarity is crime. Vulgarity is the conduct of others. *Phrases and Philosophies for the Use of the Young, The Chameleon* (*Works*, p1244)

2383. Starvation, not sin, is the parent of modern crime. That indeed is the reason why our criminals are, as a class, so absolutely uninteresting from any psychological point of view. They are not marvelous Macbeths and terrible Vautrins. They are merely what ordinary, respectable, commonplace people would be if they had not got enough to eat. *The Soul of Man* (*OWC*, p14)

2384. One is absolutely sickened, not by the crimes that the wicked have committed, but by the punishments that the good have inflicted;

and a community is infinitely more brutalised by the habitual employment of punishment, than it is by the occasional occurrence of crime. *The Soul of Man* (*OWC*, pp13–4)

2385. There is this to be said in favour of the despot, that he, being an individual, may have culture, while the mob, being a monster, has none. *The Soul of Man* (*OWC*, p29)

2386. There are three kinds of despots. There is the despot who tyrannizes over the body. There is the despot who tyrannizes over the soul. There is the despot who tyrannizes over the soul and body alike. The first is called the Prince. The second is called the Pope. The third is called the People. *The Soul of Man* (*OWC*, p30)

2387. Despotism is unjust to everybody, including the despot, who was probably made for better things. Oligarchies are unjust to the many, and Democracies are unjust to the few. High hopes were once formed of democracy; but democracy means simply the bludgeoning of the people by the people for the people. It has been found out. *The Soul of Man* (*OWC*, p13)

2388. Those who try to lead the people can only do so by following the mob. *The Critic as Artist* (*Works*, p1140)

2389. I have been a king, and now I want to be a beggar. *Quoted in Oscar Wilde: His Life and Wit* (*HBP*, p327)

2390. There would be no bad kings in the world if there were no bad ministers like you. *Vera, or the Nihilists* (*Works*, p716)

2391. The systems that fail are those that rely on the permanency of human nature, and not on its growth and development. The error of Louis the XIV was that he thought human nature would always be the same. The result of his error was the French Revolution. *The Soul of Man* (*OWC*, pp31–2)

2392. In philosophy she [Elizabeth Barrett Browning] she was a Platonist, in politics an Opportunist. She attached herself to no particular party. She loved the people when they were king-like, and the kings when they showed themselves to be men. *English Poetesses* (*Uncollected*, p62)

2393. The only consolation we can offer to the timid and the Tories is that as long as so much strength is employed in blowing the

trumpet, the sword ... will probably remain sheathed. *Quoted in Oscar Wilde: His Life and Wit* (*HBP*, p112)

2394. I am so much interested in his political career. I think he's sure to be a wonderful success. He thinks like a Tory, and talks like a Radical, and that's so important now-a-days. *Lady Windermere's Fan* (*Plays*, p32)

2395. Lying! I should have thought that our politicians kept up that habit. *The Decay of Lying* (*Works*, p1072)

2396. ... only people who look dull ever get into the House of Commons, and only people who are dull ever succeed there. *An Ideal Husband* (*Plays*, p322)

2397. The Lords Temporal say nothing, the Lords Spiritual have nothing to say, and the House of Commons has nothing to say and says it. *The Soul of Man* (*OWC*, p23)

2398. We in the House of Lords are never in touch with public opinion. That makes us a civilised body. *A Woman of No Importance* (*Plays*, p138)

2399. Really, now that the House of Commons is trying to become more useful, it does a great deal of harm. *An Ideal Husband* (*Plays*, p227)

2400. ... the House of Parliament really does very little harm. You can't make people good by an Act of Parliament. *A Woman of No Importance* (*Plays*, p137)

2401. ... in England a man who can't talk morality twice a week to a large, popular, immoral audience is quite over as a serious politician. There would be nothing left for him as a profession except Botany and the Church. *An Ideal Husband* (*Plays*, p265)

2402. What is it? Nothing about politics, I hope! They don't interest me. There is hardly a single person in the House of Commons worth painting, though many of them would do the better for a little whitewashing. *The Picture of Dorian Gray* (*SC*, p88)

2403. ... whenever a community or a powerful section of a community, or a government of any kind, attempts to dictate to the artist what he is to do, Art either entirely vanishes, or becomes stereotyped, or degenerates into a low and ignoble form of craft. *The Soul of Man* (*OWC*, pp16–7)

2404. ... to have great work we must be worthy of it. Commercialism, with its vile cheapness, its callous indifference to the worker, its innate vulgarity of temper, is our enemy. To gain anything good we must sacrifice something of our luxury — must think more of others, more of the State, the commonweal.... *Mr. Morris on Tapestry Pall Mall Gazette* (*Works*, p974)

2405. For there can be no great sculpture without a beautiful national life, and the commercial spirit of England has killed that; no great drama without a noble national life, and the commercial spirit of England has killed that too. *The English Renaissance of Art lecture* (*Uncollected*, p18)

2406. Without a beautiful national life, not sculpture merely, but all the arts will die. *Lecture to Art Students at the Royal Academy* (*Uncollected*, p128)

2407. People sometimes inquire what form of government is most suitable for an artist to live under. To this question there is only one answer. The form of government that is most suitable to the artist is no government at all. Authority over him and his art is ridiculous. *The Soul of Man* (*OWC*, p29)

2408. It is better for the artist not to live with princes. *The Soul of Man* (*OWC*, p30)

2409. ... art could not live and flourish under a tyrant. Art was an expression of the liberty-loving sentiment of the people. *Oscar Wilde Discovers America* (*HBC*, p225)

2410. The grandest art of the world has always been the art of republics. *Oscar Wilde Discovers America* (*HBC*, p177)

2411. If we are tempted to make war upon another nation, we shall remember that we are seeking to destroy an element of our own culture, and possibly its most important element. As long as war is regarded as wicked, it will always have its fascination. When it is looked upon as vulgar, it will cease to be popular. *The Critic as Artist* (*Works*, p1153)

2412. Art shall be again the most glorious of all the chords through which the spirit of a great nation finds its noblest utterance. *Art and the Handicraftsman lecture* (*Uncollected*, p112)

2413. What is inhuman in modern life is officialism. Authority is as destructive to those who exercise it as it is to those on whom it is exercised. *Letter to the Editor of The Daily Chronicle* (*Letters*, p848)

2414. All authority is quite degrading. It degrades those who exercise it, and it degrades those over whom it is exercised. *The Soul of Man* (*OWC*, p13)

2415. There is only one thing worse than Injustice, and that is Justice without her sword in her hand. When Right is not Might, it is Evil. *Quoted in Oscar Wilde: His Life and Wit* (*HBP*, p178)

2416. A right is an articulated might. *Letter to Robert Ross* (*Letters*, p819)

2417. It is often said that force is no argument. That, however, depends entirely on what one wants to prove. *The Soul of Man* (*OWC*, p23)

2418. ... there is no necessity to separate the monarch from the mob; all authority is equally bad. *The Soul of Man* (*OWC*, p30)

2419. To toil for a master is bitter, but to have no master to toil for is more bitter still. *The Young King* (*Works*, p220)

2420. Of course authority and compulsion are out of the question. All association must be quite voluntary. It is only in voluntary associations that man is fine. *The Soul of Man* (*OWC*, p6)

2421. Man has sought to live intensely, fully, perfectly. When he can do so without exercising restraint on others, or suffering it ever, and his activities are all pleasurable to him, he will be saner, healthier, more civilised, more himself. *The Soul of Man* (*OWC*, p36)

2422. Discontent is the first step in the progress of a man or a nation. *A Woman of No Importance* (*Plays*, p173)

2423. Society often forgives the criminal; it never forgives the dreamer. *The Critic as Artist* (*Works*, p1136)

2424. The only use of our *attaches* is that they supply their friends with excellent tobacco. *The Critic as Artist* (*Works*, p1118)

2425. All trials are trials for one's life, just as all sentences are sentences of death.... *De Profundis* (*OWC*, p156)

2426. Justice may be slow ... but it comes in the end. *A Woman of No Importance* (*Plays*, p203)

54

Prison

2427. ... even in prison, a man can be quite free. His soul can be free. His personality can be untroubled. *The Soul of Man* (*OWC*, p11)

2428. Prison has had an admirable effect on Mr. Wilfred Blunt as a poet.... *Quoted in Oscar Wilde: His Life and Wit* (*HBP*, p114)

2429. Prison soup is very good and wholesome. *Letter to the Editor of The Daily Chronicle* (*Works*, p1064)

2430. ... Prison has completely changed me. I was relying on it for that.... My life is like a work of art. An artist never begins the same work twice, or else it shows that he has not succeeded. My life before prison was as successful as possible. Now all that is finished and done with. *Quoted in Oscar Wilde: His Life and Wit* (*HBP*, p299)

2431. I am not really ashamed of having been in prison: I often was in more shameful places: but I *am* really ashamed of having led a life unworthy of an artist. *Letter to William Rothenstein* (*Letters*, p891) and similar quotations in *Letter to Selwyn Image* (Letters, p879) and *Letter to Arthur L. Humphreys* (*Letters*, p880)

2432. The fact of my having been the common prisoner of a common gaol I must frankly accept, and curious as it may seem to you, one of the things I shall have to teach myself is not to be ashamed of it. *De Profundis* (*OWC*, p100)

2433. When first I was put into prison some people advised me to try and forget who I was. It was ruinous advice. It is only by realising what I am that I have found comfort of any kind. Now I am advised by others to try on my release to forget that I have ever been in prison at all. I know that would be equally fatal. It would mean that I would always be haunted by an intolerable sense of disgrace, and that those things that are meant as much for me as for anyone else — the beauty of the sun and the moon, the pageant of the seasons, the music of daybreak and the silence of great nights, the rain falling through the leaves, or the dew creeping over the grass and making it silver — would all be tainted for me, and lose their healing power and their power of communicating joy. To reject one's own experiences is to arrest one's own development. To deny one's own experiences is to put a lie into the lips of one's own life. It is no less than a denial of the Soul. *De Profundis* (*OWC*, p100)

2434. It is unfair of people being horrid to me about Bosie and Naples. A patriot put in prison for loving his country loves his country, and a poet in prison for loving boys loves boys. To have altered my life would have been to have admitted that Uranian love is ignoble. I hold it to be noble — more noble than other forms. *Letter to Robert Ross* (*Letters*, p1019)

2435. We have known each other now for more than four years. Half of the time we have been together: the other half I have had to spend in prison as the result of our friendship. *De Profundis* (*OWC*, p72)

2436. I know more about the inside of prisons than of palaces. *Vera, or the Nihilists* (*Works*, p687)

2437. One gets accustomed to everything in time, to the food and the bed and the silence. One learns the rules, and knows what to expect and what to fear.... *Oscar Wilde, by Frank Harris* (*CG*, p196)

2438. Nerves are not treated in prison. *Letter to More Adey* (*Letters*, p815)

2439. One has to go to bed by daylight and the nights are interminable. *Oscar Wilde, by Frank Harris* (*CG*, p154)

2440. With midnight always in one's heart,
And twilight in one's cell,
We turn the crank, or tear the rope,
Each in his separate Hell,
And the silence is more awful far
Than the sound of a brazen bell.
The Ballad of Reading Gaol (*OWC*, p187)

2441. ... prison life, by its horrible isolation from all that could save a wretched soul, hands the victim over, like one bound hand and foot, to be possessed and polluted by the thoughts he most loathes and so cannot escape from. *Letter to the Home Secretary* (*Letters*, p658)

2442. ... there are times when the whole world seems to me no larger than my cell, and as full of terror for me. *Letter to Robert Ross* (*Letters*, p781)

2443. ... there are three permanent punishments authorised by law in English prisons: -
Hunger
Insomnia
Disease
Letter to the Editor of The Daily Chronicle (*Works*, p1067)

2444. The vilest deeds like prison weeds
Bloom well in prison-air:
It is only what is good in Man
That wastes and withers there:
Pale Anguish keeps the heavy gate,
And the Warder is Despair.
The Balled of Reading Gaol (*OWC*, p186)

2445. No one knows better than yourself how terrible life in an English prison is and what cruelties result from the stupidity of officialism, and the immobile ignorance of centralization. *Letter to Michael Davitt* (*Letters*, p870)

2446. There is no spirit in prison but hate, hate masked in degrading formalism. They first break the will and rob you of hope, and then rule by fear. *Oscar Wilde, by Frank Harris* (*CG*, p195)

2447. One of the tragedies of prison life is that it turns a man's heart to stone. The feelings of natural affection, like all other feelings, require to be fed. They die easily of inanition. *Letter to the Editor of The Daily Chronicle* (*Letters*, p1048)

2448. For prison-life, with its endless privations and restrictions, makes one rebellious. The most terrible thing about it is not that it breaks one's heart — hearts are made to be broken — but that it turns one's heart to stone. *De Profundis* (*OWC*, p107)

2449. Dreadful are the results of the prison system — a system so terrible that it hardens their hearts whose hearts it does not break, and brutalises those who have to carry it out no less than those who have to submit to it — yet at least amongst its aims is not the desire to wreck the human reason. *Letter to the Home Secretary* (*Letters*, p658)

2450. ... the solitary confinement that breaks one's heart, shatters one's intellect too: and prison is but an ill physician: and the modern modes of punishment create what they should cure, and, when they have on their side Time with its long length of dreary days, they desecrate and destroy whatever good, or desire even of good, there may be in man. *Letter to the Home Secretary* (*Letters*, p668)

2451. When one has been for eighteen months in a prison cell, one sees things and people as they really are. The sight turns one to stone. *Letter to Robert Ross* (*Letters*, pp669–70)

2452. One of the many lessons that one learns in prison is that things are what they are, and will be what they will be. *De Profundis* (*OWC*, p82)

2453. The thing I want is to know everything quite clearly as it really is. That is what one wants to know in prison. What kills one is uncertainty, with its accompanying anxiety and stress. *Letter to More Adey* (*Letters*, p804)

2454. To those who are in prison, tears are a part of every day's experience. A day in prison on which one does not weep is a day on which one's heart is hard, not a day on which one's heart is happy. *De Profundis* (*OWC*, p130)

2455. Have you ever learned what a wonderful thing pity is? For my part I thank God every night, yes, on my knees I thank God for having taught it to me. I went into prison with a heart of stone, thinking only of my own pleasure; but now my heart is utterly broken — pity has entered into my heart. I have learned now that pity is the greatest and the most beautiful thing in the world. And that is why I cannot bear ill-will towards those who caused my suffering and those whose condemned me; no, nor to anyone, because without them I should not have known all that. *Oscar Wilde, by Frank Harris* (*CG*, p214)

2456. During the first six months in prison I was dreadfully unhappy, so utterly miserable that I wanted to kill myself; but what kept me from doing so was looking at the others, and seeing that they were as unhappy as I was, and feeling sorry for them. Oh dear! What a wonderful thing pity is, and I never knew it. *Oscar Wilde, by Frank Harris* (*CG*, p214)

2457. I have no bitterness at all, but I have learnt pity: and that is worth learning, if one has to tramp a yard for two years to learn it. *Letter to Michael Davitt* (*Letters*, p870)

2458. Prisoners are, as a class, extremely kind and sympathetic to each other. Suffering and the community of suffering makes people kind.... *Letter to the Editor of The Daily Chronicle* (*Letters*, p164)

2459. For us [in prison] there is only one season, the season of Sorrow. The very sun and moon seem taken from us. Outside, the day may be blue and gold, but the light that creeps down through the thickly-muffled glass of the small iron-barred window beneath which on sits is grey and niggard, It is always twilight in one's cell, as it is always midnight in one's heart. And in the sphere of thought, no les than in the sphere of time, motion is no more. The thing that you personally have long ago forgotten, or can easily forget, is happening to me now, and will happen to me again to-morrow. *De Profundis* (*OWC*, pp83–4)

2460. ... we who live in prison, and in whose lives there is no event but sorrow, have to measure time by throbs of pain, and the record of bitter moments. We have nothing else to think of. Suffering — curious as it may sound to you — is the means by which we exist, because it is the only means by which we become conscious of existing; and the remembrance of suffering in the past is necessary to us as the warrant, the evidence, of our continued identity. *De Profundis* (*OWC*, p54)

2461. The prisoner looks to liberty as an immediate return to all his ancient energy, quickened into more vital forces by long disuse. When he goes out, he finds he still has to suffer. His punishment, as far as its effects go, lasts intellectually and physically, just as it lasts socially. He still has to pay. One gets no receipt for the past when one walks out into the beautiful air. *Letter to Frank Harris* (*Letters*, p896)

2462. I never saw sad men who looked
With such a wistful eye
Upon that little tent of blue
We prisoners call the sky
And at every careless cloud that passed
In happy freedom by.
   The Ballad of Reading Gaol (*OWC*, p182)

2463. Kind words are much in prison, and a pleasant "good morning" or "good evening" will make one as happy as one can be in prison. *Letter to the Editor of The Daily Chronicle* (*Works*, p1062)

2464. I have learnt in prison-cells to be grateful. That, *for me*, is a great discovery. *Letter to Selwyn Image* (*Letters*, p879)

2465. I learnt in prison to be grateful. I used to think gratitude a burden. Now I know that it is something that makes life lighter as well as lovelier for one. I am grateful for a thousand things, from my good friends down to the sun and the sea. I cannot make phrases about it. For *me* to use such a word shows enormous development in my nature. *Letter to Frank Harris* (*Letters*, p894)

2466. I learnt many things in prison that were terrible to learn, but I learnt some good lessons that I needed. I learnt gratitude: and though, in the eyes of the world, I am of course a disgraced and ruined man, still every day I am filled with wonder at all the beautiful things that are left to me: loyal and loving friends: good health: books, one of the greatest of the many worlds God has given to each man: the pageant of the seasons: the loveliness of leaf and flower: the nights hung with silver and the dawns dim gold. I often find myself strangely happy. *Letter to Robert Ross* (*Letters*, pp911–2)

2467. I often thought of you in the long black days and nights of my prison life, and to find you just as wonderful and dear as ever was no surprise. The beautiful are always beautiful. *Letter to Ada Leverson* (*Letters*, p845)

2468. When I came out of prison *you* met me with garments, with spices, with wise council. You met me with love. *Letter to Robert Ross* (*Letters*, p859) and *Letter to Leonard Smithers* (*Letters*, p973)

2469. There is no prison in any world into which Love cannot force an entrance. *De Profundis* (*OWC*, p157)

2470. ... I said to myself: "At all costs I must keep Love in my heart. If I go into prison without Love what will become of my soul?" *De Profundis* (*OWC*, p75)

2471. Nay peace: behind my prison's blinded bars
I do possess what none can take away
My love, and all the glory of the stars.
   At Verona (*Works*, p777)

2472. In the prison in which my body is I am shown much kindness, but in the prison in which my soul is I can show myself none. *Letter to More Adey* (*Letters*, p682)

2473. I ... wish we could meet to talk over the many prisons of life — prisons of stone, prisons of passion, prisons of intellect, prisons of morality, and the rest. All limitations, external or internal, are prison-walls, and life is a limitation. *Letter to R.B. Cunningham* (*Letters*, p1021)

2474. ... for the first year of my imprisonment I did nothing else, and can remember doing nothing else, but wring my hands in impotent despair, and say "What an ending! What an appalling ending!" now I try to say to myself, and sometimes when I am not torturing myself do really and sincerely say, "What a beginning! What a wonderful beginning!" *De Profundis* (*OWC*, p126)

2475. I must try, and the details of Prison Reform will have to be worked out by others. I put the fly in motion but I cannot drive the wheels. It is enough for me that the thing is coming and that what I suffered will not be suffered by others. That makes me happy. *Letter to Georgina Weldon* (*Letters*, pp1080–1)

2476. ... I have been able to deal a heavy blow at the monstrous prison-system of English justice. There is to be no more starvation, nor sleeplessness, nor endless silence, nor eternal solitude, nor brutal floggings. The system is exposed, and, so, doomed. But it is difficult to teach the English either pity or humanity. They learn slowly. *Letter to Georgina Weldon* (*Letters*, p1080)

2477. ... the first and perhaps the most difficult task is to humanise the governors of the prisons, to civilise the warders, and to Christianise the chaplains. *Letter to the Editor of The Daily Chronicle* (*Works*, p1070)

2478. It is not the prisoners who need reformation. It is the prisons. *Letter to the Editor of The Daily Chronicle* (*Works*, p1064)

2479. If England persists in treating her criminals like this, she does not deserve to have any. *Oscar Wilde, by Frank Harris* (*CG*, p247)

55

Prophecy and Destiny

2480. The gift of prophecy is given to all who do not know what is going to happen to themselves. *Letter to Max Beerbohm* (*Letters*, p856)

2481. I wish I could look into the seeds of time and see what is coming. *Quoted in Oscar Wilde: His Life and Wit* (*HBP*, p34)

2482. As for omens, there is no such thing as an omen. Destiny does not send us heralds. She is too wise or too cruel for that. *The Picture of Dorian Gray* (*SC*, p215)

2483. It is what we fear that happens to us. *Aspects of Wilde* (*CC*, p62)

2484. ... every action has its consequence. *Letter to Carlos Blacker* (*Letters*, p947)

2485. Of course I discern in all our relations, not Destiny merely, but Doom.... *De Profundis* (*OWC*, p61)

2486. It was mad of me, but I asked Lady Brandon to introduce me to him. Perhaps it was not so mad, after all. It was simply inevitable. We would have spoken to eachother without introduction. I am sure of that. Dorian told me so afterwards. He, too, felt that we were destined to know each other. *The Picture of Dorian Gray* (*SC*, p25)

2487. Then—but I don't know how to explain it to you. Something seemed to tell me that I was on the verge of a terrible crisis in my life. I had the feeling that fate had in store for me exquisite joys and exquisite sorrows. *The Picture of Dorian Gray* (*SC*, p25)

2488. Thou knowest all; I cannot see.
I trust I shall not live in vain,
I know that we shall meet again
In some divine eternity.
The True Knowledge (*Works*, p758)

2489. But, indeed, I need not go on further with more instances of the strange Doom you seem to have brought on me in all things big or little. It makes me feel sometimes as if you yourself had been merely a puppet worked by some secret and unseen hand to bring terrible events to a terrible issue. *De Profundis* (*OWC*, p64)

2490. Why is it that one runs to one's ruin? Why has destruction such a fascination? *Letter to Carlos Blacker* (*Letters*, p921)

2491. My friends are extraordinary. They beg me to be careful. Careful? But how can I be careful? That would be a backwards step. I must go on as far as possible. I cannot go much further. Something is bound to happen ... something else. *The Three Trials of Oscar Wilde* (*UB*, p27)

2492. However, while I blame you *ab initio*, I am now in a mood of mind that makes me think that everything that happens is for the best, and that the world is not a mere chaos in which chance and cleverness clash. *Letter to Robert Ross* (*Letters*, p784)

2493. I may say candidly that I am gradually getting to a state of mind when I think that everything that happens is for the best. This may be philosophy, or a broken heart, or religion, or the dull apathy of despair. But whatever its origin, the feeling is strong with me. *Letter to Robert Ross* (*Letters*, p789)

2494. Every single work of art is the fulfillment of a prophecy. For every work of art is the conversion of an idea into an image. Every single human being should be the fulfillment of a prophecy. For every human being should be the realisation of some ideal, either in the mind of God or in the mind of man. *De Profundis* (*OWC*, p117)

2495. "Oh, I see!" said the duchess, feeling very much relieved; "He tells fortunes, I suppose?"

"And misfortunes, too." answered Lady Windermere. *Lord Arthur Savile's Crime* (*SC*, p266)

2496. Why did the sibyl say fair things? *The Three Trials of Oscar Wilde* (*UB*, p68)

2497. She was a Sibyl delivering a message to the world, sometimes through stammering lips, and once at least with blinded eyes, yet always with the true fire and fervour of lofty and unshaken faith, always with the greatest raptures of a spiritual nature, the high ardours of the impassioned soul. *English Poetesses* (*Uncollected*, p62)

2498. In her dealings with man, destiny never closed her accounts. *The Picture of Dorian Gray* (*SC*, p201)

2499. He had tried to do his duty, but it seemed as if Destiny herself had turned traitor. *Lord Arthur Savile's Crime* (*SC*, p297)

2500. My cradle was rocked by the fates. Only in the mire can I know peace. *Letter to Carlos Blacker* (*Letters*, p921)

2501. I wait on Fortune, like a discarded lover. *Letter to Reginald Turner* (*Letters*, p1133)

2502. ... every single thing had happened as I said it would happen, as far as the result goes. *De Profundis* (*OWC*, p90)

2503. You have done wonderful things for me, but the Nemesis of circumstances, the Nemesis of character, have been too strong for me.... I think I was a problem for which there was no solution. *Letter to Robert Ross* (*Letters*, p1001)

2504. Let Destiny work out his doom. He would not stir to help her. *Lord Arthur Savile's Crime* (*SC*, p297)

56

Public Opinion

2505. Public opinion exists only where there are no ideas. *A Few Maxims for the Instruction of the Over-Educated, Saturday Review* (*Works*, p1242)

2506. ... England has done one thing; it has invented and established Public Opinion, which is an attempt to organise the ignorance of the community, and to elevate it to the dignity of physical force. *The Critic as Artist* (*Works*, p1152)

2507. The public has always, and in every age, been badly brought up. *The Soul of Man* (*OWC*, p17)

2508. The problem then is, why do not the public become more civilized? They have the capacity. What stops them? *The Soul of Man* (*OWC*, p26)

2509. Which public? There are as many publics as there are personalities. *Interview in The Sketch* (*Uncollected*, p.xviii)

2510. The world is simply divided into two classes — those who believe the incredible, like the public — and those who do the improbable. *A Woman of No Importance* (*Plays*, p186)

2511. The English public like tediousness, and like tedious things to be explained to them in a tedious way. *Letter to the Editor of The Scots Observer* (*Letters*, p448)

2512. The private lives of men and women should not be told to the public. The public have nothing to do with them at all. *The Soul of Man* (*OWC*, p24)

2513. If I were you.... I would not care about being loved on false pretences. There is no reason why a man should show his life to the world. The world does not understand things. But with people whose affection one desires to have it is different. *De Profundis* (*OWC*, p144)

2514. The artist is always a munificent patron of the public. I am very fond of the public, and, personally, I always patronise them very much. *Quoted in Oscar Wilde: His Life and Wit* (*HBP*, p222)

2515. [The public] is always asking a writer why he does not write like somebody else, or a painter why he does not paint like somebody else, quite oblivious of the fact that if either of them did anything of the kind he would cease to be an artist. *The Soul of Man* (*OWC*, p20)

2516. When the public say a work is grossly unintelligible, they mean that the artist has said or made a beautiful thing that is new; when they describe a work as grossly immoral, they mean that the artist has said or made a beautiful thing that is true. *The Soul of Man* (*OWC*, p20)

2517. The one thing that the public dislike is novelty. Any attempt to extend the subject-matter of art is extremely distasteful to the public; and yet the vitality and progress of art depend in a large measure on the continual extension of subject-matter. The public dislike novelty because they are afraid of it. It represents to them a mode of Individualism, an assertion on the part of the artist that he selects his own subject, and treats it as he chooses. *The Soul of Man* (*OWC*, p19)

2518. And for the mob, despise it as I do, I hold its bubble praise and windy favours In such account, that popularity Is the one insult I have never suffered.
The Duchess of Padua (*Works*, p614)

2519. The fact is, the public make use of the classics of a country as a means of checking the progress of Art. They degrade the classics into authorities. They use them as bludgeons for preventing the free expression of Beauty in new forms. They are always asking a writer why he does not write like somebody else, or a painter why he does not paint like somebody else, quite oblivious to the fact that if either of them did anything of the kind he would cease to be an artist. *The Soul of Man* (*OWC*, pp19–20)

2520. In Art, the public accept what has been, because they cannot alter it, not because they appreciate it. They swallow their classics whole and never taste them. *The Soul of Man* (*OWC*, p19)

2521. The public are all morbid, because the public can never find expression for any-thing. The artist is never morbid. He expresses everything. *The Soul of Man* (*OWC*, p21)

2522. As for "success" on the stage, the public is a monster of strange appetites: it swallows, so it seems to me, honeycake and hellebore, with avidity: but there are many publics — and the artist belongs to none of them: if he is admired it is, a little, by chance. *Letter to an Unidentified Correspondent* (*Letters*, p626)

2523. Yes, the public is wonderfully tolerant. It forgives everything except genius. *The Critic as Artist* (*Works*, p1108)

57

Relations

2524. Relations are simply a tedious pack of people, who haven't got the remotest knowledge of how to live, nor the smallest instinct about when to die. *The Importance of Being Earnest* (*Plays*, p370)

2525. LORD GORING: Extraordinary thing about the lower classes in England — they are always losing their relations.

PHIPPS: Yes, my lord. They are extremely fortunate in that respect. *An Ideal Husband* (*Plays*, p293)

2526. To be born, or at any rate bred, in a hand-bag, whether it had handles or not, seems to me to display a contempt for the ordinary decencies of family life that reminds one of the worst excesses of the French Revolution. *The Importance of Being Earnest* (*Plays*, p368)

2527. ... I can't help detesting my relations. I suppose it comes from the fact that none of us can stand other people having the same faults as ourselves. *The Picture of Dorian Gray* (*SC*, p26)

2528. ... I dined there on Monday, and once a week is quite enough to dine with one's own relatives. *The Importance of Being Earnest* (*Plays*, p356)

2529. ... I love hearing my relations abused. It is the only thing that makes me put up with them at all. *The Importance of Being Earnest* (*Plays*, p370)

2530. No one cares about distant relatives nowadays. They went out of fashion years ago. *Lord Arthur Savile's Crime* (*SC*, p272)

2531. It is a ridiculous attachment. She has no money, and far too many relations. *The Happy Prince* (*Works*, p237)

2532. Who is she? Where does she come from? Why hasn't she any relations? Demmed

nuisance, relations! But they make one so demmed respectable. *Lady Windermere's Fan* (*Plays*, p28)

2533. And now that I think of it I have never heard any man mention his brother. The subject seems distasteful to most men. *The Importance of Being Earnest* (*Plays*, p402)

2534. Oh brothers! I don't care for brothers. My elder brother won't die, and my younger brothers seem never to do anything else. *The Picture of Dorian Gray* (*SC*, p26)

2535. I have no brother at all. I never had a brother in my life, and I certainly have not the smallest intention of ever having one in the future. *The Importance of Being Earnest* (*Plays*, p408)

2536. A mother's love is very touching, of course, but it is often curiously selfish. I mean, there is a good deal of selfishness in it. *A Woman of No Importance* (*Plays*, p178)

2537. But mothers are so weak. They give up their sons everything. We are all heart, all heart. *A Woman of No Importance* (*Plays*, p201)

2538. Her mother is perfectly unbearable. Never met such a Gorgon.... I don't really know what a Gorgon is like, but I am quite sure Lady Bracknell is one. In any case, she is a monster, without being a myth, which is rather unfair.... *The Importance of Being Earnest* (*Plays*, p369)

2539. Of course, I was influenced by my mother. Every man is when he is young. *A Woman of No Importance* (*Plays*, p173)

2540. Few parents nowadays pay any regard to what their children say to them. The old-fashioned respect for the young is fast dying. Whatever influence I ever had over mamma, I lost at the age of three. *The Importance of Being Earnest* (*Plays*, p373)

2541. Children begin by loving their parents; as they grow older they judge them; sometimes they forgive them. *The Picture of Dorian Gray* (*SC*, p82) and similar quotations in *A Woman of No Importance* (*Plays*, p174 & p216)

2542. God gave you that child. He will require from you that you make his life fine, that you will watch over him. What answer will you make to God if his life is ruined through you? *Lady Windermere's Fan* (*Plays*, p53)

2543. "My wife has a cold" but in about a month will be over it. I hope it is a boy cold, but will love whatever the gods send. *Letter to E. W. Godwin* (*Letters*, p260)

2544. It is the duty of every father to write fairy tales for his children but the mind of a child is a great mystery. It is incalculable, and who shall divine it, or bring to it its own peculiar delights? You humbly spread before it the treasures of your imagination, and they are as dross. *Quoted in Oscar Wilde: His Life and Wit* (*HBP*, p164)

2545. I was telling them [his children] stories last night of little boys who were naughty and made their mother cry, and what dreadful things would happen to them unless they became better; and do you know what one of them answered? He asked me what punishment could be reserved for naughty papas who did not come home till the early morning, and made their mother cry far more? *Quoted in Oscar Wilde: His Life and Wit* (*HBP*, p163)

2546. Ah! I know nothing about the feelings of parents. I am not a family man. *The Devoted Friend* (*Works*, p286)

2547. Oh, why will parents always appear at the wrong time? Some extraordinary mistake in nature, I suppose. *An Ideal Husband* (*Plays*, p294)

2548. Fathers should be neither seen nor heard. That is the only proper basis for family life. Mothers are different. Mothers are darlings. *An Ideal Husband* (*Plays*, p320)

2549. ... the eldest son has quarreled with his father, and it is said that when they meet at the club Lord Brancaster always hides himself behind the money article in "The Times." However, I believe that is quite a commonplace occurrence nowadays and that they have to take in extra copies of "The Times" at all the clubs in St. James Street; there are so many sons who won't have anything to do with their fathers, and so many fathers who won't speak to their sons. I think myself, it is very much to be regretted. *An Ideal Husband* (*Plays*, p283)

2550. The fact that your father loathed you, and that you loathed your father, was not a matter of any interest to the English public. Such feelings are very common in English domestic life, and should be confined to the place they characterise: the home. *De Profundis* (*OWC*, p187)

2551. Fathers have so much to learn from their sons nowadays. *An Ideal Husband* (*Plays*, p283)

2552. In know lots of people [in America] who would give a hundred thousand dollars to have a grandfather, and much more than that to have a family Ghost. *The Canterville Ghost* (*Works*, p197)

2553. The longer I live the more keenly I feel that whatever was good enough for our fathers is not good enough for us. In art, as in politics, *les grandperes sont toujours tort* [the grandfathers are always wrong]. *The Picture of Dorian Gray* (*SC*, p66)

Society, Status and Success

2554. Never speak disrespectfully of Society, Algernon. Only people who can't get into it do that. *The Importance of Being Earnest* (*Plays,* p421)

2555. Society —civilised society, at least — is never very ready to believe anything to the detriment of those who are both rich and fascinating. It feels instinctively that manners are of more importance than morals. *The Picture of Dorian Gray* (*SC,* p155)

2556. To get into the best society, nowadays, one has either to feed people, amuse people, or shock people — that is all? *A Woman of No Importance* (*Plays,* p180)

2557. A man who can dominate a London dinner-table can dominate the world. *A Woman of No Importance* (*Plays,* p179)

2558. You will never be in the best society unless you can stand on your heads. *The Devoted Friend* (*Works,* p286)

2559. ... society must be amazed, and my Neronian coiffure has amazed it. *Oscar Wilde: The Story of an Unhappy Friendship* (*GC,* p83)

2560. One can survive everything nowadays, except death, and live down anything except a good reputation. *A Woman of No Importance* (*Plays,* p147)

2561. I won't tell you that the world matters nothing, or the world's voice, or the voice of society. They matter a good deal. They matter far too much. *Lady Windermere's Fan* (*Plays,* p37)

2562. Arguments are extremely vulgar, for everybody in good society holds exactly the same opinions. *The Remarkable Rocket* (*Works,* p299)

2563. GERALD: I suppose society is wonderfully delightful!

LORD ILLINGWORTH: To be in it is merely a bore. But to be out of it simply a tragedy. *A Woman of No Importance* (*Plays,* p180)

2564. Oh, I love London society! I think it has immensely improved. It is entirely composed now of beautiful idiots and brilliant lunatics. Just what society should be. *An Ideal Husband* (*Plays,* p224)

2565. Charming ball it has been! Quite reminds me of old days. And I see that there are just as many fools in society as there used to be. So pleased to find that nothing has altered! *Lady Windermere's Fan* (*Plays,* p41)

2566. ... as far as she could see, London society was entirely made up of dowdies and dandies. *An Ideal Husband* (*Plays,* p237)

2567. Can't make out how you stand London society. The thing has gone to the dogs, a lot of damned nobodies talking about nothing. *An Ideal Husband* (*Plays,* p234)

2568. Other people are quite dreadful. The only possible society is oneself. *An Ideal Husband* (*Plays,* p292)

2569. MR. ERSKINE: I am due at the Athenaeum. It is the hour when we sleep there.

LORD HENRY: All of you, Mr. Erskine?

MR. ERSKINE: Forty of us, in forty armchairs. We are practicing for an English Academy of Letters. *The Picture of Dorian Gray* (*SC,* p60)

2570. It is always nice to be expected and not to arrive. *An Ideal Husband* (*Plays,* p293)

2571. ... when one pays a visit, it is for the purpose of wasting other people's time, not one's own. *An Ideal Husband* (*Plays,* p320)

2572. He has fought a good fight and has had to face every difficulty except popularity. *Letter to William Rothenstein* (*Letters,* p925)

2573. I have never met him in Society, though he has been in my society, which is more important. *The Three Trials of Oscar Wilde* (*UB*, pp148–9)

2574. The fact is that our Society is terribly over-populated. Really, some one should arrange a proper scheme of assisted emigration. It would do a great deal of good. *An Ideal Husband* (*Plays*, p279)

2575. ... A. came to London with the intention of opening a salon and succeeded in opening a saloon. *Aspects of Wilde* (*CC*, p104)

2576. I'm sure I don't know half the people who come to my house. Indeed, from all I hear, I shouldn't like to. *An Ideal Husband* (*Plays*, p280)

2577. I like to find people out for myself. But Lady Brandon treats her guest exactly as an auctioneer treats his goods. She either explains them away entirely, or tells one everything about them except what one wants to know. *The Picture of Dorian Gray* (*SC*, p25)

2578. ... still I feel you are there, just as in the old days there was always the aroma of poor old Lady Pollack's weak tea and literary twaddle — the "five o'clock" of their reminiscences and butter. *Letter to Frank Harris* (*Letters*, p1043)

2579. There are three inevitables — death, quarterday, and Lady Jeune's parties. *Unorthodox Reminiscences* (*Uncollected*, p115)

2580. Talk to every woman as if you loved her, and to every man as if he bored you, and at the end of the first season you will have the reputation of possessing the most perfect social tact. *A Woman of No Importance* (*Plays*, pp179–80)

2581. Society is a necessary thing. No man has any real success in this world unless he has got a woman to back him, and women rule society. If you have not got women on your side you are quite over. You might just as well be a barrister, or a stockbroker, or a journalist at once. *A Woman of No Importance* (*Plays*, p180)

2582. Success is a science; if you have the conditions, you get the result. *Letter to Marie Prescott* (*Letters*, p204)

2583. ... you must carve your way to fame. Laurels don't come for the asking. *Letter to an Unidentified Correspondent* (*Letters*, p265)

2584. OSCAR WILDE: If you wish for reputation and fame in this world, and success during your lifetime, you ought to seize every opportunity of advertising yourself. You remember the Latin word, "Fame springs from one's own house." Like other wise sayings, it's not quite true; fame comes from oneself ... you must go about repeating how great you are till the dull crowd comes to believe it.

FRANK HARRIS: The prophet must proclaim himself, eh? and declare his own mission?

OSCAR WILDE: That's it, that's it. Every time my name is mentioned in a paper, I write at once to admit that I am the Messiah. Why is Pear's soap so successful? Not because it is better and cheaper than any other soap, but because it is more strenuously puffed. The journalist is my "John the Baptist." What would you give, when a book of yours comes out, to be able to write a long article drawing attention to it in *The Pall Mall Gazette*? Here you have the opportunity of making your name known just as widely; why not avail yourself of it? I miss no chance. *Oscar Wilde, by Frank Harris* (*CG*, p61)

2585. I wanted my success when I was young. Youth is the time for success. I couldn't wait. *An Ideal Husband* (*Plays*, p261)

2586. I myself feel that I am happier with Bosie than I could be if all my laurels were given back to me. *Letter to Reginald Turner* (*Letters*, p961)

2587. Former successes will suffice me. (*Plays*, p. xxxix)

2588. If I could have the feelings appropriate to my position — or rather my lack of position — it would be better for me — but while natures alter, what is artificial is always permanent. *Quoted in Oscar Wilde: His Life and Wit* (*HBP*, p326)

2589. There is something vulgar in all success ... the greatest men fail — or seem to the world to have failed. *Quoted in Oscar Wilde: His Life and Wit* (*HBP*, p322)

2590. Moderation is a fatal thing. Nothing succeeds like excess. *A Woman of No Importance* (*Plays*, p188)

59

Travel

2591. Any place you love is the world to you.... *The Remarkable Rocket* (*Works,* p295)

2592. ... the best thing you can do is emigrate and improve your mind. *The Canterville Ghost* (*Works,* p197)

2593. Travel improves the mind wonderfully, and does away with all one's prejudices. *The Remarkable Rocket* (*Works,* p295)

2594. Sunday is such a good day for traveling, and it's always so dull everywhere, we might just as well spend it on the train. *Oscar Wilde, by Frank Harris* (*CG,* p267)

2595. I hate to fly through a country at this rate. The only true way, you know, to see a country is to ride on horseback. *Oscar Wilde Discovers America* (*HBC,* p63)

2596. I long to get back to real literary work; for though my audiences are really most appreciative I cannot write while flying from one railway to another and from the cast-iron stove of one hotel to its twin horror in the next. *Oscar Wilde Discovers America* (*HBC,* p409)

2597. Everyone wants me to go abroad. I have just been abroad, and now I have come home again. One can't keep on going abroad, unless one is a missionary, or, what comes to the same thing, a commercial traveler. *The Three Trials of Oscar Wilde* (*UB,* pp43–4)

2598. Wanderers in drear exile, and dispossessed

Of what should be our own, we can but feed on wild unrest.
Humanitad (*Works,* p825)

2599. I have never known such loneliness. There [the Atlantic] was such a broad expanse of water, a desert, as one may say, and I felt at times as though it would have been a great relief could I have seen a single fishing smack. *Oscar Wilde Discovers America* (*HBC,* p47)

2600. Dear Godwino, I am delighted to know you are somewhere. We thought you were nowhere, and searched for you everywhere, but could not find you anywhere. *Letter to E.W. Godwin* (*Letters,* p260)

2601. Even the criminal classes have gone to the seaside, and the *gendarmes* yawn and regret their enforced idleness. Giving wrong directions to English tourists is the only thing that consoles them. *Letter to Frank Harris* (*CG,* p224)

2602. Oh, [a view] is altogether immaterial, except to the innkeeper, who, of course, charges the bill. *Oscar Wilde: The Story of an Unhappy Friendship* (*GC,* p26)

2603. I love to travel and meet the best men and look at the best and most beautiful women so that when I die I will leave behind me a name that will be handed down to posterity as a lover of the beautiful. *Oscar Wilde Discovers America* (*HBC,* p313)

60

Truth and Fiction

2604. Truth, indeed, is a thing that is most painful to listen to and most painful to utter. *De Profundis* (*OWC*, p142)

2605. ... to speak the truth is a painful thing. To be forced to tell lies is much worse. *De Profundis* (*OWC*, p144)

2606. A few ordinary platitudes will do. In modern life nothing produces an effect as a good platitude. It makes the whole world kin. *An Ideal Husband* (*Plays*, p242)

2607. The things one feels absolutely certain about are never true. That is the fatality of faith, and the lesson of romance. *The Picture of Dorian Gray* (*SC*, p227)

2608. Man can believe the impossible, but man can never believe the improbable. *The Decay of Lying* (*Works*, p1089)

2609. ... as for believing things, I can believe anything, provided that it is quite incredible. *The Picture of Dorian Gray* (*SC*, p23)

2610. When people agree with me I always feel I must be wrong. *The Critic as Artist* (*Works*, p1150) and similar quotation in Lady Windermere's Fan (*Plays*, p58)

2611. Whenever people talk to me about the weather, I always feel quite certain that they mean something else. And that makes me so nervous. *The Importance of Being Earnest* (*Plays*, p361)

2612. Falsehood[s are] the truths of the people. *An Ideal Husband* (*Plays*, p292)

2613. A truth ceases to be a truth when more than one person believes in it. *Phrases and Philosophies for the Use of the Young, The Chameleon* (*Works*, p1245)

2614. ... it is a terrible thing for a man to find out suddenly that all his life he has been speaking nothing but the truth. Can you for-give me? *The Importance of Being Earnest* (*Plays*, p432)

2615. If one tells the truth, one is sure, sooner or later, to be found out. *Phrases and Philosophies for the Use of the Young, The Chameleon* (*Works*, 1244)

2616. OSCAR WILDE: I could never have dealings with Truth. If Truth were to come unto me, to my room, he would say to me, "You are too willful." And I would say to him, "You are too obvious." And I should throw him out of the window!

FRIEND: You would say to *him*. Is not Truth a woman?

OSCAR WILDE: Then I could not throw her out of the window; I should bow her to the door. *Quoted in Oscar Wilde: His Life and Wit* (*HBP*, p129)

2617. Simplicity, too, is not without its dangers. The *enfant terrible*, with his shameless love of truth, the raw country-bred girl who always says what she means, and the plain, blunt man who makes a point of speaking his mind on every possible occasion, without ever considering whether he has a mind at all, are fatal examples of what simplicity leads to. *Aristotle at Afternoon Tea, Pall Mall Gazette* (*Uncollected*, p84)

2618. Then be not spendthrift of your honesty,
But keep it to yourself....
The Duchess of Padua (*Works*, p613)

2619. You are so evidently, so unmistakably sincere, and most of all so truthful, that.... I can't believe a single word of what you say. *Quoted in Oscar Wilde: His Life and Wit* (*HBP*, p172)

2620. Is insincerity such a terrible thing? I think not. It is merely a method by which we can multiply our personalities. *The Picture of Dorian Gray* (*SC*, p156)

2621. A little sincerity is a dangerous thing, and a great deal of it is absolutely fatal. *The Critic as Artist* (*Works*, p1144)

2622. One should never take sides in anything. Taking sides is the beginning of sincerity and earnestness follows shortly afterwards, and the human being becomes a bore. *A Woman of No Importance* (*Plays*, p137)

2623. Well, the English can't stand a man who is always in the right, but they are very fond of a man who admits that he has been in the wrong. It is one of the best things in them. *An Ideal Husband* (*Plays*, p265)

2624. If one puts forward an idea to a true Englishman — always a rash thing to do — he never dreams of considering whether the idea is right or wrong. The only thing he considers of any importance is whether one believes it oneself. Now, the value of an idea as nothing whatsoever to do with the sincerity of the man who expresses it. Indeed, the probabilities are that the more insincere a man is, the more purely intellectual will be the idea be, as in that case it will not be coloured by either his wants, his desires, or his prejudices. *The Picture of Dorian Gray* (*SC*, p27)

2625. Sincerity itself, the ardent, momentary sincerity of the artist, is often the unconscious result of style.... *The Portrait of Mr. W.H.* (*Works*, p336)

2626. In unimportant matters, style, not sincerity, is the essential. In all important matters, style, not sincerity is the essential. *Phrases and Philosophies for the Use of the Young Chameleon* (*Works*, p1244) and similar quotation in *The Importance of Being Earnest* (*Plays*, p415)

2627. Truth is entirely and absolutely a matter of style. *The Decay of Lying* (*Works*, p1081)

2628. The first duty in life is to be as artificial as possible. What the second duty is no one has yet discovered. *Phrases and Philosophies for the Use of the Young, The Chameleon* (*Uncollected*, p1244)

2629. Being natural is simply a pose, and the most irritating pose I know. *The Picture of Dorian Gray* (*SC*, p22)

2630. To be natural is to be obvious, and to be obvious is to be inartistic. *The Critic as Artist* (*Works*, p1148)

2631. My dear young lady, there was a great deal of truth, I dare say, in what you said, and you looked very pretty while you said it, which is much more important.... *A Woman of No Importance* (*Plays*, p162)

2632. CECILY: This is no time for wearing the shallow mask of manners. When I see a spade I call it a spade.

GWENDOLEN: I am glad to say that I have never seen a spade. It is obvious that our social spheres have been widely different. *The Importance of Being Earnest* (*Plays*, p403)

2633. The truth is rarely pure and never simple. Modern life would be very tedious if it were either, and modern literature a complete impossibility! *The Importance of Being Earnest* (*Plays*, p355)

2634. One of the chief causes that can be assigned for the curiously commonplace character of most of the literature of our age is undoubtedly the decay of Lying as an art, a science, and a social pleasure. The ancient historians gave us delightful fiction in the form of fact; the modern novelist presents us with dull facts under the guise of fiction. *The Decay of Lying* (*Works*, p1073)

2635. Don't write what you don't mean: that is all. If anything in your letter is false or counterfeit I shall detect it by the ring at once. *De Profundis* (*OWC*, p157)

2636. Is the story about me? If so, I will listen to it, for I am extremely fond of fiction. *The Devoted Friend* (*Works*, p286)

2637. You think that is true? — I rarely think that anything I write is true. *The Three Trials of Oscar Wilde* (*UB*, p123)

2638. I need not say, though, that I shift with every breathe of thought and am weaker and more self-deceiving than ever. *Letter to William Ward* (*Letters*, p39)

2639. I am sorry about my excuse. I had forgotten I had used Nogent before. It shows the utter collapse of my imagination, and rather distresses me. *Letter to Robbie Ross* (*Letters*, p1102)

2640. I have always been of the opinion that consistency is the last refuge of the unimaginative.... *The Relation of Art to Dress lecture* (*Uncollected*, p52)

2641. If a man is sufficiently unimaginative to produce evidence in support of a lie, he might just as well speak the truth at once. *The Decay of Lying* (*Works*, p1072)

2642. Bored by the tedious and improving conversation of those who have neither the wit to exaggerate nor the genius to romance, tired of the intelligent person whose reminiscences are always based upon memory, whose statements are invariably limited by probability, and who is at any time liable to be corroborated by the merest Philistine who happens to be present, Society sooner or later must return to its lost leader, the cultured and fascinating liar. *The Decay of Lying* (*Works*, p1081)

2643. For the aim of the liar is simply to charm, to delight, to give pleasure. He is the very basis of civilized society, and without him a dinner-party, even at the mansions of the great, is as dull as a lecture at the Royal Society, or a debate at the Incorporated Authors, or one of Mr. Burnand's farcical comedies. *The Decay of Lying* (*Works*, p1081)

2644. Lying for the sake of a monthly salary is, of course, well known on Fleet Street, and the profession of a political leader-writer is not without its advantages. *The Decay of Lying* (*Works*, p1090)

2645. One should always play fairly ... when one has the winning cards. *An Ideal Husband* (*Plays*, p246)

2646. The only form of lying that is absolutely beyond reproach is lying for its own sake, and the highest development of this is.... Lying in Art. *The Decay of Lying* (*Works*, p1090)

2647. Indeed, honesty of work is essential to progress in a practical age, yet is this an honest age? This century has been marked by more dishonest workmanship and has produced more rubbish than any that preceded it. *The Decorative Arts lecture* (*Works*, p928)

2648. ... to censure an artist for forgery was to confuse an ethical with an aesthetical problem. *The Portrait of Mr. W.H.* (*Works*, p302)

2649. People have a careless way of talking about a "born liar," just as they talk about a born poet. But in both cases they are wrong. Lying and poetry are arts—arts as Plato saw,

not unconnected with each other — and they require the most careful study, the most interested devotion. *The Decay of Lying* (*Works*, p1073)

2650. ... a lad who learns any simple art learns honesty, truth-telling, and simplicity, in the most practical school of simple morals in the world, the school of art.... *Letter to Charles Godfrey Leland* (*Letters*, p170)

2651. But in modern days while the fashion of poetry has become far too common, and should, if possible, be discouraged, the fashion of lying has almost fallen into disrepute. Many a young man starts in life with a natural gift for exaggeration which, if nurtured in congenial and sympathetic surroundings, or by the imitation of the best models, might grow into something really great and wonderful. But, as a rule, he comes to nothing. He either falls into the careless habits of accuracy ... or takes to frequenting the society of the aged and well-informed ... and in a short time he develops a morbid and unhealthy faculty of truth-telling, begins to verify all statements made in his presence, and has no hesitation in contradicting people who are much younger than himself, and often ends by writing novels which are so life-like that no one can possibly believe in their probability. *The Decay of Lying* (*Works*, p1073)

2652. The English are always degrading truths into facts. When a truth becomes a fact it loses all its intellectual value. *A Few Maxims for the Instruction of the Over-Educated, Saturday Review* (*Works*, p1242)

2653. Certainly we are a degraded race, we have sold our birthright for a mess of facts. *The Decay of Lying* (*Works*, p1077)

2654. Facts are not merely finding a footing-place in history, but they are usurping the domain of Fancy, and have invaded the kingdom of Romance. *The Decay of Lying* (*Works*, p1080)

2655. ... knaves nowadays do look so honest that honest folk are forced to look like knaves so as to be different. *The Duchess of Padua* (*Works*, p655)

2656. Truth is independent of facts always.... *The Critic as Artist* (*Works*, p1166)

2657. It is so hard to use facts, so easy to accumulate them. *The Rise of Historical Criticism* (*Works,* p1238)

2658. SIR ROBERT CHILTERN: You have enabled me to tell the truth. That is something. The truth has always stifled me.

LORD GORING: Ah! the truth is a thing I get rid of as soon as possible. Bad habit, by the way. Makes one very unpopular at the club ... with the older members. They call it being conceited. Perhaps it is.

SIR ROBERT CHILTERN: I would to God that I had been able to tell the truth ... to live the truth. Ah! that is the great thing in life, to live the truth. *An Ideal Husband* (*Plays,* p270)

2659. See that thou speakest nothing but the truth,
Naught else will serve thee.
The Duchess of Padua (*Works,* p666)

2660. I urge you not to become discouraged because ridicule is thrown upon those who have the boldness to run counter to popular prejudice; in time the true aesthetic principles will prevail. Throughout the world, in all times and in all ages, there have been those who have had the courage to advocate opinions that were for the time abhorred by the public. But if those who hold these opinions have the courage to maintain and defend them, it is absolutely certain that in the end the truth will prevail. *The House Beautiful lecture* (*Works,* p925)

2661. Whatever is false will vanish; whatever is permanent will remain. I am patient, and I can wait. *Oscar Wilde Discovers America* (*HBC,* p422)

2662. For, try as we may, we cannot get behind the appearance of things to the reality. And the terrible reason may be that there is no reality apart from their appearances. *Quoted in Oscar Wilde: His Life and Wit* (*HBP,* p186)

61

Vanity and Humility

2663. To be great is to be misunderstood. *Letter to James Whistler* (*Letters*, p250)

2664. I have never given adoration for anybody except myself. *The Three Trials of Oscar Wilde* (*UB*, p129)

2665. I am fond of praise. I like to be made much of. *The Three Trials of Oscar Wilde* (*UB*, p316)

2666. Praise makes me humble. But when I am abused I know I have touched the stars. *Aspects of Wilde* (*CC*, p11)

2667. ... the only thing that ever consoles a man for the stupid things he does is the praise he always gives himself for doing them. *Quoted in Oscar Wilde: His Life and Wit* (*HBP*, p116)

2668. I like to be liked.... I like to be lionized. *The Three Trials of Oscar Wilde* (*UB*, p316)

2669. Even the disciple has his uses. He stands behind one's throne, and at the moment of one's triumph whispers in one's ear that, after all, one is immortal. *A Few Maxims for the Instruction of the Over-Educated* (*Works*, p1243)

2670. I am always thinking about myself, and I expect everybody else to do the same. *The Remarkable Rocket* (*Works*, p296)

2671. Yes; I am always astonishing myself. It is the only thing that makes life worth living. *A Woman of No Importance* (*Plays*, p186)

2672. We watch ourselves, and the mere wonder of the spectacle enthralls us. I am the only person in the world I should like to know thoroughly, but I don't see any chance of it at present. *Quoted in Oscar Wilde: His Life and Wit* (*HBP*, p124)

2673. The only thing which sustains one through life is the consciousness of the immense inferiority of everybody else, and this feeling I have always cultivated. *The Remarkable Rocket* (*Works*, p297)

2674. Geniuses talk so much, don't they? Such a bad habit! And they are always thinking about themselves, when I want them to be thinking about me. *An Ideal Husband* (*Plays*, p277)

2675. Fortune had so turned my head that I fancied I could do whatever I chose. *Oscar Wilde: The Story of an Unhappy Friendship* (*GC*, p163)

2676. I trust the glory round thy head
Has kept thine eyes from seeing clear.
   Untitled (*Works*, p765)

2677. Vanity had barred up the windows, and the name of the warder was Hate. *De Profundis* (*OWC*, p83)

2678. ... nothing makes one so vain as being told one is a sinner. Conscience makes egotists of us all. *The Picture of Dorian Gray* (*SC*, p117)

2679. Is affectation the only thing that accompanies a man up the steps of the scaffold? *The Portrait of Mr. W.H.* (*Works*, p349)

2680. It is a very unimaginative nature that only cares for people on their pedestals. A pedestal may be a very unreal thing. A pillory is a terrific reality. *De Profundis* (*OWC*, p130)

2681. The painter, Basil Hallward, worshipping physical beauty far too much, as most painters do, dies by the hand of one in whose soul he has created a monstrous and absurd vanity. *Letter to the Editor of The St. James Gazette* (*Letters*, p430)

2682. In literature mere egotism is delightful. *The Critic as Artist* (*Works*, p1108)

2683. Even in actual life egotism is not without its attractions. When people talk to us about others they are usually dull. When they talk to us about themselves they are nearly always interesting, and if one could shut them up, when they become wearisome, as easily as one can shut up a book of which one has grown wearied, they would be absolutely perfect. *The Critic as Artist* (*Works*, p1109)

2684. The egoistic note is, of course, and always has been to me, the primal and ultimate note of modern art, but *to be an Egoist one must have an Ego*. It is not everyone who says "I, I who can enter into the kingdom of art." *Letter to Lord Alfred Douglas* (*Letters*, p874)

2685. ... he was a sad example of an Egoist who had no Ego. *Oscar Wilde, by Frank Harris* (*CG*, p278)

2686. Really, Bobbie, you ride the high horse so well, and so willingly, it seems a pity that you never tried Pegasus. *Oscar Wilde, by Frank Harris* (*CG*, p313) and similar quotation in *Letter to Leonard Smithers* (*Letters*, p987)

2687. It is a sad thing, but one wearies even of praise. *Letter to the Editor of The Scots Observer* (*Letters*, p447)

2688. Anything approaching self-aggrandisation is vulgar. You must avoid it. *Oscar Wilde: The Story of an Unhappy Friendship* (*GC*, p62)

2689. It is curious how vanity helps the successful man, and wrecks the failure. In old days half of my strength was my vanity. *Letter to Robert Ross* (*Letters*, p980)

2690. The prayer of your pride has been answered. The prayer of your repentance will be answered also. I worshipped you too much. We are both punished. *The Picture of Dorian Gray* (*SC*, p170)

2691. Shyness may be a form of vanity, and reserve a development of pride.... *Aristotle at Afternoon Tea, Pall Mall Gazette* (*Uncollected*, pp84–5)

2692. All the spring may be hidden in a single bud, and the low ground-nest of the lark may hold the joy that is to herald the feet of many rose-red dawns, and so perhaps whatever beauty of life still remains to me is contained in some moment of surrender, abasement and humiliation. *De Profundis* (*OWC*, p130)

2693. That something hidden away in my nature, like a treasure in a field, is Humility.... It has come to me right out of myself, so I know that it has come at the proper time. It could not have come before, nor later. Had anyone told me of it, I would have rejected it. Had it been brought to me, I would have refused it. As I found it, I want to keep it. *De Profundis* (*OWC*, pp96–7)

2694. Of all things, [humility] is the strangest. One cannot give it away, and another may not give it to one. One cannot acquire it, except by surrendering everything that one has. It is only when one has lost all things, that one knows that one possesses it. *De Profundis* (*OWC*, p97)

2695. There is only one thing for me now — absolute Humility: just as there is only one thing for you, absolute Humility also. You had better come down in the dust and learn it beside me. *De Profundis* (*OWC*, p96)

2696. Could anything be more petty — a greater revelation of insignificance? Now for me, the highest place is where I am myself. *Aspects of Wilde* (*CC*, p71)

Vice and Virtue

2697. I can resist everything except temptation. *Lady Windermere's Fan* (*Plays*, p9)

2698. Make me an offer, if you care to, and be sure that it is a temptation, for I never resist temptation. *Letter to Lewis Waller* (*Letters*, p581)

2699. One should never do anything that one cannot talk about after dinner. *The Picture of Dorian Gray* (*SC*, p225)

2700. I like persons better than principles, and I like person with no principles better than anything else in the world. *The Picture of Dorian Gray* (*SC*, p27)

2701. I don't like principles.... I prefer prejudices. *An Ideal Husband* (*Plays*, p334)

2702. We are not sent into the world to air our moral prejudices. *The Picture of Dorian Gray* (*SC*, p89)

2703. Experience was of no ethical value. It was merely the name men gave to their mistakes. *The Picture of Dorian Gray* (*SC*, p74)

2704. There is no such thing as morality or immorality in thought. There is immoral emotion. *The Three Trials of Oscar Wilde* (*UB*, p123)

2705. ... manners before morals! *Lady Windermere's Fan* (*Plays*, p70)

2706. I never came across anyone in whom the moral sense was dominant who was not heartless, cruel, vindictive, log-stupid, and entirely lacking in the smallest sense of humanity. Moral people, as they are termed, are simple beasts. *Letter to Leonard Smithers* (*Letters*, p996)

2707. A man who moralizes is usually a hypocrite, and a woman who moralizes is invariably plain. *Lady Windermere's Fan* (*Plays*, p58)

2708. Immoral women are rarely attractive. What made her quite irresistible was that she was unmoral. *Quoted in Oscar Wilde: His Life and Wit* (*HBP*, p232)

2709. Vice and virtue are to the artist materials for an art. *The Picture of Dorian Gray* (*SC*, p18)

2710. There were moments when he looked on evil simply as a mode through which he could realise his conception of the beautiful. *The Picture of Dorian Gray* (*SC*, p159)

2711. An artist, sir, has no ethical sympathies at all. Virtue and wickedness are to him simply what the colours on his palette are to the painter. They are no more, and they are no less. He sees that by their means a certain artistic effect can be produced. *Letter to the Editor of The Scots Observer* (*Letters*, p439)

2712. Good people, belonging as they do to the normal, and so, commonplace, type are artistically uninteresting. Bad people are, from the point of view of art, fascinating studies. They represent colour, variety, and strangeness. Good people exasperate one's reason; bad people stir one's imagination. *Letter to the Editor of The St. James Gazette* (*Letters*, p430)

2713. Wickedness is a myth invented by good people to account for the curious attractiveness of others. *Phrases and Philosophies for the Use of the Young, The Chameleon* (*Works*, p1244)

2714. He hasn't a single redeeming vice. *Quoted in Oscar Wilde: His Life and Wit* (*HBP*, p171)

2715. The interesting thing surely is to be guilty and so wear as a halo the seduction of sin. *Oscar Wilde, by Frank Harris* (*CG*, p245)

2716. I am afraid you are leading a wonderfully wicked life. *The Three Trials of Oscar Wilde* (*UB*, p20)

2717. ... nothing looks so like innocence as an indiscretion. *Lady Windermere's Fan* (*Plays*, p41)

2718. Besides, we are all innocent until we are found out.... *Oscar Wilde, by Frank Harris* (*CG*, p245)

2719. One should believe evil of everyone, until, of course, people are found out to be good. But that requires a great deal of investigation nowadays. *A Woman of No Importance* (*Plays*, p184)

2720. Morality is simply the attitude we adopt towards people whom we personally dislike. *An Ideal Husband* (*Plays*, p286)

2721. ... vulgarity is simply the conduct of other people. *An Ideal Husband* (*Plays*, p292)

2722. Ethics, like natural selection, make existence possible. *The Critic as Artist* (*Works*, p1154)

2723. ... intellectual generalities are always interesting, but generalities in morals mean absolutely nothing. *A Woman of No Importance* (*Plays*, p1154)

2724. Modern morality consists in accepting the standard of one's age. I consider that for any man of culture to accept the standard of his age is a form of the grossest immorality. *The Picture of Dorian Gray* (*SC*, p172)

2725. The two weak points in our age are its want of principle and its want of profile. *The Importance of Being Earnest* (*Plays*, p421)

2726. I want to introduce you to my mother. We have founded a Society for the Suppression of Virtues. *Quoted in Oscar Wilde: His Life and Wit* (*HBP*, p22)

2727. I hope you have not been leading a double life, pretending to be wicked and being really good all the time, that would be hypocrisy. *The Importance of Being Earnest* (*Plays*, p382)

2728. Oh, now-a-days, so many conceited people go about society pretending to be good, that I think it shows rather a sweet and modest disposition to pretend to be bad. *Lady Windermere's Fan* (*Plays*, p5)

2729. As a wicked man I am a complete failure. Why, there are lots of people who say I have never really done anything wrong in the whole course of my life. Of course, they only say it behind my back. *Lady Windermere's Fan* (*Plays*, p10)

2730. If you pretend to be good, the world takes you very seriously. If you pretend to be bad, it doesn't. Such is the astounding stupidity of optimism. *Lady Windermere's Fan* (*Plays*, pp5–6)

2731. Naturally we pretend to be bad ... it is the only way to make ourselves interesting to you. Everyone believes a man who pretends to be good, he is such a bore; but no one believes a man who says he's evil. That makes him interesting. *Oscar Wilde, by Frank Harris* (*CG*, p247)

2732. ... I turned the good things of my life to evil, and the evil things of my life to good. *De Profundis* (*OWC*, p99)

2733. It may be that the things which we call evil are good, and that the things which we call good are evil. There is no knowledge of anything. *Salome* (*Plays*, p105)

2734. ... it is not the wicked only who do wrong, nor the bad alone who work evil. *Injury and Insult, Pall Mall Gazette* (*Uncollected*, p89)

2735. I don't think now that people can be divided into the good and the bad as though they were two separate races or creatures. What are called good women may have terrible things in them, mad moods of recklessness, assertion, jealousy, sin. Bad women, as they are termed, may have in them sorrow, repentance, pity, sacrifice. *Lady Windermere's Fan* (*Plays*, p68)

2736. Nobody is incapable of doing a foolish thing. Nobody is incapable of doing a wrong thing. *An Ideal Husband* (*Plays*, p273)

2737. Any preoccupation with ideas of what is right or wrong in conduct shows an arrested intellectual development. *Phrases and Philosophies for the Use of the Young, The Chameleon* (*Works*, p1245)

2738. You always find out that one's most glaring fault is one's most important virtue. You have the most comforting views of life. *A Woman of No Importance* (*Plays*, p188)

2739. Our virtues are most frequently but vices disguised. *Quoted in Oscar Wilde: His Life and Wit* (*HBP*, p177)

2740. A man may commit a sin against society and yet realize through that sin his own perfection. (*Plays*, p. xxix)

2741. We cannot go back to the saint. There is far more to be learned from the sinner. *The Critic as Artist* (*Works*, p1137)

2742. I am not in favour of this modern mania for turning bad people into good people at a moment's notice. As a man sows so let him reap. *The Importance of Being Earnest* (*Plays*, p378)

2743. It is well for our vanity that we slay the criminal, for if we suffered him to live he might show us what we had gained by his crime. It is well for his peace that that the saint goes to his martyrdom. He is spared the sight of the horror of his harvest. *Quoted in Oscar Wilde: His Life and Wit* (*HBP*, p165)

2744. Do you know I am afraid good people do a great deal of harm in this world. Certainly the greatest harm they do is that they make badness of such extraordinary importance. *Lady Windermere's Fan* (*Plays*, p8)

2745. We think that we are generous because we credit our neighbor with the possession of those virtues that are likely to be a benefit to us. The gratitude of most men is but a secret desire of receiving greater benefits. *Quoted in Oscar Wilde: His Life and Wit* (*HBP*, pp176–7)

2746. People regret their good actions. That is the point to which the moral sense ultimately arrives. *Letter to Robert Ross* (*Letters*, p1089)

2747. I regret my bad actions. You regret your good ones— that is the difference between us. *Lady Windermere's Fan* (*Plays*, p75)

2748. The gods are strange. It is not of our vices only they make instruments to scourge us. They bring us to ruin through what in us is good, gentle, humane, loving. But for my pity and affection for you and yours, I would not now be weeping in this terrible place [prison]. *De Profundis* (*OWC*, p61)

2749. ... the gods are strange, and punish us for what is good and humane in us as much as for what is evil and perverse.... *De Profundis* (*OWC*, p101)

2750. God is in what is evil as He is in what is good. *Salome* (*Works*, p105)

2751. No, no, he will not die, he is too sinful;
Honest men die before their proper time. *The Duchess of Padua* (*Works*, p636)

2752. ... they are those who are too good for hell, and too bad for heaven. *Some Literary Notes, Women's World* (*Uncollected*, p152)

2753. We are each our own devil, and we make
This world our hell. *The Duchess of Padua* (*Works*, p675)

2754. Whenever I think of my bad qualities at night, I go to sleep at once. *Quoted in Oscar Wilde: His Life and Wit* (*HBP*, p171)

2755. There is nothing calculating about him. He never thinks evil, he only does it. *Insult and Injury Pall Mall Gazette* (*Uncollected*, p88)

2756. I can only think of what has been and torment myself. Already I've been punished enough for the sins of a lifetime. *Oscar Wilde, by Frank Harris* (*CG*, p155)

2757. ... the memory of sins that were old could be destroyed by the madness of sins that were new. *The Picture of Dorian Gray* (*SC*, p196)

2758. Crimes may be forgotten or forgiven, but vices live on; they make their dwelling house in him who by horrible mischance or fate has become their victim. *Letter to the Home Secretary* (*Letters*, p658)

2759. In our friend Todd's ethical barometer, at what height is his moral quicksilver? *Letter to William Ward* (*Letters*, p28)

2760. Sin is a thing that writes itself across a man's face. It cannot be concealed. People talk of secret vices. There are no such. If a wretched man has a vice, it shows itself in the lines of his mouth, the droop of his eyelids, the moulding of his hands even. *The Picture of Dorian Gray* (*SC*, p162)

2761. His crimes seem to have had an important effect upon his art. They gave a strong personality to his style, a quality that his early work certainly had lacked. *Pen, Pencil and Poison* (*Works*, p1107)

2762. The fact of a man being a poisoner is nothing against his prose. *Pen, Pencil and Poison* (*Works*, p1106)

2763. ... poisonous things grow in the dark.... *Letter to Robert Ross* (*Letters*, p669)

2764. ... the still more poisonous influences that came from his own temperament. *The Picture of Dorian Gray* (*SC*, p133)

2765. ... he should not have touched him; if one meddles with wicked people, one is like to be tainted with their wickedness. *The Duchess of Padua* (*Works*, p668)

2766. I little thought that it was by a pariah that I was to be made a pariah myself. *De Profundis* (*OWC*, p131)

2767. People thought it dreadful of me to have entertained at dinner the evil things of life, and to have found pleasure in their company. But they, from the point of view from which I, as an artist in life, approached them, were delightfully suggestive and stimulating. It was like feasting with the panthers. The danger was half the excitement. *De Profundis* (*OWC*, p132)

2768. Do not think that I would blame *him* for my vices. He had as little to do with them as I had with his. Nature was in this matter stepmother to each of us. *Letter to Robert Ross* (*Letters*, p670)

2769. And the worst of it is, I know, if men have treated me badly, I have treated myself worse; it is our sins against ourselves we can never forgive.... *Oscar Wilde, by Frank Harris* (*CG*, p670)

2770. Sin should be solitary and have no accomplices. *Pen, Pencil and Poison* (*Works*, p1103)

2771. Sins of the flesh are nothing. They are maladies for physicians to cure, if they should be cured. Sins of the soul alone are shameful. *De Profundis* (*OWC*, p76)

2772. What is termed Sin is an essential element of progress. Without it the world would stagnate, or grow old, or become colourless. By its curiosity Sin increases the experience of the race. *The Critic as Artist* (*Works*, p1121)

2773. Sɪʀ Rᴏʙᴇʀᴛ Cʜɪʟᴛᴇʀɴ: Is it fair that the folly, the sin of one's youth, if men choose to call it a sin, should wreck a life like mine, should place me in the pillory, should shatter all that I have worked for, all that I have built up?

Lᴏʀᴅ Gᴏʀɪɴɢ: Life is never fair, Robert. And perhaps it is a good thing for most of us that it is not. *An Ideal Husband* (*Plays*, p260)

2774. Cannot repentance wipe out an act of folly? *The Importance of Being Earnest* (*Plays*, p429)

2775. Perchance my sin will be forgiven me.
I have loved much.
  The Duchess of Padua (*Works*, p680)

2776. They do not sin at all
Who sin for love
  The Duchess of Padua (*Works*, p680)

2777. I have tempted my master with evil, and his love is stronger than I am. I will tempt him now with good. *The Fisherman and His Soul* (*Works*, p256)

2778. ... don't be led astray into the paths of virtue. Reformed, you would be perfectly tedious. *Lady Windermere's Fan* (*Plays*, pp58–9)

2779. There is no use telling me you are going to be good. You are quite perfect. Pray, don't change. *The Picture of Dorian Gray* (*SC*, p221)

2780. Nothing is more painful to me than to come across virtue in a person in whom I have never expected its existence. It is like finding a needle in a bundle of hay. It pricks you. If we have a virtue we should warn people of it. *Quoted in Oscar Wilde: His Life and Wit* (*HBP*, p175)

2781. I quite sympathise with the rage of the English democracy against what they call the vices of the upper orders. The masses feel that drunkenness, stupidity, and immorality should be their own special property, and that if any one of us makes an ass of himself, he is poaching on their preserve. *The Picture of Dorian Gray* (*SC*, p26)

2782. Nowadays, with our modern mania for morality, everyone has to pose as a paragon of purity, incorruptibility, and all the other seven deadly virtues—and what is the result? You all go over like ninepins—one after the other. Not a year passes in England without somebody disappearing. Scandals used to lend charm, or at least interest, to a man—now they crush him. *An Ideal Husband* (*Plays*, pp244–5)

2783. Great heaven, they speak of smoking as if it were a crime! I wonder they don't caution the students not to murder each other on the landings. *Oscar Wilde Discovers America* (*HBC*, p189)

2784. I gave two or three of them a cigarette case. Boys of that class smoke a good deal of cigarettes. I have a weakness for presenting my acquaintances with cigarette cases. *The Three Trials of Oscar Wilde* (*UB*, p241)

2785. Too much experience is a dangerous thing. Pray have a cigarette. Half the pretty women in London smoke cigarettes. Personally I prefer the other half. *An Ideal Husband* (*Plays*, p308)

2786. A cigarette is the perfect type of a perfect pleasure. It is exquisite, and it leaves one unsatisfied. What more can one want? *The Picture of Dorian Gray* (*SC*, p94) and *The Critic as Artist* (*Works*, p1118)

2787. The tobacco is to be smoked gravely in a pipe. *Letter to Edward Strangman* (*Letters*, p916)

2788. You make up your mind that you cannot smoke, and you resign yourself to the inevitable with ease. *Oscar Wilde: The Story of an Unhappy Friendship* (*GC*, p55)

2789. ... one regrets even the loss of one's worst habits. *The Picture of Dorian Gray* (*SC*, p224)

2790. There is a fatality about all good resolutions. They are invariably made too soon. *Phrases and Philosophies for the Use of the Young, The Chameleon* (*Works*, p1245)

2791. Every impulse that we strive to strangle broods in the mind, and poisons us.... The only way to get rid of a temptation is to yield to it. Resist it, and your soul grows sick with longing for the things it has forbidden to itself, with desire for what its monstrous laws have made monstrous and unlawful. *The Picture of Dorian Gray* (*SC*, p35)

2792. Indulgence may hurt the body, Frank, but nothing except suffering hurts the spirit; it is self-denial and abstinence that maim and deform the soul. *Oscar Wilde, by Frank Harris* (*CG*, p27)

2793. All excess, as well as all renunciation, brings its own punishment. *Letter to the Editor of The St. James Gazette* (*Works*, p430)

2794. To me reformations in morals are as meaningless and vulgar as reformations in theology. But while to propose to be a better man is a piece of unscientific cant, to have become a deeper man is the privilege of those who have suffered. And such I think I have become. *Quoted in Oscar Wilde: His Life and Wit* (*HBP*, p289)

2795. ... the good and bad man alike seem to lose the power of free will; for the one is morally unable to sin, the other physically incapacitated for reformation. *The Rise of Historical Criticism* (*Works*, p1220)

2796. How securely one thinks one lives — out of reach of temptation, sin, folly. And then suddenly — Oh! Life is terrible. It rules us, we do not rule it. *Lady Windermere's Fan* (*Plays*, p65)

2797. There is the same world for all of us, and good and evil, sin and innocence, go through it hand in hand. To shut one's eyes to half of life that one may live securely is as though one blinded oneself that one might walk with more safety in a land of pit and precipice. *Lady Windermere's Fan* (*Plays*, p81)

2798. The vices of Tiberius could not destroy that supreme civilization, any more than the virtues of the Antonines could save it. It fell for other, for less interesting reasons. *The Decay of Lying* (*Works*, p1087)

2799. ... if it is Caliban for one half of the year, it is Tartuffe for the other.... *De Profundis* (*OWC*, p139)

2800. It is absurd to divide people into good and bad. People are either charming or tedious. *Lady Windermere's Fan* (*Plays*, p8)

2801. The good ended happily, and the bad unhappily. That is what fiction means. *The Importance of Being Earnest* (*Plays*, p379)

Wealth and Poverty

2802. Time is a waste of money. *Phrases and Philosophies for the Use of the Young, The Chameleon* (*Works*, p1244)

2803. Even you are not rich enough, Sir Robert, to buy back your past. No man is. *An Ideal Husband* (*Plays*, p246)

2804. Give me the luxuries and anyone can have the necessities. *Oscar Wilde, by Frank Harris* (*CG*, p36)

2805. ... we live in an age when unnecessary things are our only necessities.... *The Picture of Dorian Gray* (*SC*, p108)

2806. Sir, knowest though not that out of the luxury of the rich cometh the life of the poor? *The Young King* (*Works*, p220)

2807. The English think that a cheque-book can solve every problem in life. *An Ideal Husband* (*Plays*, p309)

2808. His reasons are so reasonable that I cannot understand them: a cheque is the only argument I recognise. *Letter to Lord Alfred Douglas* (*Letters*, p578)

2809. LORD FERMOR: Young people nowadays, imagine that money is everything.

LORD HENRY: Yes, and when they grow older they know it. *The Picture of Dorian Gray* (*SSC*, p49)

2810. My dear Sir Robert, you are a man of the world, and you have your price, I suppose. Everybody has nowadays. *An Ideal Husband* (*Plays*, p243)

2811. Every man of ambition has to fight his century with its own weapons. What this century worships is wealth. The God of this century is wealth. To succeed one must have wealth. At all costs one must have wealth. *An Ideal Husband* (*Plays*, p260)

2812. Private information is practically the source of every large modern fortune. *An Ideal Husband* (*Plays*, p260)

2813. You have never been poor, and never known what ambition is. *An Ideal Husband* (*Plays*, p262)

2814. I had the double misfortune of being well-born and poor, two unforgivable things nowadays. *An Ideal Husband* (*Plays*, p260)

2815. Misery and poverty are so absolutely degrading, and exercise such a paralysing effect over the nature of men, that no class is ever really conscious of its own suffering. They have to be told of it by other people, and they often entirely disbelieve them. *The Soul of Man* (*OWC*, p5)

2816. As for the virtuous poor, one can pity them, of course, but one cannot possibly admire them. They have made private terms with the enemy, and sold their birthright for very bad pottage. *The Soul of Man* (*OWC*, p5)

2817. If one has to suffer poverty, one had best suffer alone. But to get discomforts grudgingly as a charity is the extremity of shame. *Oscar Wilde, by Frank Harris* (*CG*, p299)

2818. There is only one class in the community that thinks more about money than the rich, and that is the poor. The poor can think of nothing else. That is the misery of being poor. *The Soul of Man* (*OWC*, p10)

2819. I have been in a position at once tragic and comic at the some time, without money, and with that detestable preoccupation with money that poverty entails—a mood of mind fatal to all fine things. *Letter to Edward Strangman* (*Letters*, p1082)

2820. Sometimes the poor are praised for being thrifty. But to recommend thrift to the poor is both grotesque and insulting. It is like advising a man who is starving to eat less. *The Soul of Man* (*OWC*, p4)

2821. Like dear St. Francis of Assisi I am wedded to poverty: but in my case the marriage is not a success: I hate the Bride that has been given to me.... *Letter to Frances Forbes-Robertson* (*Letters*, p1145)

2822. In war, the strong make slaves of the weak, and in peace the rich make slaves of the poor. *The Young King* (*Works*, p216)

2823. Each class would have preached the importance of those virtues, for whose exercise there was no necessity in their own lives. The rich would have spoken on the value of thrift, and the idle grown eloquent over the dignity of labour. *The Picture of Dorian Gray* (*SC*, p30)

2824. Have you noticed how annoyed pigs become if you do not cast pearls before them? *Quoted in Oscar Wilde: His Life and Wit* (*HBP*, p249)

2825. Yes, we are overcharged for everything nowadays. I should fancy that the real tragedy of the poor is that they can afford nothing but self-denial. Beautiful sins, like beautiful things, are the privilege of the rich. *The Picture of Dorian Gray* (*SC*, p93)

2826. The only thing that can console one for being poor is extravagance. The only thing that can console one for being rich is economy. *A Few Maxims for the Instruction of the Over-Educated, Saturday Review* (*Works*, p1242)

2827. I am so sorry my life is so marred and maimed by extravagance. But I cannot live otherwise. I, at any rate, pay the penalty of suffering. *Letter to George Alexander* (*Letters*, p633)

2828. Never buy a thing you don't want merely because it is dear. *Quoted in Oscar Wilde: His Life and Wit* (*HBP*, p171)

2829. You are penny foolish and pound foolish — a dreadful state for any financier to be in. *Letter to Robert Ross* (*Letters*, p883)

2830. People will not pay half a crown for what they can buy for a penny. *Letter to Leonard Smithers* (*Letters*, p953)

2831. He really is a miser: but his method of hoarding is a new type: spending. *Letter to Robert Ross* (*Letters*, p1192)

2832. ... the typical spendthrift ... is always giving away what he needs most. *Vera, or The Nihilists* (*Works*, p703)

2833. Ah, now-a-days we are all of us so hard up, that the only pleasant things to pay

are compliments. They're the only things we can pay. *Lady Windermere's Fan* (*Plays*, p5)

2834. As far as I can see, he is to do nothing but pay bills and compliments. *A Woman of No Importance* (*Plays*, p157)

2835. Unless one is wealthy, there is no use in being a charming fellow. *The Model Millionaire* (*Works*, p209)

2836. He has nothing, but looks everything. What more can one desire? *The Importance of Being Earnest* (*Plays*, p422)

2837. It is better to have a permanent income than to be fascinating. *The Model Millionaire* (*Works*, p209)

2838. If the poor only had profiles there would be no difficulty in solving the problem of poverty. *Phrases and Philosophies for the Use of the Young, The Chameleon* (*Works*, p1244)

2839. It is a sad fact, but there is no doubt that the poor are completely unconscious of their own picturesqueness. *London Models, English Illustrated Magazine* (*Uncollected*, p33)

2840. Man will kill himself by overwork in order to secure property, and really, considering the enormous advantages that property brings, one is hardly surprised. One's regret is that society should be constructed on such a basis that man has been forced into a groove in which he cannot freely develop what is wonderful, and fascinating, and delightful in him — in which, in fact, he misses the true pleasure and joy of living. *The Soul of Man* (*OWC*, pp7–8)

2841. TAX COLLECTOR: I have called about the taxes.

OSCAR WILDE: Taxes! Why should I pay taxes?

TAX COLLECTOR: But, sir, you are the householder here are you not? You live here, you sleep here.

OSCAR WILDE: Ah, yes; but then, you see, I sleep so badly. *Quoted in Oscar Wilde: His Life and Wit* (*HBP*, p106)

2842. What between the duties expected of one during one's life-time, and the duties exacted from one after one's death, land has ceased to be either a profit or a pleasure. It gives one position, and prevents one form keeping it up. That's all that can be said about land. *The Importance of Being Earnest* (*Plays*, p366)

2843. Property not merely has duties, but has so many duties that its possession to any large extent is a bore. *The Soul of Man* (*OWC*, p4)

2844. Indeed, so completely has man's personality been absorbed by his possessions that the English law has always treated offences against a man's property with far more severity than offences against his person, and property is still the test of complete citizenship. *The Soul of Man* (*OWC*, p7)

2845. We have as yet nothing like it in England. We call a man rich over there when he owns a share of Scotland, or a country or so. But he doesn't have such a control over ready money as does an American capitalist. *Oscar Wilde Discovers America* (*HBC*, p41)

2846. It's as much your as it is mine. You know I have no sense of property. *Oscar Wilde: The Story of an Unhappy Friendship* (*GC*, p89)

2847. ... your fine, chivalrous friendship — is worth more than all the money in the world. *Oscar Wilde: The Story of an Unhappy Friendship* (*GC*, p144)

2848. If I got nothing at the house of the rich, I would get something at the house of the poor. Those who have much are often greedy. Those who have little always share. *De Profundis* (*OWC*, p97)

2849. Who, being loved, is poor? Oh, no one. I hate my riches. They are a burden. *A Woman of No Importance* (*Plays*, p210)

2850. The poor, who love eachother, are so rich. *The Duchess of Padua* (*Works*, p630)

2851. ... what does money matter? Love is more than money. *The Picture of Dorian Gray* (*SC*, p76)

2852. I see that any materialism in life coarsens the soul.... *Letter to Carlos Blacker* (*Letters*, p912)

2853. But I don't want money. It is only people who pay their bills who want that ... and I never pay mine. *The Picture of Dorian Gray* (*SC*, p49)

2854. It is only by not paying one's bills that one can hope to live in the memory of the commercial classes. *Phrases and Philoso-*phies for the Use of the Young, *The Chameleon* (*Works*, p1244)

2855. LADY STUTFIELD: How very, very charming those gold-tipped cigarettes of yours are, Lord Alfred.

LORD ALFRED: They are awfully expensive. I can only afford them when I'm in debt.

LADY STUTFIELD: It must be terribly, terribly distressing to be in debt.

LORD ALFRED: One must have some occupation nowadays. If I hadn't my debts I shouldn't have anything to think about. All the chaps I know are in debt. *A Woman of No Importance* (*Plays*, pp141–2)

2856. ALGERNON: Of course, I'm your brother. And that is why you should pay this bill for me. What is the use of having a brother if he doesn't pay one's bills for one?

JACK: Personally, if you ask me, I don't see any use in having a brother. As for paying your bill, I have not the smallest intention of doing anything of the kind. *The Importance of Being Earnest* (*Plays*, p437)

2857. Credit is the capital of a younger son, and one lives charmingly upon it. *The Picture of Dorian Gray* (*SC*, p49)

2858. I haven't any debts at all, dear Jack. Thanks to your generosity I don't owe a penny, except for a few neckties, I believe. *The Importance of Being Earnest* (*Plays*, p434)

2859. I know that Bosie made terms with his mother, but that is not my concern. In paying debts of honour people cannot make terms. *Letter to Robert Ross* (*Letters*, p1038)

2860. I should not fancy Mrs. Cheveley is a woman who would be easily frightened. She has survived all her creditors, and she shows wonderful presence of mind. *An Ideal Husband* (*Plays*, p268)

2861. I don't feel really at liberty to take his money, though I would like it. I have never done that sort of thing, and I can't begin. It is merely the weakness of the criminal classes that makes me refuse. *Letter to Leonard Smithers* (*Letters*, p928)

2862. As for begging, it is safer to beg than to take, but it is finer to take than to beg. *The Soul of Man* (*OWC*, p4)

2863. Wherever there exists a demand, there is *no* supply. *Letter to Robert Ross* (*Letters*, p868)

2864. I am never in during the afternoon, except when I am confined to the house by a sharp attack of penury. *Letter to Robert Ross* (*Letters*, p1074)

2865. You ask me what I am writing: very little: I am always worried by that mosquito, money; bothered about little things, such as hotel-bills, and the lack of cigarettes and little silver *francs*. Peace is as requisite to the artist as to the saint: my soul is made mean by sordid anxieties. *Letter to H.C. Pollitt* (*Letters*, p1103)

2866. I think I was a problem for which there was no solution. Money alone could have helped me, not to solve, but to avoid solving the difficulty. *Letter to Robert Ross* (*Letters*, p1001)

2867. Where will you end if you go on like this? Bankruptcy is always in store for those who pay their debts. It is their punishment. *Letter to Leonard Smithers* (*Letters*, p994)

2868. And what is true of a bankrupt is true of everyone else in life. For every single thing that is done someone has to pay. *De Profundis* (*OWC*, p152)

2869. Nobody can shift their responsibilities on anyone else. They always return ultimately to the proper owner. *De Profundis* (*OWC*, p139)

2870. Sooner or later we all have to pay for what we do. *An Ideal Husband* (*Plays*, p245)

2871. How are you getting on? Are the creditors howling? If the wolf is at the door the only thing is to ask him to come in to dine. *Letter to Frank Harris* (*Letters*, p1196)

2872. ... I am rich when I count up what I still have: and as far as money, my money did me horrible harm. It wrecked me. I hope to have just enough to enable me to live simply and write well. *Letter to William Rothenstein* (*Letters*, p892)

2873. I am completely penniless, and absolutely homeless. Yet there are worse things in the world than that. *De Profundis* (*OWC*, p97)

2874. I did not sell myself for money. I bought success at a great price. *An Ideal Husband* (*Plays*, p261)

2875. There is no thing more precious than a human soul, nor any earthly thing that can be weighed with it. It is worth all the gold that is in the world, and is more precious than the rubies of the kings. *The Fisherman and His Soul* (*Works*, p238)

2876. ... man thought that the important thing was to have, and did not know that the important thing is to be. The true perfection of man lies, not in what man has, but in what man is. *The Soul of Man* (*OWC*, p7)

2877. Be Yourself. Don't imagine that your perfection lies in accumulating or possessing external things. Your perfection is inside of you. If only you could realize that, you would not want to be rich. Ordinary riches can be stolen from a man. Real riches cannot. In the treasury-house of your soul, there are infinitely precious things, that may not be taken from you. And so, try to so shape your life that external things will not harm you. *The Soul of Man* (*OWC*, p10)

2878. Nothing should be able to rob a man at all. What a man really has, is what is in him. What is outside of him should be a matter of no importance. *The Soul of Man* (*OWC*, p8)

2879. I feel that while there is much that I have lost, still there was much that was not worth keeping. *Letter to Edward Rose* (*Letters*, p863)

64

Women

2880. The history of women is the history of the worst form of tyranny the world has ever known. The tyranny of the weak over the strong. It is the only tyranny that lasts. *A Woman of No Importance* (*Plays*, pp180–1)

2881. The growing influence of women is the one reassuring thing in our political life, Lady Caroline. Women are always on the side of morality, public and private. *A Woman of No Importance* (*Plays*, p134)

2882. ... is it a sprightly lady-journalist who led him astray? Or was it one of those typical English women with their "fatal gift of duty?" *Letter to Robert Ross* (*Letters*, p1192)

2883. GERALD: But do you think women shouldn't be good?

LORD ILLINGWORTH: One should never tell them so, they'd all become good at once. Women are a fascinatingly wilful sex. Every woman is a rebel, and usually in wild revolt against herself. *A Woman of No Importance* (*Plays*, p181)

2884. JACK: Cecily and Gwendolyn are perfectly certain to be extremely great friends. I'll bet you anything you like that half an hour after they have met, they will be calling each other sister.

ALGERNON: Women only do that when they have called each other a lot of other things first. *The Importance of Being Earnest* (*Plays*, p372)

2885. Women are hard on each other. *A Woman of No Importance* (*Plays*, p205)

2886. MABEL CHILTERN: What sort of woman is she?

LORD GORING: Oh! a genius in the daytime and a beauty at night!

MABEL CHILTERN: I dislike her already. *An Ideal Husband* (*Plays*, p233)

2887. Women have no appreciation of good looks; at least, good women have not. *The Picture of Dorian Gray* (*SC*, p31)

2888. To Helen, formerly of Troy, now of London [referring to Lily Langtry]. (*Letters*, p91)

2889. A chase after a beautiful woman is always exciting. *Vera, or the Nihilist* (*Works*, p701)

2890. The only way to behave to a woman is to make love to her, if she is pretty, and to someone else, if she is plain. *The Importance of Being Earnest* (*Plays*, p371)

2891. MRS. ALLONBY: Curious thing, plain women are always jealous of their husbands, beautiful women never are!

LORD ILLINGWORTH: Beautiful women never have the time. They are always so occupied in being jealous of other people's husbands. *A Woman of No Importance* (*Plays*, p143)

2892. Certainly, more women grow old nowadays through the faithfulness of their admirers than through anything else! At least that is the only way I can account for the terribly haggard look of most of your pretty women in London. *An Ideal Husband* (*Plays*, p228)

2893. I don't think there is a woman in the world who would not be a little flattered if one made love to her. It is that which makes women so absolutely adorable. *A Woman of No Importance* (*Plays*, p146)

2894. She'll never love you unless you are always at her heels; women like to be bothered. *Vera, or the Nihilists* (*Works*, p681)

2895. Ladies should not be kept waiting, Lord Arthur.... The fair sex is apt to be impatient. *Lord Arthur Savile's Crime* (*SC*, p273)

2896. I'm afraid that women appreciate cruelty, downright cruelty, more than anything else. They have wonderfully primitive instincts. We have emancipated them, but they remain slaves looking for their masters, all the same. They love being dominated. *The Picture of Dorian Gray* (*SC*, p117)

2897. Women defend themselves by attacking, just as they attack by sudden and strange surrenders. *The Picture of Dorian Gray* (*SC*, p79)

2898. In the case of very fascinating women, sex is a challenge, not a defense. *An Ideal Husband* (*Plays*, p311)

2899. Crying is the refuge of plain women but the ruin of pretty ones. *Lady Windermere's Fan* (*Plays*, p16)

2900. ... Margaret Fuller, to whom Venus gave everything except beauty, and Pallas everything except wisdom. *Letter to Julia Ward Howe* (*Letters*, p336)

2901. Ordinary women never appeal to one's imagination. They are limited to their century. No glamour ever transfigures them. One knows their minds as easily as one knows their bonnets. *The Picture of Dorian Gray* (*SC*, p67)

2902. Ordinary women always console themselves. Some of them do it by going in for sentimental colours. Never trust a woman who wears mauve, whatever her age may be, or a woman over thirty-five who is fond of pink ribbons. It always means that they have a history. *The Picture of Dorian Gray* (*SC*, p116)

2903. One should never trust a woman who tells one her real age. A woman who would tell one that would tell one anything. *A Woman of No Importance* (*Plays*, p145)

2904. Every woman does talk too much. *Vera, or the Nihilists* (*Works*, p684)

2905. Indeed, no woman should ever be quite accurate about her age. It looks so calculating.... *The Importance of Being Earnest* (*Plays*, p423)

2906. As long as a woman can look ten years younger than her own daughter, she is perfectly satisfied. *The Picture of Dorian Gray* (*SC*, p64)

2907. She was perfectly proportioned — a rare thing in an age when so many women are either over life-size or insignificant. *Lord Arthur Savile's Crime* (*SC*, p280)

2908. In all her movements she is extremely graceful. A work of art, on the whole, but showing the influence of too many schools. *An Ideal Husband* (*Plays*, p224)

2909. ... a perfect saint amongst women, but so dreadfully dowdy that she reminded one of a badly bound hymn-book. *The Picture of Dorian Gray* (*SC*, p54)

2910. Well, like all stout women, she looks the very picture of happiness.... *An Ideal Husband* (*Plays*, p284)

2911. A woman whose size in gloves is seven and three-quarters never knows much about anything. You know Gertrude has always worn seven and three-quarters? That is one of the reasons why there was never any moral sympathy between us.... *An Ideal Husband* (*Plays*, p312)

2912. ... a woman's first duty is to her dressmaker, isn't it? What the second duty is, no one has as yet discovered. *An Ideal Husband* (*Plays*, p308)

2913. ... we should take a wider range, as well as a high standpoint, and deal not merely with what women wear, but with what they think, and what they feel. *Letter to Wemyss Reid* (*Letters*, p297)

2914. SIR ROBERT CHILTERN: You think science cannot grapple with the problem of women?

MRS. CHEVELEY: Science can never grapple with the irrational. That is why it has no future before it, in this world.

SIR ROBERT CHILTERN: And women represent the irrational.

MRS. CHEVELEY: Well-dressed women do. *An Ideal Husband* (*Plays*, p229)

2915. For so well-dressed a woman, Mrs. Cheveley, you have moments of admirable common sense. I congratulate you. *An Ideal Husband* (*Plays*, p316)

2916. My dear boy, no woman is a genius. Women are a decorative sex. They never have anything to say, but they say it charmingly. *The Picture of Dorian Gray* (*SC*, p64)

2917. It takes a thoroughly good woman to do a thoroughly stupid thing. *Lady Windermere's Fan* (*Plays*, p35)

2918. Many a woman has a past, but I am told that she has at least a dozen, and that they all fit. *Lady Windermere's Fan* (*Plays*, p13)

2919. What have women who have not sinned to do with me, or I with them? We do not understand each other. *A Woman of No Importance* (*Plays,* p205)

2920. Oh! Wicked women bother one. Good women bore one. That is the only difference between them. *Lady Windermere's Fan* (*Plays,* p56)

2921. If a woman really repents, she never wishes to return to the society that has made or seen her ruin. *Lady Windermere's Fan* (*Plays,* p21)

2922. Arthur, Arthur, don't talk so bitterly about any woman. I don't think now people can be divided into the god and the bad, as if they were two separate races or creations. What are called good women may have terrible things in them, mad moods of recklessness, assertion, jealousy, sin. Bad women, as they are termed, may have in them sorrow, repentance, pity, sacrifice. *Lady Windermere's Fan* (*Plays,* p68)

2923. How fond women are of doing dangerous things! It is one of the qualities in them that I admire most. A woman will flirt with anybody in the world as long as other people are looking on. *The Picture of Dorian Gray* (*SC,* p215)

2924. Yes; there is really no end to the consolations that women find in modern life. Indeed, I have not mentioned the most important one.... Taking some one else's admirer when one loses one's own. *The Picture of Dorian Gray* (*SC,* p117)

2925. You talk as if you had a heart. Women like you have no hearts. Heart is not in you. You are bought and sold. *Lady Windermere's Fan* (*Plays,* p52)

2926. I assure you, women of that kind are most useful. They form the basis of other people's marriages. *Lady Windermere's Fan* (*Plays,* p35)

2927. If a woman can't make her mistakes charming, she is only a female. *Lord Arthur Savile's Crime* (*SC,* p269)

2928. It is extraordinary what astounding mistakes clever women make. *An Ideal Husband* (*Plays,* p251)

2929. She is clever, too clever for a woman. She lacks the indefinable charm of weakness.

It is the feet of clay that make the gold of the image precious. Her feet are very pretty, but they are not feet of clay. White porcelain feet, if you like. They have been through the fire, and what fire does not destroy, it hardens. She has had experiences. *The Picture of Dorian Gray* (*SC,* p193)

2930. LORD AUGUSTUS: A very clever woman. Knows perfectly well what a demmed fool I am — knows it as well as I do myself. Ah! You may laugh, my boy, but it is a great thing to come across a woman who thoroughly understands one.

DUMBY: It is an awfully dangerous thing. They always end by marrying one. *Lady Windermere's Fan* (*Plays,* p56)

2931. Women have a wonderful instinct about things. They can discover everything except the obvious. *An Ideal Husband* (*Plays,* p258)

2932. No woman should have a memory. Memory in a woman is the beginning of dowdiness. One can always tell from a woman's bonnet whether she has got a memory or not. *A Woman of No Importance* (*Plays,* p188)

2933. That awful memory of women! What a fearful thing it is! And what an utter intellectual stagnation it reveals! One should absorb the colour of life, but one should never remember its details. Details are always vulgar. *The Picture of Dorian Gray* (*SC,* p116)

2934. ... women are most reliable, as they have no memory for the important. *Letter to Robert Ross* (*Letters,* p780)

2935. ... he is like a woman, sure to remember the trivial and forget the important. *Oscar Wilde, by Frank Harris* (*CG,* p284)

2936. You women live by your emotions and for them. You have no philosophy of life. *A Woman of No Importance* (*Plays,* p215)

2937. ... women are meant to be loved, not understood. *The Sphinx without a Secret* (*Works,* p205)

2938. MRS. ALLONBY: Define us as a sex:

LORD ILLINGWORTH: Sphinxes without secrets. *A Woman of No Importance* (*Plays,* p145) and *The Sphinx without a Secret* (*Works,* p208)

2939. Never marry a woman with straw-coloured hair, Dorian ... they are so sentimental. *The Picture of Dorian Gray* (*SC*, p63)

2940. You should never try to understand them. Women are pictures. Men are problems. If you want to know what a woman really means—which, by the way, is always a dangerous thing to do—look at her, don't listen to her. *A Woman of No Importance* (*Plays*, p180)

2941. LADY CAROLINE: As far as I can make out, the young women of the present day seem to make it the sole object of their lives to be playing with fire.

MRS. ALLONBY: The one advantage of playing with fire, Lady Caroline, is that one never gets even singed. It is the people who don't know how to play with it who get burned up. *A Woman of No Importance* (*Plays*, pp132–3)

2942. SIR ROBERT CHILTERN: ... she looks like a woman with a past, doesn't she?

LORD GORING: Most pretty women do. But there is a fashion in pasts just as there is a fashion in frocks. Perhaps Mrs. Cheveley's past is merely a slightly *décolleté* one, and they are excessively popular nowadays.

An Ideal Husband (*Plays*, p268)

2943. There is only one real tragedy in a woman's life. The fact that her past is always her lover, and her future invariably her husband. *An Ideal Husband* (*Plays*, p312)

65

Writers

2944. Every great man nowadays has his disciples, and it is usually Judas who writes his biography. *The Critic as Artist* (*Works,* p1109)

2945. The only writers who have influenced me are Keats, Flaubert and Walter Pater, and before I came across them I had already gone more than halfway to meet them. *Quoted in Oscar Wilde: His Life and Wit* (*HBP,* p26)

2946. Yes, poor dear Pater has lived to disprove everything that he has written. *Quoted in Oscar Wilde: His Life and Wit* (*HBP,* p28)

2947. Like most penmen, he overrates the power of the sword. *Quoted in Oscar Wilde: His Life and Wit* (*HBP,* p115)

2948. There is always something peculiarly impotent about the violence of a literary man. It seems to bear no reference to fact, for it is never kept in check by action. It is simply a question of adjectives and rhetoric, of exaggeration and over-emphasis. *Quoted in Oscar Wilde: His Life and Wit* (*HBP,* p115)

2949. I've only one fault to find with Dilke; he knows too much about everything. It is hard to have a good story interrupted by a fact. I admit accuracy up to a certain point, but Dilke's accuracy is almost a vice. (*Letters,* p108)

2950. The only fault is that she [Elizabeth Barrett Browning] overstrains her metaphors till they snap.... *Letter to William Ward* (*Letters,* p26)

2951. Ah! Meredith! Who can define him? His style is chaos illumined by flashes of lightening. As a writer he has mastered everything except language: as a novelist he can do anything, except tell a story: as an artist he is everything, except articulate.... But whatever he is, he is not a realist. Or rather I would say that he is a child of realism who is not on speaking terms with his father. *The Decay of Lying* (*Works,* p1076)

2952. Mr. James Payne is an adept in the art of concealing what is not worth finding. He hunts down the obvious with the enthusiasm of a short-sighted detective. As one turns over the pages, the suspense of the author becomes almost unbearable. *The Decay of Lying* (*Works,* p1074)

2953. Mr. Henry James writes fiction as if it were a painful duty, and wastes upon mean motives and imperceptible "points of view" his neat literary style, his felicitous phrases, his swift and caustic satire. *The Decay of Lying* (*Works,* p1074)

2954. M. Zola ... is determined to show that, if he has not genius, he can at least be dull. *The Decay of Lying* (*Works,* p1075)

2955. I have blown my trumpet against the gates of dullness, and I hope that some shaft has hit *Robert Elsmere* between the joints of his nineteenth edition. *Letter to Mrs. George Lewis* (*Letters,* p389)

2956. It has been said of [Swinburne], and with truth, that he is a master of language, but with still greater truth it may be said that language is his master. Words seem to dominate him. Alliteration tyrannises over him. Mere sound often becomes his lord. He is so eloquent that whatever he touches becomes unreal. *Quoted in Oscar Wilde: His Life and Wit* (*HBP,* p114)

2957. Similes such as these obscure; they do not illuminate. To say that Ford is like a glittering Corinthian colonnade adds nothing to our knowledge of either Ford or Greek architecture. *Ben Jonson, Pall Mall Gazette* (*Uncollected,* p161)

2958. Mr. Hall Caine, it is true, aims at the grandiose, but then he writes at the top of his voice. He is so loud that one cannot hear what he says. *The Decay of Lying* (*Works*, p1074)

2959. The man who uses italics is like the man who raises his voice in conversation and talks loudly in order to make himself heard. *Oscar Wilde, by Frank Harris* (*CG*, p100)

2960. The horses of Mr. William Black's phaeton do not soar towards the sun. They merely frighten the sky at evening into violent chromolithographic effects. On seeing them approach, the peasants take refuge in dialect. *The Decay of Lying* (*Works*, p1074)

2961. In English poetry we do not want *chaktis* for the toes, *jasams* for the elbow-bands, and *gote* and *har, bala* and *mala*. This is not local colour; it is a sort of local discolouration. It does not add anything to the vividness of the scene. It does not bring the Orient more clearly before us. *Sir Edwin Arnold's Last Volume Pall Mall Gazette* (*Uncollected*, p177)

2962. ... Mr. Saintsbury, a writer who seems quite ignorant of the commonest laws both of grammar and of literary expression, who has apparently no idea of the difference between the pronouns "this" and "that," and who has as little hesitation in ending the clause of a sentence with a preposition, as he has in inserting a parenthesis between a preposition and it's object, a mistake of which the most ordinary schoolboy would be ashamed. *Letter to the Editor of The Pall Mall Gazette* (*Letters*, p275)

2963. I was in a troublesome editorial office, receiving frantic telegrams from Lady Archie Campbell about a correction I wished to make in her article. It was a case of grammar versus mysticism, and the contest is still raging. I feel I shall have to yield. *Letter to Violet Fane* (*Letters*, p323)

2964. George Moore has conducted his whole education in public. He had written two or three books before he found out there was such a thing as English grammar. He at once announced his discovery and so won the admiration of the illiterate. A few years later he discovered that there was something architectural in style, that sentences had to be built

up into a paragraph, and paragraphs into chapters and so on. Naturally he cried this revelation, too, from the housetops, and thus won the admiration of the journalists who had been making rubble-heaps all their lives without knowing it. I'm much afraid, Frank, in spite of all his efforts, he will die before he reaches the level from which writers start. It's a pity because he has certainly a little real talent. He differs from Symons in that he has an ego, but his ego has five senses and no soul. *Oscar Wilde, by Frank Harris* (*CG*, p278)

2965. He [George Moore] brings his readers to the latrine — and locks the door. *Aspects of Wilde* (*CC*, p98)

2966. *The Chronicle of Mites* is a mock-heroic poem about the inhabitants of a decaying cheese who speculate about the origin of their species and hold learned discussions upon the meaning of evolution and the Gospel according to Darwin. This cheese-epic is a rather unsavoury production and the style is at times so monstrous and so realistic that the author should be called the Gorgon-Zola of literature. *From the Poet's Corner, Pall Mall Gazette* (*Uncollected*, p171)

2967. K.E.V.'s little volume is a series of little poems on the saints. Each poem is preceded by a brief biography of the saint it celebrates — which is a very necessary precaution as few of them ever existed ... [it] may be said to add another horror to martyrdom. Still it is a thoroughly well-intentioned book and eminently suitable for invalids. *Quoted in Oscar Wilde: His Life and Wit* (*HBP*, p112)

2968. ... it was his prose I loved, and not his piety. *Oscar Wilde, by Frank Harris* (*CG*, p28)

2969. Thank you very much for your charming book.... Here *is* my opinion. The book is a little too crowded: the motive is hardly clear enough: if Gwendolyn is the heroine we should hear more of her: if she is not, the last chapters emphasise her too much. Captain Breutnall is not a success: his death is merely the premature disappearance of a shell jacket: I decline to mourn with Gwendolyn over someone who is not properly introduced. *Letter to J.S. Little* (*Letters*, p338)

2970. ... M. Zola's character's are much worse. They have their dreary vices, and their drearier virtues. The record of their lives is absolutely without interest. Who cares what happens to them? In literature we require distinction, charm, beauty and imaginative power. We don't want to be harrowed and disgusted with an account of the doings of the lower orders. *The Decay of Lying* (*Works,* p1075)

2971. ... he seeks simply to please his readers, and desires not to prove a theory; he looks on life as a picture to be painted than as a problem to be solved; his aim is to create men and women more than to vivisect them. *Olivia at the Lyceum* (*Uncollected,* p955)

2972. As for M. Paul Bourget, the master of the *roman psychologique,* he commits the error of imagining that the men and women of modern life are capable of being infinitely analysed for an innumerable series of chapters. *The Decay of Lying* (*Works,* p1075)

2973. One incomparable novelist we have now in England, Mr. George Meredith. There are better artists in France, but France has no one whose view of life is so large, so varied, so imaginatively true. There are tellers of stories in Russia who have a more vivid sense of what pain in fiction may be. But to him belongs philosophy in fiction. His people not merely live, but they live in thought. One can see them from myriad points of view. They are suggestive. There is soul in them and around them. They are interpretive and symbolic. And he who made them, those wonderful quickly-moving figures, made them for his own pleasure, and has never asked the public what they wanted, has never cared to know what they wanted, has never allowed the public to dictate to him or influence him in any way, but has gone on intensifying his own personality, and producing his own individual work. At first none came to him. Then the few came to him. That did not change him. The many have come now. He is still the same. He is an incomparable novelist. *The Soul of Man* (*OWC,* p28)

2974. And by what a subtle objective method does Dostoyevsky show us his characters! He never tickets them with a list or labels them with a description. We grow to know them very gradually, as we know people whom we meet in society, at first by little tricks of manner, personal appearance, fancies in dress, and the like; afterwards by their deeds and words; and even then they constantly elude us, for though Dostoyevsky may lay bare for us the secrets of their nature, yet he never explains his personages away; they are always surprising us by something that they say or do, and keep to the end the eternal mystery of life. *Injury and Insult, Pall Mall Gazette* (*Uncollected,* p89)

2975. [George Bernard Shaw is] a man of real ability but with a bleak mind. Humorous gleams as of wintry sunlight on a bare, harsh landscape. He has no passion, no feeling, and without passionate feeling how can one be an artist? He believes in nothing, loves nothing, not even Bernard Shaw, and really, on the whole, I don't wonder at his indifference. *Oscar Wilde, by Frank Harris* (*CG,* p279)

2976. I like your superb confidence in the dramatic value of the mere facts of life. I admire the horrible flesh and blood of your creatures, and your preface is a masterpiece — a real masterpiece of trenchant writing and caustic wit and dramatic instinct. *Letter to Bernard Shaw* (*Letters,* pp563–4)

2977. Your prose is full of cadence and colour, and has a rhythmic music of words that makes that constant appeal to the ear, which, to me, is the very condition of literature. *Letter to Laurence Housman* (*Letters,* p923)

2978. ... by taking existence at its most fiery-coloured moments [Turgenev] can distill into a few pages of perfect prose the moods and passions of many lives. *Insult and Injury Pall Mall Gazette* (*Uncollected,* p88)

2979. It is in Keats that the artistic spirit of this century found its absolute incarnation. *Quoted in Oscar Wilde: His Life and Wit* (*HBP,* p7)

2980. ... it is in Keats that one discerns the beginning of the artistic renaissance of England. *The English Renaissance of Art lecture* (*Uncollected,* p7)

2981. Someway standing by his grave I felt that [Keats] *too* was a Martyr, and worthy to lie in the City of Martyrs. I thought of him as a Priest of Beauty slain before his time, a lovely Sebastian killed by the arrows of a lying and unjust tongue. *Letter to Lord Houghton* (*Letters*, p49)

2982. I love [Keats's] "amica silentia." What a beautiful nature the man who could feel "the *friendly* silences of the moon." *Oscar Wilde, by Frank Harris* (*CG*, p277)

2983. Byron was a rebel and Shelley a dreamer; but in the calmness and clearness of his vision, his perfect self-control, his unerring sense of beauty and his recognition of a separate realm for the imagination, Keats was the pure and serene artist, the forerunner of a pre-Raphaelite school, and so of the great romantic movement.... *The English Renaissance of Art lecture* (*Uncollected*, p7)

2984. Balzac, besides, is essentially universal. He sees life from every point of view. He has no preferences and no prejudices. He does not try to prove anything. He feels that the spectacle of life contains its own secret. *Balzac in English, Pall Mall Gazette* (*Uncollected*, p163)

2985. As for Balzac, he was a most remarkable combination of the artistic temperament with the scientific spirit. The latter he bequeathed to his disciples. The former was entirely his own. *The Decay of Lying* (*Works*, p1076)

2986. Mrs. Ratcliffe, who introduced the romantic novel, and has consequently much to answer for. *English Poetesses Queen* (*Uncollected*, p66)

2987. WARDER: Excuse me sir, but Charles Dickens, sir: would he be considered a great writer now, sir?

WILDE: Oh, yes, a great writer indeed: you see he is no longer alive.

WARDER: Yes, I understand, sir. Being dead he would be a great writer, sir.... Now, sir, John Strange Winter, sir: would you tell me what you think of him, sir?

WILDE: A charming lady, he is a charming lady; but I would rather talk to her than read her books.

WARDER: Thank you, sir. I did not know he was a lady, sir.... Excuse me, sir, but Marie

CORELLI: would she be considered a great writer, sir?

WILDE: Now don't think I have anything against her *moral* character, but from the way she writes *she ought to be here* [prison].

WARDER: You say so, sir, you say so. *Quoted in Oscar Wilde: His Life and Wit* (*HBP*, pp285–6)

2988. Their light touch and exquisite ear, and delicate sense of balance and proportion, would be of no small service to us. I can fancy women bringing a new manner into our literature. *English Poetesses Queen* (*Uncollected*, p64)

2989. It is only fair to state that Mr. Knight's work is much better than that of his predecessors in the same field. His book is, on the whole, modestly and simply written; whatever its other faults may be, it is at least free from affectation of any kind; and it makes no serious pretence at being either exhaustive or definitive. Yet the best we can say of it is that it is just the sort of biography Guildenstern might have written of Hamlet. *A Cheap Edition of a Great Man, Pall Mall Gazette* (*Uncollected*, p96)

2990. Henry Wadsworth Longfellow was one of the first true men of letters America produced, and as such deserves a high place in any history of American civilisation. To a land out of breath in its greed for gain he showed the example of a life devoted entirely to the study of literature.... *Great Writers by Little Men, Pall Mall Gazette* (*Uncollected*, p92)

2991. There is a healthy bank-holiday atmosphere about this book which is extremely pleasant. Mr. Quilter is entirely free from affectation of any kind. He rollicks through art with the recklessness of the tourist and describes its beauties with the enthusiasm of the auctioneer. To many, no doubt, he will seem to be somewhat blatant and bumptious, but we prefer to regard him as simply being British. *A "Jolly" Art Critic, Pall Mall Gazette* (*Uncollected*, p132)

2992. Formerly we used to canonise our heroes. The modern method is to vulgarise them. Cheap editions of great books may be delightful, but cheap editions of great men are absolutely detestable. *The Critic as Artist* (*Works*, p1109)

2993. Between them, Hugo and Shakespeare have exhausted every subject. Originality is no longer possible, even in sin. So there are no real emotions left — only extraordinary adjectives. *Quoted in Oscar Wilde: His Life and Wit* (*HBP*, p71)

66

Writing and Literature

2994. ... one should not be too severe on English novels: they are the only relaxation of the intellectually unemployed. *Quoted in Oscar Wilde: His Life and Wit* (*HBP*, p109)

2995. The aim of our modern novelists seems to be, not to write good novels, but to write novels that will do good. *Quoted in Oscar Wilde: His Life and Wit* (*HBP*, p109)

2996. Eloquence is a beautiful thing but rhetoric ruins many a critic.... *Ben Jonson, Pall Mall Gazette* (*Uncollected*, p159)

2997. ... keep literature for your finest, rarest moments. *Letter to an Unidentified Correspondent* (*Letters*, p265)

2998. A nice letter is like a sunbeam and should not be treated as an epistle needing a reply. Besides your invitations are commands. *Letter to Violet Fane* (*Letters*, p216)

2999. No telegram can kill or mar a man with anything in him. *Letter to Norman Forbes-Robertson* (*Letters*, p159)

3000. The unread is always better than the unreadable. *Letter to Leonard Smithers* (*Letters*, p1003)

3001. I bought the book, and before I had read very far, I came on this sentence: "The birds were singing on every twig and on every little twiglet." Now, you know, when an artist comes on a sentence like that in a book it is impossible for him to go on reading it. *Aspects of Wilde* (*CC*, p96)

3002. I quite admit that modern novels have many good points. All I insist on is that, as a class, they are quite unreadable. *The Decay of Lying* (*Works*, p1076)

3003. I am too fond of reading books to care to write them.... *The Picture of Dorian Gray* (*SC*, p59)

3004. I have a horror of going out into life without a single book of my own. *Letter to Robert Ross* (*Letters*, p790)

3005. Anybody can write a three-volume novel. It merely requires a complete ignorance of both life and literature. *The Critic as Artist* (*Works*, p1120)

3006. I dislike modern memoirs. They are generally written by people who have either entirely lost their memories, or have never done anything worth remembering; which, however, is, no doubt, the true explanation of their popularity, as the English public always feels perfectly at ease when a mediocrity is talking to it. *The Critic as Artist* (*Works*, p1108)

3007. The nineteenth century may be a prosaic age, but we fear that, if we are to judge by the general run of novels, it is not an age of prose. *Quoted in Oscar Wilde: His Life and Wit* (*HBP*, p109)

3008. The difficulty under which the novelists of our day labour seems to me to be this: if they do not go into society, their books are unreadable; if they do go into society, they have no time left for writing. *Quoted in Oscar Wilde: His Life and Wit* (*HBP*, p109)

3009. To introduce real people into a novel or a play is a sign of an unimaginative mind, a coarse, untutored observation and an entire absence of style. *Interview in The Sketch* (*Uncollected*, p. xix)

3010. To be put into fiction is always a tribute to one's reality. *Quoted in Oscar Wilde: His Life and Wit* (*HBP*, p109)

3011. Life by its realism is always spoiling the subject-matter of art. The supreme pleasure in literature is to realise the non-existent. *Letter to the Editor of The St. James Gazette* (*Letters*, p430)

3012. I hate vulgar realism in literature. The man who could call a spade a spade should be compelled to use one. It is the only thing he is fit for. *The Picture of Dorian Gray* (*SC*, p206)

3013. The only form of fiction in which real characters do not seem out of place is history. In novels they are detestable. *Quoted in Oscar Wilde: His Life and Wit* (*HBP*, p110)

3014. I never travel anywhere without [*Studies in the History of the Renaissance*]. But it is the very flower of decadence: the last trumpet should have sounded the moment it was written. *Quoted in Oscar Wilde: His Life and Wit* (*HBP*, p27)

3015. Anybody can make history. Only a great man can write it. *The Critic as Artist* (*Works*, p1121)

3016. I see by the papers that you are still making mortals immortal, and I wish you were working for a Paris newspaper, that I could see your work making *kiosques* lovely. *Letter to William Rothenstein* (*Letters*, p1024)

3017. Yet one had ancestors in literature as well as in one's own race, nearer perhaps in type and temperament, many of them, and certainly with an influence of which one was more absolutely conscious. *The Picture of Dorian Gray* (*SC*, p157)

3018. We sincerely hope that there will soon be an end to all biographies of this kind. They rob life of much of its dignity and its wonder, add to death itself a new terror, and make one wish that all art were anonymous. *A Cheap Edition of Great Men The Pall Mall Gazette* (*Uncollected*, p98)

3019. Literature always anticipates life. It does not copy it, but moulds it to its purpose. The nineteenth century, as we know it, is largely an invention of Balzac. *The Decay of Lying* (*Works*, p1084)

3020. People sometimes say that fiction is getting too morbid. As far as psychology is concerned, it has never been morbid enough. We have merely touched the surface of the soul, that is all. *The Critic as Artist* (*Works*, p1150)

3021. This age has produced wonderful prose styles, turbid with individualism, and violent with excess of rhetoric. *Mr. Pater's "Appreciations," Speaker* (*Uncollected*, p149)

3022. [The Picture of Dorian Gray] is poisonous if you like; but you cannot deny that it is also perfect, and perfection is what we artists aim at. *Oscar Wilde, by Frank Harris* (*CG*, p69)

3023. I am sending you a book of mine: when it comes out — in about three weeks — you will get it. It is a fanciful, absurd comedy, written when I was playing with that tiger Life. I hope it will amuse you. *Letter to Louis Wilkinson* (*Letters*, pp1122–3)

3024. Movement, that problem of the visible arts, can be truly realised by Literature alone. It is Literature that shows us the body in its swiftness and the soul in its unrest. *The Critic as Artist* (*Works*, p1124)

3025. On a shelf of the bookcase behind you stands the *Divine Comedy*, and I know that, if I open it at a certain place, I shall be filled with a fierce hatred of some one who has never wronged me, or stirred by a great love for some one whom I shall never see. There is no mood of passion that Art cannot give us, and those of us who have discovered her secret can settle beforehand what our experiences are going to be. We can choose our day and select our hour. *The Critic as Artist* (*Works*, p1132)

3026. ... horrible as all the physical privations of modern prison life are, they are as nothing compared to the entire privation of literature to one to whom Literature was once the first thing of life, the mode by which perfection could be realised, by which, and by which alone, the intellect could feel itself alive. *Letter to the Home Secretary* (*Letters*, p657)

3027. ... there is no literary public in England for anything except newspapers, primers, and encyclopaedias. Of all people in the world the English have the least sense of the beauty of literature. *The Picture of Dorian Gray* (*SC*, p59)

3028. Pray never speak lightly of *Bootle's Baby* — Indeed pray never speak of it at all — I never do. *Letter to Robert Ross* (*Letters*, p869)

3029. To tell people what to read is, as a rule, either useless or harmful; for the appreciation of literature is a question of temperament not of teaching. *Letter to the Editor of the Pall Mall Gazette* (*Letters*, p276)

3030. In old days books were written by men of letters and read by the public. Nowadays books are written by the public and read by nobody. *A Few Maxims for the Instruction of the Over-Educated, Saturday Review* (*Works*, p1242)

3031. Old fashions in literature are not so pleasant as old fashions in dress. I like the costume of the age of powder better than the poetry of the age of Pope. *English Poetesses, Queen* (*Uncollected*, p66)

3032. He has become a classic, you see, and classics are what everybody talks about, but nobody reads. *Oscar Wilde: The Story of an Unhappy Friendship* (*GC*, p43)

3033. ... this age of ours, an age that reads so much that it has no time to admire, and writes so much that it has no time to think. *Letter to the Editor of the Pall Mall Gazette* (*Letters*, p276)

3034. Pray write constantly, especially when there is no necessity to do so. *Letter to Leonard Smithers* (*Letters*, p1006)

3035. But do write clearly. Otherwise it looks as if you had nothing to conceal. *Letter to Robert Ross* (*Letters*, p791)

3036. But life has also, my dear boy, little seemingly-unimportant duties, and it is these little duties, trivial as they may seem to many, that really make life tedious. Amongst your duties of this kind is to write me, from time to time. *Letter to Reginald Turner* (*Letters*, p878)

3037. Write me a letter *about yourself entirely.* Then it is sure to be long, and written with interest, affection and admiration. At least it should be if you took *my* view of the subject. *Letter to Reginald Turner* (*Letters*, p878)

3038. It is most distasteful to me to have to write business letters, and yours is the only firm that has ever forced me to do so. *Letter to John Lane* (*Letters*, p548)

3039. I long to get back to real literary work; for though my audiences are really most appreciative I cannot write while flying from one railway to another and form the cast-iron

stove of one hotel to its twin horror in the next. *Oscar Wilde Discovers America* (*HBC*, p409)

3040. I am not doing what I ought to do; I ought to be putting black upon white — black upon white. *Oscar Wilde: The Story of an Unhappy Friendship* (*GC*, pp101–2)

3041. I never write plays for anyone. I write plays to amuse myself. After, if people want to act in them, I sometimes allow them to do so. *Aspects of Wilde* (*CC*, p200)

3042. I don't write to please cliques. I write to please myself. Besides, I have always had grave suspicions that the basis of all literary cliques is a morbid love of meat teas. That makes them sadly uncivilized. *Interview in The Sketch* (*Uncollected*, p. xviii)

3043. My dear Aleck, I am not satisfied with myself or my work. I can't get a grip of the play yet: I can't get my people real. The fact is I worked at it when I was not in the mood for work, and must first forget it, and then go back quite fresh to it. I am very sorry, but artistic work can't be done unless one is in the mood; certainly my work can't. Sometimes I spend months over a thing, and don't do any good: at other times I write a thing in a fortnight. *Letter to George Alexander* (*Letters*, p463)

3044. What I can't understand is how such a man could sit down to work on the same book regularly for hours, day after day, during a year, or two or three years. Now, when I start a thing I must write desperately day and night till it is finished. Otherwise I should lose interest in it, and the first bus passing in the street would distract me from it. *Aspects of Wilde* (*CC*, pp 31–2)

3045. I see that romantic surroundings are the worst possible surroundings for a romantic writer. *Letter to Robert Ross* (*Letters*, p789)

3046. ... what is important in all great writers is not so much the results they arrive at as the methods they pursue. *The Rise of Historical Criticism* (*Works*, p1227)

3047. I wish I could write them down, these little coloured parables or poems that live for a moment in some cell of my brain, and then leave to go wandering elsewhere. I hate writing: the mere act of writing a thing down is troublesome to me. I want some fine medium, and look for it in vain. *Letter to Adela Shuster* (*Letters*, p621)

3048. You had left my letters lying about for blackmailing companions to steal, for hotel servants to pilfer, for housemaids to sell. That was simply your careless want of appreciation of what I had written to you. *De Profundis* (*OWC*, pp77–8)

3049. Wilde: I suppose you have come about my beautiful letter to Lord Alfred Douglas? If you had not been so foolish as to send a copy of it to Mr. Beerbohm Tree, I would gladly have paid you a very large sum of money for the letter, as I consider it to be a work of art.

ALLEN: A very curious construction could be put on that letter.

WILDE: Art is rarely intelligible to the criminal classes.

ALLEN: A man offered me 60 pounds for it.

WILDE: If you take my advice you will go to that man and sell my letter to him for 60 pounds. I myself have never received so large a sum for any prose work of that length; but I am glad to find that there is someone in England who considers a letter of mine worth 60 pounds. *The Three Trials of Oscar Wilde* (*UB*, p117)

3050. EDWARD CARSON: You are of the opinion, I believe, that there is no such thing as an immoral book?

OSCAR WILDE: Yes.

EDWARD CARSON: May I take it that you think "The Priest and the Acolyte" was not immoral?

OSCAR WILDE: It was worse; it was badly written. *The Three Trials of Oscar Wilde* (*UB*, p121)

3051. There is no such thing as a moral book or an immoral book. Books are well written, or badly written. That is all. *The Picture of Dorian Gray* (*SC*, p18)

3052. The books that the world calls immoral books are books that show the world its own shame. *The Picture of Dorian Gray* (*SC*, p229)

3053. The flower is a work of art. The book [*The Green Carnation*] is not. *Letter to the Editor of The Pall Mall Gazette* (*Letters*, p617)

3054. [Leonard Smithers] is so fond of "suppressed" books that he suppresses his own. *Letter to Robert Ross* (*Letters*, p1019)

3055. Smithers knows all about bad wine and bad women, but on books he is sadly to seek. *Letter to Robert Ross* (*Letters*, p956)

3056. To know the vintage and quality of a wine one need not drink the whole cask. It must be perfectly easy in half an hour to say whether a book is worth anything or worth nothing. Ten minutes are really sufficient, if one has the instinct for form. Who wants to wade through a dull volume? One tastes it, and that is quite enough — more than enough, I should imagine. *The Critic as Artist* (*Works*, p1120)

3057. ... there is a great deal to be said in favour of reading a novel backwards. The last page is, as a rule, the most interesting and when one begins with the catastrophe or *denouement* one feels on pleasant terms with the author. It is like going behind the scenes of a theatre. One is no longer taken in, and the hairbreadth escapes of the hero and the wild agonies of the heroine leave one absolutely unmoved. *Quoted in Oscar Wilde: His Life and Wit* (*HBP*, p111)

3058. If one cannot enjoy reading a book over and over again, there is no use reading it at all. *The Decay of Lying* (*Works*, p1078)

3059. I sit by his side and read him passages from his own life. They fill him with surprise. Everyone should keep someone else's diary; I sometimes suspect you of keeping mine. *Letter to Ada Leverson* (*Letters*, p618)

3060. I keep a diary in order to enter the wonderful secrets of my life. If I didn't write them down I should probably forget all about them. *The Importance of Being Earnest* (*Plays*, p378)

3061. ALGERNON: Do you really keep a diary? I'd give anything to look at it. May I?

CECILY: Oh, no. You see it is simply a very young girl's record of her own thoughts and impressions, and consequently meant for publication. *The Importance of Being Earnest* (*Plays*, p394)

3062. I never travel without my diary. One should always have something sensational to read in the train. *The Importance of Being Earnest* (*Plays,* p403)

3063. I write because it gives me the greatest possible artistic pleasure to write. If my work pleases the few, I am gratified. If it does not, it causes me no pain. As for the mob, I have no desire to be a popular novelist. It is far too easy. *Letter to the Editor of The Scots Observer* (*Letters,* p438)

3064. I am glad to have provided a permanent employment to many an ink-stained life. *Oscar Wilde Discovers America* (*HBC,* p422)

3065. Not that I agree with everything that I have said in this essay. There is much with which I entirely disagree. The essay simply represents an artistic standpoint, and in aesthetic criticism attitude is everything. *Quoted in Oscar Wilde: His Life and Wit* (*HBP,* p109)

3066. My pen is horrid, my ink bad, my temper worse.— Write soon, and come to London. *Oscar Wilde: The Story of an Unhappy Friendship* (*GC,* p84)

3067. ... even prophets correct their proofs. *Mr. Pater's "Appreciations," Speaker* (*Uncollected,* p144)

Youth and Age

3068. ... youth is the one thing worth having. *The Picture of Dorian Gray* (*SC*, p38)

3069. The world belongs to you [youth] for a season.... *The Picture of Dorian Gray* (*SC*, p39)

3070. It is a kind of genius to be twenty-one. *Quoted in Oscar Wilde: His Life and Wit* (*HBP*, p172)

3071. Youth! There is nothing like it. *The Picture of Dorian Gray* (*SC*, p227)

3072. For there is such a little time that your youth will last — such a little time. The common hill-flowers wither, but they blossom again. The laburnum will be as yellow next June as it is now. In a month there will be purple stars on the clematis, and year after year the green night of its leaves will hold the purple stars. But we never get back our youth. The pulse of joy that beats in us at twenty becomes sluggish. Our limbs fail, our senses rot. We degenerate into hideous puppets, haunted by the memory of the passions of which we were too much afraid, and the exquisite temptations that we had not the courage to yield to. Youth! Youth! There is absolutely nothing in the world but youth! *The Picture of Dorian Gray* (*SC*, pp39–40)

3073. Remember that you've got on your side the most wonderful thing in the world — youth. *A Woman of No Importance* (*Plays*, p177)

3074. His night had been untroubled by any images of pleasure or of pain. But youth smiles without any reason. It is one of its chiefest charms. *The Picture of Dorian Gray* (*SC*, p174)

3075. To get back one's youth, one has merely to repeat one's follies. *The Picture of Dorian Gray* (*SC*, p57)

3076. Your reckless extravagance was not a crime. Youth is always extravagant. It was your forcing me to pay for your extravagances that was disgraceful. *De Profundis* (*OWC*, p146)

3077. Nay, let us walk from fire unto fire,
From passionate pain to deadlier delight, -
I am too young to live without desire,
Too young art thou to waste this summer
　　night.
Panthea (*Works*, p830)

3078. And no hand can gather up the fallen
　　withered
petals of the rose of youth.
Bittersweet Love (*Works*, p844)

3079. Those whom the gods love grow young. *A Few Maxims for the Instruction of the Over-Educated, Saturday Review* (*Works*, p1243)

3080. ... the things which the English public never forgives: Youth, power, and enthusiasm. *Oscar Wilde Discovers America* (*HBC*, p58)

3081. I like people who are young, bright, happy, careless and original. I do not like them sensible, and I do not like them old. *Quoted in Oscar Wilde: His Life and Wit* (*HBP*, p257)

3082. EDWARD CARSON: What enjoyment was it to you to entertain grooms and coachmen?

OSCAR WILDE: The pleasure to me was being with those who are young, bright, happy, careless, and free. I do not like the sensible and I do not like the old. *The Three Trials of Oscar Wilde* (*UB*, p143)

3083. Maurice has won twenty-five games of bezique and I twenty-four: however as he has youth, and I have only genius, it is only natural that he should beat me. *Letter to Leonard Smithers* (*Letters*, p1030)

3084. EDWARD CARSON: What was there in common between this young man and yourself? What attraction had he for you?

OSCAR WILDE: I delight in the society of people much younger than myself. I like those who may be called idle or careless. I recognise no social distinctions at all of any kind; and to me youth, the mere fact of youth, is so wonderful that I would sooner talk to a young man for half-an-hour than be — well, cross-examined in Court. *The Three Trials of Oscar Wilde* (*UB*, p145)

3085. It is absurd to talk of the ignorance of youth. The only people to whose opinions I listen now with any respect are people much younger than myself. They seem in front of me. Life has revealed to them her latest wonder. *The Picture of Dorian Gray* (*SC*, p227)

3086. I am afraid that you have been listening to the conversation of some one older than yourself. That is always a dangerous thing to do, and if you allow it to degenerate into a habit you will find it absolutely fatal to any intellectual development. *The Critic as Artist* (*Works*, pp1113–4)

3087. ... I don't think as a rule that people ever mind much what advice friends *of the same age* give them. After all, for effect and persuasion there is nothing like wrinkles and either gray hair or baldness. *Letter to William Ward* (*Letters*, p36)

3088. The old believe everything: the middle-aged suspect everything: the young know everything. *Phrases and Philosophies for the Use of the Young, The Chameleon* (*Works*, p1245)

3089. There is nothing like youth. The middle-aged are mortgaged to Life. The old are in Life's lumber room. But youth is the Lord of Life. Youth has a kingdom waiting for it. *A Woman of No Importance* (*Plays*, p177)

3090. LORD ILLINGWORTH: ... I have so many bad qualities.

MRS. ALLONBY: Ah, don't be so conceited about them. You may lose them as you grow old.

LORD ILLINGWORTH: I never intend to grow old. The soul is born old but grows young. That is the comedy of life.

MRS. ALLONBY: And the body is born young and grows old. That is life's tragedy. *A Woman of No Importance* (*Plays*, p147)

3091. Rudderless, we drift athwart a tempest, and when
once the storm of youth is past,
Without lyre, without lute or chorus, Death the
silent pilot comes at last.
Bittersweet Love (*Works*, p844)

3092. Life seems to be slipping from me. Events do not loom half as large as they once did. Age is not yet with me but its shadow is in the doorway. *Quoted in Oscar Wilde: His Life and Wit* (*HBP*, p325)

3093. For you, at least, are young; "no hungry generations tread you down," and the past does not weary you with the intolerable burden of its memories nor mock you with the ruins of a beauty, the secret of whose creation you have lost. *The English Renaissance of Art lecture* (*Uncollected*, p19)

3094. The tragedy of old age is not that one is old, but that one is young. *Quoted in Oscar Wilde: His Life and Wit* (*HBP*, p177)

3095. Thirty-five is a very attractive age. London society is full of women of the very highest birth who have, of their own free choice, remained thirty-five for years. Lady Dumbleton is an instance in point. To my own knowledge she has been thirty-five ever since she arrived at the age of forty, which was many years ago now. *The Importance of Being Earnest* (*Plays*, p424)

3096. She was now forty years of age, childless, and with that inordinate passion for pleasure which is the secret of remaining young. *Lord Arthur Savile's Crime* (*SC*, p266)

3097. The youth of the present day are quite monstrous. They have absolutely no respect for dyed hair. *Lady Windermere's Fan* (*Plays*, p57)

3098. I am so sorry but neither my wife or I ever go to dances: I am not sure whether we are too old or too young, but we never tread any measures now. *Letter to W. Graham Robertson* (*Letters*, p337)

3099. The gods bestowed on Max [Beerbohm] the gift of perpetual old age. *Aspects of Wilde* (*CC*, p78)

Bibliography

Douglas, Lord Alfred. *The Complete Poems of Lord Alfred Douglas.* London: Martin Secker, Ltd, 1928.

Harris, Frank. *Oscar Wilde.* New York: Carroll and Graf, 1916.

Holland, Merlin, and Rupert Hart-Davis. *The Complete Letters of Oscar Wilde.* New York: Henry Holt and Co., 2000.

Holland, Merlin, ed. *Collins Complete Works of Oscar Wilde.* New York: Harper Collins, 1999.

Hyde, H. Montgomery, ed. *The Three Trials of Oscar Wilde.* New York: University Books, 1948.

Jackson, John Wyse, ed. *The Uncollected Oscar Wilde.* London: Fourth Estate Limited, 1991.

Lewis, Lloyd, and Henry Justin Smith. *Oscar Wilde Discovers America.* New York: Harcourt Brace and Co., 1936.

Murray, Isobel, ed. *The Soul of Man and Prison Writings.* Oxford: Oxford World's Classics, 1999.

O'Sullivan, Vincent. *Aspects of Wilde.* London: Constable, 1936.

Pearson, Hesketh. *Oscar Wilde: His Life and Wit.* New York: Harper and Brothers, 1946.

Sherard, Robert H. *Oscar Wilde: The Story of an Unhappy Friendship.* London: Greening, 1908.

Wilde, Oscar. *The Picture of Dorian Gray and Selected Stories.* New York: Signet Classic, 1962.

Wilde, Oscar. *The Plays of Oscar Wilde.* New York: Vintage Books, 1988.

Keyword and Subject Index